Panaflex Users' Manual

Second Edition

Panaflex Users' Manual
Second Edition

David W. Samuelson

Focal Press

Boston   Oxford   Johannesburg   Melbourne   New Delhi   Singapore

Focal Press is an imprint of Butterworth–Heinemann.

 A member of the Reed Elsevier group

 Recognizing the importance of preserving what has been written,
Butterworth–Heinemann prints its books on acid-free paper whenever
possible

Library of Congress Cataloging-in-Publication Data
Samuelson, David W.
 Panaflex users' manual, second edition / David W. Samuelson.
  p.   cm.
 Includes index.
 ISBN 0-240-80267-5 (pbk. : alk. paper)
  1. Panaflex motion picture camera--Handbooks, manuals, etc.
 I. Title.
 TR883.P36S262 1996
 778.5'3--dc20   96-21775
                                                          CIP

British Library Cataloguing-in-Publication Data
A catalogue record for this book is available from the British Library.

The publisher offers special discounts on bulk orders of this book.
For information, please contact:

Manager of Special Sales
Butterworth–Heinemann
313 Washington Street
Newton, MA 02158-1626
Tel: 617-928-2500
Fax: 617-928-2620

For information on all Focal Press publications available, contact our
World Wide Web home page at: http://www.bh.com/fp

10 9 8 7 6 5 4 3 2 1

Printed in the United States of America

Contents

THE DIRECTORS OF PHOTOGRAPHY'S PANAFLEX

THE CAMERA OPERATORS' PANAFLEX

THE CAMERA ASSISTANTS' PANAFLEX

USING PANAFLEX AND PANASTAR CAMERA ACCESSORIES

THE SOUND RECORDISTS' PANAFLEX

THE PRODUCTION MANAGERS' PANAFLEX

Foreword to the First Edition

When PANAVISION developed its 'system' of cinematography the goal was to create a system where crews could be absolutely assured that the cameras, lenses and all accessories would always fit together to provide a complete solution to their needs, irrespective of where in the world the equipment was being used. This consistency has enabled the equipment to become an integral part of the craft of film making. Surprising as it may seem, to this day in 1989, PANAVISION is the only system in the world where this applies.

From the very beginning, PANAVISION has not considered itself to be just another rental company, nor do we consider ourselves to be simply a manufacturing company. Our concept has always been to develop equipment in a partnership with the motion picture industry. We grew as a company by insisting that we be technically involved in the actual production of movies. This ongoing collaboration has allowed us to develop unique equipment that addresses the needs of the cinematographers and their crews. The majority of PANAVISION equipment has in fact been developed in response to the suggestions and ideas of filmmakers over the years; and we would like to thank these people for their contributions to the finely tuned systems described in the manual.

For PANAVISION's staff, this partnership with filmmakers has fostered a feeling of participation in the making of motion pictures, and therefore a sense of responsibility and pride in their own skills. The dedication felt by every employee at PANAVISION is way beyond the scope of this foreword, but it is the passion for craft, and the continuous desire to provide the finest quality motion picture equipment and service, that has made PANAVISION what it is today.

Because PANAVISION doesn't sell the equipment it manufactures, the prime concern is to provide the highest quality and functionality, without the compromises required to meet a sales price. We can assure you that PANAVISION will continue its leadership for many years to come. It is our firm belief that the future of the motion picture industry is just as rich as its past. Our role, along with film manufacturers and laboratories, is to provide the cinematographer with an ever expanding palette of creative choices. The newest generation of PANAVISION Primo-L lenses is one illustration of the major advances we can all still achieve.

PANAVISION is honored to have David Samuelson write about our camera systems. The PANAFLEX USERS' MANUAL is a great accomplishment that could only be undertaken by someone with David's wealth of knowledge and experience. We would like to pay tribute to his willingness to give his time, so that we all may be better informed and educated.

John Farrand
President and C.E.O.,
PANAVISION Inc.
April 1989

Introduction

PANAVISION Inc. was founded by Robert E. Gottschalk in 1954, shortly after the introduction of the CinemaScope wide screen format, to fulfill the need for high quality anamorphic projection lens attachments.

Within a year of the introduction of the CinemaScope format, ordinary 4 x 3 (1.37:1) pictures quickly looked old fashioned and theatre owners frantically sought a source of good anamorphic lens attachments to enable them to show the new films without the need to modify their theatres or to be beholden to one supplier.

At that time Gottschalk owned a camera store in Westwood Village where he numbered among his customers many professional photographers and cinematographers. Among his acquaintances was an optical engineer who helped him to design a prism type de-anamorphoser which proved to be superior to the original CinemaScope projection lenses.

Within a short while he and a small staff, which included Frank Vogelsang, Tak Miyagishima, George Kraemer and Jack Barber, produced and delivered some 35,000 lenses until the market became saturated.

Other founder participants were Harry Eller, who owned the Radiant Screen Company in Chicago, the largest screen manufacturers in the U.S., William Mann, an optical manufacturer, Richard Moore and Meridith Nicholson, both Directors of Photography, and Walter Wallin, an optical designer. All of this group dropped out of the company soon after the initial demand for projection lenses was satisfied.

In 1957, at about the same time that the demand for projection lenses was falling off, Gottschalk was asked by MGM to develop a set of anamorphic lenses with a 1.33:1 squeeze ratio for 65mm cameras for a forthcoming production, Raintree County, starring Elizabeth Taylor and Montgomery Clift and in which they were attempting to outdo Gone With the Wind. The system was called CAMERA 65.

Another CAMERA 65 picture of the period was Ben Hur (1959) the first PANAVISION lensed picture to win an Academy Award for Cinematography.

The CAMERA 65 system was later further developed, changed to a 1.25:1 squeeze ratio and called ULTRA PANAVISION.

Building upon this success PANAVISION developed a system of non-anamorphic 65mm cameras and lenses, called SUPER PANAVISION, and such pictures as Exodus, West Side Story, Lawrence of Arabia and My Fair Lady all bore this label.

The next step was 35mm 2:1 anamorphic lenses and PANAVISION 35 was born. The lenses were called AUTO PANATARS, a name which has endured to this day.

These lenses incorporated patented counter-rotating focusing elements, developed by Walter Wallin, which eliminated what had become known as 'anamorphic mumps', the swelling of faces in close-ups, which upset many famous Hollywood actors and actresses and made them reluctant to appear in CinemaScope films.

Those who were in the screening room at MGM when the first tests of the new lenses were screened recalled that the entire audience clapped and cheered at what they saw. It was the dawning of a new age of anamorphic cinematography and since that time almost every truly major picture shot in the anamorphic format has been photographed using PANAVISION AUTO PANATAR lenses.

In 1958 PANAVISION Inc. received an Academy Award for Scientific and Technical Achievement and in 1993 won an Oscar© for the development of these lenses.

Even Twentieth Century Fox, who pioneered the whole process of CinemaScope 2.35:1 anamorphic cinematography, quickly changed to PANAVISION lenses when they saw the improvement in image quality.

Among the early pictures shot using the PANAVISION 35 system and blown-up to 70mm for road show presentation were Beckett, The Cardinal and Doctor Zhivago.

The next logical step was to provide cameras to go with their lenses and PANAVISION rapidly became well known for their innovative modifications to existing Mitchell and Arriflex cameras.

In the early 60's, with television making inroads to their traditional movie theatre business and with so many of their pictures being photographed with cameras and lenses supplied by PANAVISION, MGM and many other major studios decided to close down their camera departments and most sold off their entire inventory of cameras and lenses to PANAVISION.

This gave the company an abundance of Mitchell BNC 35mm cameras which they rebuilt as the PANAVISION SILENT REFLEX CAMERA, incorporating mirror shutter reflex viewfinding, crystal controlled motors, quietness of operation, lightness of weight and interchangeability of lenses between all cameras within the system, thus rendering all other Mitchell BNCs obsolescent.

The PSR cameras were immensely successful and rapidly became the industry standard.

Robert Gottschalk realized that good though the PSR was, it was not hand-holdable and set about designing and building a hand-holdable silent reflex support camera.

The result was the PANAFLEX motion picture camera.

The rest, as they say, is history.

This book is dedicated to the memories of
Robert E. Gottschalk
1917 - 1982,
Frank P. Vogelsang
1934 - 1988
and
George Kraemer
1927 - 1993

Academy Technical or Scientific Awards won by PANAVISION Inc.
(1958 - 1978)

1958. Class II
"PANAVISION Inc. for the design and development of the Auto Panatar anamorphic photographic lens for 35mm CinemaScope photography."

1959. Class II
"DOUGLAS G. SHEARER of Metro-Goldwyn-Mayer Inc., and ROBERT E. GOTTSCHALK and JOHN R. MOORE of PANAVISION Inc. for the development of a system of producing and exhibiting wide-film motion pictures known as CAMERA 65."

1966. Class III
"PANAVISION Inc. for the design of the Panatron Power Inverter and its application to motion picture camera operation."

1967. Class III
"PANAVISION Inc. for a Variable Speed Motor for Motion Picture Cameras."

1968. Class II
"PANAVISION Inc. for the conception, design and introduction of a 65mm hand-held motion picture camera."

1969. Class III
"PANAVISION Inc. for the design and development of the Panaspeed Motion Picture Camera Motor."

1970. Class II
"PANAVISION Inc. for the development and engineering of the Panaflex motion picture camera."

1976. Class III
"PANAVISION Inc. for the design and development of super-speed lenses for motion picture photography."

1977. Class III
"PANAVISION Inc. for the concept and engineering of the improvements incorporated in the Panaflex Motion Picture Camera."

1977. Class III
"PANAVISION Inc. for the design of the Panalite, a camera-mounted controllable light for motion picture cameras."

1977. Class III
"PANAVISION Inc. for the engineering of the Panahead gearhead for motion picture cameras."

Note: With effect from the 51st Annual Academy Awards, for achievements during 1978 the classification of awards was changed. Class designations were discontinued. The "Class 1" Award became: *Academy Award of Merit*, "Class II" became: *Scientific and Engineering Award* and "Class III" became: *Technical Achievement Award.*

1978: Academy Award of Merit (Oscar ©)
"PANAVISION Inc. and its engineering staff under the direction of ROBERT E. GOTTSCHALK, for the concept, design and continuous development of the Panaflex Motion Picture Camera System."

Academy Technical or Scientific Awards won by PANAVISION Inc.
(1990 - 1995)

1990. Technical Achievement Award
"PANAVISION Inc. for the optical design, mechanical design and concept & development of the Primo-L Series™ of spherical prime lenses for 35mm cinematography."

1991. Scientific and Engineering Award
"PANAVISION Inc. for the optical design, mechanical design and for the concept & development of the Primo-L Zoom™ Lens for 35mm cinematography."

1992. Scientific and Engineering Award
"PANAVISION Inc. for the camera design, the optical design, the opto-mechanical design and technical support in developing the Panavision System-65 Studio Sync Sound Camera for 65mm motion picture photography."

1992. Technical Achievement Award
"PANAVISION Inc. for the optical design and mechanical design of the Panavision Slant Focus Lens for motion picture photography."

1993. Award of Merit (Oscar®)
"PANAVISION Inc. for the Auto-Panatar photographic lens system."

1994. Scientific and Engineering Award
"PANAVISION Inc. for the optical design, the mechanical design and development of the 11:1 Primo Zoom™ lens for motion picture photography."

1995. Scientific and Engineering Award"
"PANAVISION Inc. for the optical design, the mechanical design and development of the 3:1 Primo Zoom™ lens for motion picture photography."

Acknowledgments

My association with PANAVISION Inc. goes back to 1965 when they were a small lens manufacturing and rental company in Los Angeles and my brothers and I owned a small equipment rental company in London and we became the first PANAVISION overseas representatives.

It was a turning point in all our lives. We have grown and matured together.

Since that time I have always had a close personal and working relationship with both the management and the technical staff at PANAVISION and for this reason it was particularly gratifying, having retired from the Samuelson Group, to have been asked to become a consultant for the company.

Out of this special relationship has come this PANAFLEX USERS' MANUAL.

I wish to thank all at PANAVISION for their help, their cooperation and their knowledge, so freely shared, which has contributed to the writing of this, 'their' book.

In particular I wish to thank John Farrand, the President and C.E.O. of Panavision who gave me the opportunity and Benjamin Bergery who has been the Los Angeles coordinator whenever I have needed information from thousands of miles away.

Nearer home I wish to thank Karl Kelly of the Samuelson Group who read an early version of the manuscript and made many useful suggestions.

Regrettably, it is no longer possible to thank Bob Gottschalk who taught me to think the PANAVISION way.

I only hope that he would have approved of what I have written.

David Samuelson
London
April 1989

Seven years have passed since I wrote the first edition of the PANAFLEX USERS' MANUAL and like the cameras and lenses we make and talk about, we are all just that little bit older and more mature.

As before I am grateful to all those members of the PANAVISION fraternity, both in Los Angeles and in London who have given me their unstinting help.

In particular I wish to thank Iain A. Neil, Senior Vice-President of Optics, and Jonathan Maxwell of Imoerial College, London, for all the help they have given in compiling the new Lens Data section. Between us I believe we have put into print much useful information that has never before been available to the cinematographer on the studio floor.

David Samuelson
London
April 1996

The
Film Producers'
PANAFLEX

PANAVISION Cameras for All Types of Film Making

The PANAVISION system of motion picture cinematography, and especially the PANAVISION PANAFLEX system, offers the Film Producer the widest possible range of creative possibilities and most efficient means of transferring a script to film. It matters not if that film is a multi-million dollar movie or a low budget project; a TV Series production, a TV Commercial or a Visual Music project; or whether it is shot in a local studio or on a far away location. Whatever and wherever, to go PANAVISION is the most cost-efficient way to do it.

The PANAFLEX system
The PANAFLEX "SYSTEM" includes the following:
• The PLATINUM PANAFLEX, a 35mm, truly silent, reflex camera.
• The very quiet GII GOLDEN PANAFLEX, the latest upgraded version of the original Academy Award winning PANAFLEX camera and incorporating many of the features of the PLATINUM PANAFLEX but at a greatly reduced price.
• The GOLDEN PANAFLEX, the workhorse camera of the PANAFLEX range.
• The PANAFLEX-X, a 'fixed-eyepiece' type economical 'second camera' which is similar to, and just as quiet as, a GOLDEN PANAFLEX.
• The PANASTAR, a state-of-the-art high speed camera for all purposes, including Special Effects.
• The LIGHTWEIGHT PANAFLEX, especially made for Steadicam and remote control camera crane use where weight is at a premium.
Note: All PANAFLEX cameras, except the PANAFLEX-X, may be used either hand-held or mounted on a tripod etc.

Other PANAVISION cameras
Other cameras available from PANAVISION include:
• The SUPER PSR (an advanced studio type camera based on the Mitchell NC), the regular PSR, now very inexpensive and much used for TV situation comedy multi-camera shoots.
• Various 'special shot' cameras, including Mitchells and Arriflexes, etc., all with hard front PANAVISION lens mounts.
• Large format PANAVISION 65mm cameras for the ultimate in screen image quality and for special effects work. The full range includes reflex studio, handholdable and highspeed type cameras.
• For 16mm PANAVISION has the studio-quiet PANAFLEX 16 camera.

All PANAVISION cameras have available for them a full range of compatible PANAVISION lenses.

2

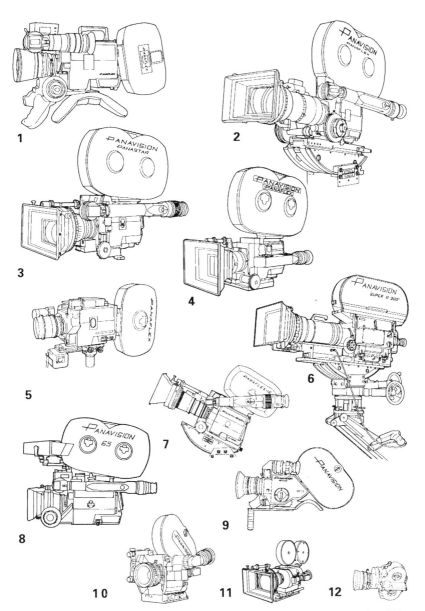

1. Hand held PANAVISION PLATINUM PANAFLEX camera,   2. PANAVISION GII/
GOLDEN PANAFLEX camera, 3. PANAVISION PANASTAR highspeed camera,
4. PANAVISION PANAFLEX-X, 5. PANAVISION LIGHTWEIGHT camera for floating
camera systems,   6. PANAVISION Super PSR studio camera,   7. PANAVISION
PANAFLEX 16 camera,   8. PANAVISION 65mm studio camera, 9. PANAVISION
65mm hand-held and high speed cameras, 10. PANAVISION Arri 3 camera,
11. PANAVISION Mitchell S35 camera,   12. PANAVISION Eymo camera.

3

PANAVISION Lenses for All Formats

Long before PANAVISION was known for its state-of-the art cameras, it was famous for its fine lenses. Such films as *Lawrence of Arabia, Dr. Zhivago and My Fair Lady,* among others, won Oscars for Cinematography using PANAVISION crafted lenses.

PANAVISION'S wide choice of formats and lenses
PANAVISION offers the greatest universe of presentation possibilities:
   You can go 'PANAVISION ANAMORPHIC' and have your picture photographed in the "2.4:1" anamorphic ratio giving your film a broad canvas. PANAVISION's PRIMO-L series are the very latest anamorphic lenses and the culmination of 35 years of continuous development.
   Alternatively, for 2.4:1 release prints, you can go 'PANAVISION SUPER-35', using spherical (non-anamorphic) lenses but extending the picture into the soundtrack area of the "Academy" negative to achieve greater image area (2/3 that of a normal Anamorphic frame).
   With either of these systems you can have 70mm prints made for exhibition in large theatres and drive-in movie houses and when it comes to making transfers for cable, cassette, network and satellite TV, and even in-flight movie presentation, you will have a product where the close-ups of your major artists will be relatively as large on a small screen as they are in the theatre. (See page 7)
   Alternatively you can choose 'PANAVISION SPHERICAL' using the regular Academy frame which can be projected by any 35mm projector anywhere in the world, can be masked down to 1.66:1 or 1.85:1 and can be used for direct transfer to video for television presentation in either the normal or the 16:9 format and for reduction to 16mm.
   Whichever format you choose, the credits 'FILMED IN PANAVISION' or 'FILMED WITH PANAVISION CAMERAS AND LENSES' will say to your distributors, exhibitors and prospective filmgoers and video viewers that yours is a carefully crafted movie.
   PANAVISION's new PRIMO-L lenses, both spherical and anamorphic, are the first complete sets of lenses especially conceived, designed and manufactured solely for motion picture usage to be commissioned in over a decade. The Primos highlight PANAVISION's place at the forefront of lens manufacturers. These magnificent lenses have unique features about them which give the cinematographer the greatest possible scope for creativity, whether the photography be by natural or highly stylized lighting, or anything in between.
   In conjunction with PANAVISION cameras, these state-of-the-art lenses provide the cinematographer with the ultimate image forming equipment.

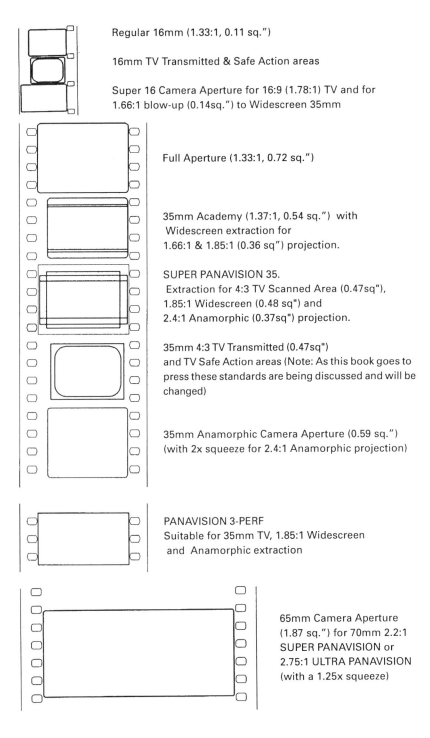

Regular 16mm (1.33:1, 0.11 sq.")

16mm TV Transmitted & Safe Action areas

Super 16 Camera Aperture for 16:9 (1.78:1) TV and for
1.66:1 blow-up (0.14sq.") to Widescreen 35mm

Full Aperture (1.33:1, 0.72 sq.")

35mm Academy (1.37:1, 0.54 sq.") with
Widescreen extraction for
1.66:1 & 1.85:1 (0.36 sq") projection.

SUPER PANAVISION 35.
Extraction for 4:3 TV Scanned Area (0.47sq"),
1.85:1 Widescreen (0.48 sq") and
2.4:1 Anamorphic (0.37sq") projection.

35mm 4:3 TV Transmitted (0.47sq")
and TV Safe Action areas (Note: As this book goes to
press these standards are being discussed and will be
changed)

35mm Anamorphic Camera Aperture (0.59 sq.")
(with 2x squeeze for 2.4:1 Anamorphic projection)

PANAVISION 3-PERF
Suitable for 35mm TV, 1.85:1 Widescreen
and Anamorphic extraction

65mm Camera Aperture
(1.87 sq.") for 70mm 2.2:1
SUPER PANAVISION or
2.75:1 ULTRA PANAVISION
(with a 1.25x squeeze)

5

Anamorphic or Spherical?

For theatrical release, to shoot 'anamorphic' or 'spherical' is a technical decision the Producer must make. Put simply, 'going anamorphic' involves photography with anamorphic lenses which squeeze a wide scene area onto a narrow film format. The film is subsequently projected in the theatre using a complementary anamorphic lens which unsqueezes the image to give a picture on the screen which is almost 2.4 times as wide as it is high. Television, and other forms of electronic presentation, be it for the normal 4:3 format, for the later 16:9 format or for any other video screen shape that may be dreamed up in the future, is achieved by extracting an appropriate width image from the anamorphic original at the time the film is transferred to video tape.

Going 'spherical' means photographing the film in a normal manner with an image which is a little more than 1 1/3 times as wide as it is high (1.37:1) and from this losing a great deal of the top and bottom of the image for 1.85:1 Widescreen presentation in the theatre. In this format almost all of the original image is used for subsequent television and video presentation.

A third alternative is to go 'PANAVISION SUPER-35'. This involves photographing the film with spherical lenses across the full with of the film, including the sound track, to give the largest possible 35mm image area in the first place. From this a normal interpositive is made and from this, in turn, optical printing is used to make a series of internegatives to suit each and every presentation format. This can include 70mm and anamorphic negatives from which theatrical release prints can be made, 1.85:1 for Widescreen presentation, 4:3 and 16:9 for television and video, and even 16mm if required. With the modern generation of fine grain filmstocks and improved optics image quality is not an overwhelming problem from this format and it has the advantage that the tele-cine transfers can be made directly from the original without the need to "pan and scan" the original picture composition.

Counting the costs

So far as the PANAVISION equipment is concerned, whether the production is to be shot Anamorphic or Spherical, the camera rental cost is the same.

While anamorphic lenses cost more to rent than spherical, the chances are that fewer will be taken, if for no other reason than the range of focal lengths is limited compared to spherical.

Straightforward Academy format for 1.85:1 release has its additional costs as higher sets and more ceiling pieces will be required and with Super-35 an important consideration is the additional cost of making the optically printed internegatives. Both of these costs help to offset the additional costs of anamorphic lenses.

The original scene

THE ACADEMY (WIDESCREEN) ROUTE	THE SUPER 35 ROUTE	THE ANAMORPHIC ROUTE
v	v	V

AS SEEN IN THE THEATRE

(1.85:1)

(2.4:1 Anamorphic print from an internegative)

or

(1.85:1 Widescreen print from an internegative)

(2.4:1 Anamorphic original)

AS SEEN ON TELEVISION

(4:3 transfer from an Academy original)

or

(16:9 "Letterbox" transfer)

(4:3 transfer from a normal or an optical print)

or

(16:9 "Letterbox" transfer)

(Panned and scanned from an anamorphic original)

or

 or

(Anamorphic cropped to 16:9)   (Original framing)

7

The Pros and Cons of Academy, Anamorphic & Super-35 Cinematography

Academy cinematography

For theatrical release, the great advantage of spherical cinematography is that the same original image can be used for all forms of presentation.

The disadvantages are that the image must be framed top and bottom to suit both the 1.85:1 Widescreen and the 4:3 television formats. This will entail additional cost in ceiling pieces, keeping lights higher and being careful that dolly tracks to not appear in the television picture. When shooting it will mean framing close-ups in such a manner that artists' heads do not go through the top of the wide screen format, thus losing much of their impact when shown on television with all the additional head and foot room.

Anamorphic cinematography

The super-wide screen ratio of anamorphic presentation (often called '2.35:1' but actually 2.4:1) is particularly good for pictures which contain many panoramic exterior scenes and for those which have many stretches of conversation between important characters, all of whom need to be seen in close-up to add importance to what they are saying.

There are two schools of thought on which is the most preferable means of transferring an anamorphic original to video.

In the past 'panning and scanning' the image at the time of tele-cine transfer in order to centre the image on the most important element or character has been the norm. This method maintains the power and the impact of all the close-ups.

The alternative, which is becoming more popular with the advent and acceptance of "Widescreen" television, is to have a "letter box" scan done whereby the original framing decided upon by the Director is preserved, leaving a blank area at the top and bottom of the frame.

Super-35 cinematography

Super-35 is cinematography using the largest possible frame area, what used to be called the "Silent" or "Full" frame. Then, at a later stage, when the film has been edited and finished, a series of optical internegatives are made to suit all the different methods of presentation.

Given that in all cases all presentation prints will be made from one or more internegatives made from a master interpositive, this means that final prints can be made to suit particular forms of presentation.

8

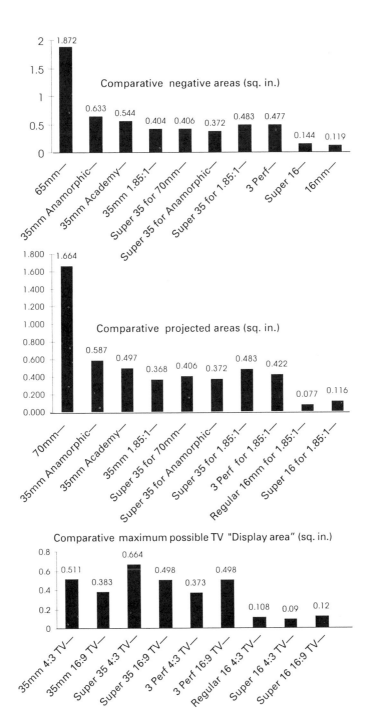

Comparative negative areas (sq. in.)

65mm	1.872
35mm Anamorphic	0.633
35mm Academy	0.544
35mm 1.85:1	0.404
Super 35 for 70mm	0.406
Super 35 for Anamorphic	0.372
Super 35 for 1.85:1	0.483
3 Perf	0.477
Super 16	0.144
16mm	0.119

Comparative projected areas (sq. in.)

70mm	1.664
35mm Anamorphic	0.587
35mm Academy	0.497
35mm 1.85:1	0.368
Super 35 for 70mm	0.406
Super 35 for Anamorphic	0.372
Super 35 for 1.85:1	0.483
3 Perf for 1.85:1	0.422
Regular 16mm for 1.85:1	0.077
Super 16 for 1.85:1	0.116

Comparative maximum possible TV "Display area" (sq. in.)

35mm 4:3 TV	0.511
35mm 16:9 TV	0.383
Super 35 4:3 TV	0.664
Super 35 16:9 TV	0.498
3 Perf 4:3 TV	0.373
3 Perf 16:9 TV	0.498
Regular 16 4:3 TV	0.108
Super 16 4:3 TV	0.09
Super 16 16:9 TV	0.12

9

PANAVISION's Special Equipment

PANAVISION is always interested in supplying custom engineered camera systems and accessories to suit the special needs of their customers. Over the years PANAVISION has designed and supplied many unique cameras, accessories and lenses from the special mirage effect lens that was used to shoot the desert mirage sequence in Lawrence of Arabia to various 35mm and 65mm 3D lenses and camera systems.

In keeping with this tradition of supplying innovative lenses in recent times PANAVISION have developed a Slant Lens, which enables the point of focus to be varied across the width of the frame, a Perspective Lens, which can return buildings to an upright position and the PANAVISION/FRAZIER lens which has almost infinite depth of focus, low angle capability and can be panned and rotated about the optical axis independently of the camera, while keeping the image upright.

Cost saving equipment

It has always been a part of PANAVISION's philosophy to reduce costs and this has very often been achieved through innovation without sacrificing quality, usability or reliability.

Not least of the accessories which are available with all PANAVISION cameras are those which directly reduce production costs.

For productions where negative filmstock and processing costs are a significant part of the budget PANAVISION can supply cameras fitted with their 3-PERF camera movement, saving 25% on these costs and reducing short-end wastage and camera reloading time. The 3-PERF system, together with time code (see pages 216 - 227), is particularly suitable for film productions where the original negative is transferred directly to tape for post-production purposes.

Another cost saving/time saving item is the 2000ft magazine: 22 minutes of film at normal frame rates, nearly 30 with 3-PERF.

The PANAVID range of video-assist systems are well known and a great cost saver. PANAVISION engineers have developed an entirely new concept of color flicker-free/freeze frame video assist systems which use CCD image sensors of immense sensitivity and which scan in synchronization with the film, giving new possibilities for SFX shooting. The image quality of the CCD PANAVID is so high that it can be used for off-line video editing which can later be conformed by the use of PANAVISION's AATONCODE time code system.

Laboratory equipment

Although relatively unknown to cinematographers, PANAVISION also supplies many leading film processing laboratories and special effects companies with a wide variety of optical printer lenses.

1

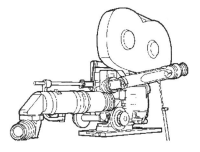

2

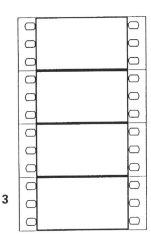

3

4

5

1. The special shimmer effect lens made by PANAVISION for the mirage sequence in *Lawrence of Arabia,* 2. The PANAVISION/FRAZIER lens system, 3. 3–PERF film, 4. PANAVISION PANAVID video viewfinder systems, 5. PANALUX night sight camera viewfinder system.

PANAVISION's New Technologies

Many of the new generation of PANAVISION's senior design personnel have had recent experience in the aerospace, electronics and computer industries and have successfully integrated into the design team to work alongside all of those who are long established cinematographic engineers with many years of experience. With this formidable combination Film Producers can be assured that the latest technologies are available to them and that the means of making films has not been left to wallow in the horse and buggy era.

Time code
For Producers seeking to use new technology as a means to reduce post-production time and costs, PANAFLEX cameras can be fitted with the PANAVISION AATONCODE time code system. This 35mm system is based upon the well established AATON 16mm system which combines SMPTE time code with legible, 'man-readable' information on every frame of negative and print.

With a PANAVISION AATONCODE time code generator fitted inside your camera, alongside each frame of film there will be a series of computer-readable dots, known as the "SMPTE time code". This "time stamp" records the precise date and time that the film was exposed (accurate to 1/100 sec. over an 8 hour period), together with the Production No. (very useful when shooting an episodic TV production), the type of filmstock used and the camera No. and ID letter. In addition, the date, the time, the "start frame", the Production No., the filmstock type and the camera No. and ID information, will all be displayed in "man readable" numbers and letters once every second.

The impact of the PANAVISION AATONCODE time-code system is greatest in the video post production stage of film making where the cost savings can be quite substantial.

PANAVISION welcomes the opportunity to discuss the use of time-code and other new and emerging technologies with all who handle the image and sound, in whatever form, from when it leaves the camera until it reaches the screen as a finished product.

Research and development
As this book goes to press PANAVISION have announced that they have recently entered into alliances to jointly develop products with such companies as Lightstorm Technologies, Hughes Aircraft, Mantis Wildlife Films and Lockheed Missiles & Space (now Lockheed Martin). These and future partnerships, along with an ever accelerating in-house research program, will ensure that PANAVISION continues to introduce new and innovative products well into the next century.

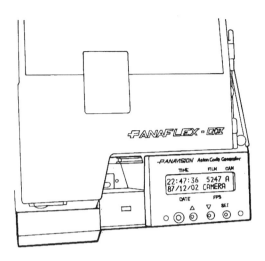

1

Direction of Travel >

| Date | Time | Start |

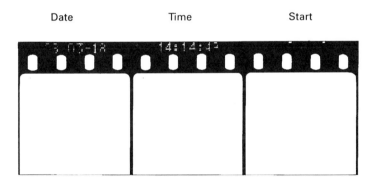

2

1. PANAVISION AATONCODE camera unit fitted to a PANAFLEX GII camera,
2. PANAVISION AATONCODE time code film clip showing man-readable figures interspersed with computer-readable time code information.

PANAVISION and Future Technologies

PANAVISION cameras are continuously updated 'state-of-the-art' devices which incorporate more desirable features than any other motion picture camera. Every feature is there either because it makes pictures look better on the screen or because it makes it less expensive to make pictures, especially when shooting sync sound in confined conditions.

Development work never stops. The PANAVISION management team knows that if they were ever to sit back on their past laurels and not continue to spend vast sums of money on R&D they would quickly lose their leadership in the field. Because PANAVISION cameras and lenses are never sold but only leased on a picture by picture basis they are in the ideal position to constantly manufacture new items, to upgrade and service existing items and to withdraw those that become passé. You never get a noisy "yesterday's" camera from PANAVISION.

PANAVISION at the cutting edge of technology

For the ultimate in image quality, especially in so far as being able to have your picture projected using very much higher screen brightness levels you can shoot with PANAVISION cameras at 29.97 fps and because the cameras are so quiet in the first place you can do so without the camera noise becoming obtrusive. With this system images have freedom from flicker, faster pans and tilts are possible without strobing and there is finer grain and greater image detail.

Shooting at 29.97 fps is also advantageous for ultimate image quality when film is transferred to NTSC video; for shooting scenes which contain many in-shot video monitors and for transfer to High Definition TV (whichever system may prevail in the future).

Irrespective of what generations of video origination, recording and display systems may be invented, and later relegated into disuse in the years to come, a transparent image on film will always be usable and marketable at any time in the future. This is more than can be said for productions that were recorded, even comparatively recently, on now obsolete video recorders. There is always a future for film.

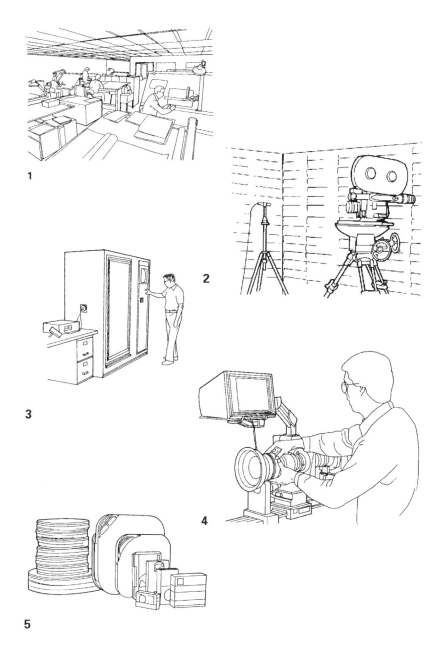

1. PANAVISION's engineering design department, 2. PANAVISION's sound test room, 3. PANAVISION's environmental test chamber, 4. PANAVISION's MTF optical test bench, 5. Video formats may come and go but rolls of film virtually last forever.

The Hidden Economies of
"Going PANAVISION"

Every element of the PANAVISION system of Cinematography is interchangeable. PANAVISION equipment is designed to minimize any possibility of downtime due to camera malfunction. PANAVISION's worldwide Distributor support network ensures that adequate backup is never more than a phone call away.

Since PANAVISION cameras, lenses and related equipment are never sold and only leased on a picture-by-picture basis, the Producer can take only the minimum amount of equipment actually needed for a specific project and then only for the period it is required. For low budget projects there are always lower cost options available and PANAVISION's client liaison personnel can always suggest alternative equipment whose bottom line cost will be less than any other.

Producers know that the very latest equipment, fully updated with all modifications will be available to him and his production technicians; they know that equipment-for-equipment PANAVISION has no equal; that the services offered have full backup support and that, in the final analysis, PANAVISION is the economic, reliable and responsible choice.

It is arguable as to whether it is more important to go "PANAVISION" on a big picture, when the financial stakes are greatest and visual impact on the screen must match the magnitude, or on a modest picture, when even a small hold-up can cause expensive delays. PANAVISION has proven itself the most cost effective camera system for films of all budgets.

"Going PANAVISION" is like taking out a low cost insurance policy.

PANAVISION credits
Of the 135 films in Variety's 1996 ALL-TIME FILM RENTAL CHAMPS list, ten were either animation or pre-PANAVISION's time (GWTW) and of the rest more than 86% were photographed with PANAVISION lenses and cameras. With PANAVISION you are not guaranteed to have a box-office winner but it doesn't hurt.

Since the first film to be filmed in 'PANAVISION', Raintree County in 1958, and the first PANAFLEX picture, Steven Spielberg's Sugarland Express, PANAVISION equipped pictures have won more Oscars for Best Picture than any others using other lenses and cameras.

With PANAVISION you are always in good company.

16

Variety ALL-TIME FILM RENTAL CHAMPS
OF THE US-CANADA MARKET
Photographed with PANAVISION lenses and cameras (Feb 26th 1996)

E.T. THE EXTRA-TERRESTRIAL	U 1982	$399,804,539
JURASSIC PARK	U 1993	357,067,947
FORREST GUMP	Par 1994	329,689,600
STAR WARS	Fox 1977	322,740,142
JAWS	U 1977	260,000,000
BATMAN	WB 1989	251,188,924
RAIDERS OF THE LOST ARK	Par 1981	242,374,454
GHOSTBUSTERS	Col 1984	238,600,000
BEVERLY HILLS COP	Par 1984	234,760,478
THE EMPIRE STRIKES BACK	Fox 1980	222,674,266
MRS DOUBTFIRE	Fox 1993	219,195,051
BACK TO THE FUTURE	U 1985	208,242,016
INDIANA JONES & THE LAST CRUSADE	Par 1989	197,171,806
DANCES WITH WOLVES	Orion 1990	184,208,848
BATMAN FOREVER	WB1995	184,031,112
THE FUGITIVE	WB 1993	183,875,760
INDIANA JONES & THE TEMPLE OF DOOM	Par 1984	179,870,271
PRETTY WOMAN	BV 1990	178,406,268
TOOTSIE	Col 1982	177,200,000
TOP GUN	Par 1986	176,781,728
CROCODILE DUNDEE	Par 1986	174,634,806
HOME ALONE 2	Fox 1992	173,585,516
RAIN MAN	MGM/UA 1992	172,825,435
APOLLO 13	U 1995	172,070,496
THE EXORCIST	WB 1973	165,000,000
BATMAN RETURNS	WB 1992	162,831,698
THE SOUND OF MUSIC	Fox 1965	160,476,831
THE FIRM	Par 1993	158,340,292
FATAL ATTRACTION	Par 1987	156,645,693
THE STING	U 1973	156,000,000
WHO FRAMED ROGER RABBIT	BV 1988	154,112,492
BEVERLY HILLS COP 2	Par 1987	153,665,036
GREASE	Par 1978	153,112,492
RAMBO: FIRST BLOOD II	TriStar 1985	150,425,432
GREMLINS	WB 1984	148,168,459
LETHAL WEAPON 2	WB 1989	147,253,986
THE SANTA CLAUSE	BV 1994	144,833,357
LETHAL WEAPON 3	WB 1992	144,731,527
ANIMAL HOUSE	U 1978	141,600,000
A FEW GOOD MEN	Col 1992	141,340,178
LOOK WHO'S TALKING	TriStar 1989	140,088,813
TEENAGE MUTANT NINJA TURTLES	New Line 1990	135,265,915
SUPERMAN	WB 1978	134,218,018
THE ROCKY HORROR PICTURE SHOW	Fox 1975	130,198,189

"Best Picture" Academy Awards

Every year five pictures are nominated for the honor of being selected as the "Best Picture" of the year. By definition "Best Picture" is what it says it is and PANAVISION is proud that year after year this singular honor falls to pictures whose Producers have put their faith and trust in PANAVISION equipment.

**"BEST PICTURE" Academy Award pictures
Photographed with PANAVISION lenses and cameras (1958 - 1995)**

AMADEUS	Zaentz-Orion
ANNIE HALL	Rollins-Joffe-UA
THE APARTMENT	Mirisch-UA
BEN HUR	MGM
BRAVEHEART	Mel Gibson-Alan Ladd Jnr.-Bruce Davey-Icon Productions/Ladd Company
BUTCH CASSIDY AND THE SUNDANCE KID	20th Century Fox
DANCES WITH WOLVES	Tig Production-Orion
THE DEER HUNTER	EMI-Cimino-Universal
DOCTOR ZHIVAGO	Ponti-MGM
DRIVING MISS DAISY	Zanuck Company-Warner Bros
FORREST GUMP	Steve Tish/Wendy Finerman-Paramount
THE FRENCH CONNECTION	D'Antoni-Schine-Moore-20th Century Fox
GANDHI	Indo-British films-Columbia
THE GODFATHER PART II	Coppola Company-Paramount
THE GRADUATE	Embassy
IN THE HEAT OF THE NIGHT	Mirisch-UA
KRAMER vs. KRAMER	Columbia
LAWRENCE OF ARABIA	Horizon-Columbia
A MAN FOR ALL SEASONS	Highland-Columbia
M*A*S*H	20th Century Fox
MY FAIR LADY	Warner Bros
OLIVER!	Romulus-Columbia
ONE FLEW OVER THE CUCKOO'S NEST	Fantasy-UA
ORDINARY PEOPLE	Universal
PATTON	20th Century Fox
RAIN MAN	Gruber-Peters Company-UA
ROCKY	Chartoff-Winkler-UA
THE STING	Bill/Phillips-Hill-Zanuck/Brown-Universal
TERMS OF ENDEARMENT	Brooks-Paramount
UNFORGIVEN	Warner Bros-Warner Bros
WEST SIDE STORY	Mirisch-UA

18

Academy Accolades

In 1960, for the first time, films shot with PANAVISION lenses, *Anatomy of a Murder, Ben Hur* and *The Diary of Anne Frank,* received Academy Award Nominations for Best Picture of the Year. Since then, over a period of 36 years, and out of a total of 180 nominated pictures, no less than 30 serviced by PANAVISION have won the most coveted of all Oscars.

Producers who have won Oscars and Oscar Nominations for films photographed with PANAVISION cameras and/or lenses:
(winners in bold)

IRWIN ALLEN	The Towering Inferno
ROBERT ALTMAN	Nashville
TAMARA ASSAYEV	Norma Rae
RICHARD ATTENBOROUGH	**Gandhi**
ROBERT ALAN ARTHUR	All That Jazz
WARREN BEATTY	Heaven Can Wait
WARREN BEATTY	Bugsy
LAWRENCE BENDER	Pulp Fiction
CLAUDE BERRI	Tess
TONY BILL	**The Sting**
WILLIAM PETER BLATTY	The Exorcist
JOHN BOORMAN	Deliverance
RON BOZMAN	**The Silence of the Lambs**
JOHN BRABOURNE	A Passage to India
MARTIN BREST	Scent of a Woman
JAMES L. BROOKS	**Terms of Endearment**
DAVID BROWN	The Verdict
DAVID BROWN	Jaws
DAVID BROWN	A Few Good Men
TIMOTHY BURRILL	Tess
JOHN CALLEY	The Remains of the Day
ROBERT CHARTOFF	The Right Stuff
ROBERT CHARTOFF	**Rocky**
MICHAEL CIMINO	**The Deer Hunter**
WALTER COBLENZ	All the President's Men
ROBERT F. COLESBERRY	Mississippi Burning

Producers who have won Oscars and Oscar Nominations for films photographed with PANAVISION cameras and/or lenses
(continued):

FRANCIS FORD COPPOLA	American Graffiti
FRANCIS FORD COPPOLA	**The Godfather Part II**
FRANCIS FORD COPPOLA	The Godfather Part III
BRUCE DAVEY	**Braveheart**
PHILIP D'ANTONI	**The French Connection**
MICHAEL DEELEY	**The Deer Hunter**
MICHAEL DOUGLAS	One Flew over the Cuckoo's Nest
CLINT EASTWOOD	**Unforgiven**
ROBERT EVANS	Chinatown
EDWARD S. FELDMAN	Witness
WENDY FINERMAN	**Forrest Gump**
JOHN FOREMAN	Prizzi's Honor
JOHN FOREMAN	Butch Cassidy and the Sundance Kid
CARL FOREMAN	The Guns of Navarone
MELVIN FRANK	A Touch of Class
GRAY FREDERICKSON	**The Godfather Part II**
STEPHEN J. FRIEDMAN	The Last Picture Show
MEL GIBSON	**Braveheart**
BRUCE GILBERT	On Golden Pond
RICHARD GOODWIN	A Passage to India
CHARLES GORDON	Field of Dreams
LAWRENCE GORDON	Field of Dreams
HOWARD GOTTFREID	Network
BRIAN GRAZER	Apollo 13
RICHARD GREENHUT	Hannah and Her Sisters
MICHAEL GRILLO	The Accidental Tourist
STEVEN HAFT	Dead Poets Society
JEROME HELLMAN	Coming Home
NORMA HEYMAN	Dangerous Liaisons
A. KITMAN HO	Born on the Fourth of July
A. KITMAN HO	JFK
ROSS HUNTER	Airport
STANLEY R. JAFFE	Fatal Attraction
STANLEY R. JAFFE	**Kramer vs. Kramer**
NORMAN JEWISON	A Soldier's Story
NORMAN JEWISON	Fiddler on the Roof
NORMAN JEWISON	The Russians Are Coming

20

Producers who have won Oscars and Oscar Nominations for films photographed with PANAVISION cameras and/or lenses
(continued):

CHARLES H. JOFFE	**Annie Hall**
MARK JOHNSON	**Rain Man**
MARK JOHNSON	Bugsy
QUINCY JONES	The Color Purple
ANDREW KARSCH	The Prince of Tides
LAWRENCE KASDAN	The Accidental Tourist
KATHLEEN KENNEDY	The Color Purple
KATHLEEN KENNEDY	E.T. The Extra-Terrestrial
ARNOLD KOPELSON	The Fugitive
KEVIN COSTNER	**Dances with Wolves**
STANLEY KRAMER	Guess Who's Coming to Dinner?
STANLEY KRAMER	Ship of Fools
GARY KURTZ	Star Wars
GARY KURTZ	American Graffiti
ALAN LADD Jr.	**Braveheart**
SHERRY LANSING	Fatal Attraction
LAWRENCE LASKER	Awakenings
ARTHUR LAURENTS	The Turning Point
BARRY LEVINSON	Bugsy
JOSHUA LOGAN	Fanny
FRANK MARSHALL	The Color Purple
FRANK MARSHALL	Raiders of the Lost Ark
FRANK McCARTHY	**Patton**
ISMAIL MERCHANT	**Howards End**
ISMAIL MERCHANT	The Remains of the Day
BILL MILLER	Babe
GEORGE MILLER	Babe
HOWARD G. MINSKY	Love Story
WALTER MIRISCH	**In the Heat of the Night**
DOUG MITCHELL	Babe
HANK MOONJEAN	Dangerous Liaisons

21

RALPH NELSON	Lilies of the Field
MIKE NICHOLS	The Remains of the Day
CHARLES OKUN	The Accidental Tourist
PATRICK PALMER	Children of a Lesser God
PATRICK PALMER	A Soldier's Story
WALTER F. PARKES	Awakenings
JOHN PEVERALL	**The Deer Hunter**
JULIA PHILLIPS	**The Sting**
MICHAEL PHILLIPS	**The Sting**
MARTIN POLL	The Lion in Winter
SYDNEY POLLACK	Tootsie
CARLO PONTI	Dr. Zhivago
INGO PREMINGER	M*A*S*H*
OTTO PREMINGER	Anatomy of a Murder
ROBERT B. RADNITZ	Sounder
BOB RAFELSON	Five Easy Pieces
ROB REINER	A Few Good Men
DICK RICHARDS	Tootsie
FRED ROOS	**The Godfather Part II**
ALEX ROSE	Norma Rae
AARON ROSENBERG	Mutiny on the Bounty
HERBERT ROSS	The Turning Point
ROBERT ROSSEN	The Hustler
RICHARD ROTH	Julia
ALBERT S. RUDDY	**The Godfather**
JONATHAN SANGER	The Elephant Man
EDWARD SAXON	**The Silence of the Lambs**
ANDREW SCHEINMAN	A Few Good Men
BERNARD SCHWARTZ	Coal Miner's Daughter
RONALD L. SCHWARY	A Soldier's Story
RONALD L. SCHWARY	**Ordinary People**
MICHAEL SHAMBERG	The Big Chill

**Producers who have won Oscars and Oscar Nominations for films
photographed with PANAVISION cameras and/or lenses
(continued):**

.

STEVEN SPIELBERG	The Color Purple
STEVEN SPIELBERG	E.T. The Extra-Terrestrial
SAM SPIEGEL	Nicholas and Alexandra
SAM SPIEGEL	**Lawrence of Arabia**
RAY STARK	The Goodbye Girl
RAY STARK	Funny Girl
STEVE STARKEY	**Forrest Gump**
GEORGE STEVENS	The Diary of Anne Frank
OLIVER STONE	Born on the Fourth of July
OLIVER STONE	JFK
BARBRA STREISAND	The Prince of Tides
BURT SUGARMAN	Children of a Lesser God
TONY THOMAS	Dead Poets Society
STEVE TISCH	**Forrest Gump**
LAWRENCE TURMAN	The Graduate
KENNETH UTT	**The Silence of the Lambs**
HAL B. WALLIS	Anne of a Thousand Days
HAL B. WALLIS	Beckett
JACK L. WARNER	**My Fair Lady**
RICHARD WECHSLER	Five Easy Pieces
BILLY WILDER	**The Apartment**
JIM WILSON	**Dances with Wolves**
IRWIN WINKLER	The Right Stuff
IRWIN WINKLER	**Rocky**
ROBERT WISE	The Sand Pebbles
ROBERT WISE	**West Side Story**
PAUL JUNGER WITT	Dead Poets Society
JOHN WOOLF	**Oliver!**
SAUL ZAENTZ	**Amadeus**
SAUL ZAENTZ	**One Flew over the Cuckoo's Nest**
DARRYL F. ZANUCK	The Longest Day
LILI FINI ZANUCK	**Driving Miss Daisy**
RICHARD D. ZANUCK	The Verdict
RICHARD D. ZANUCK	Jaws
RICHARD D. ZANUCK	**Driving Miss Daisy**
SAM ZIMBALIST	Ben Hur
FRED ZINNEMANN	**A Man for All Seasons**
FREDERICK ZOLLO	Mississippi Burning

......and more to come

23

Selecting PANAVISION Equipment

When you decide to shoot a film with PANAVISION equipment you have the option of many alternative types of equipment with an equally wide range of prices appropriate to all types of productions and budgets. PANAVISION's customer liaison personnel are always available and ready to guide you through all the choices, to discuss the costs with you and to quote you for the most suitable and best equipment your budget can support. Nothing is impossible and never assume that PANAVISION equipment is too expensive for your picture.

Conditions of business
PANAVISION equipment is leased subject to standard production-by-production contracts, copies of which are available upon request.

The attention of all clients is drawn to the fact that PANAVISION Inc. and its Distributors supply equipment, materials and services only in accordance with their respective conditions of business. Copies of these Conditions of Business, *which include Clauses which exclude, limit or modify the liability of the company and provide for an indemnity from the customer in certain circumstances* are available on request.

Typical PANAVISION Equipment Choices

At first glance the variety of choice of PANAVISION equipment options is overwhelming; but by the time the pros and cons of the various demands and aspirations of the script, the Director and Director of Photography have been weighed the most economical option begins to come clear. To help you in your choice the PANAVISION staff are always ready to discuss your requirements and to supply you with a well documented catalogue.

Here is a headline guide to some of the possible choices:

The very finest, and quietest, camera system in the world:
PANAVISION PLATINUM PANAFLEX camera
PANAVISION GII/GOLDEN PANAFLEX "reduced cost" camera

The lightweight camera for Steadicam and remote camera use:
PANAVISION LIGHTWEIGHT PANAFLEX

The non-handholdable PANAFLEX system:
PANAVISION PANAFLEX-X camera

Low cost studio style cameras for low budget pictures:
SUPER PANAVISION SILENT REFLEX camera

High speed cameras:
PANAVISION PLATINUM PANASTAR 2-120 fps camera

PANAVISION PRIMO-L (™) lenses, the best there are:
10, 14.5, 17.5, 21, 27, 35, 40, 50, 75, 100 & 150mm T1.9
17.5 - 75mm T2.3, 24 - 275 & 135 - 420mm T2.8 zoom lenses

PANAVISION PRIMO ANAMORPHIC lenses:
35, 40, 50, 75 & 100mm T2 lenses
48 - 550 & 270 - 840mm T4.5 zoom lenses

A selection of PANAVISION's enormous range of lenses:
14 - 180mm "Z" series lenses (Zeiss glass, PANAVISION mechanics) T1.3 - 1.4
14 - 150mm PANAVISION ULTRA SPEED T1.0 - T1.9 lenses
8 - 1000mm PANAVISION NORMAL SPEED lenses
27 - 68mm PANAVISION LIGHTWEIGHT ZOOM lens
20 - 100mm T3.1 COOKE/PANAVISION 5:1 ZOOM lens
25 - 250mm T4 COOKE/PANAVISION 10:1 SUPER PANAZOOM lens
25 - 250mm T4 ANGENIEUX/PANAVISION 10:1 ZOOM lens
24 - 2000mm PANAVISION ANAMORPHIC lenses

Desirable additional equipment:
PANAVISION PANAHEAD geared tripod head
Sealed lead acid batteries with built-in chargers
Reversible magazines for the PLATINUM and PANASTAR PANAFLEXES
PANAVISION CCD Flicker free PANAVID video systems
PANAVISION/AATONCODE TIME CODE system

The
Film Directors'
PANAFLEX

The 'Go PANAVISION' Decision

To 'go PANAVISION' is an early and an important decision on any film.

With the security of PANAVISION the Director is assured that, so far as the camera is concerned, he has the best possible chance of delivering the film on time, within budget and with the maximum image impact on the screen.

In the environment of a film production set the omnipresence of a friendly camera can contribute much to creating an atmosphere of quiet professionalism. The PANAFLEX camera is sleek and small and doesn't get in the way. It has been a design aim of the PLATINUM PANAFLEX that it should be 'transparent' on the set.

PANAVISION cameras don't need blankets over them to keep the Sound Recordist quiet

Always quiet and efficient, PANAFLEX cameras do not need blankets thrown over them to pacify the sound recordist.

Changing a lens on a PANAFLEX is simple and swift, nothing extra is needed to bottle up the camera noise, so your camera crew will not mind how many alternative set-ups you try before you settle on just the right one.

Somehow, there is a touch of humanity about the PANAFLEX camera which helps to keep your actors and actresses relaxed. Maybe it is the soft contours or its discrete color, maybe because it is only seen and never heard, or maybe it's because the crew never have to take it apart just when you are ready to go for an important take. PANAFLEX cameras never draw attention to themselves.

For whatever reason, everyone gets on well together around a PANAFLEX.

Customized equipment

PANAVISION has a long history of supplying hardware solutions to shooting problems. Typical examples are:

A lightweight AUTO PANATAR anamorphic lens to use on a skydiver's helmet.

A rifle sight that can be deployed in front of the camera lens during a take.

A mesmerizer lens to create a mystical dreamlike experience.

A camera body on a self-propelled platform to run under a big truck.

Various single and two-camera 3D systems.

Some very special underwater camera equipment ... about which more later!

If your script has some special equipment need to make a point more effectively talk to PANAVISION. The chances are they will be able to come up with a solution....

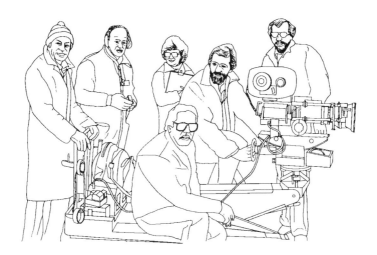

1.

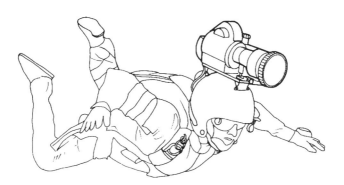

2.

1. A PANAFLEX camera is a central part of the film making team,
2. A PANAVISION AUTO PANATAR anamorphic lens mounted on a lightweight camera on a skydiver's helmet.

PANAVISION Formats to Suit the Script

The range of PANAVISION camera equipment is vast. There is no script or budget camera demand that PANAVISION cannot satisfy.

65mm
PANAVISION has a full range of 65mm cameras with reflex, handholdable, studio-quiet, high speed and underwater capabilities.

Anamorphic large screen formats
35mm PANAVISION Anamorphic lenses are readily available for pictures destined for large screen theatrical release. Many Directors like to shoot in this format because it gives them a wide canvas that makes their movie more special in the theatre and yet gives a sense of intimacy to a group shot.

Academy, TV and Widescreen formats
PANAVISION has the widest range of spherical lenses to cover the Academy frame, which encompasses both the TV and the Widescreen (1.85:1) formats, available anywhere in the world. For Directors who wish to ensure that their pictures are correctly shown on theatrical screens PANAVISION cameras may be supplied with a hard matte. A TV image can still be extracted from a 1.66:1 hard matted negative.

Super-35
PANAVISION cameras can be supplied to shoot with spherical lenses across the full width of the 35mm frame. This format gives an adequate negative area for large screen 70mm and Anamorphic prints and yet the video format can be extracted without the need to pan and scan the image.

PANAVISION 3-PERF
PANAVISION's 3-PERF three perforation pull-down system reduces film production costs by saving more than 25% of all camera filmstock costs and processing charges. It is especially suitable for films destined only for video post-production and presentation but may also be used for films destined for theatrical presentation.

Regular 16 and Super 16
For both Regular 16 and Super 16 shooting, where the sound track area is included in the 16mm frame area to give a larger negative for 1.66:1 and 1.85:1 35mm blow-up prints, the PANAFLEX 16 is the ideal camera.

Television
To shoot film is to shoot "future proof" TV.

30

1. 65mm

2. Typical scene relative to a 2.35:1 frame.

3. The same scene relative to a TV Transmitted area frame.

4. Head & shoulders C.U. relative to a 1.85:1 frame.

5. Same size C.U. relative to a TV Transmitted Area frame.

6. 1.85:1 image area relative to an Academy frame.

7. TV Transmitted area relative to an Academy frame.

8. 1.85:1 and TV Transmitted relative to an Academy frame.

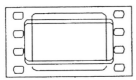

9. 2.35:1, 1.85:1 & TV image areas relative to a SUPER PANAVISION 35 frame.

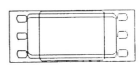

10. 2.35:1, 1.85:1 & modified TV image areas relative to a PANAVISION 3-PERF frame.

11. 1.66:1 Super 16 image area.

12. 1.66:1 image area derived from Regular 16.

13. Comparison of 1.66:1 image areas derived from Super 16 and Regular 16.

PANAVISION Cameras to Suit the Script

PANAVISION is able to supply the quietest handholdable sync camera, floating cameras, high speed or single shot cameras, plate cameras, underwater cameras, and so on. PANAVISION has them all, off the shelf.

PANAFLEX cameras

PANAVISION's computer-age camera is the PLATINUM PANAFLEX, an advanced technology instrument to make filming easier, quicker and quieter.

The GII GOLDEN PANAFLEX is an updated version of the GOLDEN at an economy price. It is very quiet and can be used with all the same lenses and most of the same accessories as the PLATINUM.

The GOLDEN PANAFLEX is the standard camera of the PANAFLEX range of cameras. It has practically all of the features required for general day-to-day cinematography, is quiet enough for most shooting environments and is very competitively priced compared to any other make of camera.

In close support of these cameras is the PANAFLEX-X, basically similar to the GII/GOLDEN PANAFLEXES but which has a fixed viewfinder. It does, however, use the same magazines, matte boxes and most other accessories and is proportionately less expensive. Directors often choose an X as a second camera.

The PANAFLEX LIGHTWEIGHT is specially designed and made for Steadicam and long-reach remote control camera crane use.

Complementing the PANAFLEX range of cameras are the PLATINUM PANASTAR and the PANASTAR single frame to 120 fps cameras especially designed for action unit and special effects cinematography. Where extraordinary image steadiness, the choice of ultra fast and ultra slow camera speeds and camera ruggedness are all at a premium, the 'STARS' perform perfectly. The PLATINUM STAR is incredibly quiet for a SFX camera and at 24 fps is quite suitable for second camera use in many exterior sync-sound shooting conditions.

SUPER PSR cameras

Even less expensive than the X is the Super PSR camera. Based on Mitchell movements these cameras are the answer when the overriding need is for a studio camera at the least possible cost. They are particularly useful for multi-camera shoots including TV Situation Comedies.

Panavised support cameras

PANAVISION can supply a wide variety of Arriflex and Mitchell cameras, all fitted with PANAVISION lens mounts to make all cameras take all PANAVISION lenses.

1. The GII/GOLDEN PANAFLEX
A much quieter version of an old
friend now principally used as a
support camera

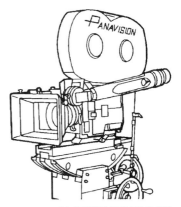

2. The PLATINUM PANAFLEX
The quietest camera in the world
and incorporating every possible
'Production Value' facility

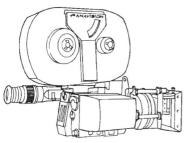

3. The PANASTAR
Single frame to 120 fps
Crystal controlled 12 to 120 fps

4. The PANAFLEX-X
An economy version
of the PANAFLEX GII

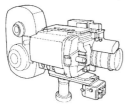

5. The LIGHTWEIGHT PANAFLEX
Perfect for *Steadicam* and similar
usage

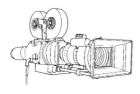

6. The Super PSR. Especially
good for multi-camera shooting

7. 'Pan' Mitchells & Arris
Ideal as support cameras

33

PANAVISION Lenses to Suit the Script

The scene-by-scene choice of lenses can make an enormous difference to the way a story is told. PANAVISION has lenses in profusion.

PANAVISION spherical lenses

Top of the range of non-anamorphic lenses are the fantastic PRIMO-L series of lenses. Their undoubted superiority in definition, contrast, freedom from distortion and color balance between lenses makes them the No. 1 choice not only when the script demands crisp, gutsy images but also when the requirement is to produce soft and subtle images in conditions of harsh backlighting, diffusion and smoke.

The range of PRIMO-L fixed focal length lenses extends from 10mm to 150mm, 210mm with a PANAVISION matched range extender.

PRIMO zoom lenses are equal even to PRIMO fixed focal length lenses in image quality.

Of particular interest to the Director is the variety of special purpose PRIMO lenses. There is the distortion-free 10mm Wide Angle PRIMO-L lens. There are Close Focusing and Macro PRIMO lenses, Slant Focus PRIMO lenses and View Camera type lenses. There are 17.5 - 75mm Wide Angle, normal 24.5 - 275mm 11:1 and 135 - 420mm Long Focal Length PRIMO zoom lenses. A Lightweight zoom lens especially designed and made for Steadicam and similar usage.

There are some extreme wide aperture lenses that almost see in the dark.

There is the PANAVISION/FRAZIER lens system, which does all manner of unique tricks, and so on.

PANAVISION anamorphic lenses

PANAVISION has long held a unique position in the supply of anamorphic lenses. No one else has ever come near and in recognition of this achievement PANAVISION Inc. was awarded an Oscar by the Academy of Motion Picture Arts and Sciences.

With the introduction of the PRIMO range of Anamorphic lenses PANAVISION have well aligned themselves to remain in the lead well into the twenty-first century

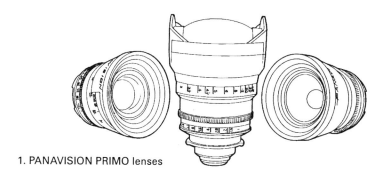

1. PANAVISION PRIMO lenses

FOCAL LENGTH	LENS ANGLES (Academy camera aperture)	
	HORIZONTAL	VERTICAL
150mm	8.3°	6.1°
100mm	12.5°	9.1°
75mm	16.6°	12.1°
50mm	24.7°	18.1°
40mm	30.6°	22.5°
35mm	34.8°	25.7°
27mm	44.2°	33.0°
21mm	55.1°	41.7°
17.5mm	64.1°	49.1°
14.5mm	74.2°	57.7°
10mm	95.3°	77.3°

2. PANAVISION PRIMO SPHERICAL lens focal length/lens angle chart

3. PANAVISION PRIMO ANAMORPHIC lens

35

PANAVISION Viewfinding Aids

The part of the film camera with which the Director has the closest relationship is the viewfinder. It therefore matters to him that the viewfinder system, and the video assist system, if fitted, are bright and clear.

Optical viewfinder systems
The optical viewfinders on all PANAVISION PANAFLEX cameras are particularly bright and are sometimes referred to as being 'brighter than life'.

All PANAFLEX viewfinders incorporate a PANAGLOW illuminated ground-glass reticle which enables the markings to be seen, even in the dark.

All PANAFLEX and PSR cameras, (except the 'X'), have a viewfinder magnification system which enables the Director to zoom in on the ground glass image to take a closer look at a particular part of the scene.

All PANAFLEX and PSR viewfinders have a white bezel around the eyepiece focus ring where individuals can mark their own personal focus setting.

A new and interesting item is the "VID-Stick" a cooperative development between PANAVISION and Lightstorm Technologies Inc. This item is essentially a combination of a "mass balanced" portable viewfinder, a video assist and a video transmitter. It enables a Director to go through the camera movements that he wishes the camera to follow while at the same time transmitting the image to a video monitor and/or a video recorder for the benefit of the camera, the Steadicam and the camera crane operator.

For normal usage the PANAFINDER portable viewfinder accessory is also available. It can be used with any lens and the Director can carry it around and hold it in his hands to use as an aid to determining a camera setup.

PANAVID video assist viewfinders
PANAVID video-assist systems can be fitted to any PANAFLEX camera.

The PANAVID CCD system gives high quality, flicker-free images, even in very low light levels. It incorporates a FRAME GRAB facility to exactly superimpose the present setup with a previous one. The quality of the CCD system is good enough to use for off-line video editing.

All PANAVID video assists can be made even more efficient by exchanging the camera's mirror shutter for a fixed pellicle mirror, a feature unique to PANAVISION.

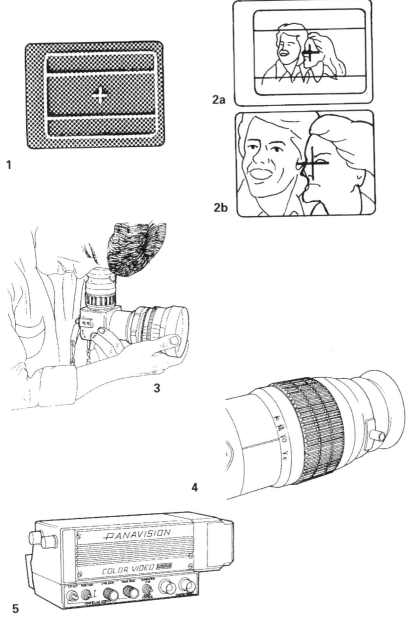

1. PANAGLOW illuminated ground glass markings, 2.a. Normal image through the viewfinder showing the ground glass markings, 2.b. Enlarged image through the viewfinder, 3. PANAFINDER viewfinder, 4. PANAFLEX eyepiece marker ring for personal setting marks, 5. PANAVISION COLOR CCD video assist and character generator system.

PANAVISION Equipment to Give Added Production Values

PANAVISION not only supplies cameras and lenses but can also supply a wide range of complementary specialist equipment.

Image control filters
PANAVISION have developed some very special matte-boxes beyond the normal multi-stage filter holders. To give added production values filters can be slid, rotated and tilted, in-shot, if required.

Inclining prism low angle attachment
An INCLINING PRISM placed in front of the taking lens enables a low angle shot to be taken from ground level. With it, it is even possible to take a shot looking upwards as though a hole had been cut in the floor to accommodate the camera. With an INCLINING PRISM there is no loss of exposure, definition or image orientation.

PANAFLASHER light overlay accessory
The PANAFLASHER gives the film a very low overall exposure which has the effect of increasing the exposure in the shadow areas and reducing image contrast. If the light is colored it has the effect of tinting the shadows and leaving the highlights, and most of the skin tones, unaffected.

PANAVISION/FRAZIER lens system
An extremely versatile lens system with almost infinite depth of field. Other attributes are an articulated front section which enables panning to be done independently of the camera, the ability of the lens to rotate the image about the optical axis (as with a dutch head or a turnover mount) and a unique cranked low-angle configuration.

PANAVISION slant focus lenses
Allows the focal plane to be angled to one side or the other so that the plane of focus, and the available depth of field, may be set at a slope to the film plane. This is particularly useful when shooting with little depth of field and a close object on one side of the picture is required to be in as sharp focus as a more distant object on the other side.

PANATATE turnover camera mount
The interpretation of a script sometimes calls for creative camera angles, even to the point of the camera turning upside down in space. This can be achieved with the PANATATE turnover mount which fits onto any PANAHEAD.

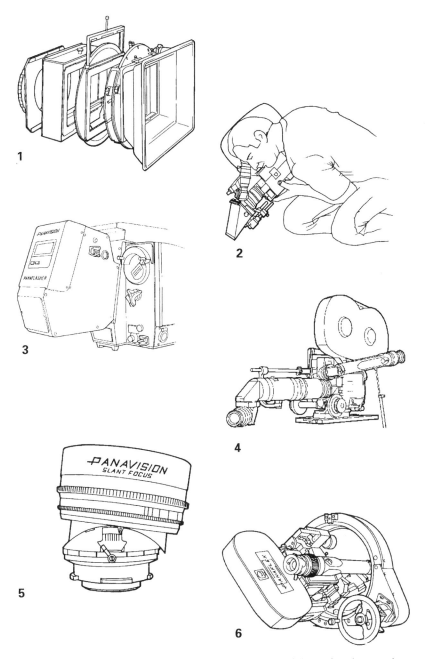

1. PANAVISION special facilities 6.6" matte-box, 2. Inclining prism low angle lens attachment, 3. PANAFLASHER light overlay accessory, 4. PANAVISION/FRAZIER lens system, 5. PANAVISION slant focus lens, 6. PANATATE turnover camera mount.

39

The equipment is the last thing in the world the Director wants to worry about

PANAVISION's Credentials

The Director's job is all about concentration. Concentration on the artists, concentration on interpreting the script and how a sequence is finally going to cut together on the screen, concentration on maintaining the mood to keep the audience absorbed, and so on. He or she has a great deal to think about.

For this reason it is of the utmost importance to the Director that all involved in the making of the picture, including the camera and sound crews, are efficient in themselves and are equipped in such a manner that they can give their best. The results of this will undoubtedly show on the screen.

From David Lean to Steven Spielberg there is not a great contemporary Director of motion picture films who has not put his trust in PANAFLEX cameras and PANAVISION lenses. Directors can have confidence with PANAVISION.

Directors who have won Oscars and Oscar Nominations
for films photographed with
PANAVISION cameras and/or lenses
(Winners in **BOLD**)

WOODY ALLEN	Annie Hall
WOODY ALLEN	Interiors
WOODY ALLEN	Broadway Danny Rose
WOODY ALLEN	Hannah and Her Sisters
WOODY ALLEN	Crimes and Misdemeanors
WOODY ALLEN	Bullets over Broadway
ROBERT ALTMAN	M*A*S*H*
ROBERT ALTMAN	Short Cuts
HAL ASHBY	Coming Home
RICHARD ATTENBOROUGH	**Gandhi**
JOHN G. AVILDSEN	**Rocky**
HECTOR BABENCO	Kiss of the Spider Woman
WARREN BEATTY	Heaven Can Wait
ROBERT BENTON	**Kramer vs. Kramer**
BRUCE BERESFORD	Tender Mercies
PETER BOGDANOVITCH	The Last Picture Show
JOHN BOORMAN	Deliverance
KENNETH BRANAGH	Henry V
MARTIN BREST	Scent of a Woman
JAMES L. BROOKS	**Terms of Endearment**
MICHAEL CIMINO	**The Deer Hunter**
FRANCIS FORD COPPOLA	The Godfather, Part III
KEVIN COSTNER	**Dances with Wolves**
CHARLES CRICHTON	A Fish Called Wanda
GEORGE CUKOR	**My Fair Lady**

JONATHAN DEMME	**The Silence of the Lambs**
CLINT EASTWOOD	**Unforgiven**
FEDERICO FELLINI	Satyricon
MIKE FIGGIS	Leaving Las Vegas*
MILOS FORMAN	**One Flew over the Cuckoo's Nest**
MILOS FORMAN	**Amadeus**
STEVEN FREARS	The Grifters
WILLIAM FRIEDKIN	The Exorcist
MEL GIBSON	**Braveheart**
BUCK HENRY	Heaven Can Wait
GEORGE ROY HILL	Butch Cassidy and the Sundance Kid
GEORGE ROY HILL	**The Sting**
JOHN HOUSTON	Prizzi's Honor
JAMES IVORY	Howards End
JAMES IVORY	The Remains of the Day
NORMAN JEWISON	Fiddler on the Roof
STANLEY KUBRICK	2001: A Space Odyssey
AKIRA KUROSAWA	Ran
DAVID LEAN	**Lawrence of Arabia**
DAVID LEAN	Doctor Zhivago
DAVID LEAN	A Passage to India
BARRY LEVINSON	**Rain Man**
BARRY LEVINSON	Bugsy
GEORGE LUCAS	Star Wars
SIDNEY LUMET	Dog Day Afternoon
SIDNEY LUMET	Network
SIDNEY LUMET	The Verdict
ADRIAN LYNE	Fatal Attraction
JOSEPH L. MANKIEWICZ	Sleuth
MIKE NICHOLS	**The Graduate**
MIKE NICHOLS	Silkwood
CHRIS NOONAN	All the President's Men
ALAN J. PAKULA	Babe
ALAN PARKER	Midnight Express
ALAN PARKER	Mississippi Burning
ROMAN POLANSKI	Chinatown
SYDNEY POLLACK	They Shoot Horses, Don't They?
SYDNEY POLLACK	Tootsie
MICHAEL RADFORD	Il Postino (The Postman)
ROBERT REDFORD	**Ordinary People**
CAROL REED	**Oliver!**
MARTIN RITT	Hud
TIM ROBBINS	Dead Man Walking
JEROME ROBBINS	**West Side Story**
HERBERT ROSS	The Turning Point

* Super16 Aaton supplied by PANAVISION HOLLYWOOD

41

MARK RYDELL	On Golden Pond
FRANKLIN J. SCHAFFNER	**Patton**
JOHN SCHLESINGER	Darling
JOHN SCHLESINGER	Sunday Bloody Sunday
BARBET SCHROEDER	Reversal of Fortune
MARTIN SCORSESE	Raging Bull
STEVEN SPIELBERG	Close Encounters of the Third Kind
STEVEN SPIELBERG	Raiders of the Lost Ark
STEVEN SPIELBERG	E.T. the Extra-Terrestrial
OLIVER STONE	**Born on the Fourth of July**
OLIVER STONE	JFK
QUENTIN TARANTINO	Pulp Fiction
FRANCOIS TRUFFAUT	Day for Night
PETER WEIR	Witness
ROBERT WISE	**West Side Story**
WILLIAM WYLER	**Ben Hur**
ROBERT ZEMECKIS	**Forrest Gump**
FRED ZINNEMANN	Julia

.... and more to come

The
Directors of Photography's
PANAFLEX

The Directors of Photography's
PANAFLEX

Although the Producer and the Director may feel especially comfortable selecting PANAVISION cameras and lenses, the decision to 'GO PANAVISION' is crucial to the Director of Photography.

PANAVISION has the widest range of lenses available anywhere. The widest apertures, the widest angles, the longest telephotos, the broadest choice of zooms. Lenses that have good contrast and excellent resolution and lenses that are as free of distortion, color aberration and flare as it is possible to be. Good lenses and lots of them.

PANAFLEX cameras have many wonderful features. They are exceptionally quiet, even for close close-ups; they can be tripod or dolly mounted or hand held; they can be compact or low profile and have three sizes of magazines, any of which can be used either on top of the camera body or at the rear. It's not just a camera, it's a comprehensive system for cinematography.

Every possible facility and control
PANAFLEX cameras have in-shot adjustable shutters, behind the lens filters, full fitting register pins for 'plate steady' image steadiness, pitch control to set the pull-down stroke for maximum quietness, crystal controlled speeds, variable speeds from 4-36 fps, the possibility of single shot and slow running.

On the PLATINUM PANAFLEX it is possible to use the computer measured camera shutter opening and speed control systems to shoot with HMI lights at any camera speed, enabling speeded up and slowed down action to be shot without fear of light flicker.

The adjustable shutter system of all PANAFLEX cameras, combined with the wide range of electronic synchronizing units, makes it possible to shoot with HMI, and other discharge lamps, in absolute safety; to film TV screens at 24 or 25 fps with 144, 172.8 or 180° shutter opening and to synchronize with process projectors and every possible TV scanning speed.

When you "GO PANAVISION" a full palette of additional possibilities becomes available.

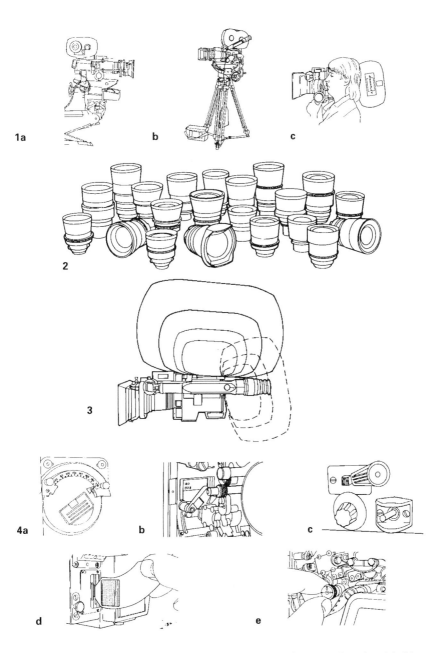

1. a., b. & c. PANAFLEX cameras may be dolly or tripod mounted, or hand-held,
2. PANAVISION PRIMO-L lenses, the latest additions to the wide range of
spherical and anamorphic lenses, 3. PANAFLEX film magazines may be mounted
on top or at the rear of the camera, 4. PANAFLEX cameras have: a. an 'in-shot'
adjustable shutter, b. full-fitting register pins, c. integral variable speed control,
d. behind-the-lens filtering and e. adjustable pitch control.

45

Panaccessories to Help the Cinematographer

Every accessory for PANAFLEX cameras, many of them unique and exclusive to PANAVISION, are thought through as an integrated part of the system:

PANABALL leveller/hi-hat for any Mitchell type tripod head
PANACLEAR heated mist-free eyepiece
PANAFLASHER in-camera negative flashing device
PANAGLOW illuminated ground glass reticle
PANAHEAD pan and tilt head
PANALAB advanced technology optical design and lens testing department
PANALENS LIGHT lens calibration illuminating light
PANALEVELLER eyepiece levelling device
PANALITE constant color temperature/variable intensity Obie lamp
PANANODE ADAPTOR for nodal panning and tilting on a PANAHEAD
PANAPOD lightweight yet rugged tripod
PANAREMOTE remote control system for any PANAHEAD
PANAROCK near ground level pan and tilt device
AUTO PANATAR anamorphic lenses
PANATAPE ultrasonic range finding device
PANATATE 360° nodal turnover mount
PANATILT tilt/balance plate
PANAVID video-assist systems
PANAZOOM zoom lenses

Additional optional accessories include frame cutters, car rigs for rugged tracking, rain deflectors, splash boxes, weather proof covers, remote focus, zoom, aperture and shutter controls, camera and lens heaters, multi-stage matte boxes and companion cameras which accept all PANAVISION lenses.

As if all that is not enough there is the **PANAVISION 3-PERF** camera movement and the **PANAVISION AATON CODE** time code system.

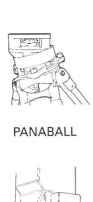

PANABALL

PANACLEAR

PANAFINDER

PANAFLASHER

PANAGLOW

PANAHEAD

PANALAB

PANALENSLIGHT

PANALEVELLER

PANALITE

PANANODE

PANAPOD

PANAMOTE

PANAROC

PANATAPE

AUTO PANATAR

PANATATE

PANATILT

PANAVID

PANAZOOM

47

PANAVISION Lenses

Long before they supplied and manufactured cameras PANAVISION Inc. were providers of fine lenses. Films such as *Ben Hur, Lawrence of Arabia* and *My Fair Lady,* among many others, were all photographed through PANAVISION lenses. In 1994 the Academy of Motion Picture Arts and Sciences awarded PANAVISION Inc. their Award of Merit, an "Oscar," in recognition of this achievement.

PRIMO-L "Spherical" lenses
Acknowledged to be the finest lenses ever designed and made for cinematography, the PRIMO-L range of fixed focal length and zoom lenses are unique.

A set of 11 lenses, ranging from a 10mm distortion free super-wide angle to a 150mm telephoto, all with the same optical characteristics (high contrast and resolution, good field illumination, negligible veiling glare, ghosting and distortion), all color matched and all with the same T1.9 maximum aperture. They are in a class by themselves. As if that were not enough, they are complemented by three zoom lenses which are equally as good.

PRIMO Anamorphic lenses
PANAVISION Auto PANATAR anamorphic lenses were the first such lenses to make it possible to photograph close-ups without distortion — "Anamorphic Mumps" — as it was called. The PRIMO Anamorphic series are a marriage of the latest prime lenses with the latest anamorphic lens technologies.

Close Focusing and Macro lenses
Close Focusing PRIMO lenses are regular PRIMO lenses especially mounted to allow close focusing down to a magnification ratio of 1:3 — i.e. an object 2½" wide can be photographed to fill the screen width.

Macro lenses can be focused closer still, some to greater than 1:1, producing an image on film larger than the object itself.

Slant Focus and Perspective lenses
Slant Focus lenses allow the plane of focus to be tilted in any direction, either before or during a take. Typically these lenses can be used to photograph a flat object set diagonally to the camera and to keep it all in focus, from one side to the other.

Perspective lenses allow a lens to be moved off the optical axis of the camera. Typically such a lens would be used to photograph a building with the camera tilted upwards at a severe angle. The Perspective lens can be used to counter the "falling over backwards" look.

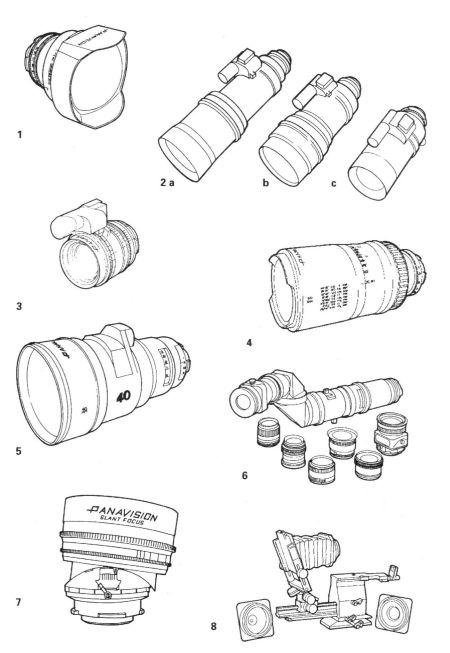

1. 10mm T1.9, distortion free, super-wide angle Primo-L Spherical lens, 2. Primo zoom lenses: a. 17.5 - 75mm T2.3: b.24 - 275mm T2.8: c. 135 - 420mm T2.8, 3. 27 - 68mm T2.8 Lightweight zoom lens, 4. 90mm 1:0.7 Macro lens, 5. Primo Anamorphic lenses, 6. PANAVISION/FRAZIER lens, 7. Slant Focus lens, 8. View camera lens system (VCLS).

49

Ground Glasses and Hard Masks

PANAVISION ground glasses are multipurpose. In the first place they delineate the image area and secondly, the lines are reflective to provide the illuminated reticle lines which make it easy to see the edges of the frame against a dark background.

Choice of Ground Glass markings — the options

Whether the prime format be for Anamorphic or Spherical release, Super 35 or 3-PERF, Roadshow 70mm blow-up or Jumbo Jet video, protecting the Action Area for all possible releases can be a nightmare. A decision has to be made at the outset of shooting and adhered to throughout the production. It is an amusing thought that the format most thought of, 35mm "Academy," is the one least likely ever to be used for presentation purposes.

Basically the choice lies between the principal theatrical options — Anamorphic, 1.85 Widescreen, Super 35 for Anamorphic and Super 35 for Widescreen — with protection markings for TV.

Complications come in if protection for 1.66:1 is desired for overseas release and if the TV markings should be "TV Transmitted" or "TV Safe Action," or both.

Yet another choice is for "Common Headroom" or "Symmetrical." Common Headroom, together with one theatrical marking and one TV marking is often a good choice as it eliminates the need for many ceiling pieces in sets, making it easier and less expensive to light. puts most heads and faces in the top third of the screen irrespective of the presentation format and means that only the tracks and the floor need to be looked at vis-à-vis the Video and TV releases.

Hard masks

When shooting for 1.85:1 Widescreen presentation PANAVISION can fit a hard mask or matte into the aperture plate to prevent any unprotected area being shown, either by inattention or on purpose because the lower part of the image may be more interesting than the top. A 1.66:1 hard mask is often a good choice as this allows the TV area to be scanned and eliminates all else.

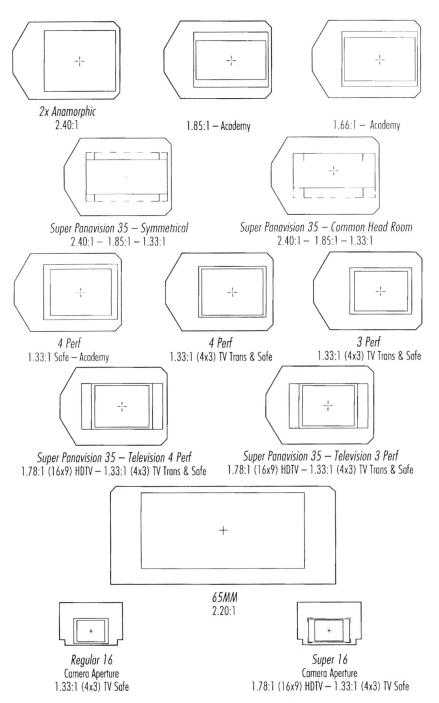

2x Anamorphic
2.40:1

1.85:1 – Academy

1.66:1 – Academy

Super Panavision 35 – Symmetrical
2.40:1 – 1.85:1 – 1.33:1

Super Panavision 35 – Common Head Room
2.40:1 – 1.85:1 – 1.33:1

4 Perf
1.33:1 Safe – Academy

4 Perf
1.33:1 (4x3) TV Trans & Safe

3 Perf
1.33:1 (4x3) TV Trans & Safe

Super Panavision 35 – Television 4 Perf
1.78:1 (16x9) HDTV – 1.33:1 (4x3) TV Trans & Safe

Super Panavision 35 – Television 3 Perf
1.78:1 (16x9) HDTV – 1.33:1 (4x3) TV Trans & Safe

65MM
2.20:1

Regular 16
Camera Aperture
1.33:1 (4x3) TV Safe

Super 16
Camera Aperture
1.78:1 (16x9) HDTV – 1.33:1 (4x3) TV Safe

A partial selection of PANAVISION's available ground glasses.

51

Light Efficiency

With a maximum shutter opening of 200° and a wide range of ultra wide aperture lenses ranging from T1.0 and T1.3 (Spherical) and T1.1 and T1.4 (Anamorphic) PANAFLEX cameras are the most 'light efficient' cameras available. At T1.0 and rating the film at EI 500 less that 1 foot candle of light is necessary to give full exposure.

The 200° shutter passes 1/6 stop more light than a 175 - 180° shutter and only requires to be closed down to 100° to reduce the exposure by one full stop and to 50° to reduce one stop again. The minimum shutter opening on the PANAFLEX is 50°.

In addition to transmitting more light, the PANAFLEX 200° shutter opening reduces the possibility of image strobe during fast pan movements

Note: The shutter angle of the LIGHTWEIGHT PANAFLEX is 180° and is not adjustable.

Sharper and steadier images
PANAFLEX cameras have a focal plane shutter which moves across the shortest side of the frame and in the opposite direction to the travel of the film. This adds very considerably to the camera's light capping efficiency. Very precise shutter timing ensures that all light is completely cut off before the film begins to move and remains so until it has come to a stop and has been held securely in position by the registration pins. Unlike many other cameras there is absolutely no movement of the film while even the smallest part of the frame is uncovered, even at high speed.

Another important point is that PANAFLEX registration pins are full fitting and no compromise is made to quiet the camera. Furthermore, the pins are positioned on both sides of the film and engage in the perforations immediately below the frame line, the same as on all optical printers.

You can safely use any PANAFLEX camera to shoot plates for multi-exposure SFX scenes.

EXPOSURE CONTROL BY SHUTTER ADJUSTMENT

EXPOSURE	SHUTTER OPENING (°)	
	PANAFLEX	PANASTAR
Full open	200	180
-1/3 stop	160	144
-2/3 stop	126	114
-1 stop	100	90
-1 1/3 stop	80	72
-1 2.3 stop	63	57
-2 stops	50	45

180/200° EXPOSURE ADJUSTMENT

	200° EXPOSURE SETTING FOR 180° EXPOSURE READING									
180° Reading	1	1.4	2	2.8	4	5.6	8	11	16	22
200° Setting	1.05	1.46	2.21	2.29	4.2	5	8.4	11.5	16.8	23.1

CAMERA SPEED / SHUTTER ANGLE / EXPOSURE TIMES

CAMERA SPEED (fps)	SHUTTER ANGLE								
	45	50	60	90	120	144	172.8	180	200
	EXPOSURE TIME (sec)								
3	0.0417	0.0463	0.0556	0.0833	0.1111	0.1333	0.16	0.1667	0.1852
4	0.0313	0.0347	0.0417	0.0625	0.0833	0.1	0.12	0.125	0.1389
6	0.0208	0.0231	0.0278	0.0417	0.0556	0.0667	0.08	0.0833	0.0926
9	0.0139	0.0154	0.0185	0.0278	0.037	0.0444	0.0533	0.0556	0.0617
12	0.0104	0.0116	0.0139	0.0208	0.0278	0.0333	0.04	0.0417	0.0463
18	0.0069	0.0077	0.0093	0.0139	0.0185	0.0222	0.0267	0.0278	0.0309
24	0.0052	0.0058	0.0069	0.0104	0.0139	0.0167	0.02	0.0208	0.0231
25	0.005	0.0056	0.0067	0.01	0.0133	0.016	0.0192	0.02	0.0222
32	0.0039	0.0043	0.0052	0.0078	0.0104	0.0125	0.015	0.0156	0.0174
48	0.0026	0.0029	0.0035	0.0052	0.0069	0.0083	0.01	0.0104	0.0116
60	0.0021	0.0023	0.0028	0.0042	0.0056	0.0067	0.008	0.0083	0.0093
96	0.0013	0.0014	0.0017	0.0026	0.0035	0.0042	0.005	0.0052	0.0058
120	0.001	0.0012	0.0014	0.0021	0.0028	0.0033	0.004	0.0042	0.0046

To convert the above decimal parts of a second into fractions of a second use a pocket calculator to divide the above into 1.

Optical Accessories

There is more to creative cinematography than setting the lights and getting the exposure correct. PANAVISION has developed a whole series of accessories to put the cinematographer's imagination on the screen.

Filters

PANAVISION can supply the widest possible range of image control filters and "clever" matte boxes to put them in. To keep the number of filters required to cover their lenses to a minimum most PANAVISION lenses are covered by the standard size, 4 x 5.650", filters. However, there are occasions when a cameraman wishes to slide and rotate filters, especially graduated filters, and to accommodate this PANAVISION also supplies multi-stage matteboxes which take 6.6" sq. filters.

PANAVISION tests its filters on its optical test bench to ensure that their optical quality is every bit as good as its lenses.

Even the 10mm wide angle PRIMO-L lens has a specially designed clip-on filter holder to utilize standard 6.6" sq. filters, thus eliminating the need to handle exceptionally large, awkward, and additional filters.

Diopters

A very useful accessory, especially with zoom lenses, is a full cover 'diopter' lens which is placed in front of the normal taking lens for closer focus-sing. PANAVISION can supply diopter lenses to cover all their zoom lenses.

Split diopters are another very useful accessory, especially for Anamorphic cinematography, as these make it possible to have two planes of focus in a single shot. Split diopters are full diopters cut in half and are placed in front of the normal lens so that the close-up part of the scene is photographed through the diopter.

When using split diopters it is usual to lose the dividing line between the two planes of focus by placing the edge of the diopter coincident with a vertical object such as a pillar or the corner of a room.

Diffusion

PANAVISION has a wide range of standard and customized sliding diffusers available to enable Directors of Photography to control the amount of diffusion as a scene progresses, usually as they pan to, from and between close-ups where one artist in a scene requires more diffusion than another.

Special matte boxes

PANAVISION can supply matte boxes with filter trays which slide, rotate and tilt to make the most use of a particular type of filter.

54

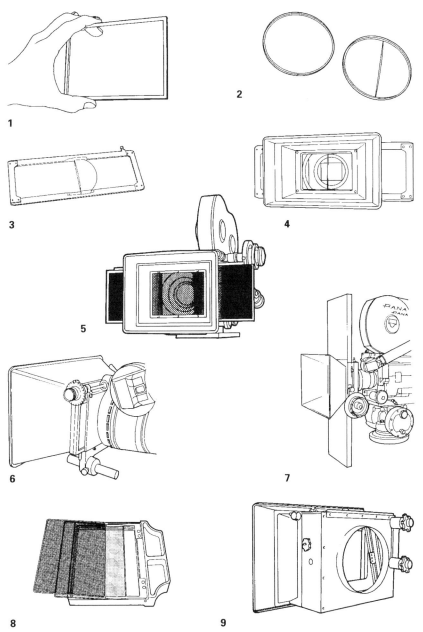

1. Standard 4 x 5.650" filter which covers most PANAVISION lenses, 2. Full cover and split diopters for zoom lenses, 3. Split diopter mounted on a slide, 4. Sliding split diopter mounted in front of an anamorphic lens, 5. Contra-direction sliding graduated ND light attenuator, 6. Standard sliding diffuser fitted to the rear of a standard mattebox, 7. Custom made sliding diffuser, 8. Antireflection triple filter holder, 9. Mattebox fitted with a tiltable filter stage.

Light Control Accessories

The ways to make PANAFLEX cameras interface with the lighting add much, not only to the way the image photographs, but also to the way in which the camera can be operated.

The PANALITE onboard Obie light
PANALITES are a shadowless fill-light which fits onto the camera just above the mattebox and which can be dimmed to almost nothing without affecting the color temperature of the light. The Mk.I version (650/1000w tungsten) works by changing a row of cylindrical reflectors, from black to white, which reflect the light. The Mk.II version (dimmable HMI) incorporates a disk type variable density filter.

PANAFLEX micro precision adjustable shutter
The in-shot ADJUSTABLE FOCAL PLANE SHUTTER has always been one of the most important of all PANAFLEX features. The advent of the onboard micro computer has enabled the ADJUSTABLE SHUTTER of the PLATINUM PANAFLEX to be controlled to greater accuracy than ever before. This has made it possible to fine tune the shutter opening to suit any HMI Lighting Power Supply Hz/Camera Speed combination without fear of HMI flicker.

The effective exposure time = (shutter angle/360) x (1/fps)

PANAVISION Smart Shutter II system
The Smart Shutter II system is an electronic shutter control device which can be interlinked with the camera speed and/or the lens aperture. With it, it is possible to change the camera speed without affecting the exposure. Up to two stops difference it will do it by changing the shutter alone, beyond this it will change both the shutter and the T stop. Equally it can change the depth of field in shot without affecting the exposure, control the exposure while panning from a dark to a light area, or vice versa, or do an in-camera fade-in or fade-out.

Motorized graduated filters
Among the "clever" facilities that are available for the PANAVISION MULTI-STAGE MATTEBOX are the motorized slides which enable two opposing graduated filters to be slid towards (or away) from one another to give an overall transitional effect.

Anti-reflection triple filter holder
For shooting with multiple filters in conditions where there are bright lights shining directly into the lens the PANAVISION anti-reflection triple filter holder is a useful accessory. This gadget sandwiches up to three filters tightly together so that reflected light does not have space to bounce between the surfaces, thus eliminating multiple reflections.

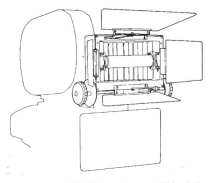
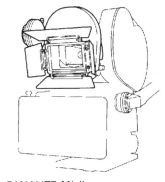

1 a. PANALITE Mk.I on-board Obie light   b. PANALITE Mk.II

HMI FRAMES PER SECOND / SHUTTER ANGLE TABLES

Power	OPTIMUM SHUTTER ANGLES (°) FOR HMI LIGHTING								
	6-25 fps								
Supply	6	8	10	12	16.667	20	22	24	25
60 Hz	180	144	180	144	150	180	198	144	150
50 Hz	172.8	172.8	180	172.8	180	144	158.4	172.8	180
	24-60fps								
	24	25	30	32	33.333	40	48	50	60
60 Hz	144	150	180	192	200	120	144	150	180
50 Hz	172.8	180	108	115.2	120	144	172.8	180	432

2. Optimum shutter openings are shown in bold. With these settings any opening is possible if the camera fps and the power supply Hz are extremely precise.

3. Smart Shutter II adjustable shutter system, 4. Sliding graduated ND filter mattebox.

In-Camera Light Control and Enhancement Accessories

In addition to offering the means to control the light entering the camera, PANAFLEX cameras also provide facilities to manipulate the light inside the camera.

Behind the lens filters
There are many advantages to placing at least one of the light control filters (usually the 85) behind the lens; for one, it makes room for one more fog, diffuser, low-contrast or other filter in the mattebox. Behind the lens filtering has always been a feature of all PANAFLEX and PANASTAR cameras.

PANAFLASHER light overlay accessory
Since the very beginnings of photography, film has been "flashed" with a very low brightness light either before or after exposure, to reduce contrast or increase exposure in the shadow areas, or to put a color bias into the darker tones without greatly affecting the highlights.

In the past it was a process normally carried out by a film laboratory at a price per foot of film and with no-scene-by-scene control by the cinematographer.

The effect is to give the film a basic exposure below the toe of the sensitometric curve. This overcomes the exposure inertia so that all light falling on the film during a take appears on the screen

The PANAVISION PANAFLASHER fits onto whichever PANAFLEX magazine port is not in use. (If the magazine is on the top of the camera the PANAFLASHER fits on the rear and vice versa.)

The PANAFLASHER unit is small enough to be used while the camera is hand-held and does not require a main power source.

The PANAFLASHER incorporates an extremely sensitive exposure meter so that the effect can be very closely monitored and controlled.

White light will control image contrast and bring out details in the shadows that would otherwise be plain black. Colored light will tint the darker parts of the image leaving the highlights untouched and having very little effect on light skin tones.

PANAVISION can also supply the necessary interface units to fit a Lightflex light overlay system to any PANAFLEX camera.

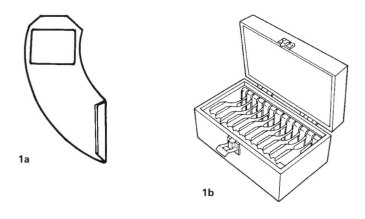

1a

1b

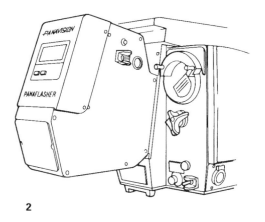

2

1.a. Behind the lens gelatin filter holder and b. box of filters, 2. PANAFLASHER unit fitted to the rear of a PANAFLEX camera.

Camera Angle Control Accessories

Not every shot has to be taken with the camera at eye level and perfectly horizontal. With PANAVISION it is possible to have fun with camera angles.

PANAVISION/FRAZIER lens system

The PANAVISION/FRAZIER lens system is unique in many ways. It has the capability of holding everything in focus from macro magnification to infinity, it has an articulated front element, or "swivel tip", which enables the front part of the lens to pan across a subject without the camera being moved and can rotate the image about the optical axis, like a Panate, without need to rotate the camera. It creates the possibility to probe deep into a miniature, like a probe or a snorkel lens, and then to move around and all the while holding everything in focus.The system comprises seven interchangable lenses (12-35mm) of which two lenses have perspective and slant focus capability and a third has perspective control only.

Inclining prisms

An INCLINING PRISM placed in front of the taking lens enables either very low or very high angle shots which would otherwise be impossible. More than this, it enables the camera to look upwards from below floor level or down from above ceiling height without cutting a hole in either.

An INCLINING PRISM works by reflecting and refracting the light and because the light is bent twice the image is the correct way around. Other optical advantages are that there is virtually no loss of transmission, the planes of the front and rear of the prism are perfectly flat so there is no chance of optical distortion and by using a glass of high refractive index it is possible to cover a much wider angle lens than would otherwise be possible.

The PANAFLEX LIGHTWEIGHT camera system

The possibility of taking the camera off the tripod, or other rigid support system, and moving it about with all the fluidity of human movement is a feature of modern cinematography brought about both by the Steadicam floating camera system and the long reach portable crane with a remotely controlled camera. The advantage of these systems is that they make unobtrusive gliding camera movements possible without the audience being aware.

The PANAVISION LIGHTWEIGHT PANAFLEX is tailor made for either of these situations.

PANATATE turnover camera mounts

PANATATE turnover camera mounts enable the camera to rotate longitudinally (about the lens axis) during a take. They also incorporate a nodal mounting system so that a camera can be panned, tilted and rotated simultaneously without displacing the entrance pupil.

60

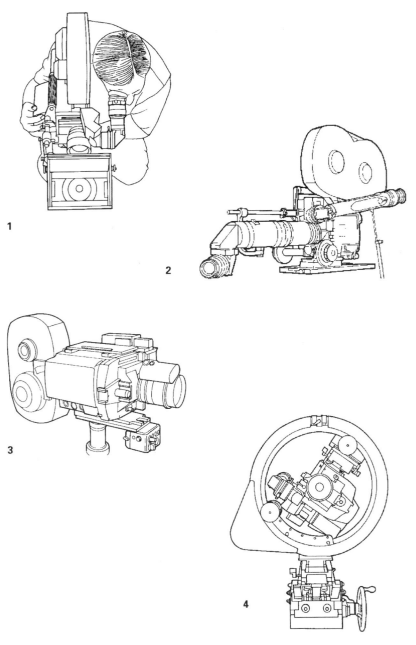

1. Inclining prism low angle attachment fitted to a hand-held PANAFLEX camera for a ground-level shot, 2. PANAVISION/FRAZIER lens system, 3. LIGHTWEIGHT PANAFLEX camera system, 4. PANATATE turnover camera mount.

Environmental Protective Equipment

Creative cinematography often demands that a camera must continue to work perfectly under conditions of intense cold, desert heat and dust, driving rain, sea and storm, severe vibration, stress and 'g' forces and in dangerous places.

Intense cold

PANAFLEX cameras and magazines are fitted with internal heaters which ensure that they run freely and quietly under even the coldest conditions.

Additional heater barneys are available to cover and give additional warmth to the camera, the magazines and the lenses (especially zoom lenses) and are advisable for use when the camera is set up in an exposed position where the wind chill factor is likely to be significant. Where camera heaters and heater barneys are likely to be used intensively, additional camera batteries should be ordered.

Lenses kept in a cold truck and taken into a warm building for use should be stored in plastic bags to prevent internal misting up.

Heat and dust

Thanks to their light color, smooth finish and good sealing PANAFLEX cameras operate exceptionally well in conditions of extreme heat and dust.

Dust should be brushed away from the camera, not cleared with an aerosol air spray which only blows it into inaccessible places.

Rain, storm and water

Waterproof covers are available to protect the camera from rain, etc.

Spinning disk spray deflectors/waterproof covers are available for use in storm conditions. These devices incorporate high speed rotating glass disk fronts which throw off water as quickly as it falls on them, thus keeping the camera lenses clear of water.

Water boxes are available for shallow water filming (up to 1' deep) and are useful for surface filming in water tanks, swimming pools, etc.

If a camera is contaminated with salt water all traces of salt should be washed away with fresh water at the earliest possible opportunity and the camera returned to PANAVISION, or its representative, for emergency servicing. Nothing can damage a camera more than salt water.

Vibration, stress, high "g" forces and dangerous places

Automobile mounts and clamp rigs are available to give additional camera and magazine security in rugged conditions, as when filming car chases.

Cameras in protective boxes and "disposable" cameras are available for placing in highly hazardous positions.

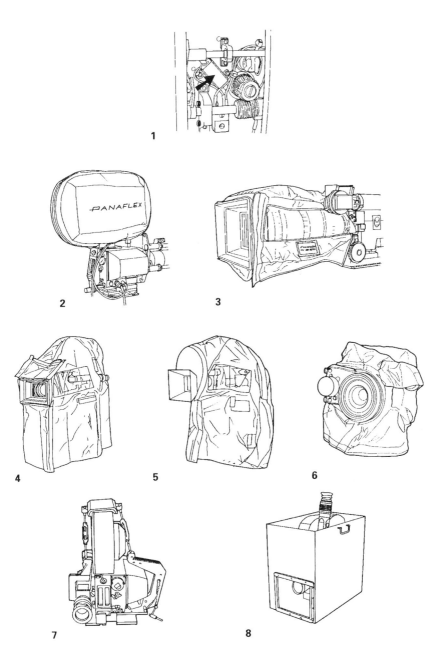

1. Internal heater elements arranged around a camera bearing, 2. Magazine heater/cover showing power supply arrangements, 3. Zoom lens heater/cover, 4. Normal waterproof camera cover, 5. Rain deflector waterproof cover, 6. Handholdable rain deflector, 7. Camera clamp rig, 8. Water-box shallow water housing.

PANAVISION People

Of special note are the dedicated PANAVISION PEOPLE who use all their experience to prepare the equipment for your shoot with all the efficiency and enthusiasm it is possible to muster. They like to be considered to be a part of your extended crew.

They will gather all the equipment together for you and your crew to make the most exacting tests you can devise. They will listen to any comments you have to make and change or modify anything with which you are not entirely happy. They will want to hear from you while you are away and when you return. In particular they will want to know if anything at all went wrong.

They will welcome suggestions as to what can be done to improve and extend the PANAVISION product range even further. PANAVISION's policy of constant updating ensures that today's new idea will be incorporated into every existing camera.

If the PANAFLEX range is not already your ideal camera system they would even like to know what else needs to be done to make it so.

The PANAVISION PEOPLE are your constant partners in progressive cinematography and every time a Director of Photography wins or is nominated for an Oscar using PANAFLEX cameras and lenses which they have conceived, designed, manufactured and prepared, they quietly share in your personal pleasure and satisfaction.

**Cinematographers who have won Oscars and Oscar Nominations
for Best Cinematography using PANAVISION cameras and/or lenses (1958-95):**
(Winners in **bold**)

NESTOR ALMENDROS	**Days of Heaven**
NESTOR ALMENDROS	Kramer vs. Kramer
NESTOR ALMENDROS	The Blue Lagoon
NESTOR ALMENDROS	Sophie's Choice
JOHN A. ALONZO	Chinatown
ADRIAN BIDDLE	Thelma & Louise
JOSEPH BIROC	**The Towering Inferno**
PETER BIZIOU	**Mississippi Burning**
RALPH D. BODE	Coal Miner's Daughter
DON BURGESS	Forrest Gump
STEPHEN H. BURUM	Hoffa
BILL BUTLER	One Flew Over the Cuckoo's Nest
GHISLAIN CLOQUET	**Tess**
JACK COUFFER	Jonathan Livingston Seagull
JAMES CRABE	The Formula
JORDAN CRONENWETH	Peggy Sue Got Married

64

Cinematographers who have won Oscars and Oscar Nominations for Best Cinematography using PANAVISION cameras and/or lenses, (continued):

MICHAEL CHAPMAN	The Fugitive
DEAN CUNDY	Who Framed Roger Rabbit
ALLEN DAVIAU	E.T. the Extra-Terrestrial
ALLEN DAVIAU	The Color Purple
ALLEN DAVIAU	Empire of the Sun
ALLEN DAVIAU	Avalon
ALLEN DAVIAU	Bugsy
ERNEST DAY	A Passage to India
CALEB DESCHANEL	Right Stuff
CALEB DESCHANEL	The Natural
DANIEL L. FAPP	Ice Station Zebra
DANIEL L. FAPP	**West Side Story**
WILLIAM A. FRAKER	Looking for Mr. Goodbar
WILLIAM A. FRAKER	Heaven Can Wait
WILLIAM A. FRAKER	1941
WILLIAM A. FRAKER	Wargames
WILLIAM A. FRAKER	Murphy's Romance
FREDDIE FRANCIS	**Glory**
OSAMI FURUYA	Tora! Tora! Tora!
LEE GARMES	The Big Fisherman
STEPHEN GOLDBLATT	The Prince of Tides
STEPHEN GOLDBLATT	Batman Forever
JACK N. GREEN	Unforgiven
CONRAD HALL	**Butch Cassidy and the Sundance Kid**
CONRAD HALL	The Day of the Locust
CONRAD HALL	Tequila Sunrise
CONRAD HALL	Searching for Bobby Fischer
SINASAKU HIMEDA	Tora! Tora! Tora!
RICHARD H. KLINE	King Kong
FRED KONEKAMP	Patton
FRED KONEKAMP	**The Towering Inferno**
JOSEPH LaSHELLE	The Apartment
ERNEST LASZLO	It's a Mad, Mad, Mad, Mad World
ERNEST LASZLO	Logan's Run
PHILIP LATHROP	Earthquake
SAM LEAVITT	Exodus
JOSEPH MacDONALD	The Sand Pebbles
OSWALD MORRIS	Oliver!
OSWALD MORRIS	**Fiddler on the Roof**
ASAKAZU NAKAI	Ran
SVEN NYKVIST	The Unbearable Lightness of Being
MIROSLAV ONDRICEK	Amadeus

65

DON PETERMAN	Flashdance
DON PETERMAN	Star Trek IV: The Voyage Home
TONY PIERCE-ROBERTS	Howards End
ROBERT RICHARDSON	Born on the Fourth of July
ROBERT RICHARDSON	**JFK**
OWEN ROIZMAN	The Exorcist
OWEN ROIZMAN	Network
OWEN ROIZMAN	Tootsie
OWEN ROIZMAN	Wyatt Earp
PHILIPPE ROUSSELOT	**A River Runs Through It**
TAKAO SAITO	Ran
MESAMICHI SATOH	Tora! Tora! Tora!
JOHN SEAL	Witness
JOHN SEAL	Rain Man
DOUGLAS SLOCOMBE	Travels with my Aunt
DOUGLAS SLOCOMBE	Julia
DOUGLAS SLOCOMBE	Raiders of the Lost Ark
HAROLD E. STINE	The Poseidon Adventure
HARRY STRADLING	**My Fair Lady**
HARRY STRADLING Jr.	1776
HARRY STRADLING Jr.	The Way We Were
ROBERT SURTEES	**Ben Hur**
ROBERT SURTEES	Mutiny on the Bounty
ROBERT SURTEES	The Last Picture Show
ROBERT SURTEES	Summer of '42
ROBERT SURTEES	The Sting
ROBERT SURTEES	The Hindenberg
ROBERT SURTEES	A Star Is Born
ROBERT SURTEES	The Turning Point
RONNIE TAYLOR	**Gandhi**
JOHN TOLL	**Legends of the Fall**
JOHN TOLL	**Braveheart**
MASAHARU UEDA	Ran
GEOFFREY UNSWORTH	Murder on the Orient Express
GEOFFREY UNSWORTH	**Tess**
HASKELL WEXLER	One Flew Over the Cuckoo's Nest
HASKELL WEXLER	**Bound for Glory**
CHARLES F. WHEELER	Tora! Tora! Tora!
BILLY WILLIAMS	On Golden Pond
BILLY WILLIAMS	**Gandhi**
GORDON WILLIS	Zelig
JAMES WONG HOWE	**Hud**
JAMES WONG HOWE	Funny Lady
FREDDIE YOUNG	**Lawrence of Arabia**
FREDDIE YOUNG	**Doctor Zhivago**
FREDDIE YOUNG	**Ryan's Daughter**
FREDDIE YOUNG	Nicholas and Alexandra
VILMOS ZSIGMOND	**Close Encounters of the Third Kind**
VILMOS ZSIGMOND	The Deer Hunter
VILMOS ZSIGMOND	The River

. . . and more to come

The
Camera Operators'
PANAFLEX

The Camera Operators' PANAFLEX

The aspects of camera design that affect the Camera Operator most — the control of pan and tilt movements, the large, comfortable, eyepiece and the quality of the viewfinder system, and the fact that the film magazines may be fitted on top or at the rear, which together with the ergonomic shape, the good balance and the comfort pads makes hand holding almost effortless — are all areas where the PANAFLEX camera system is particularly superior.

PANAHEAD facilities

With PANAVISION Operators have the choice of two PANAHEADS, the "Regular" model which is suitable for most PANAFLEX camera and lens combinations and the "Super" version which is preferable for PANAFLEX and PSR cameras in combination with particularly heavy lenses.

The PANAHEAD pan and tilt camera head derives its unique smoothness of movement from the patented tooth belt drive system which translates the smallest hand movement to a camera movement without the problems of gear cogging and wear in one section of the tilt quadrant which are unavoidable problems inherent in all traditional geared heads with metal quadrants.

The PANAHEAD offers the Camera Operator a choice of three pan and tilt speeds in the "geared head" mode. It may also be used as a free head, as a gyro head and as a remote head.

With a PANAHEAD it is possible to film at any angle, from 90° directly up to 90° directly down, encompassing the widest possible range of tilt.

PANAFLEX viewfinder facilities

The 'Brighter than Life' viewfinders of PANAFLEX cameras give the brightest ground glass images of any film camera. For most models there is a choice of three viewfinder lengths, short for hand-holding, intermediate for when the operator wants to be close to the camera when it is on a PANAHEAD or a fluid head, and long when he wishes to stand back from the camera. On the PANAFLEX-16 the viewfinder can be swung out for left eye viewing.

Other much appreciated viewfinding features are the patented PANAGLOW system, which lights up the viewfinder markings when shooting against a dark background, the patented PANALEVELLER which keeps the eyepiece at eye level irrespective of how much the camera is tilted up or down, the PANACLEAR heated eyepiece which positively prevents the viewfinder optics from misting up in cold conditions, the ocular marker ring, image magnification, a choice of two contrast filters and a de-anamorphoser which makes the image larger, not smaller.

All PANAFLEX cameras have facilities for fitting video-assist systems of exceptional sensitivity which may be flicker-free if required.

On all PANAFLEX cameras there is even a place for the Operator, or anyone else for that matter, to park their spectacles while looking through the viewfinder!

68

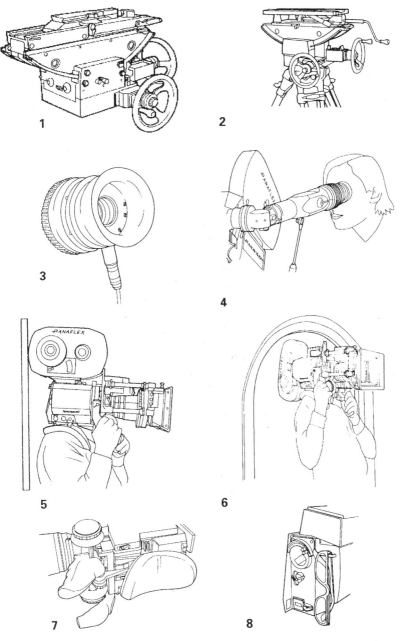

1. Regular PANAHEAD, 2. Super PANAHEAD with adjustable tilt, 3. The large, comfortable, PANAFLEX eyepiece, 4. The swing-out viewfinder facility of the PANAFLEX-16, 5. Hand-holding a PANAFLEX in a confined space, 6. Hand-holding a PANAFLEX with little headroom, 7. The PANAFLEX shoulder pad and ergonomic handgrips for comfortable handholdability, 8. The PANAFLEX spectacle park.

Sharper Images and Faster Pans with a PANAFLEX

Of the very many features which differentiate the PANAFLEX camera system from many others are the light capping efficiency of the focal plane shutter, which makes for sharper images on the film, and the maximum shutter opening of 200° which maximizes the exposure time and makes it possible to pan faster without fear of strobing.

Panning speeds

Camera Operators should be aware that due to the efficiency of the focal plane shutter of the PANAFLEX camera and the fact that the registration pins do not disengage until the film is completely capped, or the shutter begin to open until the film is firmly held in position once more, the images on the film tend to be crisper and sharper than on cameras which are not so light-efficient and this may affect the maximum safe panning speed.

On the other hand, the 200° maximum shutter opening of the PANAFLEX camera maximizes the image blur on the leading and trailing edges of the image, making it possible to pan faster than with a smaller shutter opening. The vertical movement of the shutter across the film makes it possible to pan in either direction equally fast.

How fast is a safe 'across frame' panning speed (the time it takes for a fixed object to travel from one side of the frame to the other irrespective of lens focal length) is a subjective judgement which Operators take note of every time they see dailies. It is part of the skill of Camera Operating.

As a starting point, most Operators consider that at 24/25 fps and with the shutter at 180° a 5 sec. 'across frame' movement is quite safe with spherical lenses, 7 secs. with anamorphic. These times will be longer when the shutter is closed down, less when it is fully opened to 200°.

CAMERA SPEED / MINIMUM "ACROSS FRAME" PAN TIME TABLE

(Modified safe "across frame" pan time with a normal shutter angle
but wiith a modified camera speed)

Modified camera speed (fps)	Normal 24fps/180° safe "across frame" pan time (sec)					
	4	5	6	7	8	10
	New minimum safe "across frame" pan time (sec)					
6	16	20	24	28	32	40
8	12	15	18	21	24	30
10	9	12	14	16	19	24
12	8	10	12	14	16	20
16	6	7	9	10	12	15
20	4	6	7	8	9	12
24	4	5	6	7	8	10
30	3	4	4	5	6	8
40	2	3	3	4	4	6
60	1	2	2	2	3	4
80	1	1	1	2	2	3
100	0	1	1	1	1	2
120	0	1	1	1	1	2

CAMERA SPEED / MINIMUM SHUTTER ANGLE TABLE

(To pan at the normal "across frame" pan time but with a modified
camera speed, using the adjustable shutter to compensate)

Modified camera speed (fps)	6	8	10	12	16	20	24	25	26.6
New minimum shutter angle	45	60	75	90	120	150	180	188	200

SHUTTER ANGLE / MINIMUM SAFE "ACROSS FRAME" PAN TIME TABLE

(Minimum safe "across frame" pan time table at normal camera speed
but with a modified shutter angle)

Modified shutter angle (°)	Normal 24fps/180° safe "across frame" pan time (secs)					
	4	5	6	7	8	10
	New safe "across frame" pan time (sec)					
45	16	20	24	28	32	40
50	15	18	22	26	29	36
60	12	15	18	21	24	30
90	8	10	12	14	16	20
100	8	9	11	13	15	18
144	5	7	8	9	10	13
180	4	5	6	7	8	10
200	4	5	6	7	8	9

Note: All the above figures have been rounded off to the nearest whole number
for the sake of simplicity.

PANAVID Viewfinder Systems

PANAVISION has always been at the forefront in developing video assist systems and embracing the most advanced video technologies as they emerge. The various systems they offer, the PANAVISION CCD COLOR VIDEO ASSIST systems, the SUPER CCD B&W PANAVID and the various LIGHTWEIGHT PANAVID CCD VIDEO ASSIST systems all represent the 'state of the art' in the use of miniature CCD video cameras as viewfinders for film cameras.

The Color CCD flicker-free Video Assist

PANAVISION 's COLOR PANAVID video assist systems use a 740 x 488 pixel high resolution CCD camera and give a flicker-free video image at sync sound camera speeds. This makes it very much more pleasant for the Operators to view and gives a truer rendition of light and shade. The extreme sensitivity of the system and the automatic gain control make it possible for the Operator to see action in dark sections of a scene and yet the image does not burn out when confronted with a bright light source.

For normal lighting conditions the B&W PANAVID CCD incorporates an infrared filter to ensure best balance color rendition across the full grey-scale but for low light conditions this filter may be removed. On the color versions a neutral density filter may be interposed in the CCD light path to reduce the amount of light.

Particularly useful accessories which are incorporated into some models and are available add-ons to others are FRAMELINE and CHARACTER GENERATORS. The FRAMELINE GENERATOR displays bold format markings and has an adjustable outside mask, the CHARACTER GENERATOR displays camera information such as camera speed, footage and PANATAPE II data.

The EYEPIECE VIDEO is a compact CCD camera which can be plugged into the viewfinder system in place of an optical finder.

The LIGHTWEIGHT PANAVID uses a coherent bundle of optical fibres to reduce the image size from that of a 35mm film format to that of a CCD chip. It is particularly intended for Steadicam and similar usage.

Image grabbing

PANAVISION's high quality, distortion free video images are particularly suitable for image grabbing, i.e., recording a single frame from a scene to be held in store and used as an electronic matte or cut frame for alignment with another setup in the future.

Equally, when shooting a scene for subsequent optical or digital treatment it is possible to overlay the current image onto a previously shot background plate in exactly the same manner as it will appear in the composite scene.

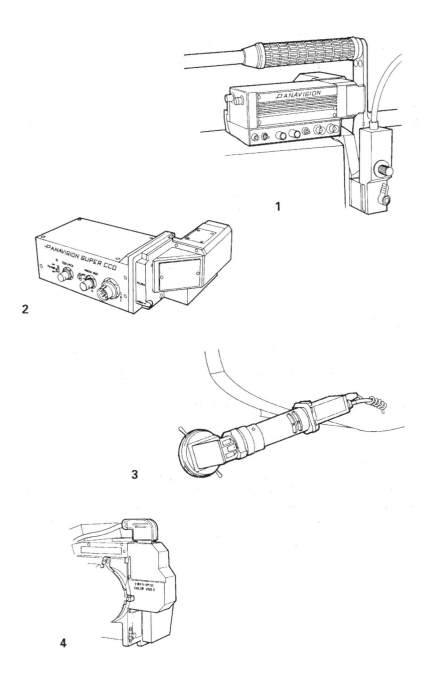

1. PANAVISION color video-assist which also incorporates frameline and character generators, 2 PANAVID B&W CCD video-assist, 3. PANAVISION eyepiece color video-assist, 4. PANAVISION fibre-optic color video-assist.

The PANAVISION PANAHEAD

The normal tilt range of the PANAHEAD is 30° up or down. It goes without saying that it can do a 360° pan around and around many times over. Three handwheel speed ratios make possible the full 30° of tilt in 15, 8 or 4 turns of the hand wheel respectively and a 360° pan in approximately 75, 41 or 21 turns.

The handwheel finger knobs can be preset in a precise position to suit a specific shot by returning the ratio selector lever to 'N' and setting the knob as required before finally selecting the desired ratio.

Note: It is very important to lock the tilt before setting the tilt selector to the 'N' position, or even passing through it.

Additional features that enhance the PANAHEAD'S user friendliness

Where to put the exposure meters safely, keep the rolls of camera tape handy, put the measuring tape where it can be found quickly, and even put the PANAVISION CINEMATOGRAPHERS' COMPUTER PROGRAM where an eye can be kept on it, was a problem that PANAVISION solved for all when they made it possible to attach an accessory box to the front of the PANAHEAD. So simple and so useful!

At the front of the PANAHEAD are two studs which may be used to support an accessory box. PANAVISION Inc. can supply adaptor plates to interface with clients' own accessory boxes.

There are two bushed holes on either side of the PANAHEAD tilt section which may either be used to pass a bar through for carrying purposes or for attaching lashing down cables when maximum rigidity is required as when shooting background plates and other SFX shots.

The camera body may be slid backwards and forwards on the head to achieve perfect tilt balance at all times (i.e., when exposed film is transferred from the front to the rear of the magazine).

Sliding base plates are available to use a PANAFLEX camera fitted with a PANAFLEX type dovetail attachment slide with any flat-top tripod head fitted with a standard 3/8" 16 TPI thread.

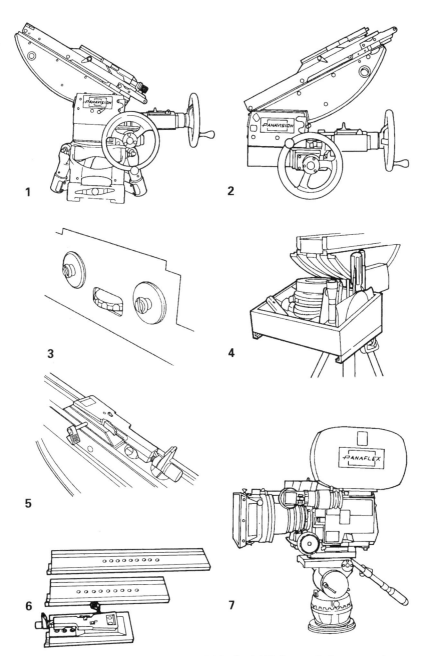

1. PANAHEAD tilted 30° up, 2. PANAHEAD tilted 30° down, 3. Accessory box studs on the front of a PANAHEAD, 4. Assistant's accessory box fitted to the front of a PANAHEAD, 5. Sliding base unit on top of a PANAHEAD, 6. O'Connor Sliding Base system for use with fluid heads, etc., 7. PANAFLEX camera mounted on a flat-top type tripod head.

Additional Camera Tilt, Up or Down

An adjustable tilt plate for exaggerated tilt up or down makes possible shots with the camera pointing 90° up or 90° down.

To adjust the tilt plate for additional tilt down

For additional tilt DOWN release the rear tilt plate locking lever that is just in front of the rear pan handle socket and press the safety catch at the rear of the tilt plate on the left. For small amounts of additional tilt, press in whichever of the three safety stops at the rear right hand side of the dovetail slideway is appropriate and lock the sliding block in such a manner that the safety stop remains in position. Greater amounts of tilt may be achieved by additionally pressing one of the three safety stops at the front and adjusting the forward block accordingly.

To adjust the tilt plate for additional tilt up

For additional tilt up loosen both the front and the rear tilt plate locking levers, depress either the front or back lower dovetail slide safety stops to release, slide out and reverse the entire tilt plate subassembly, reverse the camera attachment plate so that the entire subassembly operates in the opposite direction and proceed as for additional tilt DOWN.

The PANAROCK and the PANATILT accessories

For additional tilt at ground level or close to any flat surface the PANAROCK and the PANATILT are two very useful accessories.

The PANAROCK is a semicircular shaped device which fits to the underside of a PANAFLEX camera and enables the camera to be positioned very close to the floor or other flat surface and tilted up and down in shot by a rocking motion.

The PANATILT is an adjustable wedge unit which may also be fitted to the underside of a PANAFLEX camera to give additional tilt movement in close proximity to a flat surface. The PANATILT unit provides a rather more rigid support than the PANAROCK and is not suitable for in-shot camera movements.

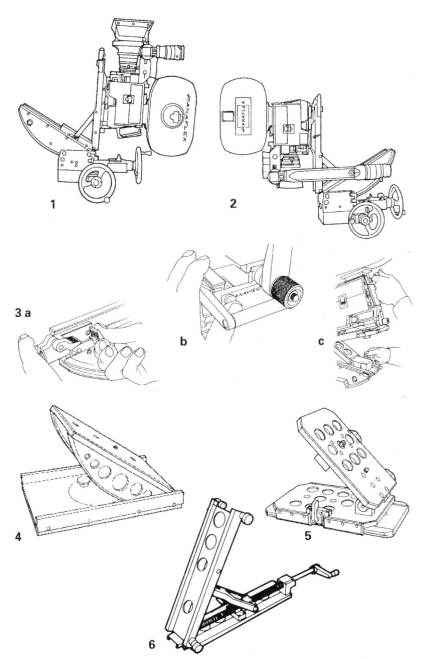

1. PANAHEAD tilted 90° up, 2. PANAHEAD tilted 90° down, 3. Adjusting a PANAHEAD for additional tilt up or down: a. release the side locking lever, b. press in the safety catch, c. raise the dovetail slide and securely lock off, 4. PANAROCK, 5. PANATILT, 6. Geared tilt plate.

Fine Tuning PANAHEAD Pan and Tilt Movements

The amount of friction or "feel" applied to the pan and tilt movements may be adjusted by the levers at the rear and side of the PANAHEAD. These levers may be fully tightened to positively lock the PANAHEAD when shooting Special Effects and background plates.

Later model PANAHEADS have tilt locking levers on either side to make the tilt lock-off even more positive for shooting plates.

Any gross backlash in the pan movement may be smoothed out by releasing a small set screw at the rear right hand side of the head and adjusting a knob at the rear. Take care not to set the gears so tight that they bind. This adjustment is correctly set before a PANAHEAD leaves the PANAVISION plant or that of any of its representatives, but a small amount of adjustment may be required during the course of a long location shoot, especially if the head is used constantly with the keyway in one position relative to the scene so that gear wear is maximized over a short segment.

Take care also not to completely undo the pan adjusting knob and disengage the pan gears as these are very meticulously lapped together relative to one another at the factory. Should this setting be upset it will be necessary to remove the bottom cover plate from the PANAHEAD and note that the small index marks on the worm wheel and drive gears coincide when they come together. This is not a job that should be attempted in the field.

The tension of the belt drive may be adjusted by turning the wheel at the front of the PANAHEAD to the right. This also should rarely require adjustment in the field.

Emergency servicing
Should a PANAHEAD become immersed in sea water or subject to a sandstorm then it will be necessary to completely strip down, clean and re-lubricate the unit before it is fit for further use.

In the case of sea water immediately submerge the head in fresh water and wash away all traces of salt.

In the case of sand BRUSH away all traces of sand. DO NOT USE AN AIRLINE OR AN AEROSOL AIRSPRAY to remove the sand as this will only drive the sand further into the bearings and between the gears and will inevitably cause even more damage.

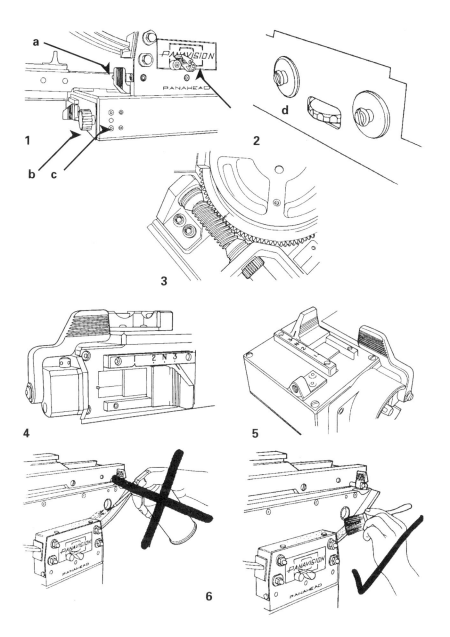

1. PANAHEAD adjustment controls: a. Pan feel (drag) adjustment/lock lever, b. Pan gear meshing adjustment and c. Release set screw, d. Tilt feel adjustment lever and quadrant lock, 2. Tilt tension adjustment wheel at front of PANAHEAD, 3. Index marks on pan gears which must be realigned if ever they become disengaged, 4. Pan gear ratio selector and pan lock, 5. Tilt gear ratio selector and tilt lock, 6. When a PANAHEAD has been in a dusty environment it is better to brush away grit rather than blow it further into the gear teeth.

Special PANAHEAD Facilities

The skills of a Camera Operator may be greatly enhanced by making use of some of the additional features of the PANAHEAD in order to customize the head to the requirements of a particular shot without the need to exchange the head for another type.

Using the PANAHEAD as a free or friction head
For very fast "whip pans" the PANAHEAD may be used as a free head by attaching a pan bar to the rear of the head. An auxiliary pan bar may also be fitted to the front of the head. In this mode the gearing should be set to neutral. Resistance or "feel" may be introduced by tightening the "feel" adjusting levers.

Using the PANAHEAD as a gyro head
For long smooth pans the PANAHEAD may be used as a gyro head by using it as a free head but with the hand wheels fitted and the gearing set to the highest ratio to maximize the effect. The finger knob of the tilt wheel may be reversed to eliminate the possibility of it snagging on the operator's clothing. (Press the button at its center to release.)

Using the PANAHEAD as a remote head
For reasons of safety, or to get shots that would otherwise be impossible with a Camera Operator in close proximity to the camera, the PANAHEAD may be used as a remote controlled head by use of the PANAREMOTE remote control system. In this mode slave motors are fitted in place of the PANAHEAD hand wheels and the camera controlled by remote handwheels, the aid of a Video Assist and remote lens and camera controls. The Operator may be 150 ft. away from the camera and still be able to operate the camera with all the subtlety of a hands-on situation.

The PANAREMOTE system also incorporates facilities to control the focus, zoom focal length and aperture of the lens and the camera on/off operation. All the controls, together with the video assist image, a video picture of the lens settings and film and other camera data can be passed to the operating position along a single cable.

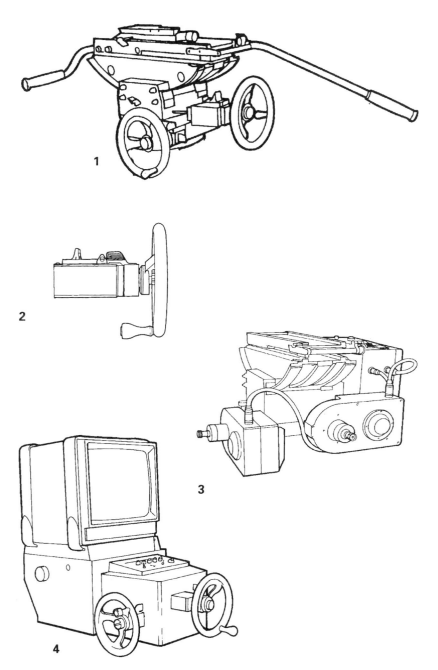

1. PANAHEAD with pan handles attached, 2. Tilt handwheel with knob turned round when PANAHEAD is in gyro-head mode, 3. PANAREMOTE remote pan and tilt system, with remote control motors fitted in place of normal pan and tilt handles, 4. PANAREMOTE system, control console.

81

PANABALL LEVELLERS

Yet another useful PANAVISION accessory is the PANABALL LEVELLER which eliminates the need to level a Mitchell type flat-top tripod by shortening or lengthening, or kicking, individual legs until the head is level.

For general use the regular PANABALL LEVELLER is fitted between the top of a Mitchell type tripod top and the underside of a PANAHEAD and gives 15° of levelling capability in any direction. Equally it can be used to tilt the camera by 15° in any direction.

The three short feet on the underside of a PANABALL LEVELLER may be removed when it is fitted to an extra wide tripod, dolly or camera crane interface. (When doing so, unscrew the feet and screw them in from the top side so they do not get lost).

The PANABALL leveller as a hi-hat
A PANABALL LEVELLER may be placed on the ground or fitted to any flat surface and used as a levelling hi-hat. The three short feet have holes in them for retaining screws.

The PANABALL nodal leveller
For SFX use, the PANABALL NODAL LEVELLER may be used in conjunction with a PANANODE adaptor so that the entrance pupil of the lens does not move in space as the camera is levelled or tilted. The tilt range of the PANABALL NODAL LEVELLER is 3° in any direction.

82

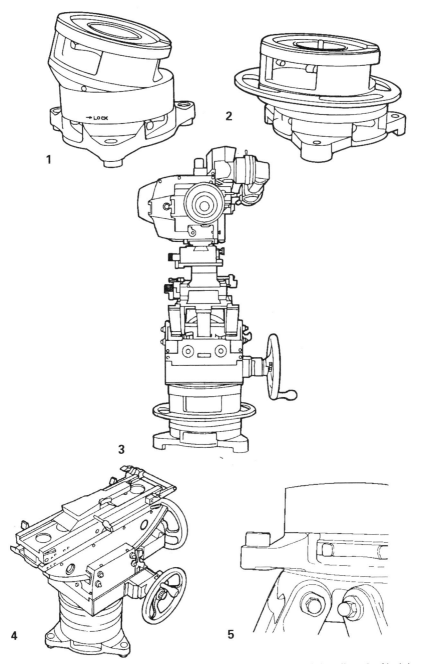

1. Regular (15°) PANABALL leveller, 2. Nodal (3°) PANABALL leveller, 3. Nodal PANABALL leveller/PANAHEAD/PANANODE/PANAFLEX assembly, 4. PANABALL leveller used as a hi-hat on the ground, 5. PANABALL foot reversed.

83

Nodally Mounting PANAFLEX and PANASTAR Cameras

Many aspects of the PANAFLEX CAMERA SYSTEM make it especially suitable for film productions with a major SFX content. Not least of these is where the lens is mounted relative to the pan and tilt movement.

For normal usage PANAFLEX and PANASTAR cameras are mounted centrally on a PANAHEAD and as low as is practical. However, for SFX work, especially when shooting miniatures and for Front Projection work, it is of crucial importance that the camera be mounted nodally on the head, that is, with the front entrance pupil of the lens (the point inside the lens where the bundle of light rays entering the lens appear to meet) is set exactly above the center of rotation of the pan axis and in the exact center of the tilt axis (the center of the quadrant).

To achieve this it is necessary to mount the camera about two inches higher than normal, about 4" to one side and to be able to slide the camera rearward on the head until the entrance pupil of the lens (which is in a different place on every lens) is directly above the center of the pan axis, regardless of what this does to the balance and the "feel" of the head.

Setting the camera in a nodal position

The easy way to check if a camera and lens are mounted nodally is to place a post in front of the camera and note through the viewfinder its position relative to the studio wall or to the horizon. If the camera is correctly mounted it will be possible to pan and tilt the camera without changing the relative positions of the post and the mark on the studio wall.

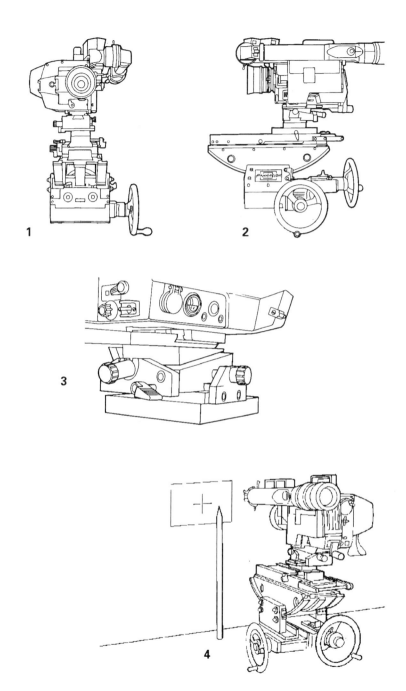

1. Camera mounted nodally above the pan axis and about the rotational axis,
2. Camera mounted nodally above the pan axis and about the tilt axis, 3.
PANANODE micro-adjustment unit, 4. Setting a camera nodally by the use of
two markers.

The PANATATE TURNOVER MOUNT

PANATATE TURNOVER MOUNT enables the camera to be turned sideways or upside down, or even rotated, about the optical axis during a take.

The camera attachment unit incorporates a PANANODE NODAL ADAPTOR for fine height and sideways adjustment and the entire unit may be slid longitudinally on the PANAHEAD to make three dimensional nodal positioning possible, making it an ideal instrument with which to photograph miniatures.

The unit is fitted with a regular PANAHEAD three-speed gearbox and handwheel. The handwheel may be interchanged with a PANAREMOTE actuator unit for remote control.

Camera Operators may find it easier to operate this unit with the aid of a PANAVID VIDEO ASSIST system, with a small monitor set on the unit, rather than try to look through the camera viewfinder as the camera is rotated.

The PANATATE system can also be used with a 65mm camera.

Fitting a camera to a PANATATE turnover mount

When fitting a PANAFLEX or PANASTAR camera to the PANATATE TURNOVER MOUNT the film magazine must be fitted in the rear position.

The camera battery, control and video cables should be arranged so as to leave the unit from directly behind the camera and not allowed to wrap around the camera as it is rotated.

Balancing weights may be placed around the turnover ring to balance the camera radially, making it easier to turn the camera through 360° and control it. Other weights may be fitted to the front of the unit to counterbalance the mass when it is moved rearwards on the head to nodally align the entrance pupil of the lens with the center of the pan and tilt axes.

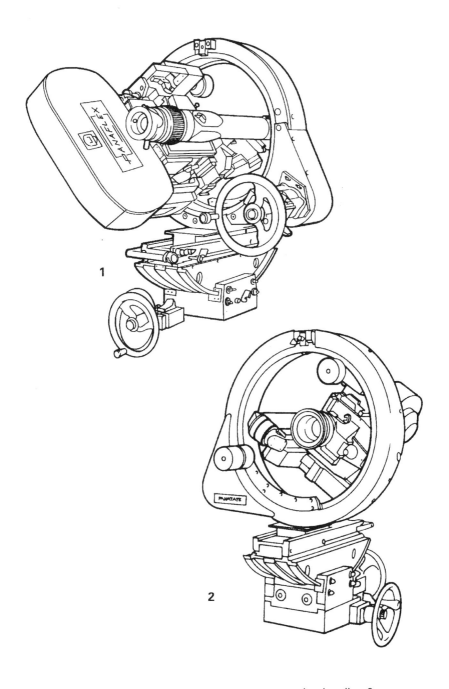

1. PANATATE unit, rear view showing turn-over operating handle, 2. PANATATE unit, front view showing counter weights.

What you see is what you get ... especially with a PANAFLEX

PANAFLEX Viewfinder Eyepieces

PANAFLEX (not PANAFLEX-X) cameras are fitted with INTERCHANGEABLE EYEPIECES. A short eyepiece is used when the camera is hand held and supported on the operator's shoulder. A long length viewfinder, incorporating an IMAGE MAGNIFIER, is for normal use when the camera is mounted on a pan and tilt head and when the Operator needs to stand back from the camera when doing fast pans, etc. There also is an optional medium length which is somewhere between the two.

Fitting and interchanging eyepieces

To remove an eyepiece first unplug the PANACLEAR heated eyepiece and release the eyepiece leveller if fitted. Rotate the eyepiece until it is pointing directly upwards, tighten the friction lock at the front 'elbow' of the viewfinder system by turning it counter-clockwise, press the thumb lock with left thumb and turn the locking ring to the right until the reference lines coincide and then gently lift the eyepiece straight up to remove.

Fit an eyepiece by pressing it into position with the reference lines aligned and turn the locking ring to the left until an audible click indicates that the eyepiece is double locked in position. Do not over tighten.

Note: it is good practice to orient the viewfinder directly upwards when changing an eyepiece. This supports the weight of the extension eyepiece while it is unlocked.

Rotate friction lock clockwise to unlock.

At this point the image in the eyepiece will appear to be upside down. To correct, press in the thumb control below the horizontal arrow, while rotating the eyepiece counter-clockwise until it faces downwards.

Release the thumb control, return the eyepiece (clockwise) to the upright position until an audible click is heard, and return to the shooting position.

Lock the friction ring if the eyepiece is to be self supported, leave it unlocked if it is to be attached to the eyepiece leveller or linked to the camera door hinge.

88

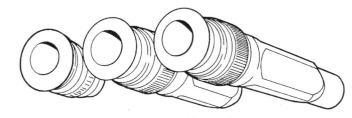

1

1. Set of three PANAFLEX interchangeable eyepieces.

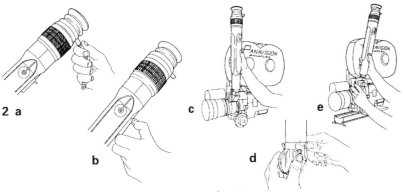

2 a

b

c

d

e

2. Removing a PANAFLEX eyepiece, stage by stage.

a. Unplug the PANACLEAR, b. Release the eyepiece leveller, c. Set eyepiece pointing directly up, d. Press in the thumb lock and turn locking ring to the right until reference lines coincide, e. Remove eyepiece.

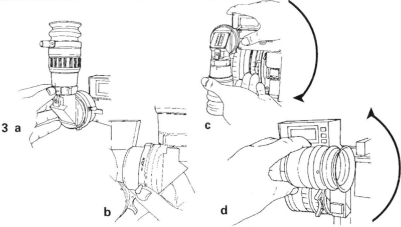

3 a

b

c

d

3. Fitting an eyepiece

a. Position eyepiece with reference marks aligned and turn locking ring to left, b. Release friction lock, c. Press thumb control and rotate eyepiece clockwise until pointing directly downwards, d. Release the thumb control and rotate the eyepiece counter-clockwise, past the position where a click is heard, to the shooting position.

PANAVISION Eyepiece Special Facilities

Ventilators in PANAFLEX rubber eyepiece cups prevent the discomfort of suction pulling on the operator's eye and also prevents water and dirt from entering the viewfinder optical system.

The ocular marker ring

PANAFLEX eyepieces have a WHITE MARKER BEZEL around their front rim so that the individual eyepiece settings of all the various people who must look through the camera may be marked with a pencil for easy future reference. This saves a great deal of time and petty aggravation when people with diverse eyesight are constantly using the viewfinder.

The image magnifier

The IMAGE MAGNIFIER enlarges the center of the ground glass image when it is necessary to carefully examine only a part of the scene. It may be used by the Director to check a particular performance during a rehearsal, by the Director of Photography to examine a lighting detail, by the Operator to study picture composition and especially by the Assistant when eye-focusing.

The PANACLEAR eyepiece demister

In cold weather conditions the PANAFLEX viewfinder optics may be heated by means of a PANACLEAR eyepiece heater to eliminate fogging. The problem of an eyepiece fogging during a take due to the comparative warmth of the operator's body or breath is a serious one and the PANACLEAR heated viewfinder is a complete cure.

The PANACLEAR draws its power from the camera and is connected by a coiled cable plugged into a socket on the magazine port handle. As this handle is usually over the top magazine port (and the magazine is on the rear) when the short eyepiece is fitted for hand holding and on the rear when a medium or long eyepiece is fitted, only a short connecting cable is necessary. A small switch and indicator light by the side of the outlet socket switches the heater unit ON and OFF.

Ocular diopters

Diopters can be supplied and fitted into the eyepiece system to suit user requirements.

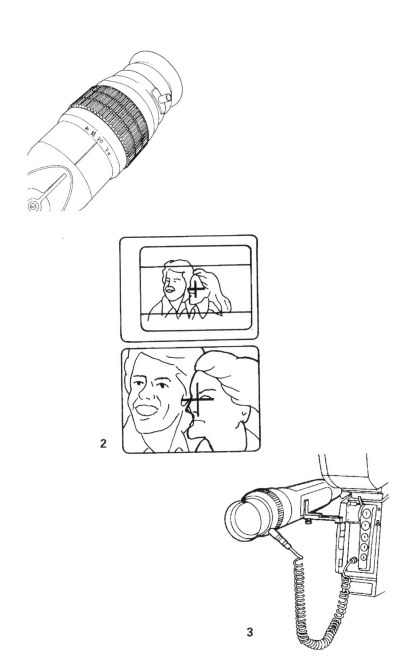

1. PANAFLEX eyepiece bezel showing multiple personal setting marks, 2. Simulated view through a PANAFLEX eyepiece showing normal and enlarged pictures using the magnification facility, 3. PANACLEAR power supply cable connected to an outlet on the magazine port handle.

PANAFLEX Viewfinder Special Facilities

The Viewfinder Tube is that part of the viewfinder system which is attached to the camera.

The PANAGLOW illuminated reticle

PANAGLOW is PANAVISION's patented and unique illuminated reticle system which, when switched ON, causes the ground glass markings to glow red so that the camera operator can clearly see the outline of the acceptable picture area, even in very low light conditions. It is an essential accessory when filming with low-key lighting.

The secret of the PANAGLOW system is its special ground glass focusing screen which uses discrete mirrors instead of etched lines to delineate the picture area. These mirrored lines reflect light to the operator from a small red lamp set in the viewfinder system. It is turned ON by a switch on the left side of the camera.

The intensity of the PANAGLOW light may be adjusted by a screw set behind a cover-screw on the front of the camera to the right of the engraved 'PANAFLEX' nameplate. To alter the brightness, remove the protective cover-screw and use a small screwdriver to gently turn the adjusting screw. Take care not to set the brightness too high as this may cause the ground glass to 'blush-out' with an overall red flare.

Later model PLATINUM PANAFLEXES have a knob to adjust the PANAGLOW brightness level.

ND contrast viewing filters

All PANAFLEX cameras are fitted with two CONTRAST-VIEWING FILTERS which can be introduced into the viewfinder system to assist the Director of Photography in selecting the overall contrast and lighting balance of a scene. The filters normally supplied are ND 0.6 and 0.9. Alternative filters may be fitted on request. The Viewing-Filters are activated by a lever on the viewfinder tube. Press down for ND 0.6, up for ND 0.9.

De-anamorphoser and light cutoff

A lever on the side of the viewfinder tube may be set horizontal for spherical viewing, vertical for anamorphic viewing, or directly down for light cutoff.

92

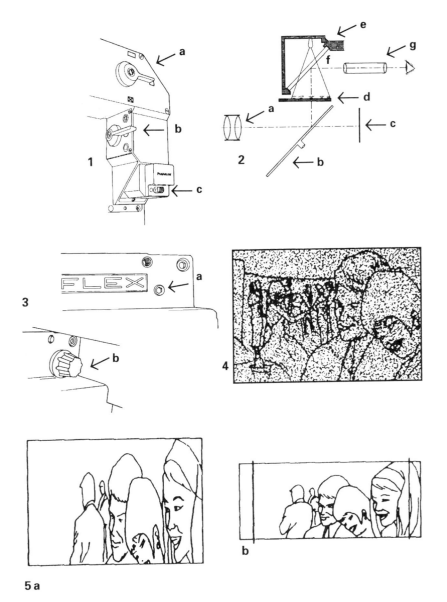

1. Front of PANAFLEX viewfinder system showing: a. the de-anamorphoser, normal and light cutoff, b. the viewing filter, and c. the PANAGLOW controls, 2. The way the PANAGLOW system works: a. Camera taking lens, b. mirror shutter, c. film, d. ground glass with mirrored markings which reflect light from the red LED lamp (e), f. partial mirror passes light from the LED to mirrored markings on the ground glass and at the same time reflects the ground glass image to the viewfinder eyepiece (g), 3. a. Normal PANAGLOW brightness control and (b.) later model PLATINUM PANAFLEX type, 4. Effect of a viewfinder contrast filter, 5. Effect of the viewfinder de-anamorphoser: a. anamorphic image, b. unsqueezed image (note the 70mm frame lines).

Digital Displays

Digital Displays on all PANAFLEX and PANASTAR cameras indicate the actual running speed of the camera and function only when the camera is switched on and operating. Digital Footage Displays indicate the number of feet or meters of film shot since the counter was last reset.

PLATINUM PANAFLEX displays

The Digital Display on the PLATINUM PANAFLEX is double sided so that it can be viewed from either side of the camera. These two displays can be switched independently and may be set to show footage (feet or meters), camera speed, camera shutter angle, whether a behind-the-lens gelatin filter is fitted and time code information.

In addition, the PLATINUM PANAFLEX and the PANAFLEX 16 cameras each have an ANNUNCIATOR PANEL, a row of LED warning lights which warn of LOW BATTERY VOLTAGE, INCORRECT CAMERA SPEED, FILM JAM, LOW FILM and OUT OF FILM.

PANAFLEX GII displays

On the PANAFLEX GII and earlier PANAFLEX and PANASTAR cameras the display is activated during operation and will remain lit for approximately five seconds after the camera is switched off. The footage shot display may be recalled by pressing the recall button on the top of the read-out unit marked with a red '0'. It may be reset by pressing the reset button at the left front end of the display, marked with a white 'X', simultaneously with the recall button.

Between the displays are two LED lights. The lower green lamp indicates that power is ON: the top, red light flashes when the battery voltage is 21-22 volts or less.

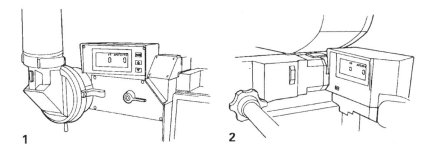

1. PLATINUM PANAFLEX digital displays and beam splitter cover plate
2. Digital display on the reverse side of a PLATINUM PANAFLEX

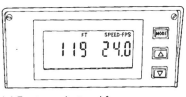

(a) Footage shot and fps

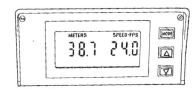

(b) Meters shot and fps

(c) Shutter angle and fps

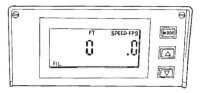

(d) Behind-the-lens filter in position

3. Alternative PLATINUM PANAFLEX displays

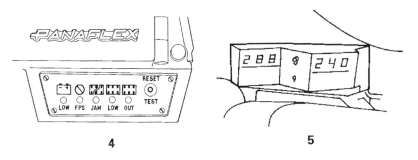

4. PLATINUM PANAFLEX annunciator panel (the PANAFLEX 16 is very similar),
5. PANAFLEX GII footage counter display.

PANAFLEX Lightweight Camera

The PANAFLEX LIGHTWEIGHT camera is especially intended for use with Steadicam and with extended remote camera crane equipment.

With a body made of magnesium, and with all nonessential items stripped off it, it is as light as a serious, register-pin, camera can be.

To save weight the PANAFLEX LIGHTWEIGHT camera has a fixed opening shutter (180° is the norm but 172.8° and 144° are readily available and any other can be made to order). For the same reason the digital display unit (DDR) is not normally fitted but can be plugged into the top of the camera for checking the fps, the footage used and the battery condition when required. Also, to keep weight to a minimum, the LIGHTWEIGHT camera has only a rear magazine position.

An inherent advantage of the PANAFLEX camera system is the fact that the rear magazine position is vertical, ensuring that there is no change in the camera's center of gravity as the film passes through.

Add-on items

An available item for the LIGHTWEIGHT camera is a special LIGHTWEIGHT zoom lens (27-68mm, T2.8) which weighs only 2lbs stripped or 3lbs with a remote controlled zoom motor. As with the lightweight remote focus and T-Stop control the remote zoom control can be operated either by a cable or a radio link.

Also available are custom lightweight 500' magazines.

The LIGHTWEIGHT camera is supplied with a B&W Video Assist as standard but if required a PANAVISION FIBRE-OPTIC color CCD camera can be fitted instead. The fibre-optic unit consists of a coherent bundle of fibre optics which cover the full height and width of the ground glass and which are then extruded to cover only the face of a CCD chip without losing their coherence. This arrangement is both lighter in weight and gives better image quality than an optical system.

Steadicam Clamp Plates are available for normal or for underslung (low angle) mounting.

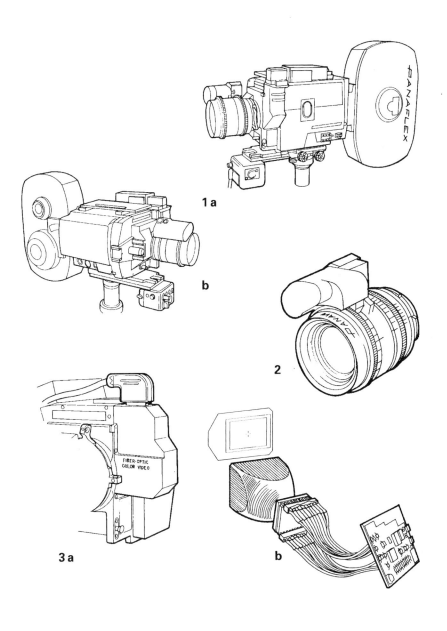

1 a. & b. PANAFLEX LIGHTWEIGHT camera, 2. PANAVISION LIGHTWEIGHT zoom lens, 3 a. PANAVISION FIBRE-OPTIC lightweight color video-assist, b. The coherent fibre-optic bundle; the CCD microchip and the tiny circuit board.

The PANAVISION Pedestal System

There are many well documented reasons why a Producer might wish to shoot a purely TV show on film, of which the "look" and the archivability are but two, but when it comes to the actual shooting those involved may wish the process to "feel" more like the TV production process.

To meet these requirements PANAVISION have developed, and can supply, a complete multi-camera setup.

Typically it will consist of three or four PANAFLEX-X cameras, all with 2000' magazines, using video viewfinders, focusing and zooming by panhandle controls and all mounted on video pedestals.

Special facilities

For the Pedestal System setup PANAFLEX-X cameras are used as they give the brightest possible video viewfinder image and are fitted with a continuous image pellicle reflex system to ensure that the image is also flicker-free.

The 2000' magazines enable just over 22 minutes of continuous filming, almost 30 minutes if the 3-PERF mode is used.

The FTZSAC Focus, T-Stop and Zoom control system is used together with a panhandle control unit to emulate video camera lens control.

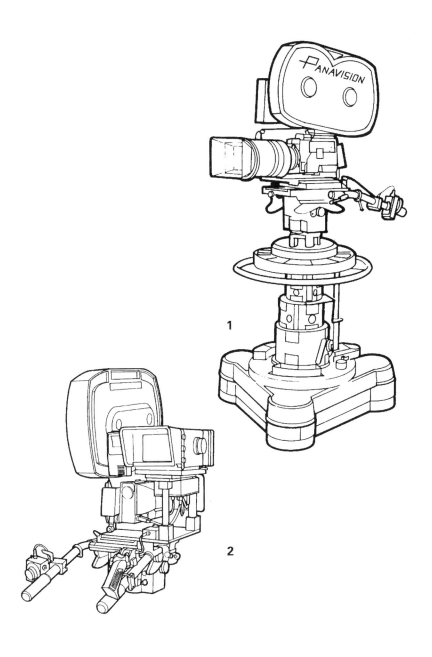

1 & 2. Pedestal mounted PANAFLEX-X cameras fitted with 2000 ft. magazines, high quality color CCD video assist systems and large viewing monitors, panhandle mounted FTZAC focus, T-Stop and Zoom lens controls and all the other "bells and whistles" that are common in a TV studio.

The
Camera Assistants'
PANAFLEX

The Camera Assistants' PANAFLEX

PANAFLEX CAMERAS have been designed to simplify the mechanical side of the Camera Assistant's responsibilities and to allow him to concentrate on those aspects most directly concerned with creative film making.

The following section details the procedures for assembling, loading and operating PANAVISION PANAFLEX EQUIPMENT. We hope that even the most experienced PANAUSER will discover a few valuable tricks and ideas.

Checking that the equipment is all there and is as required

Before starting on any operations to do with the camera, it is the Assistant's responsibility to check that the camera supplied by PANAVISION Inc., or by one of its representatives worldwide, as ordered by your Production company, is complete and is suitable to meet all the demands of the Production ahead. Remember that, although the camera will have been meticulously checked out in the shop, the technicians carrying out that task may not have been informed of any special requirements and additional features.

Assistants are advised to ask their Production Manager beforehand for a list of the equipment to be made available to them and to report any changes, additions or deletions that are made to the list during the testing period.

The Assistant should also look to see if the camera is fitted with an aperture matte, and if so that it is the correct one, and that a correctly marked ground glass is fitted.

Check list

PANAVISION technicians take particular pride in preparing cameras for use by clients and are required to sign a special 'check list' form to confirm that the flange focal depth setting and the collimation to the ground glass are both within 1/10,000" of standard, that the camera runs free of scratches, that it has been tested for quiet running in the sound test room, that the electronics, the mechanics and the video are all operating as normal and that the film transport movement is clean.

They must even sign that the camera is 'cosmetically' up to PANAVISION's high standard. It is all part of the pride of PANAVISION.

This card is included with the camera outfit when it leaves the shop and on the reverse the user is asked to state if all the equipment was delivered on time, if it was in a satisfactory condition and if the user has any comments to make.

PANAVISION particularly asks users to tell them if they detect the slightest thing going wrong with their equipment as this enables them to make sure it is put right before it goes to another user, it being much easier to detect the beginnings of any malfunction when it is actually in use than in the shop.

Users are then asked to return the card to the head of the Camera Service Dept.

PANAVISION is always grateful for user feedback.

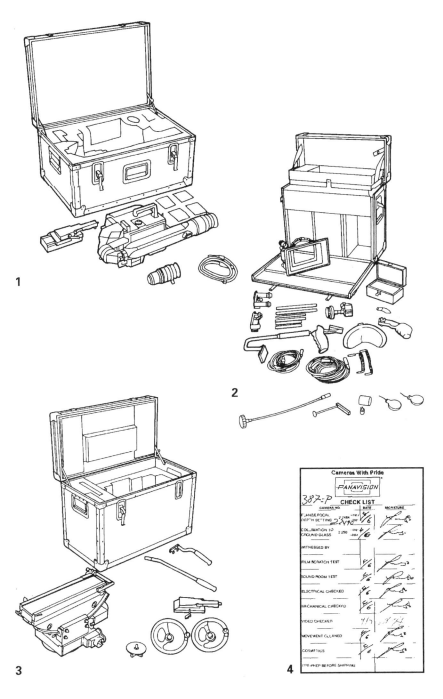

1. The contents of a PANAFLEX camera case, 2. The contents of a PANAFLEX camera accessory case, 3. The contents of a PANAHEAD case, 4. Check list.

103

Setting up a PANAVISION PANAHEAD

The PANAVISION PANAHEAD geared head fits on any regular tripod, dolly or camera crane equipped with a standard Mitchell type interface.

When setting the PANAHEAD in place be sure that the male locating key on the underside of the head is properly located in the keyway of the tripod etc. and secure it by using the locking knob supplied.

Attach the pan and tilt handwheels by the central locking knobs after aligning the keyways correctly. The handwheel with the removable finger knob should be fitted in the tilt (rear) position.

Release the pan and tilt locking levers and check for smoothness of movement in all three speed ratios. In the gyro head mode the handwheels act as flywheels to smooth out the pan and tilt movements. The finger knob of the tilt handwheel may be reversed by pressing its centre section and fitting it in the rear side of the flywheel so that it does not snag on the operator.

A two-way level is fitted to the rear of the PANAHEAD to check that it is set level.

A PANABALL leveller may be used between the head and a tripod to make it easier to level the head or to shoot with a tilted camera. A PANABALL leveller may also be used as a hi-hat for fitting a head to a flat surface.

Fitting the tilt plate

Additional up or down tilt movements are possible by adjusting the tiltplate system which may be located either way round. It is normally fitted with the panhandle socket to the rear giving additional downwards tilt. It may be reversed, with the panhandle socket located at the front, to give additional tilt up.

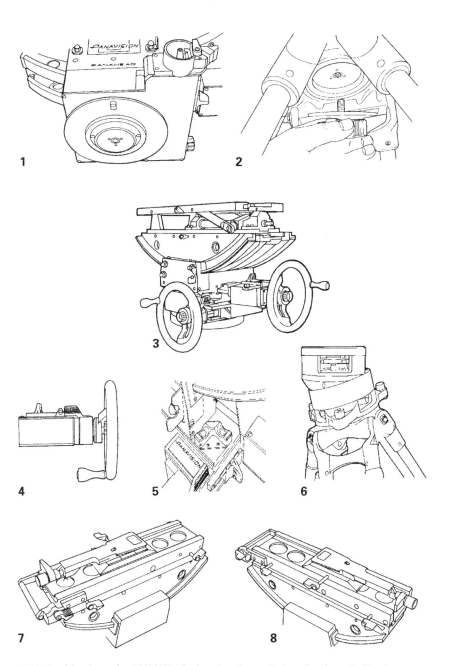

1. Underside view of a PANAHEAD showing the male locating key, 2. Head
secured by means of a central locking knob, 3. (Super) PANAHEAD handwheels,
4. Reversed tilt handwheel knob, 5. Two-way level, 6. PANABALL leveller,
7. Tiltplate with pan handle socket at the rear (normal) for additional tilt down,
8. Tiltplate with pan handle socket at the front for additional tilt up.

Fitting a PANAFLEX Camera to a Pan and Tilt Head

BEFORE FITTING A CAMERA TO A SLIDING BASE PLATE FIRST MAKE SURE THAT THE BASE PLATE IS SECURELY LOCKED IN ITS SLIDE.

To attach a PANAFLEX camera body to a PANAHEAD or a Sliding Base Plate make sure that the tail lock is completely withdrawn by fully turning it counter-clockwise and downwards, place the camera body squarely on the front of the dovetail shaped interface and push forwards until an audible click is heard indicating the camera is firmly in position; rotate the tail lock knob clockwise and tighten until the rubber pad is firmly against the rear of the camera.

Earlier PANAHEADS and Sliding Base Plates have a tail lock which must be pulled downwards to release rather than turned to one side.

When the camera has been completely assembled with a loaded magazine, a lens and other appropriate accessories, the entire unit may be slid forwards and backwards to bring it into balance by releasing the balancing slide lock lever on the left side of the dovetail plate.

Securely lock off the balancing slide when proper balance is achieved.

To remove a PANAFLEX camera from a PANAHEAD or Sliding Base Plates, position the viewfinder fully forward (resting on the matte box) hold the camera body firmly by the handle on top of the camera, release and turn the tail lock counter-clockwise until it is clear of the camera, pull the release catch at the side of dovetail, move camera back and lift carefully off the base, using both hands to do so.

Using a sliding base plate

PANAFLEX cameras may be fitted to any other flat top tripod head (O'Connor, Ronford, Sachtler, Vinten, etc.) by the use of an optional Sliding Base Plate assembly which provides an interface between a standard 3/8" 16 TPI tripod screw and the PANAVISION Dovetail attachment system. Note: A Sliding Base Plate is always supplied and is to be found in the camera case.

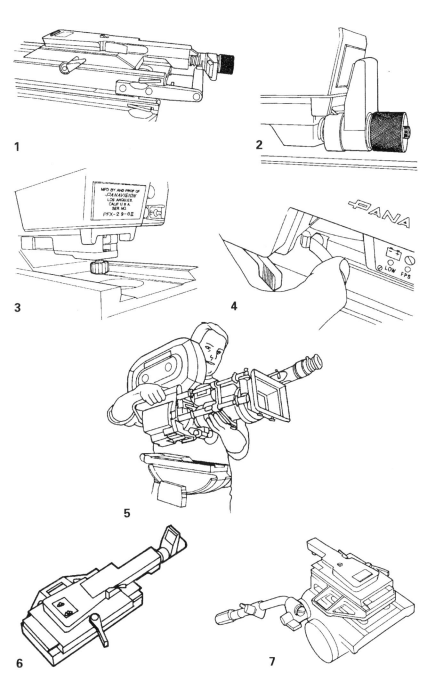

1. Top of PANAHEAD with tail lock set to one side, 2. Tail lock set tight, 3. Earlier type tail lock, 4. Side release lever, 5. Removing camera from a PANAHEAD using two hands, 6. Sliding base plate, 7. Sliding base plate on fluid head.

107

Preparing a PANAFLEX Camera for Hand Holding

Before converting a PANAFLEX camera from a mounted configuration to a hand-held mode it is necessary to have the following items at hand:
1. 500' or 250' magazine (usually)
2. Right hand grip
3. Left hand grip
4. Shoulder rest
5. Short eyepiece
6. Belt or onboard battery.

If the camera is to be used in the hand-held mode (except for the PANAFLEX-X, which is not intended for hand-held use) first change from the long to the short eyepiece. If the camera is mounted on a PANAHEAD it is usually easier to make this change before dismounting the camera. Similarly, it may be found easier to change from a 1000' top mounted magazine to a 250' or 500' rear mounted configuration and to fit the right hand grip while the camera is still on a PANAHEAD.

Attaching the handgrips and shoulder rest

Attach the right hand grip to the slide situated at the front of the camera to the left of the lens mount, turning the locking lever clockwise to secure.

Turn the camera onto its side and fit the left hand grip into the dovetail slide (located underneath) until there is an audible click indicating it is safely locked in position. Then slide the shoulder rest into the slideway located crosswise at the top of the 'cave' in the middle underside of the camera.

Both handgrips and the shoulder rest are adjustable for operator comfort.

An optional extension for added control is available for the left hand grip.

The right hand grip is fitted with both a camera toggle and pressure type on-off switches. Note: If the right hand grip is not properly secured to the camera, the camera may stop running or run intermittently.

Magazine considerations for hand-held shooting

For most hand-held shooting it will be found most convenient to use a 500' magazine mounted on the rear of the camera. However, when weight is an important consideration a 250' magazine can be used and if a very long take is envisioned, a 1000' magazine can be fitted.

While it is preferable to mount the magazine on the rear of the camera for optimum balance, it may be mounted on top if it is necessary for the operator to get as far back as possible.

108

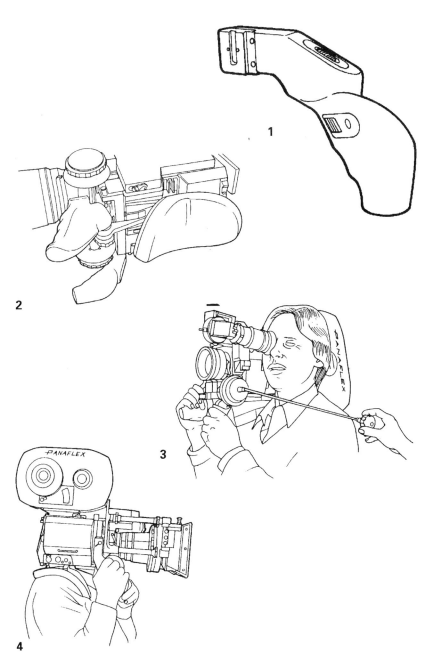

1. Right-hand grip, showing switches, 2. Underside of camera showing hand grips and shoulder rest fitted, 3. Hand held camera with a rear mounted 500' magazine and with a follow-focus extension fitted, 4. Hand held camera with magazine on top.

Camera Movement Lubrication

In general, camera movements should be lightly lubricated at the start of each working day using one drop of the special oil supplied by PANAVISION in each oil well.

If more than 20,000' of film (6000m) is shot per day then it is advisable to oil the camera more often.

When cameras are run at speeds greater than 24 fps they should be lubricated more often.

If, when lubricating a camera, a regular clockwise progression is made there is less chance that any oil well will be missed.

With most PANAFLEX camera types it will be found easier, or necessary, to remove the gate pressure pad in order to access the register pin oil points.

IMPORTANT: DO NOT OVER-LUBRICATE CAMERA MOVEMENTS.

PANAFLEX lubrication points

There are 12 lubrication points on all 35mm PANAFLEX movements irrespective of model type.

In addition, the thin metal strip between the bottoms of the pull-down claw slots in the register plate should be lightly pressed to check that the felt pads at the bottom of each slot are slightly moist. These pads are designed to smear a minute amount of silicone liquid onto the undersides of the pull down claws and, if dry, should be carefully moistened using a drop of PANAVISION silicone liquid.

IT IS VERY IMPORTANT NOT TO SPILL ANY SILICONE LIQUID ONTO THE CAMERA MOVEMENT AS THIS MAY CAUSE THE CAMERA TO SEIZE UP.

PANASTAR lubrication points

There are eight lubrication points on PANASTAR camera movements.
When the camera is run faster than 24 fps it should be oiled more often, every 1000', and at maximum speed it should be oiled before every take.

PANAFLEX 16 lubrication points

There are 12 lubrication points on PANAFLEX 16 cameras.

To lubricate the eccentric pivot arm it is necessary to remove the aperture plate.

To lubricate the lower register pin bush it is necessary to remove the pressure plate.

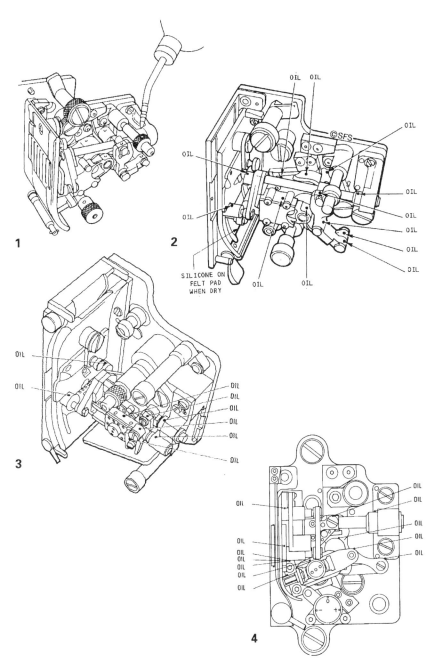

OIL OIL

OIL

©SFS

OIL

OIL

OIL

OIL

OIL

OIL

OIL

OIL

OIL

OIL

1

2

SILICONE ON
FELT PAD
WHEN DRY

OIL

OIL

OIL

OIL

OIL

OIL

OIL

OIL

OIL

OIL

3

OIL

OIL

OIL

OIL

OIL

OIL

OIL

OIL

OIL

OIL

OIL

OIL

4

1. Use only one drop of PANAVISION oil in each oil well from the dispenser
provided with each camera, 2. PANAFLEX lubrication points, 3. PANASTAR
lubrication points, 4. PANAFLEX 16 lubrication points.

111

SUPER PSR, PAN-MITCHELL Mk.II and PANAVISION 65 Lubrication

Like the PANAFLEX and PANASTAR cameras, the SUPER PSR, PAN-MITCHELL Mk.II and PANAVISION 65mm cameras should be lubricated daily in a routine manner so that no oil wells are overlooked.

In addition, the pair of skew gears on the main drive shaft on the motor side of these cameras should be lubricated with a light grease about once per month with average use.

SUPER PSR lubrication points
There are 13 lubrication points on all types of PSR cameras.

PAN-MITCHELL Mk.II lubrication points
There are seven lubrication points on PAN-MITCHELL Mk.II cameras.

When these cameras are run faster than 24 fps they should be oiled more often and at maximum speed should be oiled before every take.

PANAVISION 65mm lubrication points
There are eight lubrication points on a Standard type PANAVISION 65mm camera.

In addition a single drop of oil should be applied to each end of the pressure plate rollers.

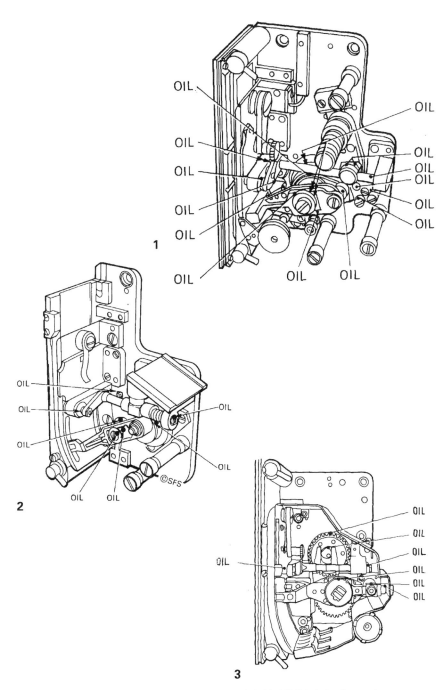

OIL

OIL

OIL

OIL

OIL

OIL

OIL

OIL

OIL

OIL

OIL

OIL

OIL

OIL

OIL

1

OIL

OIL

OIL

OIL

OIL

OIL

OIL

©SFS

2

OIL

OIL

OIL

OIL

OIL

OIL

OIL

3

1. SUPER PSR lubrication points,   2. PAN-MITCHELL Mk.II lubrication points,
3. PANAVISION 65mm lubrication points.

113

Removing and Replacing Camera Movements

Movements may be removed from the camera body for lubricating and cleaning provided that the flange focal depth is checked before use. Otherwise movements should be cleaned and oiled while still in the camera.

Removing and replacing a PANAFLEX camera movement

Tilt the camera slightly up to ensure the camera door remains open on its own.

Inch camera until the pulldown claws are at the bottom of the stroke and fully withdrawn from their slots, stopping just before the pulldown claw arm obstructs the lower movement lockdown screw.

Gently use a wide screwdriver to loosen the two short length knurled-head "capture" screws which secure the movement plate. Unscrew approximately five turns until they go loose in their bushings. Remove movement by pulling on the pitch control knob, wiggling to loosen. Please be gentle.

To replace the movement, inch the camera until the pins of the motor coupling are horizontal with the witness mark downwards and similarly align the movement shaft so that they match. Hold the movement with both hands using the left hand for support and the right hand to guide the movement into position.

Hold the movement with the thumb on the pitch control knob and the forefinger on the top aperture dog-lock, slide the entire unit into the camera interior, engage coupling in camera body with the witness marks aligned, secure with short knurled-head capture screws and tighten with a wide screwdriver.

Check the flange focal depth, see page 150, before reusing the camera.

Note: The interface between the motor drive coupling and the movement coupling is offset so they cannot be assembled incorrectly. If the movement does not seat, inch camera back and forth slightly until they fit snugly together. If it still does not seat remove and check the drive and movement couplings for possible damage.

Removing and replacing a PANASTAR camera movement

The method of removing and replacing the movement of a PANASTAR camera is similar to that of a PANAFLEX except that pull down claws should be set in the middle of the pull-down movement and then withdrawn by pushing the retraction knob downwards.

In addition to the two movement retaining screws there is also a cam at the rear of movement plate which must be released before the movement can be removed and replaced and tightened afterwards.

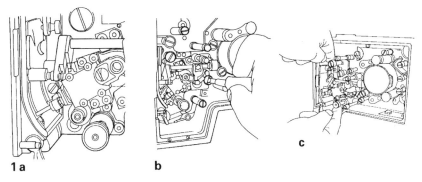

1 a   b

1. Removing a PANAFLEX movement: a. Position the claws at the bottom of the pull-down stroke stopping just before the link arm covers the lower captive screw, b. Loosen the two captive screws with a broad screwdriver, c. Pull gently on the pitch control to remove the movement.

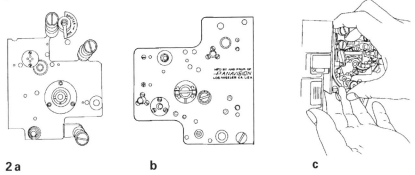

2 a   b   c

2. Replacing a PANAFLEX movement: a. Inch camera until witness mark on the movement coupling is directly downwards, b. Align the movement until the witness mark is directly downwards, c. Hold movement correctly to replace.

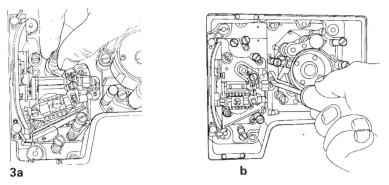

3a   b

3. Removing a PANASTAR movement: a. Pull down claws should be in the middle of the pull-down movement and then withdrawn by pushing the retraction knob downwards, b. In addition to loosening the captured screws a cam at the rear of the movement plate must also be released with a screwdriver.

115

PANAFLEX Power Supplies

All PANAVISION cameras, except the PSR, operate from a 24 volt DC power source.

All PANAVISION camera to battery cables use the same 3 pin connector at the battery end of the cable (pin 1 is 24v+, pin 2 is ground) although the connector at the camera end may differ depending upon the camera and the model.

On PANAFLEX 16 (and on some PLATINUM PANAFLEX) cameras the power supply is attached to the camera via a 2-pin LEMO connector, the right hand one of three sockets situated at the bottom left hand corner of the right hand side of the camera. (Pin 1 is 24v+, pin 2 is ground.)

On other PANAFLEX and PSR cameras the power supply is attached to the camera via a 3-pin LEMO connector, the centre one of three sockets situated at the bottom left hand corner of the right hand side of the camera. (Pin 1 is 24v+, pin 2 is ground.)

Camera power requirements

The minimum power requirement is 21v. DC., the maximum 28v. DC. Under normal circumstances most cameras draw approximately 2 amps but in very cold conditions may draw as much as 9 amps.

The battery packs normally supplied are 10-16 Ah. Lightweight 4 & 6 Ah shoulder-slung, belt and onboard batteries are also available.

On the PLATINUM PANAFLEX a LOW BATTERY battery warning light, situated on the left hand side of the annunciator panel, shows when the power supply is low or inadequate (21 volts or less).

On the GII/GOLDEN PANAFLEX a green battery condition light, adjacent to the footage/fps display, shows when the power supply is adequate, a red light indicates that power is low (21 volts or less).

Camera power notes

The camera must NEVER be switched on or off by connecting or disconnecting the power supply. Use only the power switch which is located at the rear of the camera, the handgrip switch or the optional side or remote control switches.

The camera ON-OFF switch only disconnects power to the camera motor. It does NOT disconnect battery power to the camera.

There is always a small drain on the battery caused by the electronic circuits whenever the battery is connected.

DO NOT change the circuit boards or touch the electronics while the battery is connected.

Disconnect the camera from the battery during long breaks.

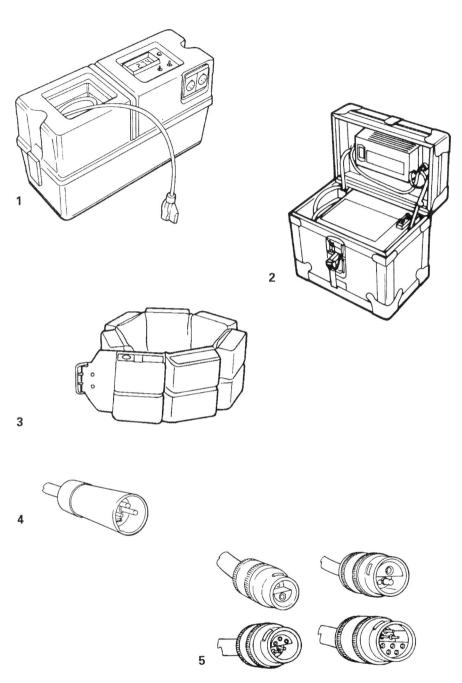

1. Regular LA 'purse' battery complete with charger, 2. Block battery with built-in charger, 3. Battery belt, 4. Universal 3 pin battery connector, 5. Various LEMO connectors.

Recharging Nicad Batteries

PANAVISION cameras may be supplied either with Nickel Cadmium or Sealed Lead Acid batteries. Both types have a good power to weight ratio, are maintenance free and hold their charge well under normal temperature conditions. From the users' point of view the principal differences are in the voltage of the individual cells, the type of charger that needs to be used and the effect of habitual overcharging.

Nickel cadmium batteries

PANAVISION supply two types of Nicad Batteries, the normal type being made up of cylindrical cells and the higher capacity type which uses rectangular nickel-cadmium alkaline cells.

Cylindrical cells, being smaller, are most usually used for battery belts and for onboard batteries.

All Nicad batteries hold their charge best when kept cool and deliver best when warm. They self-discharge quite rapidly at temperatures above 95°F (35°C) but below 32° (0°C) can hold their charge for years.

They give of their maximum at 85-95°F (30-35°C). At 32°F (0°C) they give only half capacity and at -40° may not operate at all.

The nominal voltage of Nicad cells is 1.2v. When charging is just completed, for a short period, the voltage may be as high as 1.5v per cell. For this reason they should be rested for at least two hours after charging to allow the voltage to stabilize.

On discharge Nicad cells maintain a very constant 1.2v per cell until they come to the end of their charge when the voltage drops rapidly. They should not be discharged below 1v per cell.

Nicad batteries must only be recharged using a constant current type charger designed especially for recharging Nicad type cells.

If Nicad batteries are frequently recharged before they have been fully discharged they will suffer from what is known as 'memory effect' and will cease to hold their full capacity. This state can be corrected by discharging the batteries to 1v per cell several times between full charging. It is very bad practice to recharge Nicad batteries when they are already fully charged.

PANAVISION Inc. in Tarzana has a special nicad battery testing rig which plots the current flow of batteries as they are fully discharged under controlled conditions. On this device any malfunction, even of a single cell, is plotted on a graph so that any faulty cell may be identified and replaced.

118

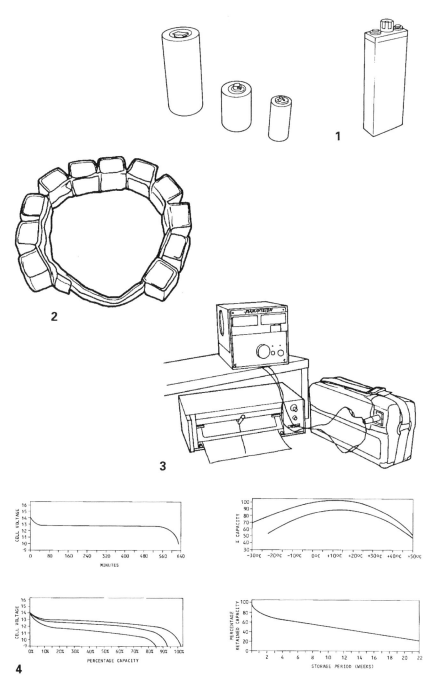

1. Cylindrical and rectangular Nicad battery cells, 2. Battery belt made up of Nicad cells, 3. Nicad battery test rig, 4. Nicad battery graphs.

Recharging Sealed Lead Acid Batteries

The sealed lead acid (LA) batteries supplied by PANAVISION for the purpose of powering cameras and camera accessories are far removed from the lead acid type batteries used for automobiles. Unlike the common lead acid battery the sulphuric acid electrolyte of LA batteries is solid and cannot be spilled. From the outside they look very similar to cylindrical type Nicad batteries but that is where the similarity ends.

The nominal voltage of LA cells is 2 volts. Twelve LA cells are required to make up a 24v battery compared to twenty Nicad cells.

LA batteries must be charged at approximately 2.5v per cell using a constant voltage charger. For this reason constant current chargers designed to be used with Nicad batteries are not suitable for use with LA batteries, and vice versa. Only chargers supplied by PANAVISION for use with particular types of batteries should be used with those batteries. Many batteries supplied by PANAVISION incorporate chargers within the battery case so there can be no confusion.

Charge retention and performance
Like Nicad batteries, LA batteries store their charge best when kept in a cool atmosphere but unlike Nicads should only be stored in a fully charged state. They will, however, store their charge better than Nicads in warm conditions and will continue to perform at temperatures slightly lower than Nicads.

Unlike Nicad batteries, LA batteries do not suffer from the memory effect. Furthermore, under-discharging between recharging will increase the number of charge-discharge cycles to be expected from the life of a particular battery.

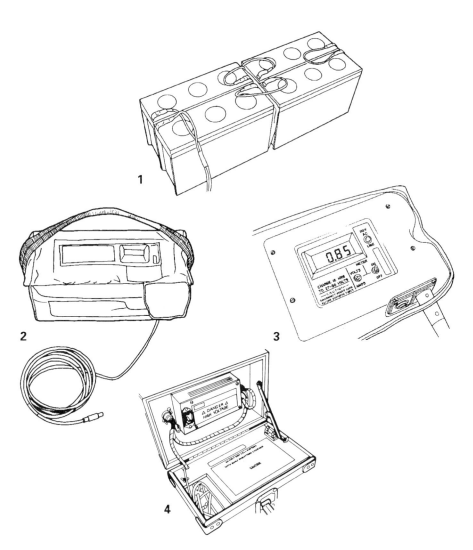

1. Connected blocks of LA cells, 2. LA battery with built-in charger, 3. The voltage/amperage meter of an LA battery, 4. Block battery with built-in charger.

SEALED LEAD ACID BATTERY TEMPERATURE v CAPACITY TABLE

Temperature		Capacity
°C	°F	
61	140	110%
38	100	105%
20	68	100%
0	32	85%
-12	10	50%
-40	-40	15%

Setting the Camera Speed

Before running the camera, especially for the first time during the day, it is a wise precaution to check that the camera speed (fps) is set as required.

The 24/25, 24/29.97 or 24/30 crystal control fps switch is situated in the recess in the centre underside of the camera (the cave). On most cameras this switch may be configured to switch between either 24 and 25 fps or 24 and 29.97/30 fps by means of a switch on the crystal/tach circuit board. The latest circuit boards allow you to switch between all four speeds.

PLATINUM PANAFLEX speed controls

The PLATINUM can be set to run under crystal control at any speed (4 - 36 fps) in increments of 1/10 fps by a switch at the rear of the camera. (The 29.97 fps switch is in the cave.) Lift the cover to set the speed and check that it is exactly as required by running the camera and observing the digital display panel. (Note: At 29.97 fps the display will show 29.9 and flash.)

To vary the camera speed continuously and smoothly over the full range a special Variable Speed Control Unit is an available accessory.

GII and earlier PANAFLEX speed controls

The crystal control/variable speed switch of these cameras is located at the rear of the camera providing 4-36 fps variable speeds. Push the slide switch to the 'VARY' position (a safety catch prevents this from being done inadvertently) and turn the knurled black knob to vary the speed. On some cameras the maximum speed may be achieved by turning the knob fully clockwise and then backing off very slightly. Running speed is confirmed by the LED display.

PANASTAR speed controls

A switch at the rear of PANASTAR cameras may be used to set the camera to operate at crystal controlled speeds of 6, 12, 18, 24, 36, 48, 60, 72, 96 and 120 fps.

The 24 fps selection may be set to run at 25 fps by means of a switch in the cave and on some cameras this setting may in turn be set to operate at 30 fps by a switch on the crystal/tach board.

Other preset crystal controlled speeds, and infinitely variable speeds may be selected by means of an external speed control unit.

On PLATINUM PANASTAR cameras a digital switch may be used to set the camera to run at any crystal controlled speed between 4 and 120 fps.

Precision speed control

An electronic Precision Speed Control is available to run any camera at any speed, in increments of $\frac{1}{1000}$ fps, under crystal control.

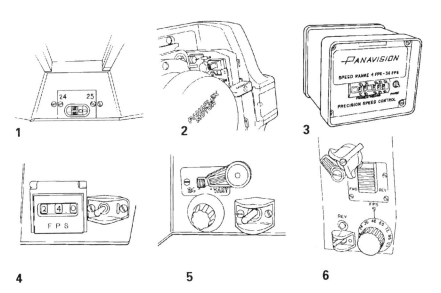

1. 24/25, 24/29.97 or 24/30 fps switch set in camera cave, 2. 25/30 or 25/29.97/30 fps configuration switch on the circuit board, 3. Precision Speed Control accessory, 4. PLATINUM digital speed selector and rear ON/OFF switch, 5. GII/GOLDEN crystal control (24, 25, 29.97 or 30 fps)/variable speed switch, variable speed control and rear ON/OFF switch, 6. PANASTAR speed control.

HMI FLICKER-FREE CAMERA SPEEDS

	LIGHT PEAKS	SHUTTER ANGLE (º)								
	PER	50	80	100	120	144	160	172.8	180	200
Hz	EXPOSURE	FRAMES PER SECOND (to nearest 0.001 fps) at 50Hz								
50	0.5	27.778	44.444	55.556	66.667	80	88.889	96	100	111.111
50	1	13.889	22.222	27.778	33.333	40	44.444	48	50	55.556
50	1.5	9.259	14.815	18.519	22.222	26.667	29.63	32	33.333	37.037
50	2	6.944	11.111	13.889	16.667	20	22.222	24	25	27.778
50	2.5	5.556	8.889	11.111	13.333	16	17.778	19.2	20	22.222
50	3	4.63	7.407	9.259	11.111	13.333	14.815	16	16.667	18.519
		FRAMES PER SECOND (to nearest 0.001 fps) at 60Hz								
60	0.5	33.333	53.333	66.667	80	96	106.667	115.2	120	133.333
60	1	16.667	26.667	33.333	40	48	53.333	57.6	60	66.667
60	1.5	11.111	17.778	22.222	26.667	32	35.556	38.4	40	44.444
60	2	8.333	13.333	16.667	20	24	26.667	28.8	30	33.333
60	2.5	6.667	10.667	13.333	16	19.2	21.333	23.04	24	26.667
60	3	5.556	8.889	11.111	13.333	16	17.778	19.2	20	22.222

Note: The above speed settings are dependent upon very accurate frequency and shutter settings. Where a speed is rounded off it is advisable to use a micro shutter control and a look-through device to ensure safe flicker-free operation (see page 121).

A 200º (or any other) shutter opening is safe at 24 fps with a 60 Hz AC power supply providing that both the camera speed and the 60Hz power supply are very precise.

" 0.5 Light Peaks per Exposure" is one light peak during the exposure period but none during the viewfinder period.

Running the Camera

Under normal circumstances the camera is turned ON and OFF by a switch at the rear of the camera.

On the PLATINUM PANAFLEX an optional additional ON/OFF switch may be situated on the viewfinder side of the camera just below the PANAGLOW switch.

An extension power switch for remote control is an optional accessory and slides into the dovetail situated to the side of the lens port.

Certain of the optional electronic accessories also provide camera ON/OFF capabilities.

Slack film in the rear side of the magazine may be taken up by pressing in the inching knob on the rear of the camera.

On the PLATINUM, additional inching and run switches are situated inside the camera film compartment, just below the main sprocket, to make it easier for the assistant to check that the film is threaded properly and the camera is running correctly before closing the camera door.

Running the camera at the beginning of the day
Prior to each day's shooting, run the camera without film for a short period to ensure that the mechanism is functioning smoothly. If the camera is fitted with a micro switch situated at the bottom right-hand corner of the film compartment opening this must be depressed to run the camera with the door open.

Running a PLATINUM PANAFLEX or a PANASTAR in reverse
PLATINUM PANAFLEX and some PANASTAR cameras may be run in reverse using special reverse running magazines. It should be noted that the film winds on or off the rear roll of film in the magazine in the opposite direction to normal.

Reverse running may be used either for shooting a scene to run backwards on the screen (in which case there must be sufficient unexposed film loaded in the rear of the magazine) or for rewinding the film between normal direction multiple exposures.

To run the camera in reverse a special switch to the left of the rear ON/OFF switch must be set to the REV position.

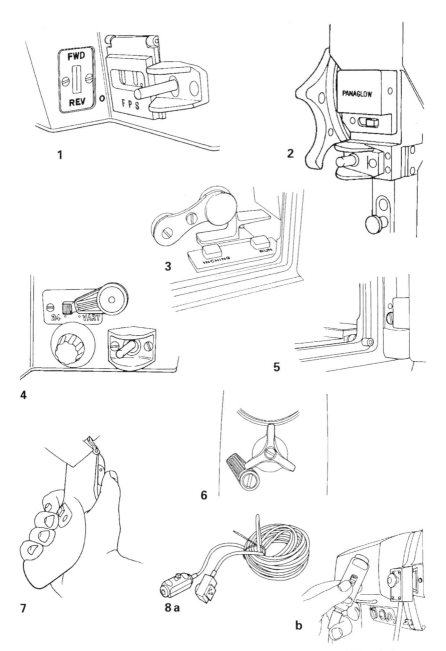

1. PLATINUM reverse running, digital speed selector and rear ON/OFF switch, 2. PLATINUM optional side ON-OFF switch, 3. PLATINUM internal INCHING and RUN switches, 4. GII ON-OFF switch, 5. Micro switch at bottom R. corner of camera body (GII and earlier cameras), 6. Inching knob, 7. Camera handle switches, 8 a.&b. Camera extension switch.

Setting the Shutter Opening

A feature of all PANAFLEX cameras is that they have separate focal plane and mirror shutters. The advantages of this configuration are that the exposure time can be adjusted, in shot if necessary, by adjusting the shutter opening to any angle between 50° and 200°, giving up to two stops of exposure control and allowing the exposure period to be set accurately to suit HMI lighting and synchronization with video and computer displays.

On PANASTAR cameras the adjustable shutter range is 40-180°.

The opening of the focal plane shutters of all PANAFLEX cameras (except the LIGHTWEIGHT which does not have an adjustable shutter) may be adjusted by use of a quadrant control at the top rear of the camera to the right of the rear magazine port. For coarse adjustment the lever may be set according to the engraved markings and locked-off as required.

Adjustable limit stops at either end of the quadrant make possible in-shot exposure adjustment from one shutter opening to another without the need to look at the quadrant markings while so doing.

For the most critical adjustment of the shutter opening, as when synchronising the exposure period to exactly match the scan period of a video monitor or a computer, an Aperture Viewing Mirror is available which can see through the lens exactly as the film does. To use this device the camera must be run at the shooting speed with the film and the pressure plate removed.

Adjusting a PLATINUM PANAFLEX or PANASTAR shutter

Before adjusting the variable shutter on a PLATINUM PANAFLEX or PLATINUM PANASTAR it is first necessary to open the camera door and release the shutter locking lever situated just above the movement.

For precise adjustment press the MODE button on the Digital Indicator repeatedly until it displays the SHUTTER ANGLE. Run the camera and adjust the shutter using the quadrant control at the rear of the camera. When the digital display indicates the precise shutter angle required lock off the shutter setting by means of the shutter locking lever inside the camera.

Adjusting a GII and earlier PANAFLEX shutter

On the GII and earlier cameras a micro adjustment device which screws onto the shutter adjustment quadrant is available for precise setting of the shutter opening.

Adjusting a PANASTAR shutter

PANASTAR cameras have a locking screw on the shutter adjustment control at the rear of the camera. To set the shutter, release the locking screw, set the shutter as required and relock.

Certain frequently used precise shutter openings are engraved on the shutter blades and may be seen by removing the film and the pressure plate.

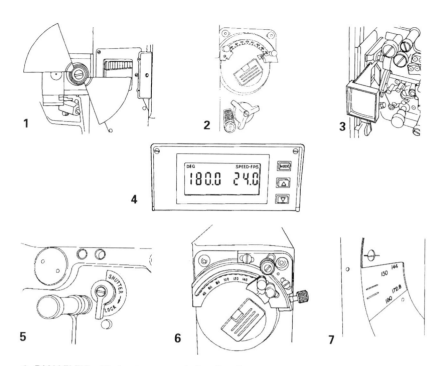

1. PANAFLEX with front removed showing focal plane and mirror shutters, 2. PANAFLEX shutter control quadrant on rear of camera, 3. Aperture Viewing Mirror in position, 4. PLATINUM PANAFLEX digital shutter-angle display, 5.PLATINUM PANAFLEX shutter release lever, 6. Shutter quadrant micro adjuster, 7. Shutter openings engraved on the shutter blade of a PANASTAR camera.

SAFEST SHUTTER ANGLE/CAMERA SPEED SETTINGS

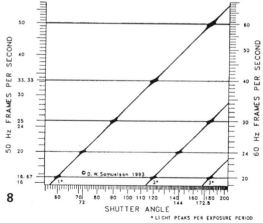

© D. W. Samuelson 1993

SHUTTER ANGLE

* LIGHT PEAKS PER EXPOSURE PERIOD

8. The horizontal lines are safe camera speeds irrespective of the shutter opening, the oblique lines are safe shutter angle/camera speed combinations. The nodes where the lines cross are the SAFEST windows of operation.

Changing the PANAFLEX Reflex System

An additional advantage of PANAVISION's dual focal plane and mirror shutter system is the possibility it affords to exchange the normal rotating reflex mirror for a fixed pellicle reflex mirror.

Although now superseded by the PANAVISION flicker-free PANAVID CCD video assist system, PANAFLEX and PANASTAR cameras can achieve a greatly enhanced, flicker-free video assist image by replacing the spinning mirror, which reflects light to the reflex viewing system intermittently for only 44% of the exposure/pulldown time with a membrane-thin partial mirror which reflects approximately 33% of the light all of the time. It is particularly advantageous when using a Steadicam floating camera system when an optimum quality video assist image is very important.

To compensate for the light that is diverted to the viewfinder by the pellicle reflex system the lens stop must be opened by 1/3 stop.

Changing and handling a pellicle mirror

Changing the reflex system must be done before a production commences by a PANAVISION technician. PANAVISION or its representatives worldwide will give instructions on the use and handling of pellicle reflex mirrors whenever one is requested.

Camera Assistants must be most careful when using a pellicle reflex to ensure that it remains perfectly dust free (a blob of dirt will cast a shadow on the film) and that they do not poke their finger through it when changing the ground glass or for any other reason. The camera should be handled with extra care lest the pellicle mirror be shattered.

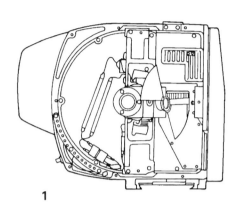

1

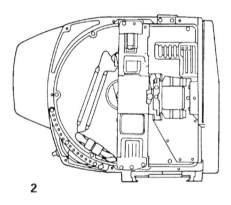

2

Third stop increments
1
1.1
1.3
1.4
1.6
1.8
2
2.2
2.5
2.8
3.2
3.6
4
4.5
5
5.7
6.3
7.1
8
9
10.1
11.3
12.7
14.3
16
18
20.2
22.6
25.4
28.5
32

3

1. PANAFLEX camera with front removed showing spinning mirror reflex,
2. PANAFLEX camera with front removed showing pellicle mirror reflex,
3. Table showing $\frac{1}{3}$ stop exposure changes.

129

Changing the Ground Glass and Putting in a Cut Frame

Unless otherwise requested PANAFLEX cameras are normally supplied with an Academy or an Anamorphic ground glass depending upon the lens type ordered.

If it is an Academy frame it will show the reticle engraved to the ISO/ANSI CAMERA APERTURE dimensions. If it is known that the production is primarily intended for Theatrical release it will also be engraved with the 1.85:1 dimensions and if for Television with an inner rectangle showing the SAFE ACTION TELEVISION AREA. Ground glasses with many other markings, with combinations of markings, with and without center crosses and with special markings are available upon request.

The reticle markings of a PANAFLEX ground glass are mirrored to enable the PANAGLOW system to operate.

Removing and replacing the ground glass

To remove the ground glass from a PANAFLEX camera GENTLY withdraw the ground glass straight out of the camera, using a cotton swab or a lens tissue to protect the glass surfaces. Do not use pliers or any other metal tool to hold the ground glass as this causes chipping.

When replacing the ground glass insert it with the ground glass (dull) side towards the mirror.

Putting a cut frame into the viewfinder system

A frame cut from a previous take may be placed immediately in front of the ground glass for aligning SFX shots.

The selected frame must first be cut using a special frame cutter supplied by PANAVISION and then carefully inserted into a special ground glass holder, marked with an 'M', in front of the ground glass.

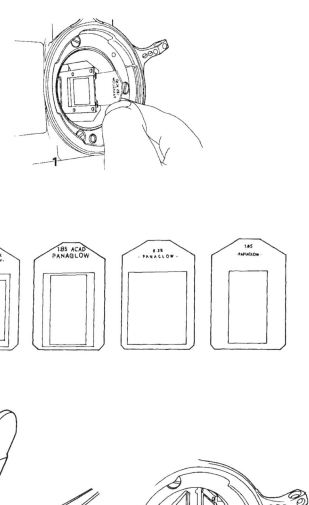

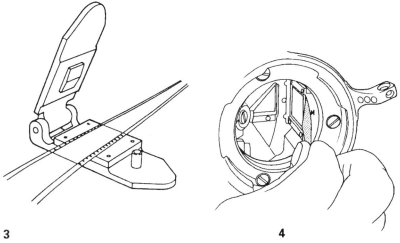

1. Removing a ground glass, 2. Various ground glass markings, 3. Cutting a frame with a cutter, 4. Putting a cut frame into a ground glass holder marked with an 'M'.

The Camera Heater

PANAFLEX cameras are fitted with internal heaters to keep the bearings warm in cold environments. The heaters, which are thermostatically controlled at 70°F, 21°C, draw 2½ to 6 amps.

Whenever the internal heaters are likely to be used care should be taken in advance to ensure there will be an adequate supply of fully charged batteries or a battery eliminator available, bearing in mind the increased amperage required to power the heaters when they are in use. A yellow 'heater-on' light to the right of the power supply socket on the rear of the camera indicates when the heaters are operating. A red LED warning light on the Annunciator Panel will indicate if the power supply is inadequate.

A 24 volt battery separate from that which powers the camera is plugged into a 2-pin LEMO socket to the right of the camera power socket. On the PLATINUM PANAFLEX a flashing red light, or on others a green/red light, between the two sockets indicates the condition of the heater battery and an amber light indicates when the heaters are functioning.

On all models power for the magazine heater is connected internally to the camera heater supply. An amber light on the magazine indicates when the heaters are operating.

In conditions of severe cold it may be necessary to supplement the internal heaters with heated barneys (see pages 58 - 59).

The eyepiece optic may be kept clear from fogging by the PANACLEAR heated eyepiece. To operate, connect the power lead to the accessory power supply outlet on the magazine port cover.

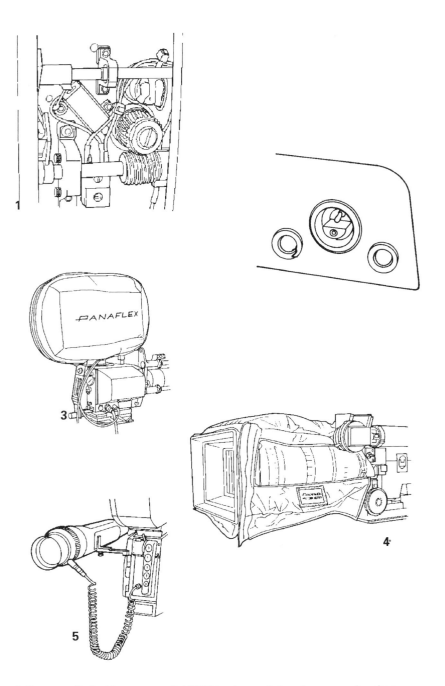

1. Heater units inside camera, 2. LEMO heater socket and green and amber warning lights, 3. Magazine heater barney, 4. Zoom lens heater barney, 5. PANACLEAR heated eyepiece.

PANAFLEX Magazines

Magazines for PANAFLEX cameras are available in 250, 500, 1000 and 2000' (75, 150, 300 and 600m) capacities. The same magazines may be used on the top or the rear of the camera. (Note: The 2000' type is normally only used in the top position.)

A special spacer unit is required when using a 250' magazine in the top position when a PANAVID video assist unit is fitted.

PLATINUM PANAFLEX magazines may be used on GII and other model PANAFLEX cameras, and vice versa, but may not be used with PANASTAR cameras which, because of their higher operating speeds, require special (500 & 1000') magazines. Note: The PLATINUM PANAFLEX magazine digital footage display will not operate when this type of magazine is fitted to a GII/GOLDEN PANAFLEX.

The 1000' and 500' magazines incorporate a mechanical 'footage remaining' indicator which may be operated by pressing a lever on the rear of the magazine.

Unexposed film must be wound EMULSION-IN on a 2" center core.

Exposed film normally winds EMULSION-OUT, also on a 2" core, except in the case of PLATINUM PANAFLEX and PANASTAR reversing magazines (see below).

Locks on each spindle hold the cores firmly in position.

A single magazine lock, which is recessed to prevent accidental opening, locks the lid simultaneously in four places.

Reverse running magazines

Special reversing type magazines, which may be run in either direction, are available for the PLATINUM PANAFLEX and the PANASTAR cameras.

Reverse running magazines may be loaded in the normal manner, with the unexposed film loaded in the left-hand side, and the film run first forwards and then in reverse or the unexposed film may be loaded directly into the right-hand side of the magazine and the camera run in reverse from the beginning of the roll.

When a camera is run in reverse the film will take up EMULSION-IN.

Camera carrying handles

A magazine port cover, which incorporates a camera carrying handle and an outlet for the PANACLEAR eyepiece heater, must be fitted over whichever port is not in use.

A long top carrying handle, and a special rear magazine port cover to which it can be attached, is an accessory supplied for use with top mounted magazines. An alternative top carrying handle and rear port cover are available for use when a PANAVID unit is fitted to the top of the camera.

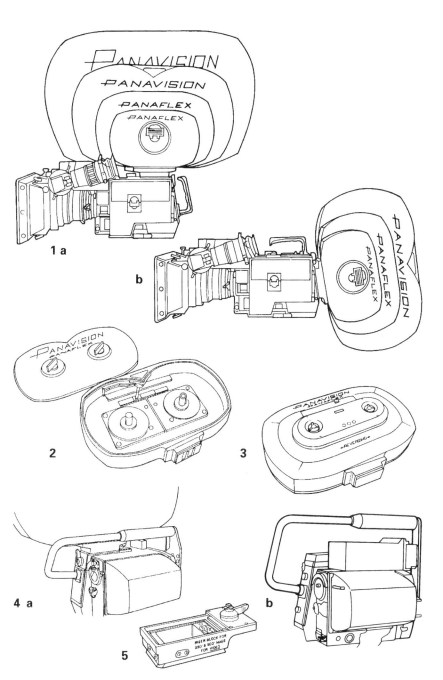

1 a. & b. PLATINUM PANAFLEX showing 7 magazine positions/sizes, 2. Interior of normal magazine, 3. Exterior of reversing magazine, 4 a. Normal long camera carrying handle, b. Special long camera carrying handle for use when a PANAVID is fitted, 5. Spacing unit used when a 250' magazine is used in the top position.

135

Magazine Systems

Electric contacts on PANAFLEX and PANASTAR camera magazine ports supply power to the magazine take-up motors and motor heaters and to the PANACLEAR and PANAFLASHER accessories.

The contacts which are common to all PANAFLEX cameras are as follows: 1. Ground, 2. Magazine motor+, 3. 24v+ to PANACLEAR and other accessories.

Other contacts are used for supplying power to the magazine heaters and for the switching, reverse running, footage counter, etc. circuits on the various cameras.

When power is not connected to a magazine, loose film on either the supply or on the take-up side can be tightened by pushing in the center of the motor and clutch covers on the back of the magazine and turning clockwise.

Footage and take-up running indicators

PLATINUM PANAFLEX and PANASTAR magazines incorporate an automatic shut-off switch which switches off the camera when there is 4' of film remaining on the PLATINUM, 5 - 10' on the PANASTAR. On the PLATINUM camera LED low-film warning lights on the annunciator panel will indicate when there is approximately 50' of unexposed film remaining in the magazine and when it is out.

PLATINUM PANAFLEX magazines incorporate an electronic 'footage shot' indicator. This may be reset to zero by pressing the right hand of three resetting buttons, the other two being used to reset the indicator slowly or quickly to predetermined footages.

On PLATINUM PANAFLEX magazines a blinking amber light indicates that the magazine is running. It is NOT a heater light.

On the magazines for GII and earlier PANAFLEX cameras the internal take-up motors incorporate a spiral indicator which shows when the take-up is running. If the camera is switched on and the spiral indicator runs comparatively slowly this shows that film is running through the camera. If the indicator runs very rapidly and continuously this signals that the film has passed through the camera and the camera has not yet been switched off.

Magazines incorporate a mechanical footage remaining indicator. It operates by means of a lever which may be pressed against the roll of film on the supply side of the magazine. In the case of reversing magazines this indicates how much film is in the left hand side of the magazine, whether it is exposed or not.

Magazine heaters

All PANAFLEX magazines incorporate electric heaters to keep the take-up motors in good working order in cold ambient conditions. On PLATINUM PANAFLEX magazines the heaters function automatically when power is applied to the camera heater. On earlier PANAFLEX magazines an amber light indicates when the heater is on.

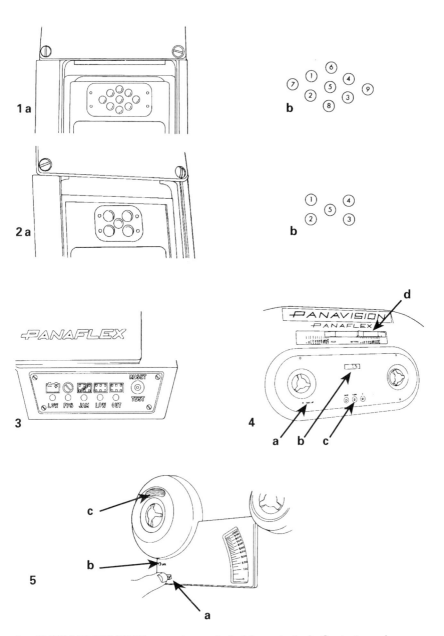

1 a. PLATINUM PANAFLEX magazine port electric contacts, b. Contact numbers,
2 a. Standard magazine port electric contacts, b. contact numbers, 3. PLATINUM
PANAFLEX annunciator panel, 4. PLATINUM PANAFLEX magazine indicators:
a. take-up running LED, b. digital footage shot indicator, c. digital indicator
reset buttons, d. manual footage remaining indicator, 5. Standard magazine
indicators: a. manual footage remaining indicator actuator, b. magazine heater
indicator LED, c. spiral take-up running indicator.

137

Magazine Loading

Check that you have the correct type of magazine, i.e., PLATINUM PANAFLEX or PANASTAR or other, 1000, 500 or 250ft capacity and, if it is a reversing type, if it is required to run a PLATINUM PANAFLEX or a PANASTAR in reverse.

Check to see that no film remains in the magazine from a previous loading before removing a magazine door in the light. Hinge the door catches out of their recesses and turn both counter-clockwise to release.

Transfer the plastic center core from the supply side of the magazine and place it on the take-up spindle with film slot facing counter-clockwise. If there is not a spare core in the magazine one must be provided.

Push back the top lock of the supply side spindle.

Things to be done in the dark
Extinguish the room light or seal up the changing bag and remove the unexposed film from its can.

For normal use set the film on the left side of the magazine with the film coming off the roll in a clockwise direction.

In the case of reversing magazines the unexposed film must go into the left-hand side of the magazine if the first run is in a forward direction or into the right-hand side of the magazine (and unwind anti-clockwise) if the first run is in reverse.

Take the end of the film between the thumb and first two fingers to curve slightly and push between the two front rollers until it comes out of the magazine throat (rear two for reversing magazines).

Move the roll of film over, slide the center core onto the spindle, and lock down. Pull the end of the film out of the magazine and press down on the spindle until an audible click is heard indicating that the spring loaded key is securely fitted in the keyway of the core.

Pull down approximately 2-3' of film, bend the end of the film again and pass between the rear magazine rollers until it is inside the magazine. Pull the film to the right hand side of the core, locate the end in the core slot, turn the take-up core counter-clockwise and wind on two or three turns of film. (Left hand side and clockwise on reversing magazines.) For normal forward running magazines the film path is in the form of a '99' and for reverse running magazines it is '9P'.

Reinstall the magazine lid (with locks vertical and turned fully counter-clockwise) by placing it flat on the body of the magazine (it is not necessary to engage any lugs) until it seats properly. Turn both locks clockwise and snap down into their recesses to double lock in position.

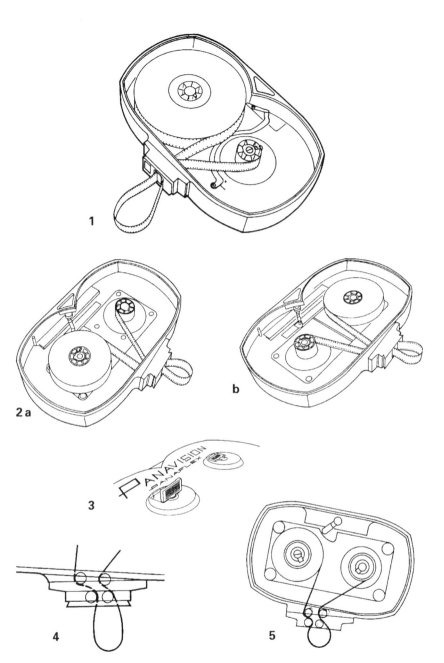

1. Normal magazine showing the normal '99' film loading path, 2 a. Reversing magazine showing the '9P' loading path to run the film in a forward direction, 2 b. Reversing magazine showing the '9P' loading path to run the film in a reverse direction, 3. Magazine lid locks, 4. The route through the light trap rollers, 5. PANAFLEX 16 magazine loading path.

139

Checking the Aperture Plate and Matte

Before operating any PANAFLEX or PANASTAR camera check that the aperture plate is clean, that the matte (if fitted) is appropriate to the shoot and that the gate is clean.

Removing PANAFLEX, PANAFLEX 16 and PSR aperture plates

To remove the aperture plate, inch the camera until the pull-down claw is at the bottom of its stroke, after it is disengaged from the film, and the registration pins are fully engaged.

Pull out the spring loaded register pin retraction knob and slide it back to clear the register pins from the film perforations.

Turn the gate top dog lock clockwise and turn the bottom thumb lock counter-clockwise. Hold the bottom lock horizontally between the thumb and index finger, and wiggle to remove the gate plate from the camera movement.

Removing a PANASTAR aperture plate

On a PANASTAR camera, inch the camera until the pull-down claws are fully engaged and the register pins are in the back position.

Retract the pull-down claws by pulling on the spring loaded retraction knob and pushing it downwards.

Checking the matte

To check the matte for size and cleanliness the gate must be removed.

Mattes for Super 35, Academy, 1:85 and 1.66:1 are available on request. Full Aperture and Anamorphic formats do not require a matte.

Replace the aperture plate by holding the bottom lock horizontally and pushing the plate onto the top locating pin. Push the bottom lock down and set the top dog lock by pulling it out and turning counter-clockwise.

Occasionally take out the rear pressure pad to check for cleanliness and freedom from abrasion. Remove by turning the spring loaded dog at the rear outwardly and removing. Reverse the process to replace.

GREAT CARE MUST BE TAKEN WHEN REMOVING AND REPLACING THE APERTURE PLATE AND THE REAR PRESSURE PAD TO AVOID DAMAGE.

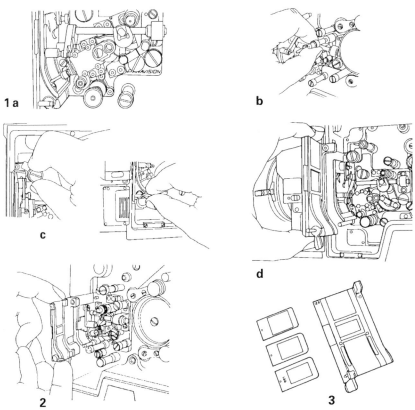

1. Removing a PANAFLEX aperture plate: a. Set the pull-down claws to bottom of stroke, b. Pull out the register pin lock and slide it back, c. Release the gate locks, d. Remove the aperture plate CAREFULLY, 2. Removing a PANAFLEX 16 aperture plate, 3. PANAFLEX 35mm aperture plate and various mattes.

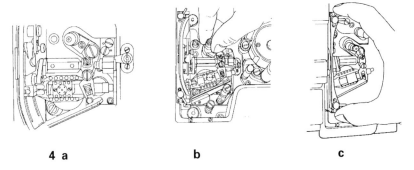

4. Removing a PANASTAR aperture plate: a. Set pull-down claws into the film with the register pins in the out position, b. Pull out the spring loaded knob and push it downwards to retract the pull-down claws, c. Release the aperture plate and remove CAREFULLY.

141

Preparing the Camera for Loading

On the PLATINUM PANAFLEX set the Digital Indicator to the desired display by pressing the MODE switch. The mode will change as follows:

CAMERA SPEED (fps) + FOOTAGE (exposed)
CAMERA SPEED (fps) + METERAGE (exposed)
CAMERA SPEED (fps) + SHUTTER ANGLE (°)
TIME CODE TIME OF DAY
TIME CODE USER BITS

(See page 93 for illustrations)

'FIL' in the bottom left corner indicates a gelatin filter holder is in place.

If an extension eyepiece is fitted, semi-tighten the friction lock at the viewfinder 'elbow' where 'LOCK' is engraved.

Release the eyepiece leveller link arm by squeezing together the pair of levers below the underside of the extension eyepiece and stow on the rest.

Disconnect the PANACLEAR eyepiece heater cable if fitted, raise the eyepiece and lock it in an upright position.

Depending upon whether it is intended to mount the magazine on the top or the rear of the camera, remove the appropriate magazine port cover and check that the other port is covered securely. An alternative rear port cover is available which incorporates an attachment point for a long carrying handle.

If a 250 or a 500' magazine is to be used in the top position together with a PANAVID video-assist system a magazine spacer unit must be fitted.

Close the top and bottom sprocket keeper rollers.

Setting PANAFLEX, PANAFLEX 16 and PSR cameras

Open the camera door and inch the movement until the pull-down claw is at the bottom of its stroke, just after it comes out of the film, and the *registration pins are fully engaged.*

Withdraw the registration pins by gently pulling out the spring-loaded retraction knob and sliding it towards the rear of the camera.

Setting PANASTAR cameras

Open the camera door and inch the movement until the pull-down claws are fully into their pull-down stroke and the register pins are fully withdrawn.

Withdraw the pull-down claws by gently pulling out the spring loaded retraction knob and sliding it downwards.

An optional safety measure

The power supply may be disconnected before threading film as a safety measure.

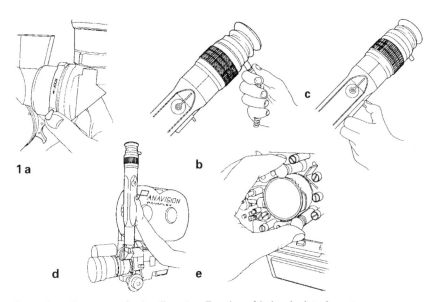

Preparing all cameras for loading: 1 a. Eyepiece friction lock to be set no more than semi-tight to enable the eyepiece to be moved clear of the camera door, b. PANACLEAR disconnected, c. Eyepiece leveller released, d. Eyepiece raised, e. Top and bottom keeper rollers closed.

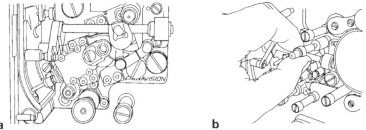

2. Setting PANAFLEX and PSR cameras: a. Set movement with pull-down claws at bottom of stroke, b. Registration pins slid back clear of the film path.

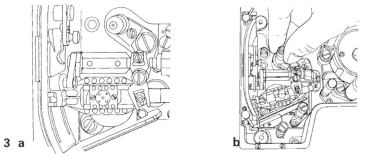

3. Setting a PANASTAR camera: a. Set movement with pull-down claw into pull-down stroke, b. Pull-down claws slid back clear of the film path.

143

Threading the Camera — Lacing the Film

Inch the camera until the pull-down claw is at the bottom of its stroke.

Check that the magazine is loaded with the appropriate film stock and pull out a very short loop from the supply (front) side of the magazine.

Rest one end of the magazine on the camera, feed the film loop through the magazine port and lock the magazine securely in position.

Special note: WHILE THREADING THE CAMERA DO NOT PRESS THE INCHING KNOB ON THE REAR OF THE CAMERA UNTIL THE FILM ON THE TAKE-UP SIDE HAS BEEN SECURELY LOCATED ON THE SPROCKET AND THE BOTTOM SPROCKET KEEPER HAS BEEN CLOSED. (Pressing in the inching knob activates the magazine motor and this is not a good thing to do until the film has been secured on the main sprocket.)

Lacing the film

Pull about 8" (20cm) of film from the front compartment of the magazine and stretch it towards the bottom left hand corner of the camera.

Open the top and bottom sprocket keepers.

Thread the film through the camera exactly as shown on the threading diagram on the inside of the camera door. Double check that it is correct.

Check that the film on the take-up side is properly seated on the underside of the sprocket and close the bottom sprocket keeper.

Set the bottom loop so that it just clears the bottom of the camera.

Press a sprocket hole onto the perforation locating pin situated just above the aperture plate. This will ensure that the perforations will be correctly aligned with the registration pins. At the same time gently press on the edge of the film to ensure the film is fully into the camera.

Set the registration pins into the perforations by gently pressing the boss at the base of the retraction pin. (Note: Pressing the base of the retraction pin has a more positive feel than pushing from the top). If it does not go easily recheck the perforation alignment.

Set the top loop by pulling the film off the perforation locating pin. The top loop should be set to clear the locating pin as per the drawings on page 141.

Engage the film on the top of the sprocket and close the top keeper.

If it has been disconnected, re-connect the camera power supply.

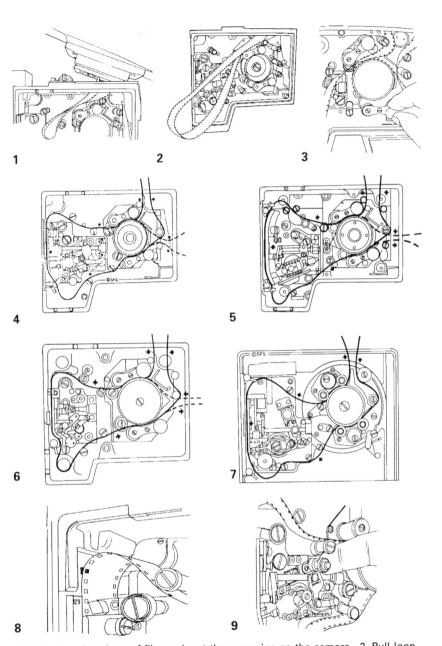

1. Pull out a short loop of film and rest the magazine on the camera, 2. Pull loop of film to bottom L.H. corner of camera, 3. Open top and bottom sprocket keepers, 4. PANAFLEX threading diagram, 5. PANASTAR threading diagram, 6. PANAFLEX 16 threading diagram, 7. SUPER PSR threading diagram, 8. Press film onto perforation locating pin, 9. Press in register pins by base of retraction pin.

Threading the Camera—Checking That It Runs Properly and Quietly

On the PLATINUM PANAFLEX press the inching switch on the inside of the camera to take up any unwound film in the magazine. On earlier cameras slide away the small lever behind the rear inching knob, press in the knob to take up any excess.

Inch the camera through a complete cycle to check the lacing. Check that the top loop does not touch the perforation locating pin and that the bottom loop does not become too tight or touch the bottom of the camera. If a loop is not correct open the corresponding sprocket roller and adjust as appropriate.

Set the switch at the rear of the camera to ON. If the camera door is open the camera will not run unless the micro switch at the bottom right-hand corner of the film compartment is depressed. (Not PLATINUM.)

Setting the camera for maximum quietness

All PANAVISION cameras (except the PANASTAR) incorporate a pitch control to align the perforations with the registration pins at the end of the pull-down stroke to ensure quiet running.

To run the camera at its operating speed while at the same time adjusting the pitch of the pull-down claws right-handed people will find it easier to hold the pitch adjustment control knob with the right hand and use the left hand to depress the micro-switch at the bottom right-hand corner of the camera body. For left-handed people it is the reverse. On the PLATINUM simply press the RUN button.

With the camera running turn the pitch control knob clockwise and counter-clockwise until the perforation noise is minimized. This adjustment may have to be made after every reload to ensure the camera runs as quietly as is possible for a camera which has full fitting registration pins and maximum image steadiness. It may even be advisable to check the pitch setting during the course of a single roll of filmstock.

In addition to adjusting the pitch of the camera to locate the perforations in relation to the register pins, PANAVISION and their representatives worldwide have a special tool available which enables them to adjust the stroke to optimize the amount of film which is pulled down each time. Cameramen using filmstock which may be slightly different than normal are advised to bring in a sample roll so that the stroke may be set to suit.

Let go the micro switch (or the RUN button), switch OFF the camera and close the camera door.

Note: It is very important, especially on the GOLD and GII PANAFLEX cameras (which have no door micro switches), to double check, before closing and locking the camera door, that the camera has switched OFF at the main camera switch. The camera is so quiet it is possible to run a whole roll of film through without realizing it.

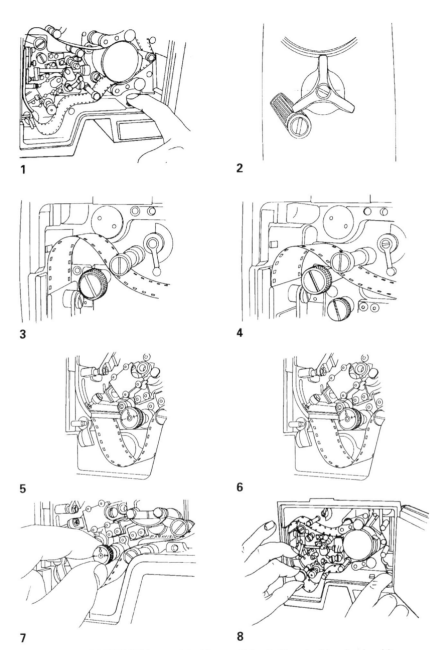

1. PLATINUM PANAFLEX internal inching switch, 2. Rear inching knob with inhibiting lever to prevent accidental operation, 3. The correct top loop with claw at bottom of stroke, 4. The correct top loop with claw at bottom of stroke, 5. The correct bottom loop with claw at top of stroke, 6. The correct bottom loop with claw at top of stroke, 7. Adjusting the pitch control, 8. Adjusting the stroke.

Threading the Camera—Final Preparation

Pull the eyepiece down to the shooting position.

If the camera is mounted on a PANAHEAD attach the eyepiece leveller link-arm to the underside of the extension eyepiece and unlock the friction lock at the eyepiece elbow.

Setting the footage counters

On the PLATINUM PANAFLEX set the digital footage/meterage counter to zero by simultaneously pressing the buttons marked with up and down arrows. Alternatively, these buttons may be used individually to preset to counter to any particular starting point.

On the GII and earlier PANAFLEX cameras zero the footage counter by pressing simultaneously the micro switches at the top and the left hand side of the digital footage read-out. Press only the top micro switch to recall the footage shot since the last resetting.

On PANASTAR reversing magazines there is a Digital Frame Counter to enable the film to be rewound to a particular frame (±1 frame) for SFX work. This may be reset by pressing the button set directly above the digital frame display. Note: This frame counter is not bidirectional and must be reset each time when reverse running.

The footage remaining in a magazine may be checked manually by a sliding actuator on PLATINUM PANAFLEX and PANASTAR magazines and by a small lever on GII and earlier magazines.

Final checks

It is good practice to check there is no slack film on either the supply or the take-up sides of the magazine by pressing in and turning the centre knobs on the back side of the magazines.

In humid and cold ambient conditions connect the power supply to the PANACLEAR heated viewfinder eyepiece.

Before shooting with a particular camera for the first time always double check the shutter setting, the fps rate and the behind-the-lens gelatin filter, if any.

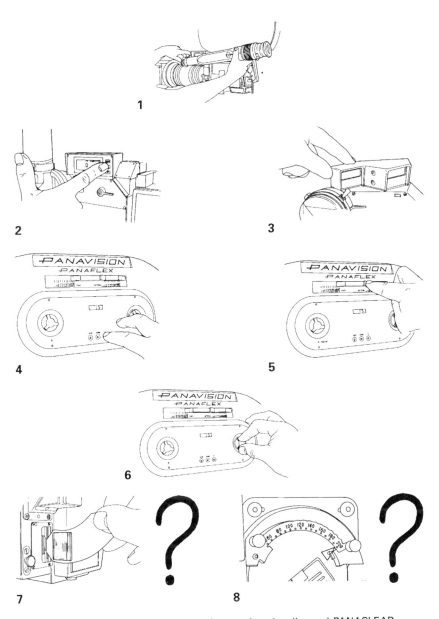

1. Reposition eyepiece and reconnect the eyepiece leveller and PANACLEAR,
2. Reset PLATINUM PANAFLEX footage counter by simultaneously pressing the up and down buttons, 3. Reset the GII footage counter by simultaneously pressing the top and left-hand side buttons, 4. Resetting the footage counter on a PLATINUM PANAFLEX magazine, 5. Checking the footage remaining on a PANAFLEX or PANASTAR magazine, 6. Tightening the roll of film inside a magazine, 7. A reminder that the gelatin filter holder must be checked, 8. A reminder that the adjustable shutter quadrant must be checked.

Fitting Lenses to the Camera

All PANAFLEX and PANASTAR cameras, together with PSR cameras and PANAVISION versions of Arriflex and Mitchell cameras are fitted with the same strongly designed PANAVISION lock ring lens mount.

To mount a lens to the camera remove the lens port cover from the camera (if fitted), and turn the lens locking ring fully counter-clockwise.

Remove the rear cover from the lens and offer up the lens to the camera with the locating pin in the downwards position, slide the lens firmly and squarely into the camera and turn the locking ring fully clockwise to secure.

Long focal length and zoom lenses may require additional support from the iris rods.

Range extenders

Range extenders are available for certain telephoto and zoom lenses which increase their focal length by a factor of 1.4 or 1.5 and 2 times.

They reduce the effective aperture by the square of their magnification. Thus a 2 X range extender working with a 400mm T4 telephoto lens converts it to an 800mm working at T8.

Range extenders certainly do not improve the optical quality of a lens and may significantly impair it. They are best used with the lens stopped down at least two stops. The image degradation sometimes looks worse through the viewfinder than it does on the screen.

PANAVISION PRIMO lens extenders have been designed to provide a 40% increase in focal length with a one stop loss in aperture and minimal loss of image quality. They may be used with most longer focal length PRIMO-L PRIME, PRIMO ZOOM, PRIMO ANAMORPHIC and PRIMO MACRO lenses and with many other PANAVISION lenses. (See the current PANAVISION price catalogue for recommended lenses to use with PANAVISION 1.4:1 range extenders together with details of increased focal lengths and resultant lens stop losses.)

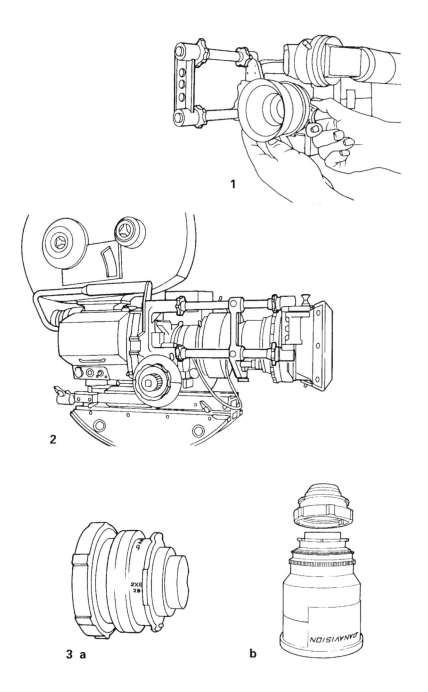

1. Fitting a lens to a camera, 2. Long lens with support, 3 a. & b. Range extender unit which may be used with zoom and many other lenses.

Testing PANAVISION Lenses

Every lens is unique and before any production commences PANAUSERS are encouraged to thoroughly test every lens they are taking with them.

It should be borne in mind that almost every lens gives of its best performance one or two stops stopped down from maximum aperture and sometimes least well at minimum aperture. Some lenses will focus on slightly different focus marks at full aperture compared to two stops stopped down. Some zoom lenses may have a focus shift over the zoom range, may have better performance at some focal lengths than others and may change their image size as the focus setting is changed. Some lenses may appear to have more, or less, depth of field than others or more, or less, depth in front, or behind, than may be expected.

Lenses incorporate many different types of glass and thus some may be warmer than others. The color of the lens coating is nothing to go by; it is the color of the image on the film that matters.

All lens design is a compromise and where one lens has less of any of these deficiencies than another then it may be at the cost of performance elsewhere. For this reason Camera Assistants are given every opportunity to get to know the capabilities of their PANAVISION lenses before a shoot in order to be able to exploit each one to its maximum.

Lenses should be tested for a combination of definition and contrast, where it focuses (both by tape and by eye) at different apertures, different distances and, with zoom lenses, at different focal lengths, for veiling glare over bright highlights, distortion of vertical and horizontal lines, depth of field and color, etc.

For optimum performance assessment Camera Assistants are invited to put their lenses through their paces in PANAVISION's Optical Test Laboratory where they may see exactly what each lens does on an MTF bench (which measures a combination of contrast and definition) and colorimetry test equipment. (Please telephone PANAVISION's optical department beforehand to make an appointment.)

Notes on understanding MTF (Modular Transfer Function) graphs

All graphs illustrated on the right are for on-axis (i.e. center of the optical axis) only.

The Diffraction Limit is the natural limit of contrast at any resolution at a given aperture of any lens.

The Average Resolution for Cinematography is as defined by the International Standards Organization (ISO).

It is worth noting that diffraction alone limits the maximum achievable contrast at any resolution (no matter what lens) and that diffraction becomes a greater limitation as the apertures become smaller, i.e. T8, T11, T16, etc. and the focal lengths become shorter, i.e. 20mm compared to 250mm.

MTF is similar to contrast when resolution is specified.

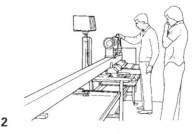

1. PANAVISION camera test room, 2. PANAVISION's MTF test bench

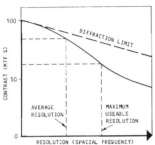
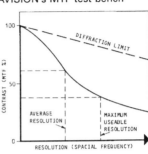

3. MTF graphs of a typical prime lens at T2.8 (left) and at T1.3 (right). (Note the greater contrast and resolution when the lens is stopped down from full aperture)

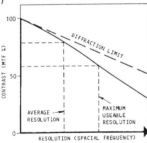
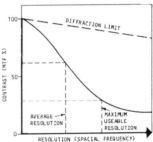

4. MTF graphs of a PANAVISION PRIMO and of a typical prime lens. (Both at T2.) (Note the considerably superior contrast/resolution characteristics of the PRIMO lens)

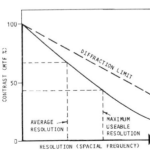
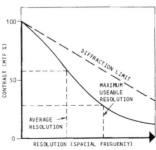

5. MTF graphs of a zoom lens (at T4) at the wide angle and at the telephoto settings. (Note the superior performance at the wide angle end of the zoom range)

153

Focusing PANAVISION Lenses

Every PANAVISION lens is calibrated individually to achieve optimum optical performance. Lenses are calibrated against a standard flange focal depth of 2.2500in, 57.15mm, at an aperture of T2.8 (or at the minimum stop above T2.8) and an index mark is engraved on the lens to indicate the best possible image at that aperture. Lenses are calibrated at all marked focus distances.

Lenses are then further calibrated at maximum aperture and any difference from the T2.8 setting is noted. If there is a significant difference between the position of the T2.8 and the full aperture mark a second (shorter) mark is engraved and this is colored blue. The apertures to which it refers are also colored blue.

This extensive calibration enables PANAVISION to spread out its lens scales to a much greater extent so that Focus Assistants can achieve maximum precision when setting focus. Unfortunately this also means that any aperture related focus shift tends to be more noticeable than on a compressed lens scale which hides focus shift. PANAVISION believes that the need to have a separate index mark for the very wide apertures only is a small price to pay for large lens barrels with big focus scales.

In general it is always preferable to use a tape measure, rather than the ground glass, to determine the focus settings for wide angle lenses at apertures greater than T2.8. This rule applies to all wide angle, wide aperture lenses on all cameras because the aperture of the viewfinder system of PANAFLEX, and all other cameras, is not as wide as a wide aperture motion picture lens and thus eye focusing will not necessarily be correct at wide apertures.

Special care should be taken by Camera Assistants when eye focusing lenses have alternative wide aperture focus markings (engraved blue and considerably shorter) for use at full aperture. When tape focusing such a lens at a blue colored aperture, the focus distance settings should be set to the blue colored index mark. When focusing these lenses by eye at apertures which are colored blue the correct distance will be that which is against the blue index mark.

Checking infinity by auto-collimator can also be inaccurate and misleading, especially with wide angle, wide aperture and long focal length lenses.

Note: Before setting lens focus by eye the focus of the ground glass through the viewfinder must first be set to suit the person who is doing the focusing.

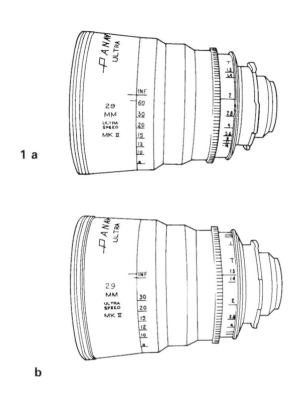

1 a

b

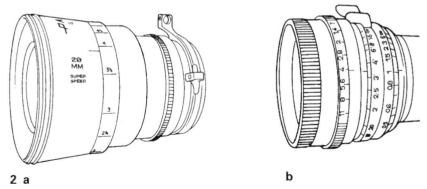

2 a

b

1. Lens scale showing the normal (yellow) and full (blue) aperture index lines a. set to the optimum infinity position for T.2 and larger apertures, and b. set to the optimum infinity position for T1.3 and T1.4,   2 a. PANAVISION spread-out lens scale, b. A typical compressed lens scale. Note how focus shift may be hidden by compressing the lens scale.

Checking and Resetting the Flange Focal Depth

To ensure the best possible image quality and the reliability of the engraved scale when setting focus with the aid of a tape measure, it is imperative that the flange focal depth of the camera be very accurately set with the aid of a depth measuring micrometer.

The correct flange focal depth setting of all PANAVISION cameras is 2.2488 ±.0001", 57.1195mm.

The only accurate method of checking the flange focal depth of a PANAFLEX camera is by the use of a depth gage and a special steel plate which is held against the camera aperture plate in place of the film. By comparison an auto-collimator is a comparatively inaccurate instrument which may give incorrect settings because it cannot make allowance for the fact that the focus must be set into the film and not on the surface, and that the film will normally run 0.0001" to 0.0003" forward from the pressure pad.

Flange focal depth gage outfits are available from PANAVISION Inc. and its representatives worldwide for use by trained technicians and it is recommended that one be taken with the equipment whenever the hire is likely to be far away from base.

The flange focal depth of PANAFLEX cameras is set by adjusting special screws set on the camera. It is not a job that should be undertaken by any Camera Assistant without special training by a PANAVISION technician. Training is available on request.

The ground glass should be set at 2.250" by collimation using a short focal length lens (no longer than 30mm) which has had its infinity mark calibrated on an MTF bench or by means of a collimator having an aperture of 1" diameter or larger.

PANAFLEX lens mounting dimensional stability

A great deal of mythology has been generated by stories of 'rubber lens mountings' on quiet cameras. On all PANAFLEX cameras both the lenses and the movements are hard mounted to the camera body. It makes no difference on a PANAFLEX if the lens is heavy or if the camera is tilted up or down. PANAVISION uses special mountings made of a hard, nonmetallic material, to isolate the pull-down mechanism from the camera body and then uses rubber mounts to isolate the motor from the mechanism. Tests, and many years of usage, have proven that the flange focal depth of PANAFLEX cameras is not affected out of tolerance by steep tilts.

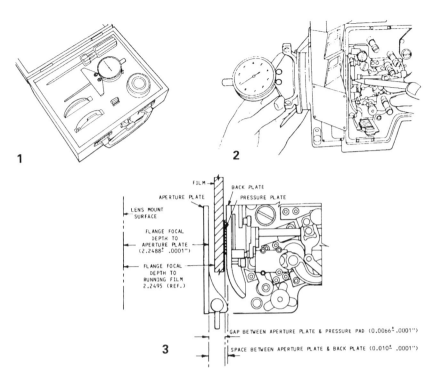

1. Flange focal depth gage set, 2. Method of using a flange focal depth gage on a camera. Note the use of a pencil to hold the gage plate in position behind the aperture plate, 3. Critical lens/film/camera distances.

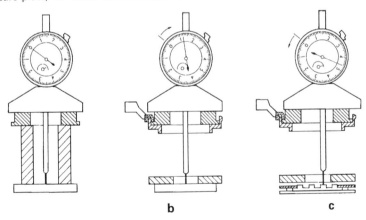

4 a   **b**   **c**

4. Flange focal depth checking procedure: a. Set the dial gage to zero with the aid of a 2.2500" gage block, plate and adaptor flange, b. With a gage plate behind the aperture, and using the adaptor flange, check the flange focal depth of the camera. It should read -.0012" ±.0001" on the dial, c. Check the depth of two center rails of the pressure plate. They should register +0054" on the dial.

157

Matte Box Features

A standard matte box is supplied with every PANAFLEX camera. It attaches to the camera by two iris rods (called "support bars" in the UK) set one above the other on the motor side of the lens.

It takes two 4 x 5.650" rectangular filters and has a 5.5960" diameter circular retainer ring which can take a 138mm Polarizing Filter or other diameter circular filter or a 4½" diameter reducing ring which can also be fitted with a "snout" which can be used with very wide angle prime lenses to clear the viewfinder optical system.

The top is especially strengthened to be fitted with a sunshade flap.

A smaller, lightweight, 'spherical' matte box, which is particularly suitable for use with physically small lenses or when hand holding the camera, is available on request. It incorporates holders for two 4 x 5.650" rectangular filters and one 4½" diameter circular filter holder.

Both matte boxes are hinged to allow them to be swung clear for lens changing. To release, lift spring loaded knob above the hinge and swing the matte box forward.

For the 20 - 100mm Super Zoom a special Wide Angle Matte Box which takes only one 4 x 5.650" filter is supplied.

All matte boxes are supplied with slip-on, lightweight, plastic mattes which fit over the front of the sunshade and have cut-outs to suit various focal length lenses. These mattes minimize the amount of stray light entering the matte box from the front. Foam rubber 'Donut' rings are supplied with all lenses. They fit between the lenses and the rear of the matte box to prevent stray light entering from behind which could reflect off the rear of the filters.

Tilting matte box
A matte box which enables the filter to be tilted forwards to eliminate distracting multiple reflections caused by automobile headlights, etc. is a very useful accessory when filming car chases at night.

Multi-stage matte box
A multi-stage matte box which takes any number of sliding and rotating 6.6" sq. filters, plus tilting and mechanically operated sliding filters, is an available extra.

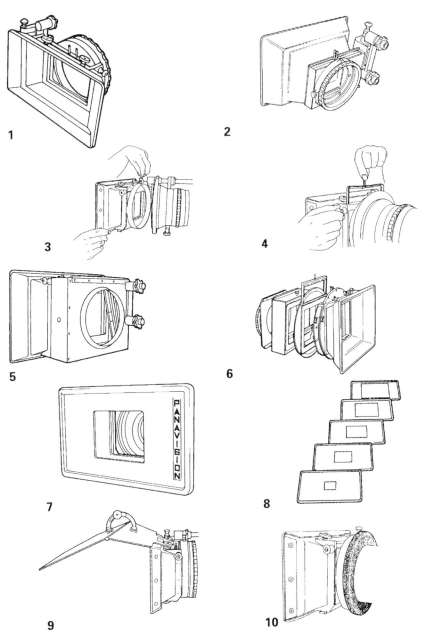

1. Standard matte box, 2. Spherical matte box, 3. Swinging a matte box open to facilitate lens changing, 4. Adjusting a sliding graduated filter tray, 5. Tilting matte box, 6. Multi stage 6.6" sq. matte box, 7. Matte box matte in position, 8. Set of matte box mattes, 9. Extension sunshade flap, 10. Donut in position between a lens and the rear of a matte box.

Iris Brackets and Rods

Two types of iris rod brackets are available to support a matte box and long and heavy lenses when appropriate. A short, lightweight, type is available for use when hand holding and a long type is for use when supporting heavy lenses.

To fit iris rods that support a matte box only, slide the short bracket into the vertical slides situated on the motor side of the lens. The iris rods and the matte box are locked in position by locking rings which should only be tightened 'finger tight.'

PANAFLEX cameras are normally supplied with three pairs of iris rods 5", 7" and 9" long. The most suitable length pair for a particular lens should be selected and fitted onto the iris rod bracket. PLATINUM and GII PANAFLEX cameras may be supplied with iris rods made of carbon fibre to give added lightness.

To support a heavy lens fit the iris rod bracket to the camera (but do not completely tighten) and select a pair of iris rods of suitable length.

Fit the lens and tighten the lens mount locking clamp in the normal manner. Initially fit only the top iris rod (remove bottom one if already fitted) and slide lens support bracket into place. Engage and lightly tighten the captured locking screw to attach the support bracket to the underside of the lens.

Thread the second iris rod through the lens support bracket and into the iris rod bracket. Tighten the iris rod bracket attachment to the camera, the lens support bracket to the lens and both iris rod locking rings, checking that no part is under any strain.

Note: In an emergency the short iris rod bracket can be used to support long and heavy lenses but it is not a recommended practice. In such an instance it is particularly important not to tighten the bracket to the camera before the lens support and both iris rods have been fitted.

160

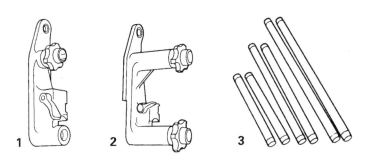

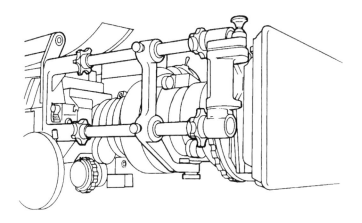

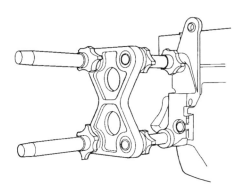

1. Short iris rod bracket, 2. Long iris rod bracket, 3. Set of iris rods, 4. Iris rods supporting a long and heavy lens, 5. Iris rod offset bracket for use with a 6.6" matte box.

Gelatin Filter Holders

In addition to places for three or four filters in the various PANAVISION matte boxes there is also a provision on all PANAFLEX cameras to place a gelatin filter just in front of the film plane and on certain PANAFLEX zoom lenses to place a gelatin filter behind the rear optical element.

PANAFLEX cameras are supplied with a box containing 12 gelatin filter holders.

Before a shoot the Camera Assistant should very carefully mount a selection of gelatin filters into the holders as requested by the Director of Photography. PANAVISION Inc. and its distributors worldwide can supply a gelatin filter punch for cutting filters to shape. Be careful to keep dust, finger marks and other blemishes off the surface of the filters. The use of a PANAVISION filter punch makes this task easier.

The use of a gelatin filter between the lens and the film affects the lens back focal distance by about 1½ thousandths (.0015) of an inch. This is not likely to have a deleterious effect on the focus of any lens unless it has a particularly short focal length and/or wide aperture. If the Director of Photography plans on using gelatin filters he may wish to request that PANAVISION technicians alter the flange focal depth setting of the camera accordingly.

To fit the gelatin filter holder into a PANAFLEX camera, slide back the dust/light/sound proof cover below the viewfinder tube, insert the filter holder inwards and upwards, close the cover slide and remind the D.P. that a behind-the-lens filter is in place so that he can make appropriate allowances in his exposure calculations.

On the PLATINUM PANAFLEX the letters 'FIL' will automatically show in the bottom left hand corner of the Digital Indicator whenever a gelatin filter is in place.

Cutter punches are also available for the circular filters that can be placed behind most PANAZOOM zoom lenses.

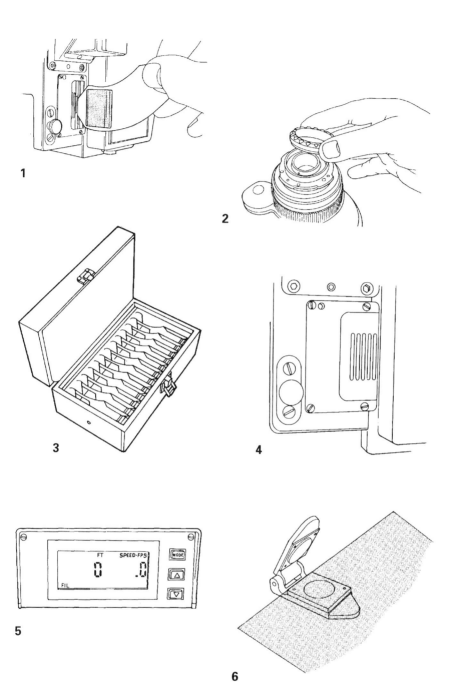

1. Putting a 'behind the lens' gelatin filter into position, 2. Fitting a filter onto the rear of a zoom lens, 3. Set of gelatin filters in a box, 4. Closed gelatin filter door, 5. 'FIL' indicator on PLATINUM PANAFLEX display, 6. Gelatin filter cutter.

163

Follow Focus Controls—Manual

A variety of follow focus, iris control and zoom control systems are available for PANAFLEX cameras and lenses.

The Standard Follow Focus unit
The Standard Follow Focus unit, which is supplied with the camera, has a single knob which can normally be operated from the left side of the camera only.

In addition, a follow focus handle, for fine control, and a follow focus extension cable, which may be used on its own or in combination with the handle, are provided to enable the focus assistant to stand a little way back from the camera.

The Standard Follow Focus unit may be operated from the right-hand side of the camera by using the follow focus extension.

It may also be operated by the camera operator's left thumb.

The Modular Follow Focus unit
The Modular Follow Focus unit is intended for use when a PANAFLEX camera is mounted on a tripod, dolly or crane and is an optional accessory which must be specially ordered as needed.

It has two large hand knobs which may be fitted to either or both sides of the camera. Adjustable limit stops make it possible to preset the near and far positions for fast focus pulls. Magnetically attached interchangeable focus disks mean that any number of discs may be marked up in advance to suit various lenses.

The knob on the viewfinder side of the unit may be replaced by a right angle knuckle and an extension knob so that the camera operator may adjust focus while he is looking through the viewfinder.

The knob on the motor side of the unit may be removed or may be replaced by an electric motor unit for remote control by cable or by radio.

Fitting and adjusting follow focus units
Both follow focus units are fitted to the camera by sliding them onto the short rod which protrudes from the camera body below the lens. After fitting, the unit must be pushed upwards to engage with the lens gearing until a spring loaded catch snaps it into position. This catch must be released every time the lens is changed. To release, pull out the flat topped knob at the bottom left hand corner of the left hand side of the camera.

The meshing of the follow focus gears may be adjusted by means of a small set screw situated near the follow focus unit attachment point.

If the lens is fitted with a range extender or a rear anamorphoser unit, either of which will move the lens meshing gears forward, it will be necessary to use the (supplied) spacing unit to make up the difference.

164

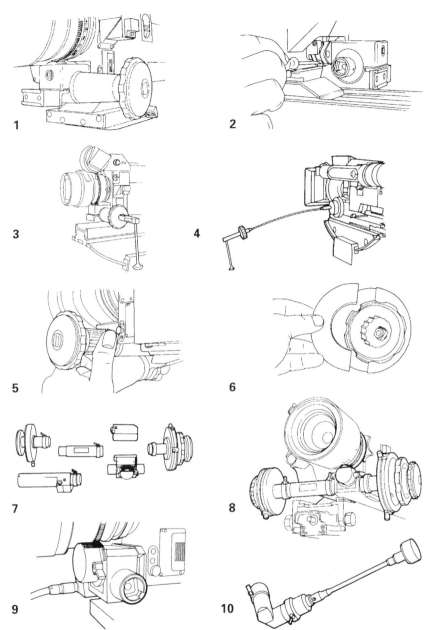

1. Standard follow focus control, 2. Adjusting standard follow focus gear meshing, 3. Follow focus with handle fitted, 4. Follow focus with extension handle fitted, 5. Using a thumb to adjust focus while hand-holding, 6. Changing follow focus lens calibration disks, 7. Modular follow focus system components, 8. Modular follow focus unit, 9. Modular horizontal slide type gear meshing adjustment, 10. Modular right-angle follow focus unit.

Follow Focus Controls—Electronic

Electronic units are available for remote focus control. Various modular systems are available to remotely operate the lens focus alone or in combination with the lens aperture, zoom focal length, camera speed, shutter angle and camera On/Off, either by a single cable or by radio.

Modular Follow Focus

Either knob of the Modular Follow Focus system may be replaced by an electric motor for remote electronic focus control. This system is particularly suitable for use with Steadicam and remote control camera crane mounted cameras.

The system may also be combined with a second motor for remote iris control in addition.

The FTZSAC system

The FTZSAC system — Focus, T-Stop, Zoom and Speed/Aperture Controller — is a modular unit to remotely control the three lens variables plus camera On/Off. Used in conjunction with the Smart Shutter accessory, all five lens and camera variables can be controlled in coordination. Only those components that are required need to be fitted or used.

The system can be used with any PANAVISION PANAFLEX (Platinum, Lightweight, GII or X), any PANASTAR, any PANAFLEX 16 or any PANAFLEX 65 camera. Connection can be by up to 300ft of ordinary TV type coaxial cable or by radio.

Interchangeable disks are fitted to the periphery of the control knobs. These can be marked by the user to match the engraved markings on the lens itself.

The full system can automatically combine camera speed (6—24 fps) with shutter angle (45—180°) for changes in camera speed without perceptible changes in depth of field. Alternatively, the shutter angle can be automatically combined with the aperture to create changes in depth of field without a variation in exposure.

The Focus control can be made to operate either in a clockwise or a counter-clockwise direction as required.

Limited focus, zoom and aperture control can be set with magnified scale movement for precision control, if required.

Limit stops on the focus and zoom controls allow crash focus and zoom pulls to preset positions and fast returns to preset start positions.

Separate T. Stop and Zoom control units may be fitted if it is required to separate the control of these functions.

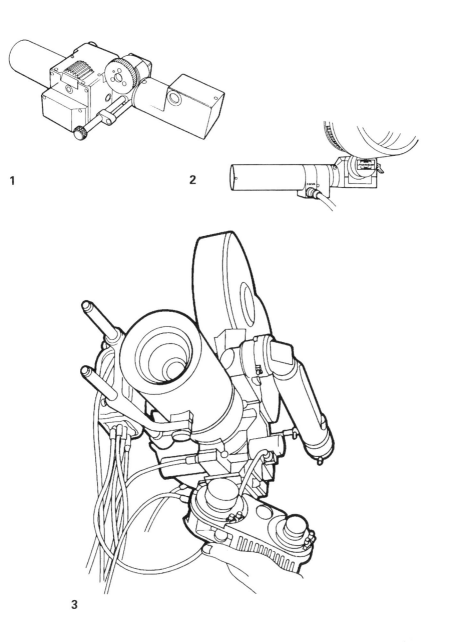

1. Combined focus and lens aperture motors, 2. Modular follow focus system
focus motor, 3. FTZSAC control system.

167

Remote Control Iris Systems

Various Iris Control units are available to remotely control lens apertures manually or electronically.

Manual Iris control
A simple mechanical iris control is available to adjust the aperture setting of a lens iris by means of a large control knob, much like a focus control. Like a focus control an extension cable can be fitted to the center of the knob if required.

Electronic Iris control
As already noted, an auxiliary motor may be used in combination with the Modular Follow Focus unit to electronically control the lens aperture setting.

As also noted, the FTZSAC lens control makes possible focus, T. Stop, Zoom and Speed/Aperture control all from one unit.

A separate T. Stop control, independent of the other controls, may be used if the DP wishes to alter exposure during the course of a shot while the Assistant is using the main unit to control other functions.

The T. Stop control can be used in combination with the camera FPS to create a change in camera speed without a change in exposure.

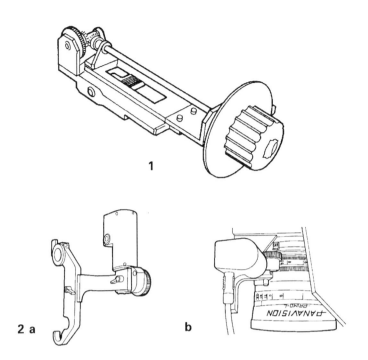

1. Optional mechanical iris control unit, 2. Optional electronic auxiliary iris control motor: a. As supplied for the iris support rods, b. As fitted to the iris control ring of a lens.

Zoom Controls

All PANAVISION zoom lenses may be operated either manually or electronically using an Electronic Zoom Control unit. A clutch on all lenses must be slid across to select whichever means of control is required (except for those lenses which have a "collar" motor).

When operating in the electronic control mode the zoom control hand unit (zoom gun) must be connected to the zoom motor by the yellow cable supplied. The zoom motor must be connected to a 24v DC power supply by one of the black cables supplied.

When drawing power from the zoom control power outlet on the front of the PANAFLEX camera use the short cable and when operating off an independent battery use the longer cable.

A switch marked IN and OUT on the back of the hand held unit determines the direction of the zoom—IN to long focal length, OUT to wide angle. A knob on the top selects the operating speed and a finger grip switches the unit ON and OFF. A button on the top of the unit, marked FAST RETURN, may be used to reset the zoom with the minimum of delay. Soft start and stop movements may be made by using the finger grip control and speed selection knob simultaneously.

Zoom control parking bracket
A special bracket which fits into the cave on the side of the camera is available to hold the zoom control unit when not in use or when it is more convenient to use attached to the camera setup.

170

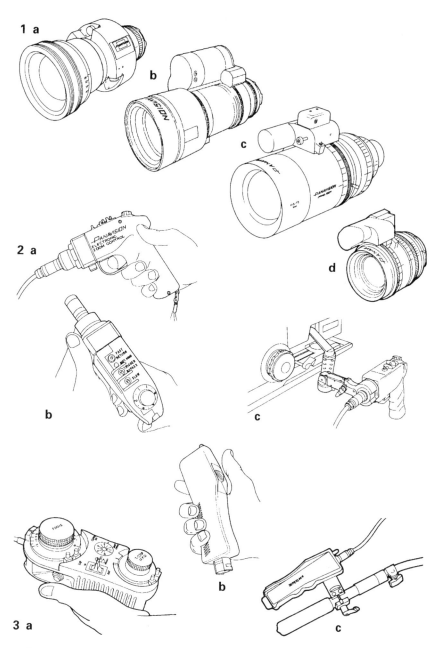

1. Zoom motor types: a. Collar type, b. Piggy-back type, c. Primo type, d. Lightweight type zoom motor, 2. Standard Zoom control: a. Hand unit (Zoom gun), b. Zoom controls in detail, c. Zoom control parked on holder unit, 3. FTZSAC Zoom controllers: a. Zoom control on combination unit, b. Super Zoom hand control, c. Super Zoom control on a pan handle.

171

"SMART SHUTTER" Shutter Angle /Camera Speed / Lens Aperture Control

The PANAVISION SMART SHUTTER II accessory is a means to control the exposure, the camera speed (FPS) or the lens depth of field without causing any change in the negative density. Typical situations that may occur are:

• It may be necessary to pan from, say, a shady area of a scene to a sunlit area in which case the exposure will need to be decreased by two stops. This can be done by closing down the shutter from 180° to 45°, leaving the depth of field unaffected.

• It may be necessary to speed up the movements of an aging actor during the course of a take without the effect showing on the screen. This can be done by using the Smart Shutter II accessory to adjust the camera speed while at the same time adjusting the camera shutter angle to compensate.

• It might be advantageous to change the depth of field during the course of a take. The Smart Shutter II accessory can change the T. Stop and the shutter angle at the same time.

For a greater range of camera speed change combined with consistent exposure throughout, it is also possible to combine a speed change with both a shutter angle and a lens aperture change (see pages 180 - 187).

An additional advantage of the Smart Shutter II system is that all three functions for change can be pre-calibrated and set so that changing one will automatically change one or both of the other two without the need to calculate what the compensatory change should be.

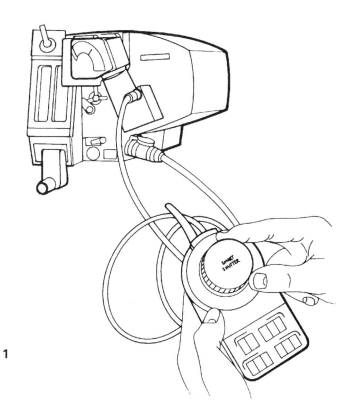

1

1. The Smart Shutter II shutter drive motor and control unit.

Electronic Servicing

Almost all of the principal electronic components of the PLATINUM PANAFLEX, including the on-board computer chips, are mounted on three (four in the case of the GII and earlier PANAFLEXES) easily changeable plug-in circuit boards mounted vertically on either side of the camera motor.

If the camera fails to function correctly, and the possibility of battery failure has been eliminated, all circuit boards can swiftly be changed in the field by the Camera Assistant.

A spare set of circuit boards (and a motor cover tool for the GII etc.), is supplied with all cameras. Experience has shown, however, that the likelihood of an electronic circuit failure is very small.

Before changing the circuit boards, the battery to camera cable should be replaced and the camera tested on a spare battery pack to ensure that the power supply to the camera is adequate.

BEFORE CHANGING ANY ELECTRONIC BOARD THE CAMERA MUST BE COMPLETELY DISCONNECTED FROM THE BATTERY.

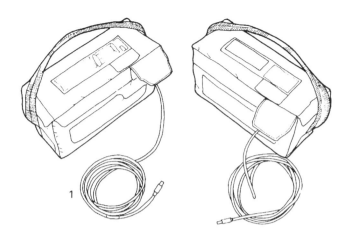

1. Camera battery and cable + Spare battery and cable. BEFORE ALL ELSE TRY USING A SPARE BATTERY AND A SPARE CABLE.

Changing the Electronic Circuit Boards

A spare set of circuit boards is supplied with every PANAFLEX camera. PLATINUM PANAFLEXES have three circuit boards, the others all have four.

To gain access to the motor compartment where the circuit boards are located it is necessary to remove the motor cover.

Before removing the motor cover the power supply to the camera must first be disconnected and the battery cable removed. THE POWER SOURCE MUST BE DISCONNECTED BEFORE CIRCUIT BOARDS ARE CHANGED. THIS IS VERY IMPORTANT.

Removing the motor cover

The motor cover of a PLATINUM PANAFLEX may be removed by undoing the screws in each corner of the motor cover and removing it gently.

The motor covers of the GII and earlier PANAFLEXES are released by turning two locks which are accessed from inside the camera.

To unlock the motor cover, push the motor cover tool through two openings in the soundproof lining. One is directly below the pitch control knob in the bottom left-hand corner of the film compartment, the other is above the buckle switch on the right-hand side. To release, turn the locks counter-clockwise as far as they will go.

To remove the motor cover lift it slightly and then pull it out from the underside.

Changing the circuit boards

Release the spring loaded retainers from the circuit boards and remove ALL boards by holding by top and bottom and pulling straight out. Replace ALL boards.

Note: The edge connectors of all boards are different so that no board can be plugged into the wrong camera or the wrong position.

Replace the motor cover and tighten securely.

In the event that a set of boards are changed the complete set of discarded boards should be returned to PANAVISION Inc. or their Distributor speedily accompanied by a note detailing the circumstances that necessitated the change. PANAVISION Inc. or its Distributor will quickly supply a replacement set.

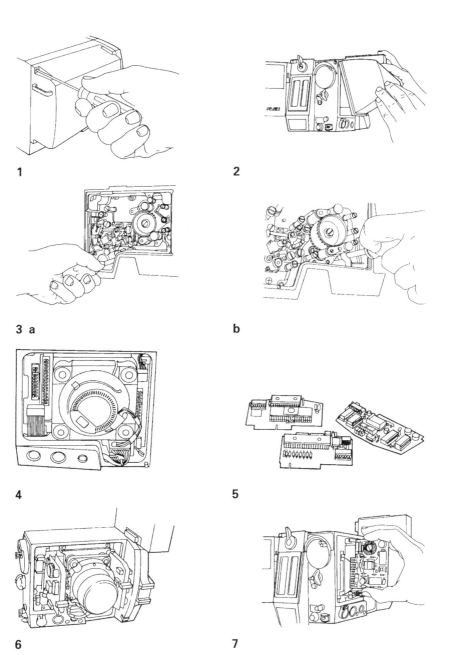

1. PLATINUM PANAFLEX motor cover release screws, 2. Removing a PANAFLEX motor cover, 3. GII motor cover locks access holes: a. below the pitch control knob, b. above the buckle switch, 4. Interior of PLATINUM PANAFLEX showing position of circuit boards, 5. Set of PLATINUM PANAFLEX circuit boards, 6. Interior of GII showing position of circuit boards, 7. Changing a circuit board.

Using
PANAFLEX and PANASTAR
Camera Accessories

The Smart Shutter II Accessory — Fitting the Shutter Motor

Note: BEFORE FITTING THE SMART SHUTTER II SYSTEM TO A PLATINUM PANAFLEX CAMERA IT IS ESSENTIAL TO FIRST RELEASE THE SHUTTER LOCKING LEVER. This can be found inside the camera just above the movement.

If using a PANASTAR I camera the speed selector must be set to "R" and on a PANASTAR II it must be set to "000."

Fitting the shutter control motor

Disconnect the power supply from the camera.

Unscrew and remove the engraved quadrant above the shutter control knob on the rear of the camera. Flip out the shutter control lever.

Mount and attach the Smart Shutter Motor (SSM) using the knurled knob on the top of the unit to align the motor with the shutter control knob.

If the required exposure change is to exceed two stops (the maximum possible by means of the shutter alone) then it will be necessary also to adjust the T-Stop. To do this fit either the Separate Remote Motor (SRM) or the Remote Focus and T-Stop Motor (RFTT) supplied with the Smart Shutter II kit. Alternatively it is possible to link into the F.T.Z.S.A.C. system. Connect the following cables:

- Shutter motor to the Smart Shutter Receiver Box (SSRB).
- T-Stop Motor, if fitted, to the SSRB.
- Camera accessory socket to the SSRB.
- 24 volt power supply from the camera or a battery to the SSRB.
- Shutter control unit to the SSRB.

Calibrating the Shutter Motor

To check the calibration reconnect the power supply to the camera, set the camera digital display to read *fps* and *shutter angle* and run the camera at 24 fps.

Turn the knurled knob until the *minimum* shutter opening is obtained.

At this point the engraved shutter angle markings (seen from the inside of the camera) should read about 5° less than the minimum shutter angle. Should the shutter angle markings not read about 5° less than the minimum shutter angle loosen the mechanical stop slide to the left of the knurled knob, turn the knob to the right as far as it will go and re-tighten. (Note: This setting operation will normally have been carried out by PANAVISION Inc. or its representatives before the equipment left their premises.)

180

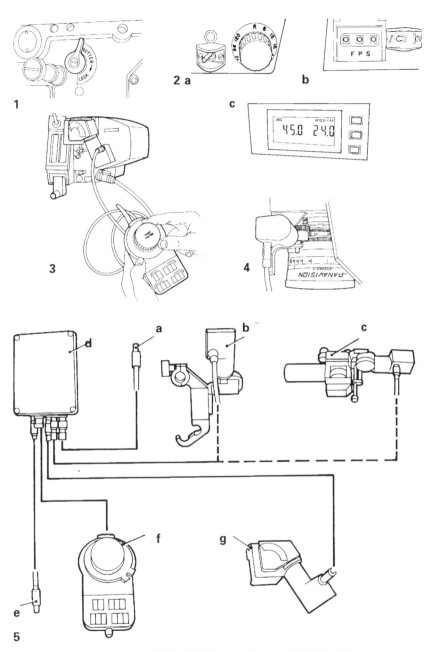

1. Shutter lock release, 2 a. PANASTAR I fps setting, b. PANASTAR II fps setting, c. Initial shutter setting display, 3. Shutter motor and control unit, 4. Separate iris control motor, 5 a. Smart Shutter II receiver box, b. Plug to camera ACC socket, c. Separate iris control motor, d. Combined focus and iris control motors, e. plug to 12v dc power supply, f. Smart Shutter II control unit, g. Shutter control motor.

The Smart Shutter II Accessory — In-shot Speed Change Below 24 fps

The rotary switch on the top of the Smart Shutter Receiver Box (SSRB) is used to set the needed mode of operation:
- FPS-SHTR/APER — for an in-shot camera speed change.
- D.O.F. — for an in-shot depth of field change.
- SHTR/APER ONLY — for in-shot exposure change.

Camera speed change below 24 fps using a PANAFLEX camera (shutter change only)
- Set the SSRB rotary switch to FPS-SHTR/APER.
- Set the LOW CAMERA SPEED selector to 6 fps.
- Set the HIGH CAMERA SPEED selector to 24 fps.
- Set the LOW SHUTTER ANGLE selector to 50°.
- Set the HIGH SHUTTER ANGLE selector to 200°.
- Press the button on the top of the SSB and hold for five seconds.
- Double check that the shutter locking lever is released.
- Apply 24v power supply and switch on the SSCB unit. The SSM wil move the shutter to the minimum shutter/fps settings. Turning the control knob to the right will set the camera to 24fps/180°. The white bezel can be marked with a pencil to note the intermediate settings.

Camera speed change with shutter *and* T. Stop compensation
- Set the SSRB rotary switch to FPS-SHTR/APER.
- Set the LOW and HIGH CAMERA SPEED selectors as above.
- Set the LOW SHUTTER ANGLE selector to 100°.
- Set the HIGH SHUTTER ANGLE selector to 200°.
- Set the shutter control knob to mid-range.
- Set the lens to T4 or larger.
- Apply power to the system (the shutter will move to minimum).
- When the shutter stops moving the aperture will start to stop down.
- As the lens reaches T5.6 press and hold down the button on the SSCB.
- Use the SSCB control to dial in T5.6 exactly.
- Release the button. The aperture will start to open up.
- As the lens reaches T4 again press and hold down the the top button.
- Again use the control to dial in T4 exactly. Release the button.
- The lens aperture can now be set as required for the shoot. With the above aperture settings (T4 and T5.6) any change to the camera speed will be compensated for by both the shutter and the aperture in equal amounts. However, if either the shutter or the aperture were to be set to different settings the change would be proportional to those maximum and minimum settings.

182

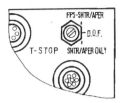 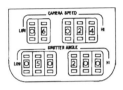 

Rotary to FPS-SHTR/APER   *6 - 24 fps, 50 - 200°*   *Aperture will remain constant at any setting*

Settings for shutter only changes on a PANAFLEX camera below 24 fps

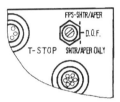 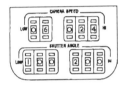  

Rotary to FPS-SHTR/APER   *6 - 24 fps, 100 - 200°*   *Aperture will adjust during the take*

Settings for shutter *and* T-Stop changes on a PANAFLEX below 24 fps

BELOW 24 fps FPS/SHUTTER ANGLE/APERTURE CHANGE TABLES

Frames per Second	SHUTTER ANGLE (°) ONLY		APERTURE CHANGE (T-Stops)
	PANAFLEX	PANASTAR	
24	200	180	
20	166.67	150	+1/3
16	133.33	120	+2/3
12	100	90	+1
10	83.33	75	+1 1/3
8	66.67	60	+1 2/3
6	50	45	+2

FPS/Shutter angle change only

Frames per Second	SHUTTER ANGLE (°) +APERTURE		APERTURE CHANGE (T-Stops)
	PANAFLEX	PANASTAR	
24	200	180	
20	182.57	164.32	+1/6
16	163.3	146.97	+1/3
12	141.42	127.28	+1/2
10	129.1	116.19	+2/3
8	115.47	103.92	+5/6
6	100	90	+1
5	91.29	82.16	+1 1/6
4	81.65	73.48	+1 1/3
3	70.71	63.64	+1 1/2
2.5	64.55	58.09	+1 2/3
2	57.74	51.96	+1 5/6
1.5	50	45	+2

FPS/Shutter angle / T-Stop change
in equal amounts

183

The Smart Shutter II Accessory — In-shot Speed Change Above 24 fps

The PANAFLEX camera system can also be used to slow down on-screen action by speeding-up the camera. To maximize this effect, above 36 fps, it is necessary to use a PANASTAR camera with its 128 fps capability.

Camera speed changes above 24 fps using a PANASTAR camera (shutter change only)

To increase the camera speed in shot from, say, 24 to 96 fps:
- Set the SSRB rotary switch to FPS-SHTR/APER.
- Set the LOW CAMERA SPEED setting to 24 fps.
- Set the HIGH CAMERA SPEED setting to 96 fps.
- Set the LOW SHUTTER ANGLE setting to 45°.
- Set the HIGH SHUTTER ANGLE setting to 180°.
- Set the lens aperture two stops open from what would normally be required at 24 fps.

When operated the camera speed will increase from 24 to 96 fps, the shutter angle will change from 45° to 180° and the exposure level will remain constant. Used the other way around the camera speed could be decreased by a similar amount.

Camera speed change with shutter *and* T. Stop compensation above 24 fps using a PANASTAR camera

To increase the camera speed in-shot from, say, 24 to 120 fps:
- Set the SSRB rotary switch to FPS-SHTR/APER.
- Set the LOW CAMERA SPEED setting to 24 fps.
- Set the HIGH CAMERA SPEED setting to 120 fps.
- Set the LOW SHUTTER ANGLE selector to 45°.
- Set the HIGH SHUTTER ANGLE selector to 180°.
- Set the shutter control knob to mid-range.
- Set the lens to T4 or larger.
- Apply power to the system (the shutter will move to minimum).
- When the shutter stops moving the aperture will start to stop down.
- As the lens reaches T5.6 press and hold down the button on the SSCB.
- Use the SSCB control to dial in T5.6 exactly.
- Release the button. The aperture will start to open up.
- As the lens reaches T4 again press and hold down the the top button.
- Again use the control to dial in T4 exactly. Release the button.
- The lens aperture can now be set as required for the shoot. With the above settings any change to the camera speed will be compensated for by both the shutter and the aperture in equal amounts. Dissimilar proportional changes can be achieved by setting either or both the shutter and/or the lens aperture to differing limits.

184

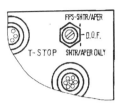

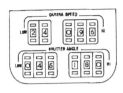

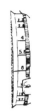

Rotary to FPS-SHTR/APER   24 - 96 fps, 45 - 180°   *Aperture will remain constant at any setting*

Settings for shutter only change above 24 fps

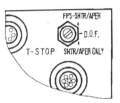

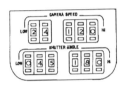

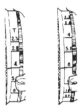

Rotary to FPS-SHTR/APER   24 - 120 fps, 45 - 120°   *Aperture will adjust during the take*

Settings for shutter + stop change above 24 fps

ABOVE 24 fps FPS/SHUTTER ANGLE/APERTURE CHANGE TABLE

Frames per Second	SHUTTER ANGLE ALONE SHUTTER (°)
24	180
32	135
40	108
48	90
64	67.5
80	54
96	45
120	(Not possible)

FPS/Shutter change alone

Frames per Second	SHUTTER ANGLE +APERTURE	
	SHUTTER (°)	APERTURE CHANGE (T-Stops)
24	180	
32	155.88	+1/6
40	139.43	+1/3
48	127.28	+1/2
64	110.23	+2/3
80	98.59	+5/6
96	90	+1
120	80.5	+1 !/6

FPS/Shutter angle/T-Stop change in equal amounts

185

The Smart Shutter II Accessory — In-shot Depth of Field and Exposure Changes

In addition to the foregoing the SSII can be used to:
- Change the depth of field.
- Change the exposure by changing the shutter opening.

Depth of field change
- Set SSRB rotary switch to D.O.F.
- Set both the LOW and HIGH CAMERA SPEED settings to 24 fps.
- Set the LOW SHUTTER ANGLE setting to 200°.
- Set the HIGH SHUTTER ANGLE setting to 50°.
- Set the lens to T8 and hold the SSCB button for five seconds.

When operated the camera speed will remain constant, the shutter angle will change from 200° to 50° and the aperture will change from T8 to T4, giving less depth of field. Used the other way around it would increase the depth of field.

Exposure change
Used on its own the adjustable shutter can be used either to increase or decrease exposure by up to two stops. Used in combination with the aperture the change can be up to four stops. For maximum effect:
- Set SSRB rotary switch to SHUT/APER ONLY.
- Set both the LOW and HIGH CAMERA SPEED settings to 24 fps.
- Set the LOW SHUTTER ANGLE setting to 50°.
- Set the HIGH SHUTTER ANGLE setting to 200°.
- Set the lens to T8 and hold the SSCB button for five seconds.

When operated the camera speed will remain constant, the shutter angle will change from 50° to 200° and the aperture will change from T8 to T4, giving four stops more exposure. Used the other way around it would decrease the exposure.

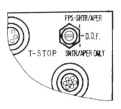
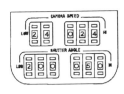

Rotary to DOF · 24 - 24 fps, 200 - 50° · If lens is set to T4 it will adjust to T8

Settings for in-shot Depth of Field change only

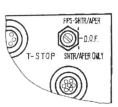
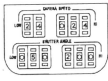

Rotary to SHUT/APER ONLY · 24 - 24 fps, 50 - 200° · If lens is set to T8 it will adjust to T4

Setting for in-shot Exposure change only

IN-SHOT DEPTH of FIELD AND EXPOSURE CHANGE TABLES

FRAMES PER SECOND	SHUTTER CHANGE	APERTURE CHANGE (T-Stops)
24	200	
24	166.67	-1/3
24	133.33	-2/3
24	100	-1
24	83.3	-1 1/3
24	66.67	-1 2/3
24	50	-2

FRAMES PER SECOND	SHUTTER CHANGE	EXPOSURE CHANGE (T-Stops)
24	50	
24	66.67	+1/3
24	83.3	"+2/3"
24	100	+1
24	133.33	+1 1/3
24	166.67	+1 2/3
24	200	+2

Shutter used to change Depth of Field with Camera Speed remaining constant

Shutter used to change Exposure with Camera Speed remaining constant

187

The Focus, T-Stop, Zoom, Speed-Aperture Controller (F.T.Z.S.A.C.)

With the F.T.Z.S.A.C. system the three principal lens functions — Focus, Aperture and Zoom — can be remotely controlled from a single unit or by separate units. Remote control can be by cable connection or via a radio link.

In addition, the T-Stop control can be linked to the camera speed to ensure constant exposure with variable camera speeds.

As an added plus the unit also has a remote camera On/Off function.

Assembling the units

Attach the combined Focus and T-Stop motor unit to the camera in place of the manual focus control system. If the T-Stop motor is not required it may be detached from the focus motor. A separate additional motor is also supplied for use with the T-Stop alone, if required. At this stage do not engage the motors with the lens gear rings.

Note that there are slightly differing attachment settings for PANAFLEX, PANASTAR amd Super-35 cameras and when a range extender or a rear anamorphoser is fitted to the lens.

Before connecting together the various units and attaching a power supply check the following:

• If using wireless control check that the channel number settings on both the transmitter and the receiving units are the same.

• The remote camera ON/OFF switch on the control unit must be "OFF."

• The Focus and T-Stop knobs on the control unit must be set to a mid-range position.

• If using a hard-wire connection connect together the following:

• Focus and T-Stop motor or T-Stop motor to the Receiver box.

• Zoom motor, if appropriate, to the Receiver box.

• Camera Accessory socket to the Receiver box (for camera ON/OFF).

• If using a cable connection, Controller unit to the Receiver box.

• If using a radio link, Controller unit to the Radio transmitter (and raise the aerials on the Radio transmitter and Receiver units).

• If required, connect the Remote Zoom Controller to the Control unit.

• If required, connect the Separate T-Stop Controller to the Control unit.

Notes:

If T-Stop, focus and/or Zoom controls are not to be used then do not connect those cables.

If separate Zoom or T-Stop Controllers are to be used be sure they are connected to the controller unit. This will automatically inhibit these controls on the Controller unit.

188

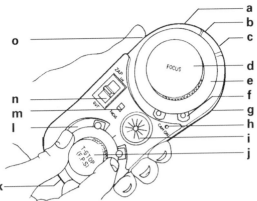

1. The F.T.Z.S.A.C. control unit: a. Calibration button, b. Socket to Receiver Unit, c. Camera ON-OFF switch, d. Focus knob, e. Focus marker disk, f. Focus stop, g. Remote focus & zoom outlets, h. Camera Running indicator, i. Zoom speed control, j. Aperture control knob, k. Minimum & maximum fps settings, l. Aperture marker disk, m. Focus direction switch, n. Zoom fast return switch, o. Zoom control.

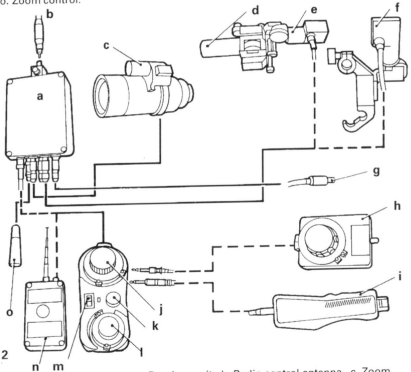

2. The F.T.Z.S.A.C. system: a. Receiver unit, b. Radio control antenna, c. Zoom motor, d. Focus motor, e. Combined iris motor, f. Alternative iris motor, g. Camera accessory plug, h. Alternative focus control, i. Alternative zoom control, j. Focus control, k. Zoom speed control, l. T-Stop control, m. Zoom fast return switch, n. Radio control transmitter, 0. 12v d.c. input plug.

189

The F.T.Z.S.A.C. System — Focus and T-Stop Control

Before the system can be used the various components must be calibrated to one another. Before commencing be sure the remote camera ON/OFF switch and the "Speed" switch are both in the OFF position.

Full range lens calibration

For a "full range" type calibration, spanning the entire focus and T-Stop range proceed as follows:

• Engage the Focus and/or T-Stop motors to mesh gently with the lens gears. If only one facility is needed the "Additional Motor" may be used for either function.

• Connect a 24v power supply to the Receiver unit. This can either be from the camera or from a separate battery. The system will then auto-calibrate.

Limited range lens calibration

For a "limited range" type calibration, say 6ft to 12ft and/or T4 to T8:

• Set the lens within the range, say 8ft and T5.6.

• Engage the Focus and/or T-Stop motors to mesh gently with the lens gears.

• Connect a 24v power supply to the Receiver unit and be ready to press the "CALIB" button.

• As the lens approaches 6ft press and hold down the CALIB button. Set the focus to exactly 6ft using the Focus Knob and then release the CALIB button.

• The lens focus will then reverse direction and move towards the 12ft mark. Repeat the operation as above.

• The lens will then move, in turn, to either end of the T-Stop scale. Repeat the operation as above.

• Use the white disks surrounding the Focus and T-Stop knobs to mark intermediate focus distances and T-Stops.

• Use the Focus Direction switch to change the rotational direction of the lens barrel, if preferred.

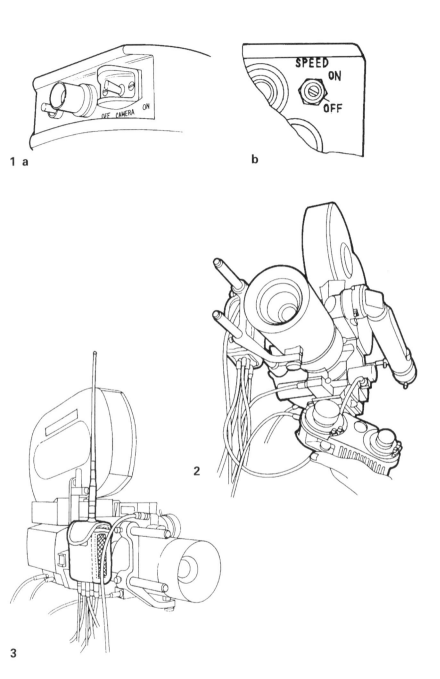

1 a

b

2

3

1. Before powering-up the F.T.Z.S.A.C. system the Camera Run switch on the control unit (a) and the "Speed" switch on the Receiver unit (b) must both be set to OFF. 2. F.T.Z.S.A.C. set up for hard-wire operation, 3. The receiver unit set for radio controlled operation.

The F.T.Z.S.A.C. System — Camera Speed/T-Stop and Zoom Control

As with the Focus and T-Stop control, before the system can be used the various components must be calibrated to one another.

Combined camera speed and T-Stop calibration

For a "Combined camera speed and T-Stop" calibration where a change in lens aperture is to maintain the correct exposure level during an in-shot change of camera speed:

• First decide what change of camera speed is required and use the tables on pages 185 and 187 to calculate what the exposure change must be to compensate. Say 24 to 6 fps and T8 to T4.

• Before powering the Receiver unit set the "SPEED" switch on the Receiver to ON. (The camera should be OFF.)

• Set the fps limit stops on the lower side of the control unit to set the camera speed range as required and move the lens T-Stop setting to be within the required range.

• Plug power into the Receiver unit. The T-Stop will start to calibrate towards the open aperture end of the scale.

• As the lens approaches the needed aperture (T4) press and hold down the "CALIB" button. Use the T-Stop knob to set the lens aperture exactly as required. Release the CALIB button.

• The lens aperture will then reverse direction and move towards the T8 mark. Repeat the operation as above.

• The camera speed/T-Stop calibration is now set and the system is ready for use.

To change the camera speed range without total re-calibration:

• Check that the camera is switched OFF.

• Reset camera speed range as required and hold down CALIB button for three seconds. The new range is now synchronized to the current T-Stop setting and ready for use.

Zoom control features

The F.T.Z.S.A.C. control incorporates zoom control features much like a normal zoom control unit. A bi-directional pressure switch actuates the zoom in either direction, a speed control knob limits the maximum zoom speed and a two-way switch enables the zoom to be operated at maximum speed in either direction.

One dedicated zoom control unit, which may be affixed to a pan bar, may be plugged into the main F.T.Z.S.A.C. control unit.

Like the focus and T-Stop controls, the zoom control may also be operated via a radio link.

192

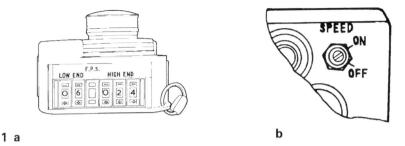

1 a

b

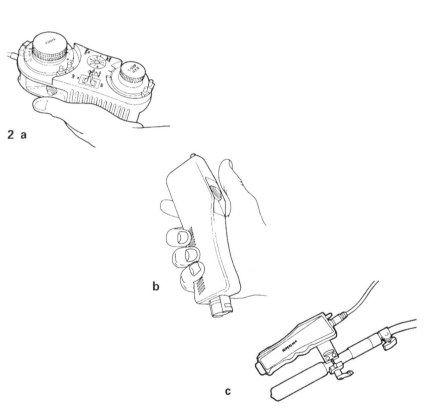

2 a

b

c

1 a. The lowest and highest fps settings required must be set on the fps limit stops and the "SPEED" switch (b) on the receiver unit which must be set to ON before making any connections, 2. Alternative forms of zoom control: a. On the main control unit. This may be hard-wired or radio control, b. Separate control, c. Pan handle control.

Electronic Synchronizer Systems

The sync speeds of PANAFLEX cameras are derived from quartz crystal oscillators to accuracies better than one frame in one hour ensuring safe synchronization with sound recorders and HMI lighting, providing they are speed controlled to a similar degree of accuracy. Even if the speeds were to drift to their maximum during the course of the longest possible take (11 minutes, the running time of a 1000 ft. roll of film) there would still be no noticeable loss of sync or discernible flicker.

In the case of the PLATINUM PANAFLEX the camera can be crystal controlled at any speed, in 0.1 fps increments, from 4 to 36 fps, including 24, 25, 29.97 and 30 fps.

There are occasions, however, when the camera must be positively synchronized with other equipment (HMI lighting, video systems or computers), or must be run in shutter phase sync with a projector (front or back projection), or with another camera (twin camera 3D), or it may be desirable to run the camera at speeds outside the normal camera speed range (time lapse, single shot), etc. In all these instances it is necessary to override the normal speed control system and sync to an outside source.

Electronic synchronizing accessories, which are totally automatic in their operation, are available for all PANAFLEX cameras. These accessories also function with PANASTAR and SUPER PSR cameras.

Phasable Synchronizer

The special feature of the PANAVISION Phasable Synchronizer system is its ability to synchronize the speed of the camera and the position of the shutter relative to an external pulse over a range of ±100° (±180° on request). The phasing is accomplished while the camera is running in a smooth manner and with only a momentary 1% change in camera speed.

The phase knob has a 'turns' counting dial and a precision 10-turn pot for accurate resetting.

Operating instructions

Phasing can be accomplished while filming and observing the effect through the viewfinder:

While filming a TV monitor, set the camera shutter to 180° and turn the phase control knob until the bar is out of sight (Field to Frame); or set the shutter to 144° and position the bar to be at its least objectionable (Video to Film).

For Front Projection, set the camera shutter to its full open position and turn the phase control knob until the least amount of light is seen through the viewfinder. The maximum amount of light is then passing to the film.

194

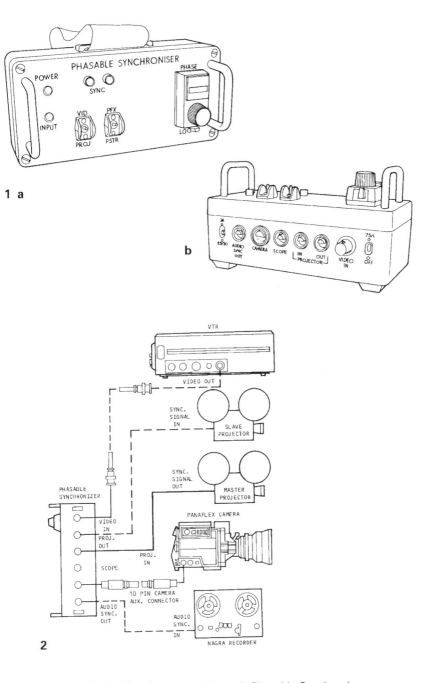

1. a. & b. Phasable Synchronizer control box. 2. Phasable Synchronizer
schematic of connections.

Electronic Synchronizer Systems — Camera to Projector Synchronizer

PANAVISION cameras can be synchronized to projectors either by means of the Phasable Synchronizer unit or by the Camera—Projector Electronic Synchronizer unit. These units not only ensure that any PANAFLEX, PANASTAR or SUPER PSR camera will operate at exactly the same speed as a film projector but will also ensure (providing that the probe is properly set on the projector) that the shutters of the two units open at precisely the same moment. It is an essential accessory for front and rear projection process filming.

To operate either synchronizer unit an electronic probe unit must be fitted in close proximity to a raised stud attached to some part of the projector which rotates once every frame. This will generate a reference pulse which will replace the internal crystal control pulse within the camera and to which the camera will automatically synchronize. A suitable probe unit for the projector can be supplied on request.

The stud and the probe unit must be set relative to one another so that they pass at the moment when the projector shutter is 48° past its closed position. It is advantageous if the probe unit can be rotated relative to the stud to allow for fine adjustment both of synchronization and of the relative exposure between the foreground and background of the process shot. If the stud can be rotated 180° relative to its normal shooting position this setting can be used during rehearsals to check the lighting balance between the projected image and the foreground.

The clearance between the stud and the probe should be approximately 1/16", 1.5mm. If it is too close double pulsing may prevent sync, and if there is too much clearance no pulse will be generated. If necessary adjust the probe in or out until the camera synchronizes properly.

The AUDIO SYNC (3-pin LEMO) connector makes available a 1 volt RMS sinewave signal that may be used as a pilotone reference for sound recording. A mating cable is supplied with bare wires on one end for this purpose. The frequencies are as follows: 60 Hz at 24/24, 30/30 and 30/24 and 50 Hz at 25/25.

Absolute synchronization may be verified by removing the film and replacing the aperture plate with an Aperture Viewing Mirror.

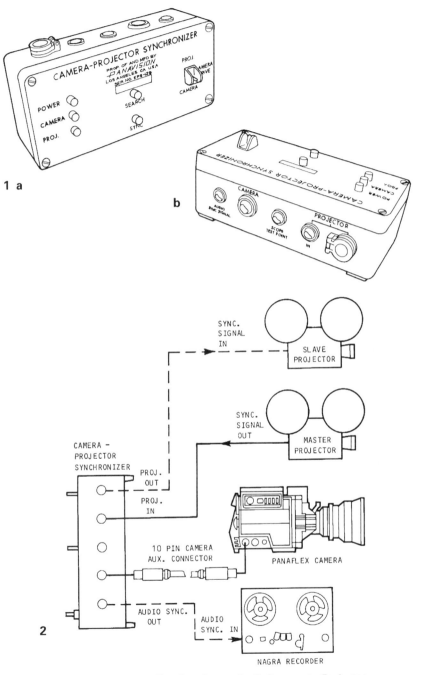

1. a. & b. Camera to Projector Synchronizer unit, 2. Camera to Projector Synchronizer schematic of connections.

Electronic Synchronizer Systems — Camera to Projector Synchronizer Operating Instructions

1. Set the camera shutter to its fully open position.
2. Connect the synchronizer to the film camera with the 10-pin LEMO cable supplied with the kit. The 10-pin connector on the Camera is located under a small gray plastic hatch. On the synchronizer the connector is labelled CAMERA.
3. Connect the sync cable from the projector shutter probe to the PROJECTOR IN socket on the rear of the synchronizer. (The PROJECTOR OUT connector is used when two or more cameras are synced to the same projector when a sync box is required for each camera).
4. If required, connect the audio pulse cable to the AUDIO SYNC SIGNAL socket and to the recorder.
5. The POWER light will come on when the battery is connected to the camera.
6. Switch the CAMERA DRIVE switch to PROJ. (When this switch is in CAMERA position, the camera runs independently of the projector).
7. Start the projector. The PROJ light will flash indicating that the shutter pulse is present.
8. Start the camera. The CAMERA light will flash. Initially the red SEARCH light will also light indicating that the camera is not yet at speed. After a few seconds the red light will go out and the green SYNC light will flash indicating that the camera is now up to speed and is in sync.
9. As a safety check, observe the projected image through the mirror shutter reflex viewfinder system of the camera. Its brightness should be minimal indicating that the maximum amount of light is being used to expose the film.

Note: It makes no difference if the camera or the projector is started first.

It is important to check that the green SYNC light continues to flash steadily during a take and that the red light does not come on. Should this not be the case it is probable that a malfunction has occurred.

198

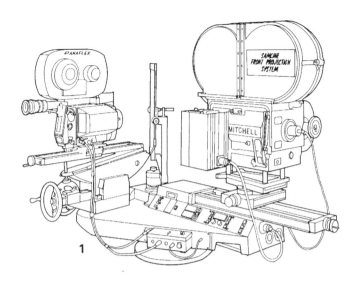

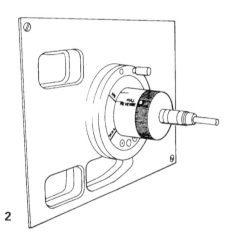

1. Front projection rig using a PANAFLEX camera and showing the projector synchronizer box in the foreground, 2. Rotatable probe unit fitted to a Front Projection projector.

Electronic Synchronizer Systems — Time-Lapse and Time Exposures

A Time-Lapse/Time Exposure speed control accessory is available which makes it possible to run PANAFLEX and PANASTAR cameras at speeds slower than the 4 fps which is the minimum speed with the normal camera speed control.

In the TIME-LAPSE mode all exposures are made as if the camera were operating at a constant rate of four frames per second. The exposure time may be controlled by using the adjustable shutter.

In the TIME-EXPOSURE mode the duration of each exposure depends on the SECONDS PER FRAME setting. Exposures longer than 640 sec. (10 2/3 min.) can be obtained by using the SINGLE FRAME button.

Note: As a precaution it is advisable to black out the magazine and camera housing with duvetine or similar material when very long time lapse sequences are envisaged or in very bright ambient light conditions.

Operating instructions

1. Set the PFX-PSTR switch to match the camera to be used. (PFX = PANAFLEX, PSTR = PANASTAR).
2. Select either TIME-LAPSE or TIME-EXPOSURE operation with the CAMERA DRIVE switch.
3. Connect the time-lapse synchronizer to the film camera with the 10-pin LEMO cable supplied with the kit. The 10-pin connector on the Camera is located under a small gray plastic hatch. On the box the connector is labelled CAMERA.
4. When power is supplied to the camera, the green POWER light should illuminate.
5. In the TIME-LAPSE mode set the switch marked X1 and X10 before selecting the frame rate. In the X10 position all of the seconds per frame settings (except .25) are multiplied by TEN.
6. Select the frame rate as required.
7. Set the camera shutter opening to control exposure.

The CAMERA light will illuminate each time the film advances.

In the TIME-EXPOSURE mode it is recommended that the shutter opening be set at 180°. At 180° the time between exposures (the film pull-down period) is fixed at 1/18 (.056) sec.

Note: A special motor cover, incorporating a blower unit, must be used with the PANASTAR camera when scenes or re-takes last for 30 minutes or longer. For long running times with a PANAFLEX camera, a special magazine that has reduced power is required.

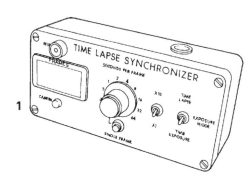

1

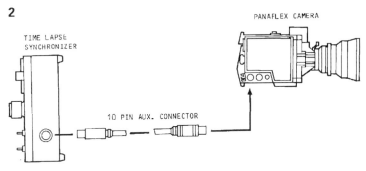

2

1. Time lapse control box, 2. Time lapse schematic of connections.

TIME-LAPSE EXPOSURE TABLE

Shutter Opening (°)											
200	180	160	144	120	100	90	80	70	60	50	45
Exposure time (sec)											
1/7	1/8	1/9	1/10	1/12	1/14	1/16	1/18	1/21	1/24	1/29	1/32
0.14	0.125	0.11	0.1	0.08	0.07	0.063	0.056	0.05	0.04	0.035	0.031

EVENT TIME/SCREEN TIME CALCULATIONS

If the elapsed time of the event and the desired screen time are known the necessary frame rate may be calculated viz.:

Seconds per frame = Event time / (Screen time x 24)

If the elapsed time of the event and the frame rate are known the screen time may be calculated viz.:

Screen time = (Event time x 24) / Seconds per frame setting

All times must be in seconds.

201

PANAFLASHER

Giving a very small, even, overall exposure to the film immediately before or after the film is exposed in the camera gate is a method of increasing effective film speed, reducing contrast, putting more information into the shadow areas and, if desired in the case of color film, of tinting the shadows without affecting the highlights. It is a technique which is as old as photography itself.

The PANAVISION PANAFLASHER unit fits onto whichever PANAFLEX or PANASTAR magazine port is not currently in use. It makes no difference if the film is flashed just before or just after the principal exposure.

The effect of flashing is most pronounced in the shadow areas. It has little or no effect in the middle tones or the white areas of the picture. In consequence scenes require less fill light and deep shadows will show more detail than they might otherwise have done.

If the flashing light is colored it will color the dark areas only. It may be used to give an overall warming or cooling effect. Moonlight, sepia and virtually any other mood may be created by using inexpensive gelatin and/or 49mm diameter screw-in filters in the PANAFLASHER.

The amount of flashing may be adjusted during the course of a scene and is particularly effective when colored flashing is being used. The effect of increasing the flashing during a take will first be seen in the darkest areas and will spread to the highlights as the PANAFLASHER iris is opened until the entire scene can have an overall colored look about it.

General guidelines

Before using the PANAFLASHER system it is important that carefully controlled photographic tests be carried out to determine what the overall effect will be in the circumstances of a particular lighting situation.

When the scene is contrasty and low-key about 10% flash exposure is likely to be a good basis for initial tests. In this situation comparatively little flash exposure is required because the shadow area comprises most of the image.

When a scene is contrasty but high key 20% flashing can be used to bring out the shadow details.

When a scene is high contrast, with equal areas of light and shade, 15% - 20% flashing should be tried.

The PANAFLASHER filter tray contains six different diffuser filters and an 80C color corrective filter that corrects the light source to 3200° K. These filters, especially the 80C, are pre-set and should not be removed.

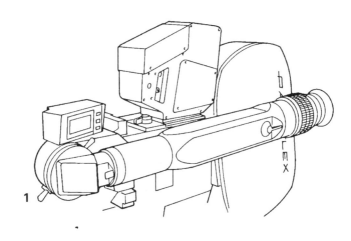

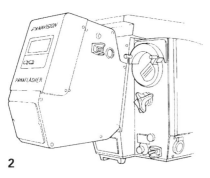

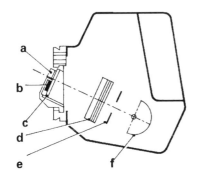

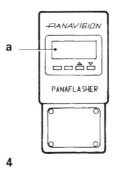

1. PANAFLASHER unit mounted on the top magazine port, 2. PANAFLASHER unit mounted in rear position, 3. The internal components: a. Fogging window, b. Meter photocell, c. Diffusion window, d. Factory set diffusion window, e. Iris, f. Light source, 4. Rear control panel: a. Meter display.

203

PANAFLASHER —
Operating Instructions

1. Put the appropriate filters in the filter tray:

NEUTRAL	As specified by PANAVISION
WARM	" " " " + 85B
COOL	" " " " + 80A
COLOR	As required and determined by tests.

2. Attach the PANAFLASHER unit to whichever magazine port is not in use.
3. If desired, plug the PANACLEAR power supply cable into the socket provided on the PANAFLASHER unit.
4. Switch ON the PANAFLASHER unit. (A green LED indicates ON.)
5. If the PANAFLASHER is mounted on the rear magazine port push the EI/TIME button to the EI position and set the EI to equal the Exposure Index of the film in use, using the up and down arrows next to the button, i.e., 5247 = EI 125.
6. If the PANAFLASHER is mounted on the top magazine port push the EI/TIME button to the EI position and set the EI according to the TOP MOUNT table opposite, i.e., 5247 = EI 40. (Note: It is necessary to make this adjustment to compensate for the fact that the PANAFLASHER unit is farther from the film in the top position than at the rear.)
7. If running the camera at any speed other than 24/25 fps reset the EI according to the CAMERA SPEED table opposite.
8. Push the EI/TIME button to the TIME position and set the speed to 1/50 sec.
9. Push in the M-CLR button and move the IRIS control back and forth to set the EV number to give the desired amount of flashing (see BASIC FLASHING INTENSITY table opposite). Note: This table is only supplied as an example. Please refer to the table supplied with the individual PANAFLASHER unit for the actual EV settings.
10. Check the EV reading before every take.

Note: The PANAFLASHER consumes very little power and it is not necessary to switch it OFF between takes.

PANAFLASHER BASIC SETTING CHART

FOR NEUTRAL FLASHING WITH AN 80C FILTER AND THE ASA (EI) SET TO EQUAL THE FILM IN USE	
%	E.V. No.
5%	2.8
10%	3.1
15%	3.5
20%	3.8
25%	4.2
30%	4.5

PANAFLASHER ASA (EI) EQUIVALENT CHART

Film ASA (EI)	Rear Magazine Port			Top Magazine Port (Video Wedge)			Top Magazine Port (No Video Wedge)		
	Neutral	Warm (85B Filter)	Cool (80A Filter)	Neutral	Warm (85B Filter)	Cool (80A Filter)	Neutral	Warm (85B Filter)	Cool (80A Filter)
500	500	800	1000	50	80	100	160	250	320
400	400	640	800	40	64	80	125	200	250
320	320	500	640	32	50	64	100	160	200
250	250	400	500	25	40	50	80	125	160
200	200	320	400	20	32	40	64	100	125
160	160	250	320	16	25	32	50	80	100
125	125	200	250	12	20	25	40	64	80
100	100	160	200		16	20	32	50	64
80	80	125	160		12	16	25	40	50
64	64	100	125			12	20	32	40
50	50	80	100				16	25	32
40	40	64	80				12	20	25
32	32	50	64				10	16	20
25	25	40	50				8	12	16
20	20	32	40					10	12
16	16	25	32					8	10
12	12	20	25						8

PANAFLASHER CAMERA SPEED CHART

F.P.S.	Film Stock EI (ASA)																
	500	400	320	250	200	160	120	100	80	64	50	40	32	25	20	16	12
	Adjusted Film EI (ASA) Number																
6	2000	1600	1200	1000	800	640	500	400	320	250	200	160	120	100	80	64	50
12	1000	800	640	500	400	320	250	200	160	120	100	80	64	50	40	32	25
18	640	500	400	320	250	200	160	120	100	80	64	50	40	32	25	20	16
24/25	500	400	320	250	200	160	120	100	80	64	50	40	32	25	20	16	12
30	400	320	250	200	160	120	100	80	64	50	40	32	25	20	16	12	
48	250	200	160	120	100	80	64	50	40	32	25	20	16	12			
72	200	160	120	100	80	64	50	40	32	25	20	16	12				
96	120	100	80	64	50	40	32	25	20	16	12						
120	100	80	64	50	40	32	25	20	16	12							

PANAHEAD Accessories

Accessory box attachment plates

Attachment plates to allow Camera Assistants to attach their own 'front' boxes to the front of a PANAHEAD are available from the store at PANAVISION (the 'PANASTORE') and from their representatives worldwide.

PANABALL leveller

An optional accessory for the PANAHEAD geared head is the PANABALL Leveller. This may be fitted between the tripod head and the PANAHEAD or used as a levelling hi-hat and stood, bolted or screwed directly to the ground or any flat surface.

To attach the PANAHEAD to the leveller tighten up the topmost of the two spoked handwheels set in the leveller.

To level or tilt the PANAHEAD, release the ball movement by turning the lower spoked handwheel in a clockwise direction. Adjust the level and re-tighten the lower handwheel.

The regular PANABALL leveller gives 15° of levelling and tilting movement. A 3° version is available to use in conjunction with a PANAVISION NODAL ADAPTOR which enables a PANAHEAD to be levelled or tilted about the nodal point of the camera lens.

If the flange onto which the PANABALL leveller is to be fitted is too wide the feet of the leveller may be removed.

Nodal adaptor

Nodal adaptors are available to fit between a PANAFLEX camera and the PANAHEAD to place the entrance pupil of the lens in the center of the pan and tilt axes of the head.

To fit a nodal adaptor remove the tilt assembly from the PANAHEAD and fit the nodal adaptor in its place, using the slide facility to place the camera and lens in the correct position.

To set the entrance pupil of the lens on the nodal point of the head place two pointers in line in front of the camera, one close to and the other further away. Looking through the viewfinder the relative positions of the pointers should not move as the camera is panned and tilted. Move the camera backwards and forwards and up and down until there is no relative movement.

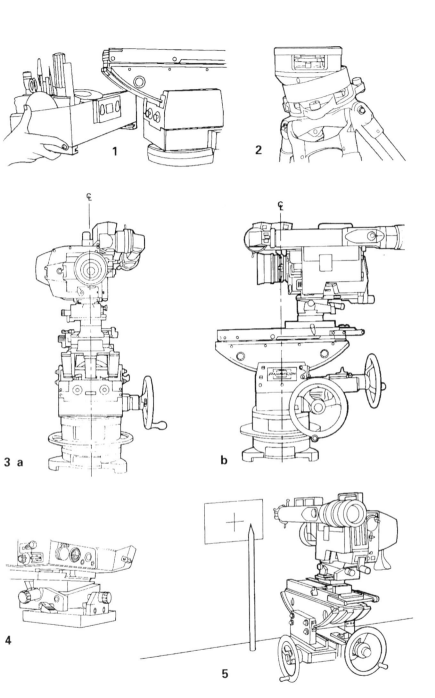

1. PANAHEAD front box attachment plate,   2. 15° PANABALL leveller on a tripod,
3 a. & b. Camera set up nodally with a 3° PANABALL leveller and a nodal adaptor
set on the ground,   4. Nodal adaptor,   5. Nodal setting up method.

PANALITE Camera Mounted Lamps

PANAVISION offers two models of their PANALITE Camera Mounted Lamps. These lamps may be mounted close to the camera lens and their brightness controlled without affecting the color quality of the light. They are mostly used to fill facial shadows.

On the Mk. I version the adjustable brightness facility works by varying the area of the reflecting surface enabling the light intensity falling on the subject to remain constant as the distance between the camera and the subject is reduced or increased during the course of a take. It uses a $4^{11}/_{16}$", 117mm, linear quartz bulb. Recommended bulbs are 120v/650w, 220v/875w and 240v/875w. These lamps may be used with an AC supply only and the color temperature is 3200K.

The Mk. II version uses a circular graduated filter to attenuate the light. It uses a 125w MSR metal halide bulb, has a high frequency, flicker free, electronic ballast and may be operated off 24v DC and any normal AC voltage.

PANALITE operation

PANALITE lamps fit onto a support bracket which is slipped over the iris rods (matte box support bars). They are supplied with an offset arm and adapters to make it possible to place them higher and further to the left or right of the lens than normal. A ball joint on the rear of the lamp housings allow them to be tilted in any direction. They are supplied with two power cables (one short and one long) fitted with in-line ON-OFF switches and a spare bulb.

Both lamps may be operated either in a soft light mode with constant color temperature brightness control or as hard lights without the brightness control.

In the soft light mode the intensity of either lamp may be adjusted by turning a knob at either side of the unit. The extension cable used for the follow focus and iris and shutter controls may also be used with a PANALITE.

In the Mk. I version a hard/bright light output may be obtained by reversing the bulb and its reflector. With the Mk. II version the light intensity control system may be separated from the lamp altogether.

PANALITE lamps are fitted with four barn doors and are supplied with a complement of gelatin filter frames which fit on support bars which swing out from the top and bottom of the lamps.

Note: In order to prevent overheating PANALITE Mk. I lamps should not be left switched on continuously but only lit during the rehearsal and take periods. This is particularly so in the case of the higher wattage 220 - 250 volt bulbs, where a maximum lit period of no more than eight minutes is recommended.

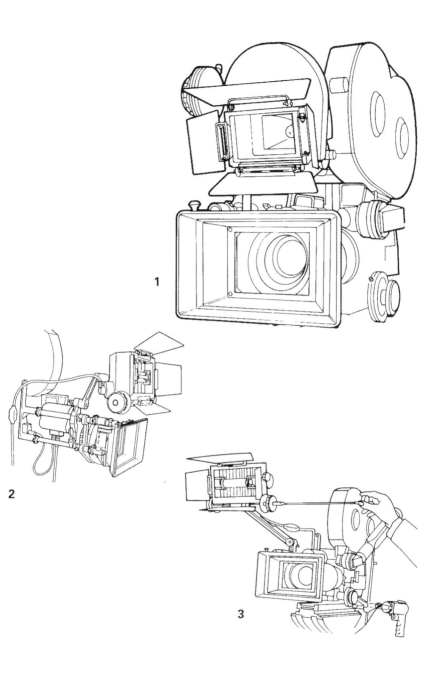

1. PANALITE Mk. II, 2. PANALITE Mk. I mounted in a normal manner, 3. Offset PANALITE mounting using a follow focus extension for remote control.

PANAPOD Tripods

PANAVISION PANAPODS are lightweight tubular tripods which are available in Standard and Baby lengths.

The Standard length makes possible lens heights between 3'9" and 6'10" (1.150-2.80m) and the Baby between 2'9" and 4'3" (0.840-1.295m), approximately, allowing for the added height of a PANAFLEX camera on a PANAHEAD and depending upon the amount of spread.

The use of a PANABALL leveller will add 6" to the height.

PANAPOD tripods should always be used with a spreader or with crows' feet for security. If the feet are fixed to the ground they should always be released before adjusting the tripod height or level to prevent the legs from becoming twisted or bent.

Three rings beneath the top plate, central with each leg, may be used for attaching tie-down chains or safety ropes.

PANAPOD tripod legs should never be overtightened as this may distort the tubular legs, making them difficult to slide up and down.

PANAPOD tripods are supplied with a shoulder pad to make it easier to carry the tripod complete with a PANAHEAD and camera, if necessary.

Cleaning PANAPOD tripod legs

If PANAPOD tripod legs become contaminated with sand or saltwater they should be stripped down and cleaned at the earliest possible opportunity. NEVER use oil to clean or lubricate tripod legs. It gets into the metal and will dirty other peoples' hands and clothing from then on.

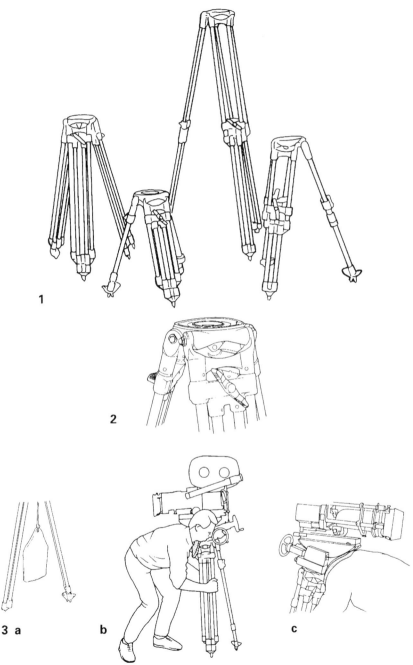

1. Standard and baby PANAPOD tripods at their shortest and most extended heights, 2. PANAPOD tripod top showing tie-down eye, 3 a, b, & c. Using a shoulder pad to carry a camera, head and tripod assembly.

211

PANATAPE II Electronic Rangefinder

The PANATAPE II electronic rangefinder measures the distance from the film plane to a selected solid object which is (usually) placed centrally in front of the camera. It is intended primarily as a system to confirm distances which have previously been eye-focused or made with a tape measure, rather than as a principal means of measurement. It is particularly useful when the camera is tracking in or out on a subject, or vice versa.

In most cases the PANATAPE II has a range of 2 - 15' (0.6 - 4.5m) with an accuracy of ±1" (25mm).

Fitting and operation

The PANATAPE II detects distances by means of two ultrasonic sensors which are mounted above the matte box by means of a bracket which fits on the iris rods (matte box support bars).

Lateral and vertical adjustments are provided to align the sensors with any particular foreground object although, in general, it is better to confine the use of the PANATAPE II to a single central object.

The digital read-out is mounted onto a wide angle matte box which is supplied with the system.

Before use, the PANATAPE II electronic rangefinder should be set up and tested at a number of distances to verify its accuracy.

Any necessary adjustments may be made by the control knob on the side of the display unit. Occasionally, the PANATAPE II may pick up spurious signals which may affect its accuracy but these errors are usually quite gross, and therefore obvious, and thus can easily be detected and discounted or compensated for.

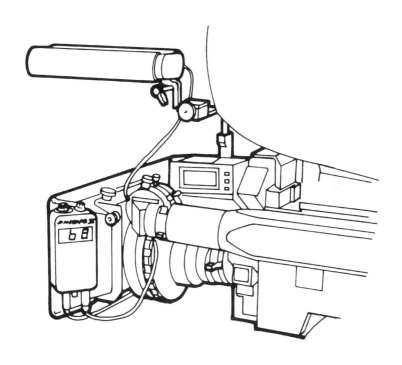

PANATAPE II electronic rangefinder

PANATATE Turnover Mount

PANATATE TURNOVER MOUNTS are available to tilt the camera about the lens axis during a shot.

Like the Nodal Adaptors, the PANATATE unit is fitted to a PANAHEAD in place of the tilt unit and can be slid backwards and forwards to place the entrance pupil of the lens in the center of the pan and tilt axes.

Fine adjustment is provided to place the camera in exactly the center of rotation so there is no displacement as the camera is rolled over.

Weights which screw into the front of the PANATATE unit are provided to partially counterweight the camera about the pan, tilt and rotational axes so that it may be panned, tilted and rotated smoothly.

Stretch the battery and any other camera cables out from the rear of the camera so they do not wrap around the PANATATE unit as it is rolled, and unwind between takes.

The Camera Operator may find it easier to operate using a video viewfinder during a take.

The PANATATE unit takes a normal PANAHEAD handwheel and has exactly the same speed change system. It may also be used with the PANAMOTE remote PANAHEAD control system.

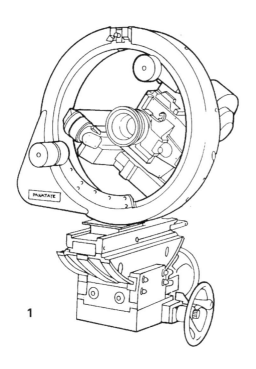

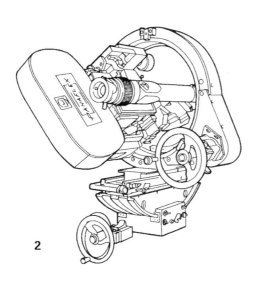

1. PANATATE turnover mount, front view showing weights, 2. PANATATE turnover mount, rear view showing handwheels.

215

PANAVISION Video Assist Systems

Since lightweight, simple-to-operate, video assist systems were first introduced PANAVISION has been at the forefront of video assist development, always advancing the state of the art and only using off-the-shelf equipment when it is advantageous to do so.

The current models include:

• PANAVISION Color Video Assist with Frameline and Character Generator. A state-of-the-art CCD system which offers flicker free "locked to the frame rate," video images at both 24 and 30 fps filming speeds. For European and other international operations a 24/25 fps PAL version is available. The Character generator will add footage, frame rate and (if fitted) PANATAPE data to the video display. This camera fits on a wedge plate which fits under the top magazine attachment plate, from which it takes its power supply.

• PANAVISION Super CCD B&W Video Assist. Gives bright, high resolution, B&W images without lag and with reduced flicker.

• PANAVID Compact CCD Bridge. A small CCD Video Assist which fits across the front of the camera that can easily be installed in the field.

• Super CCD Finder. A lightweight unit which replaces the optical finder unit for Steadicam and remote camera operations.

• Fibre optic CCD system. A super lightweight system which uses a coherent fibre optic bundle to collect the image from a 35mm size frame and reduce it down to the size of a CCD chip.

• Eyepiece video. Another CCD configuration which allows a small camera to replace the optical viewfinder tube of any regular PANAFLEX and PANASTAR camera.

• CCD Witness camera. A small video camera which can be attached or placed anywhere where visual information is required. Typical uses are to look at the lens scales of remote camera set-ups or to place alongside a focus position to check if an artist is at the expected mark, etc.

• The PANAVISION/LIGHTSTORM VID-Stick. A portable CCD viewfinder system which transmits images from a PANAFINDER type accessory.

• Frame Line Generator. A stand-alone system that displays format markings, variable intensity outside mask, camera speed and film footage. For use with color and B&W video assist systems that do not have this facility inbuilt. An advantage of this system is that it is possible to have A and B format lines and to display one or the other or both at the same time.

• As with the Frame Line Generator above, this is a stand-alone unit which superimposes footage, frame rate and PANATAPE image data on a video display.

216

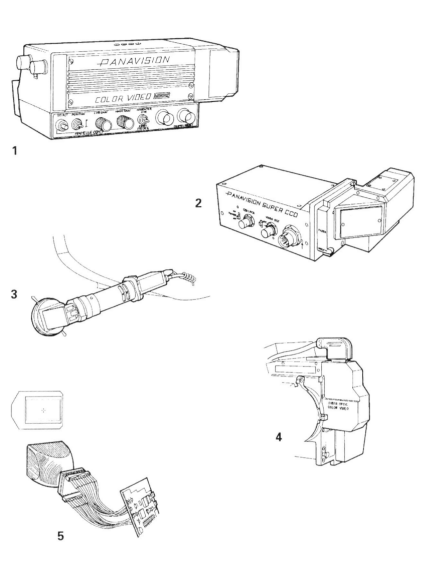

1. Combined PANAVISION CCD color video assist with character and frameline generator, 2. Super CCD B&W video assist, 3. Eyepiece CCD video assist system, 4. Lightweight video assist for Steadicam use, 5. The coherent fibre optic bundle, the CCD microchip and the tiny circuit board of the lightweight video assist.

Time Code — The AATONCODE System

The AATONCODE time code system, developed by AATON, the French camera manufacturer, is a means of encoding every frame of film with the SMPTE Time Code in a manner that can be read both by a computer and a human being.

The computer readable information may be used by a telecine machine fitted with an AATON TIME CODE READER or by an appropriately equipped film editing table to automatically synchronize picture to sound.

The secret of the AATONCODE time code marking on film lies in the method of exposing a matrix of 7 x 13 dots along the edge of the film to register both the time code and to create the normally readable alphanumeric characters.

The AATONCODE Time Code system comprises three units, The GENERATOR (fitted to the film camera), the portable ORIGIN C (used to transport the master time from the recorder to the camera) and the NAGRA IV-ST.C. fitted an AATON serial board modification.

Initializing the time code system

At the beginning of each shooting day the Camera Assistant must initialize the system by checking, and if necessary, entering the time, the date and the relevant production information into the system and synchronizing the camera and the Nagra together.

The individual clocks in both the camera and the recorder will then remain in absolute sync for at least four hours, after which they need to be briefly connected together again in order to maintain absolute sync for another four hours.

The equipment must be re-synchronised if the camera has been disconnected from a power source for 45 minutes or more.

Encoding the film during the take

Whenever the camera is running the AATONCODE system will automatically mark the exact time and then every frame number during a second, on every frame of film and on the audio tape.

Other information, such as Production number, the camera I.D. letter, etc., will be marked onto the film once every second.

A slate displaying the name of the Production and the Production Company should still be photographed onto the head of every roll of film and recorded onto every roll of tape as a means of identification.

For telecine transfer it is recommended that a traditional slate be used briefly to visually identify each scene and take, and to use the time code as a means to automatically synchronize dailies quickly, accurately and effortlessly.

218

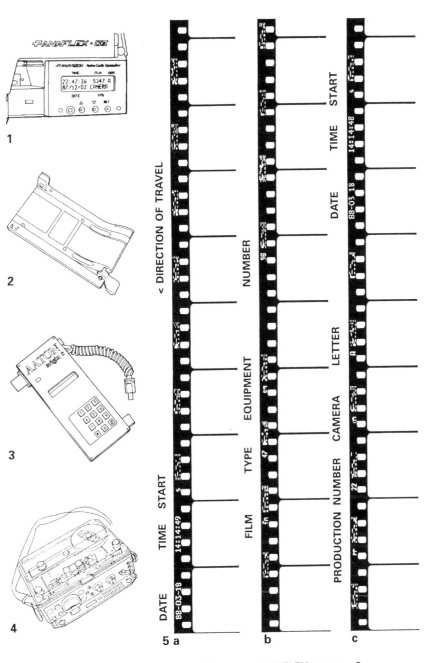

1. AATONCODE Generator or module fitted to a PANAFLEX camera, 2.
PANAFLEX aperture plate (3 PERF) showing AATONCODE exposure opening, 3.
AATON ORIGIN C module, 4. Time code panel on a NAGRA IV-ST.C. recorder,
5 a, b, & c. Strip of film showing time code edge display sequence.

Time Code — PANAVISION AATONCODE Generator Unit Overview

The PANAVISION AATONCODE Generator is fitted to the underside of a PANAFLEX camera.

The Generator, together with the special camera aperture plate and the unit which exposes the matrix of dots on the edge of the film, will have been installed into the camera before it goes onto a particular production. The Camera Assistant will not have any installation procedures to worry about.

The Generator takes its power from the film camera (it has no ON-OFF switch) and is programmed with the camera serial number before the camera leaves PANAVISION Inc.

The Generator must be synchronized with the Time Code unit within the Nagra at the start of the working day and thereafter at least every four hours, and after any period when power has been disconnected from the camera for 45 minutes or more.

If the battery has been disconnected for more than 45 minutes a red LED light will flash and a message on the LCD display will say OUT OF SYNC.

Synchronization is accomplished by transferring the time from the Nagra IV-ST.C. to the more portable ORIGIN C unit and using that to set the time in the camera.

It is good practice, when convenient, to confirm that the units are holding absolute sync.

Special note:
Productions contemplating "going Time Code" should give PANAVISION early notice as not all cameras are Time Code ready.

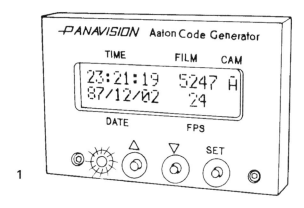

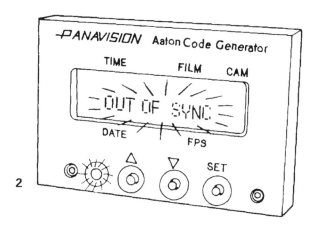

1. Generator panel displaying Time Code data settings, 2. Generator panel displaying the OUT OF SYNC message and the red LED flashing.

Time Code — PANAVISION AATONCODE Generator Unit Data Entry

The PANAVISION AATONCODE Generator will retain its real time and date settings even when the camera has been disconnected from a power source. The rest of the data need only be entered when something changes.

Entering and setting data into the AATONCODE Generator unit
Data must be entered into the Generator unit in the following sequence:

1. Set the **FILM TYPE**.

The Film Type controls the exposure of the time code 'dots' on the film (and for this reason it is imperative that it be reset correctly every time the filmstock is changed, even for a single take).

The current Film Type setting ('5247,' for instance) will always be displayed.

Press the SET button. The Film Type in the display will flash, prompting the user to set it.

Press the up and down keys to scroll backwards and forwards between the various filmstock types.

When the correct film type is displayed press the SET button.

2. Set the **CAMERA LETTER**.

After the Film Type has been set, the Camera Letter will flash.

To change the Camera Letter again press the up and down keys to scroll backwards and forwards through the alphabet.

Press the SET button when the appropriate letter is reached.

3. Set the **FPS RATE**.

After the Camera Letter has been set the FPS will flash.

As before, this is done by the use of the up and down keys and by pressing the SET button when the appropriate frame rate is displayed.

Note: At this time the system is capable of handling 24, 25, 29.97 non-drop and 30 fps time code rates. If the camera is being under or over cranked for effect the fps rate should be left at the normal production sync sound speed.

4. Set the **PRODUCTION NUMBER**.

After the fps rate has been set, the last production number entered will flash. Press the up and down keys to reach the appropriate Production Number and press the SET button.

This number will be written on the film in both machine and man readable codes.

Note: When any part of the display is flashing, waiting for an input, for longer than 30 seconds, and nothing is touched, the display will stop flashing. The SET button must then be pressed again to change the data.

222

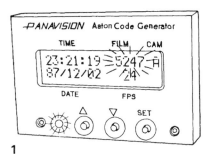

1

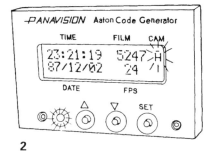

2

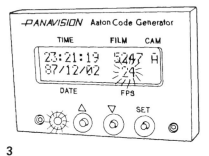

3

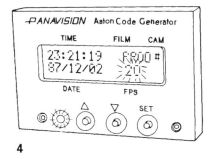

4

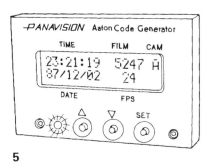

5

1. Generator panel with SET FILM TYPE display flashing, 2. Generator panel with SET CAMERA LETTER display flashing, 3. Generator panel with SET CAMERA FPS display flashing, 4. Generator panel with PRODUCTION NUMBER display flashing, 5. Generator panel with red malfunction LED flashing (call PANAVISION, or its Representative, if this happens).

Time Code —
AATONCODE/NAGRA IV-S T.C. Unit

The recommended audio recorder for Time Code operation is the stereo Nagra IV-S model fitted with a Time Code module, making it a 'Nagra IV-S T.C.'

In addition the Nagra recorder must be equipped with an AATONCODE ASCII interface board.

Checking and changing the Nagra time code settings

To operate correctly in the time code mode the frame rate must be set to that of the film camera, i.e., 24, 25 or 30 fps. This may be done by means of a rotary switch situated inside the recorder. Note: This need not necessarily be the same as the camera frame rate. At 24 fps on the camera 24 or 30 fps may be selected on the Nagra depending upon the nature of the audio post production. At 25, 29.97 non-drop or 30 fps on the camera the Nagra should be set at the same frame rate.

To check the existing Nagra time code settings press the STATUS key once to enter the status mode and then press the adjoining NEXT ST key repeatedly until the display reads either FrEE Ub or dAte Ub.

NOTE: IF FrEE Ub IS DISPLAYED, THE NAGRA WILL NOT WORK CORRECTLY WITH AATONCODE. CONSULT THE NAGRA INSTRUCTIONS TO CHANGE TO dAte Ub MODE BEFORE INITIALIZING THE NAGRA FOR AATONCODE.

Before initializing the system the Nagra must be switched to TEST.

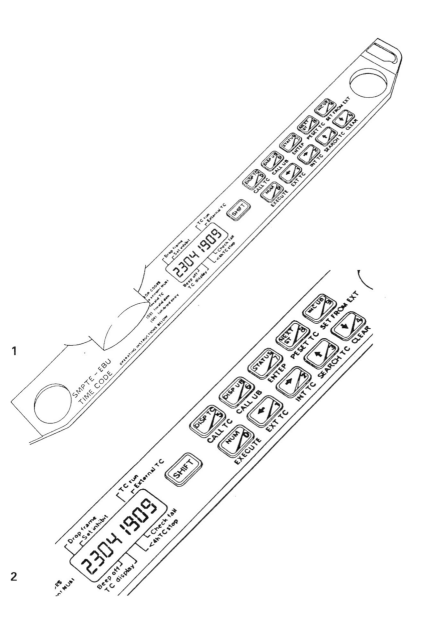

1. Nagra time code control panel,   2. Nagra time code key pad.

Time Code — Initializing the System

In practice the master time is normally taken from the time code clock inside the Nagra IV-S T.C. recorder.

Transferring data from the Nagra to the ORIGIN C unit

1. Verify that the Nagra is in dAtE Ub mode (see page 224).
2. Put the Nagra into TEST mode.
3. Switch the ORIGIN C unit ON, plug it into the Nagra recorder and press the " " key. The display should show In Control then Good. If not press the " " key again.
4. Disconnect the ORIGIN C unit from the Nagra but do not switch it OFF.

Transferring data from the ORIGIN C unit to the camera

1. Check that power is connected to the camera.
2. Plug the ORIGIN C into the camera unit socket and press the " " key.
3. The display will read bAd....REIoAd? While REIoAd is displayed again press the " " key. The display should then read In Control or Good. If it does not then press the " " key again.
4. Check the camera display to see that the code has been acquired and that the red LED is no longer flashing.
5. Repeat the process for each camera making sure that the ORIGIN C unit has not been switched off meanwhile. Note: The ORIGIN C unit will automatically switch itself off after three minutes.

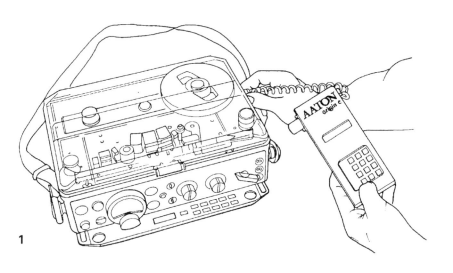

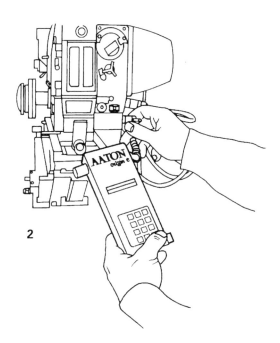

1. Transferring data between a Nagra and an ORIGIN C unit, 2. Transferring data between an ORIGIN C unit and the AATONCODE Generator on a PANAFLEX camera.

Time Code — AATON ORIGIN C Unit

The AATON ORIGIN C unit is used to carry the exact time from the time code unit in the Nagra IV-S T.C. recorder to the Generator unit in the camera.

The ORIGIN C unit may also be used to reset the date and the time settings in the Nagra, if required.

Inputting data

Original data can be entered into the ORIGIN C unit as follows:
1. Switch the unit ON.
2. The display will first ask for the Production Number (PR).
3. Enter a two digit number, i.e., '45'.
4. Press the "#" key.
5. The display will then ask for the year (Y), followed by the month, the day, the hour, the minutes and the seconds.
6. Enter two digits into each of them and press the "#" key after each entry.
7. Press the "*" key to start the clock running.
8. Press the "#" key and hold down to see the clock running.

Resetting the Nagra time and date settings

To reset the Nagra time and date settings from the ORIGIN C unit (which should already have been set correctly) plug it into the 5 pin LEMO socket on the right-hand side of the Nagra and press the "*" key. The ORIGIN C display should read bAd.....REloAd.

While REloAd is displayed again press the "*" key on the ORIGIN C. The display will say In Control....Good.

The ORIGIN C unit may then be disconnected from the Nagra and used to set the camera.

Periodically checking Time Code sync

Every two or three hours, or when convenient, the Time Code sync should be checked to be sure it is running and good:
1. Switch the unit ON and check that power is connected to the camera.
2. Plug the ORIGIN C unit into the Nagra, switch the Nagra to TEST and press the "*" key. The recorder time will be acquired by the ORIGIN C and the display will say GOOD.
3. Plug the ORIGIN C cable into the camera unit and press the "*" key. The display should also read GOOD. If it reads FAIR or BAD reload the time code into the camera by pressing the "*" again.

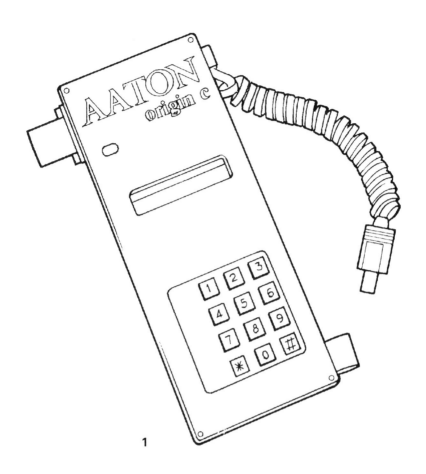

1. AATON ORIGIN C unit.

PANAVISION
PRIMO LENSES
Lens Data

PRIMO Lens Data —
Entrance Pupil Positions

All lenses have six "cardinal" points — the plane of focus (the "object plane"), the entrance pupil, the front and rear nodal points, the exit pupil and the image plane. The positioning of these six planes relative to one another is a part of the stuff that lens design is made of.

Most cinematographers are really only concerned with the plane of focus and focal plane, but for those involved in special effects work and with exacting set-ups which explore the properties of a lens to its very limits, a knowledge of where the entrance pupil falls, in particular, becomes essential.

Suffice to say that due to variations in lens design there is no consistency as to where any of the cardinal points may actually be, much less stay, as the lens is focused and zoomed. The situation is further complicated by the fact that, for practical reasons, these points are usually measured from the vertex of the front optical element but we cinematographers measure focus distances from the focal plane which, effectively, is at the other end of the lens.

With PANAVISION PRIMO *zoom* lenses the optical movements are done internally, so that although the lens lengths remain constant the principal points move separately and independently with both focus and zoom operations.

Entrance pupil positions

A knowledge of the position of the entrance pupil is particularly important to cinematographers for a number of reasons:

- It is the point about which a camera can be panned and tilted without the image being displaced. This is particularly important when shooting miniatures, ultra close-ups, front projection, glass matte shots and scenes which have to be composited at the post production stage, either digitally or in the optical printer.
- It is the point from which depth of field is calculated.
- It is also the point from which Field of View (lens angles and set-up widths and distances) is calculated.

Cardinal point positions are usually measured from the vertex of the front lens element rearwards towards the focal plane. This ensures that they remain constant to somewhere, irrespective of the focus setting. For this reason a knowledge of the overall length of a lens is also important as it enables the cinematographer to know where the cardinal point is situated relative to the tape hook.

In practice the entrance pupil position can also be found visually by mounting a camera nodally on a geared head and observing two objects, one close to the camera and one distant, as the camera is panned and tilted (see pages 206 - 207).

232

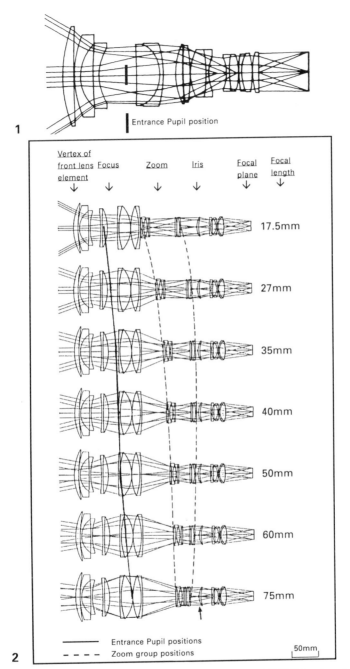

1

Entrance Pupil position

Vertex of
front lens Focus   Zoom   Iris   Focal   Focal
element   plane   length
↓   ↓   ↓   ↓   ↓   ↓

17.5mm

27mm

35mm

40mm

50mm

60mm

75mm

——— Entrance Pupil positions
- - - Zoom group positions

50mm

2

1. The Entrance Pupil position of a PANAVISION 27mm PRIMO-L prime lens,
2. The Entrance Pupil and zoom group positions of a PANAVISION 17.5 - 75mm
zoom lens throughout the zoom range.

233

PRIMO-L Lens Data —
Prime Lens Tables and Graphs

The distance of the entrance pupil forwards from the focal plane dimension is given only for guidance when setting up. With a prime lens this distance will slightly increase whenever the lens is focused closer. With a zoom lens it will probably reduce.

PANAVISION PRIMO PRIME LENS ENTRANCE PUPIL POSITIONS

Lens focal length	ENTRANCE PUPIL position rearwards from vertex of front lens element at infinity		LENGTH OF LENS from vertex of front lens element to focal plane at infinity		ENTRANCE PUPIL position forwards from focal plane at infinity	
(mm)	(in)	(mm)	(in)	(mm)	(in)	(mm)
10	1.93	48.9	7.87	199.8	5.94	150.9
14.5	1.63	41.4	6.44	163.6	4.81	122.2
17.5	1.56	39.6	5.93	150.7	4.37	111.1
21	1.91	48.4	7.02	178.4	5.11	130
27	2.15	54.6	8	203.2	5.85	148.6
35	1.9	48.2	7.58	192.5	5.68	144.3
40	2.16	54.8	7.52	191	5.36	136.2
50	2.67	67.7	8.96	227.5	6.29	159.8
75	2.02	51.3	4.51	114.6	2.49	63.3
100	2.83	71.9	5.7	144.7	2.87	72.8
150	5.23	132.8	7.66	194.5	2.43	61.7

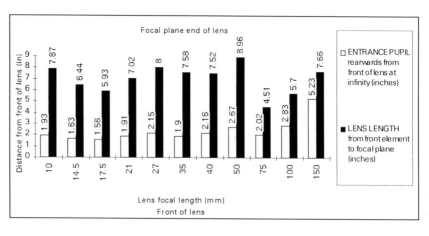

PRIMO Lens Data —
Anamorphic Lens Tables and Graphs

The positions of the principal points of PANAVISION anamorphic lenses are complicated by the fact that there are slightly different positions for both the horizontal and vertical planes, that there is an "oval" of confusion (which becomes a circle when the film is eventually projected) and by the effect of the correction optics incorporated into all PANAVISION anamorphic lenses to counter the "anamorphic mumps" effect which so afflicted pre-PANAVISION (and some later) anamorphic lenses.

ANAVISION PRIMO ANAMORPHIC LENS ENTRANCE PUPIL POSITION

Lens focal length (mm)	ENTRANCE PUPIL position *rearwards* from vertex of front lens element at infinity (in)		LENGTH OF LENS from vertex of front lens element to focal plane at infinity (in)	FRONT NODAL POINT position *reazrwards* from focal plane at infinity	
	Horizontal	Vertical		Horizontal	Vertical
35	24.75	28.28	11.36	13.39	16.92
40	24.14	27.74	11.51	12.63	16.23
50	24.02	27.92	12.91	11.11	15.01
75	21.89	27.51	10.78	11.11	16.73
100	22.54	27.64	10.15	12.39	17.49

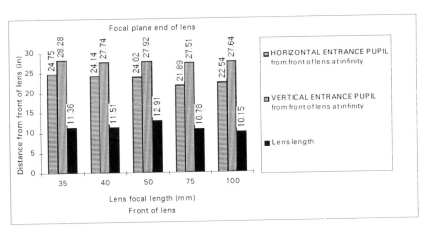

235

PRIMO Lens Data —
Zoom Lens Tables and Graphs

From the tables and graphs below the distinct design differences between a wide angle, an extended range and a telephoto type zoom lens are highlighted.

With the 17.5 - 75mm, wide angle type the entrance pupil remains fairly constant making it an ideal zoom lens to use where zooming and nodal panning must be combined.

With the 11:1, 24 - 275mm, extended range type the lens is much longer with the entrance pupil starting off about 12 inches in front of the focal plane and finishing up 10 inches behind.

The 3:1, 135 - 420mm, telephoto type zoom lens is different again. The entrance pupil starts off 11 inches behind the focal plane and finishes off somewhere behind the camera operator's head.

PANAVISION PRIMO 17.5 - 75mm, T2.3, ZOOM LENS

Length of lens from vertex of front lens element to focal plane = 13.82 in.

	FOCAL LENGTH (mm)						
	17.5	26	34	40	44	52	75
	DISTANCE (rearwards) FROM VERTEX OF FRONT LENS ELEMENT (In.)						
ENTRANCE PUPIL position at infinity	2.43	2.91	3.29	3.52	3.66	3.89	4.41
	DISTANCE (forwards) FROM FOCAL PLANE (Ins.)						
ENTRANCE PUPIL position at infinity	11.39	10.91	10.53	10.3	10.16	9.93	9.41

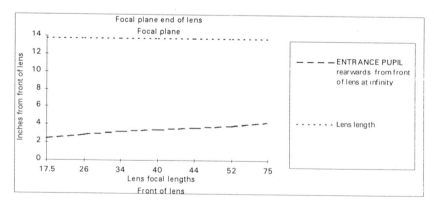

PANAVISION PRIMO 11:1, 24 - 275mm, T2.8 ZOOM LENS

Length of lens from vertex of front lens element to focal plane = 16.48 in.

	LENS FOCAL LENGTH (mm)				
	24	50	100	150	275
	DISTANCE (rearwards) FROM VERTEX OF FRONT LENS ELEMENT (In.)				
ENTRANCE PUPIL position at infinity	4.43	7.17	12.31	21.85	26.85
	DISTANCE (forwards) FROM FOCAL PLANE (Ins.)				
ENTRANCE PUPIL position at infinity	12.05	9.31	4.17	-5.37	-10.37

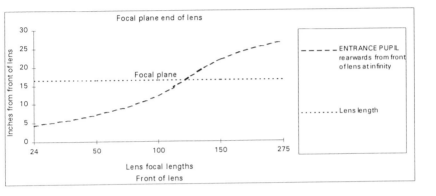

PANAVISION PRIMO 3:1, 135 - 420mm, T2.8 ZOOM LENS

Length of lens from vertex of front lens element to focal plane = 22.24 in.

	LENS FOCAL LENGTH (mm)				
	135	200	270	340	420
	DISTANCE (rearwards) FROM VERTEX OF FRONT LENS ELEMENT (In.)				
ENTRANCE PUPIL position at infinity	25.07	32.16	38.4	44.81	51.94
	DISTANCE (rearwards) FROM FOCAL PLANE (Ins.)				
ENTRANCE PUPIL position at infinity	2.83	9.92	16.16	22.57	29.7

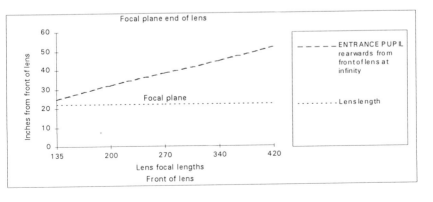

237

Subject Size/Camera Distance Tables — Academy, 1.66:1 & 1.85:1

The following tables may be used as a set-up guide to determine how far away the camera (from the focal plane) needs to be from the subject to take in a needed picture width and/or height.

35mm ACADEMY, 1.66:1 and 1.85:1

SUBJECT WIDTH / CAMERA DISTANCE

SUBJECT WIDTH	LENS FOCAL LENGTH (mm)										
	10	14.5	17.5	21	27	35	40	50	75	100	150
	LENS ANGLE (° from front entrance pupil)										
	92.7	71.7	61.8	53	42.4	33.3	29.4	23.7	15.9	12	8
	DISTANCE FROM FOCAL PLANE TO SUBJECT										
1ft							2ft 2in	2ft 4in	2ft 11in	3ft 9in	5ft 1in	7ft 4in
2ft		1ft 9in	2ft 0in	2ft 5in	3ft 1in	3ft 10in	4ft 3in	5ft 4in	7ft 4in	9ft 9in	14ft 6in
3ft	1ft 11in	2ft 6in	2ft 10in	3ft 5in	4ft 4in	5ft 6in	6ft 2in	7ft 8in	10ft 11i	14ft 7in	21ft 8in
4ft	2ft 5in	3ft 2in	3ft 8in	4ft 5in	5ft 8in	7ft 2in	8ft 1in	10ft 1in	14ft 6in	19ft 4in	28ft 10in
5ft	2ft 11in	3ft 10in	4ft 6in	5ft 5in	6ft 11in	8ft 10in	10ft 0in	12ft 5in	18ft 1in	24ft 1in	36ft 0in
6ft	3ft 4in	4ft 7in	5ft 4in	6ft 5in	8ft 3in	10ft 6in	11ft 11i	14ft 10	21ft 8in	28ft 10i	43ft 2in
7ft	3ft 10in	5ft 3in	6ft 3in	7ft 5in	9ft 6in	12ft 2in	13ft 10i	17ft 3in	25ft 3in	33ft 8in	50ft 4in
8ft	4ft 4in	5ft 11in	7ft 1in	8ft 5in	10ft 10in	13ft 10in	15ft 9in	19ft 7in	28ft 10i	38ft 5in	57ft 5in
10ft	5ft 3in	7ft 4in	8ft 9in	10ft 5in	13ft 4in	17ft 2in	19ft 6in	24ft 5in	36ft 0in	47ft 11i	71ft 9in
12ft	6ft 3in	8ft 8in	10ft 5in	12ft 5in	15ft 11in	20ft 6in	23ft 4in	29ft 2in	43ft 2in	57ft 6in	86ft 1in
15ft	7ft 8in	10ft 9in	12ft 11i	15ft 5in	19ft 10in	25ft 6in	29ft 1in	36ft 4in	53ft 11i	71ft 10i	107ft 7in
20ft	10ft 0in	14ft 3in	17ft 1in	20ft 6in	26ft 3in	33ft 10in	38ft 7in	48ft 3in	71ft 9in	95ft 8in	143ft 4in
30ft	14ft 10i	21ft 2in	25ft 5in	30ft 6in	39ft 2in	50ft 7in	57ft 8in	72ft 1in	107ft 7i	143ft 4i	214ft 11in
60ft	29ft 1in	41ft 11i	50ft 6in	60ft 6in	77ft 9in	100ft 8in	14ft 11i	143ft 8i	14ft 11i	286ft 6i	429ft 7in

35mm ACADEMY

SUBJECT HEIGHT / CAMERA DISTANCE

SUBJECT	LENS FOCAL LENGTH (mm)										
	10	14.5	17.5	21	27	35	40	50	75	100	150
	LENS ANGLE (° from front entrance pupil)										
SUBJECT	74.8	55.6	47.2	40	31.6	24.6	21.6	17.4	11.6	8.7	5.8
HEIGHT	DISTANCE FROM FOCAL PLANE TO SUBJECT										
1ft					2ft 3in	2ft 9in	3ft 1in	3ft 10in	5ft 1in	6ft 9in	10ft 0in
2ft		2ft 4in	2ft 8in	3ft 2in	4ft 1in	5ft 1in	5ft 8in	7ft 1in	10ft 1in	13ft 4in	19ft 10in
3ft	2ft 5in	3ft 3in	3ft 10in	4ft 7in	5ft 9in	7ft 4in	8ft 4in	10ft 4in	14ft 11i	19ft 10i	29ft 8in
4ft	3ft 1in	4ft 2in	4ft 11in	5ft 11in	7ft 7in	9ft 8in	10ft 11i	13ft 7in	19ft 10i	26ft 5in	39ft 5in
5ft	3ft 9in	5ft 2in	6ft 1in	7ft 4in	9ft 4in	11ft 11in	13ft 6in	16ft 10i	24ft 9in	32ft 11i	49ft 3in
6ft	4ft 5in	6ft 1in	7ft 3in	8ft 8in	11ft 1in	14ft 2in	16ft 2in	20ft 2in	29ft 8in	39ft 6in	59ft 1in
7ft	5ft 1in	7ft 0in	8ft 5in	10ft 1in	12ft 10in	16ft 6in	18ft 9in	23ft 5in	34ft 7in	46ft 1in	68ft 10in
8ft	5ft 9in	8ft 0in	9ft 6in	11ft 5in	14ft 7in	18ft 9in	21ft 5in	26ft 8in	39ft 5in	52ft 7in	78ft 8in
10ft	7ft 0in	9ft 11in	11ft 10i	14ft 2in	18ft 2in	23ft 4in	26ft 7in	33ft 3in	49ft 3in	65ft 8in	98ft 4in

35mm 1.66:1

SUBJECT HEIGHT / CAMERA DISTANCE

SUBJECT	LENS FOCAL LENGTH (mm)										
	10	14.5	17.5	21	27	35	40	50	75	100	150
	LENS ANGLE (° from front entrance pupil)										
SUBJECT	64.5	47	39.7	33.4	26.3	20.4	17.9	14.4	9.6	7.2	4.8
HEIGHT	DISTANCE FROM FOCAL PLANE TO SUBJECT										
1ft				2ft 1in	2ft 8in	3ft 3in	3ft 7in	4ft 6in	6ft 2in	8ft 2in	12ft 1in
2ft	2ft 1in	2ft 8in	3ft 2in	3ft 9in	4ft 9in	6ft 0in	6ft 9in	8ft 5in	12ft 1in	16ft 1in	23ft 12in
3ft	2ft 10in	3ft 10in	4ft 6in	5ft 5in	6ft 11in	8ft 10in	9ft 11in	12ft 5in	18ft 0in	24ft 0in	35ft 10in
4ft	3ft 8in	5ft 0in	5ft 11in	7ft 1in	9ft 1in	11ft 7in	13ft 2in	16ft 4in	24ft 0in	31ft 11i	47ft 9in
5ft	4ft 5in	6ft 2in	7ft 4in	8ft 9in	11ft 2in	14ft 4in	16ft 4in	20ft 4in	29ft 11i	39ft 10i	59ft 8in
6ft	5ft 3in	7ft 4in	8ft 8in	10ft 5in	13ft 4in	17ft 1in	19ft 6in	24ft 4in	35ft 10i	47ft 9in	71ft 6in
7ft	6ft 1in	8ft 5in	10ft 1in	12ft 1in	15ft 6in	19ft 11in	22ft 8in	28ft 3in	41ft 10i	55ft 8in	83ft 5in
8ft	6ft 10in	9ft 7in	11ft 5in	13ft 9in	17ft 7in	22ft 8in	25ft 10i	32ft 3in	47ft 9in	63ft 8in	95ft 3in
10ft	8ft 5in	11ft 11i	14ft 3in	17ft 1in	21ft 11in	28ft 2in	32ft 2in	40ft 2in	59ft 8in	79ft 6in	119ft 1in

35mm 1.85:1

SUBJECT HEIGHT / CAMERA DISTANCE

SUBJECT	LENS FOCAL LENGTH (mm)										
	10	14.5	17.5	21	27	35	40	50	75	100	150
	LENS ANGLE (° from front entrance pupil)										
SUBJECT	59.1	42.7	35.9	30.2	23.7	18.4	16.1	12.9	8.6	6.5	4.3
HEIGHT	DISTANCE FROM FOCAL PLANE TO SUBJECT										
1ft		1ft 8in	1ft 11in	2ft 3in	2ft 10in	3ft 7in	4ft 0in	4ft 11in	6ft 10in	9ft 1in	13ft 5in
2ft	2ft 3in	3ft 0in	3ft 5in	4ft 2in	5ft 3in	6ft 8in	7ft 6in	9ft 4in	13ft 5in	17ft 11i	26ft 8in
3ft	3ft 2in	4ft 3in	5ft 0in	6ft 0in	7ft 8in	9ft 9in	11ft 0in	13ft 9in	20ft 1in	26ft 9in	39ft 11in
4ft	4ft 0in	5ft 6in	6ft 7in	7ft 10in	10ft 0in	12ft 10in	14ft 7in	18ft 2in	26ft 8in	35ft 7in	53ft 2in
5ft	4ft 11in	6ft 10in	8ft 1in	9ft 8in	12ft 5in	15ft 11in	18ft 1in	22ft 7in	33ft 4in	44ft 4in	66ft 5in
6ft	5ft 9in	8ft 1in	9ft 8in	11ft 7in	14ft 9in	19ft 0in	21ft 8in	27ft 0in	39ft 11i	53ft 2in	79ft 8in
7ft	6ft 8in	9ft 4in	11ft 2in	13ft 5in	17ft 2in	22ft 1in	25ft 2in	31ft 5in	46ft 7in	62ft 0in	92ft 11in
8ft	7ft 7in	10ft 8in	12ft 9in	15ft 3in	19ft 7in	25ft 2in	28ft 8in	35ft 10i	53ft 2in	70ft 10i	106ft 1in
10ft	9ft 4in	13ft 2in	15ft 10i	19ft 0in	24ft 4in	31ft 4in	35ft 9in	44ft 8in	66ft 5in	88ft 6in	132ft 7in

Subject Size/Camera Distance Tables — Super 35

SUPER 35 - ALL FORMATS
SUBJECT WIDTH / CAMERA DISTANCE

SUBJECT WIDTH	LENS FOCAL LENGTH (mm)										
	10	14.5	17.5	21	27	35	40	50	75	100	150
	LENS ANGLE (° from front entrance pupil)										
	100.4	79.2	68.9	59.5	47.9	37.8	33.4	27	18.2	13.7	9.1
	DISTANCE FROM FOCAL PLANE TO SUBJECT										
1ft							2ft 1in	2ft 7in	3ft 4in	4ft 5in	6ft 5in
2ft		1ft 7in	1ft 10in	2ft 2in	2ft 9in	3ft 5in	3ft 9in	4ft 8in	6ft 5in	8ft 7in	12ft 8in
3ft		2ft 3in	2ft 7in	3ft 1in	3ft 10in	4ft 10in	5ft 5in	6ft 9in	9ft 7in	12ft 9in	18ft 11in
4ft	2ft 2in	2ft 10in	3ft 3in	3ft 11in	5ft 0in	6ft 4in	7ft 1in	8ft 10in	12ft 8in	16ft 11in	25ft 2in
5ft	2ft 7in	3ft 5in	4ft 0in	4ft 10in	6ft 1in	7ft 9in	8ft 9in	10ft 11in	15ft 10i	21ft 1in	31ft 5in
6ft	3ft 0in	4ft 0in	4ft 9in	5ft 8in	7ft 3in	9ft 3in	10ft 5in	13ft 0in	18ft 11i	25ft 3in	37ft 8in
7ft	3ft 5in	4ft 8in	5ft 6in	6ft 7in	8ft 4in	10ft 8in	12ft 1in	15ft 1in	22ft 1in	29ft 5in	43ft 11in
8ft	3ft 10in	5ft 3in	6ft 2in	7ft 5in	9ft 6in	12ft 2in	13ft 9in	17ft 2in	25ft 2in	33ft 7in	50ft 2in
10ft	4ft 8in	6ft 5in	7ft 8in	9ft 2in	11ft 9in	15ft 1in	17ft 1in	21ft 4in	31ft 5in	41ft 11i	62ft 8in
12ft	5ft 6in	7ft 8in	9ft 1in	10ft 11i	14ft 0in	18ft 0in	20ft 5in	25ft 6in	37ft 8in	50ft 3in	75ft 2in
15ft	6ft 9in	9ft 6in	11ft 4in	13ft 7in	17ft 4in	22ft 4in	25ft 5in	31ft 9in	47ft 1in	62ft 9in	93ft 11in
20ft	8ft 10in	12ft 6in	14ft 11i	17ft 11i	23ft 0in	29ft 8in	33ft 9in	42ft 2in	62ft 8in	83ft 7in	125ft 2in
30ft	13ft 0in	18ft 6in	22ft 3in	26ft 8in	34ft 3in	44ft 3in	50ft 5in	63ft 0in	93ft 11i	125ft 3i	187ft 8in
60ft	25ft 6in	36ft 8in	44ft 1in	52ft 11i	68ft 0in	88ft 0in	100ft 5i	125ft 6i	187ft 8i	250ft 3i	375ft 2in

SUPER 35 FOR ANAMORPHIC RELEASE

SUBJECT HEIGHT / CAMERA DISTANCE

	LENS FOCAL LENGTH (mm)										
	10	14.5	17.5	21	27	35	40	50	75	100	150
	LENS ANGLE (° from front entrance pupil)										
SUBJECT	53.1	38.1	31.9	26.8	21	16.3	14.3	11.4	7.6	5.7	3.8
HEIGHT	DISTANCE FROM FOCAL PLANE TO SUBJECT										
1ft		1ft 10in	2ft 1in	2ft 6in	3ft 2in	4ft 0in	4ft 5in	5ft 6in	7ft 8in	10ft 3in	15ft 2in
2ft	2ft 6in	3ft 4in	3ft 10in	4ft 8in	5ft 11in	7ft 6in	8ft 5in	10ft 6in	15ft 2in	20ft 3in	30ft 2in
3ft	3ft 6in	4ft 9in	5ft 7in	6ft 9in	8ft 7in	11ft 0in	12ft 5in	15ft 6in	22ft 8in	30ft 3in	45ft 2in
4ft	4ft 6in	6ft 2in	7ft 4in	8ft 10in	11ft 3in	14ft 6in	16ft 5in	20ft 6in	30ft 2in	40ft 3in	60ft 2in
5ft	5ft 6in	7ft 8in	9ft 1in	10ft 11i	14ft 0in	18ft 0in	20ft 5in	25ft 6in	37ft 8in	50ft 3in	75ft 2in
6ft	6ft 6in	9ft 1in	10ft 10i	13ft 0in	16ft 8in	21ft 6in	24ft 5in	30ft 6in	45ft 2in	60ft 3in	90ft 2in
7ft	7ft 6in	10ft 7in	12ft 7in	15ft 2in	19ft 5in	25ft 0in	28ft 5in	35ft 6in	52ft 8in	70ft 3in	105ft 2in
8ft	8ft 6in	12ft 0in	14ft 4in	17ft 3in	22ft 1in	28ft 6in	32ft 5in	40ft 6in	60ft 0in	80ft 3in	120ft 2in
10ft	10ft 6in	14ft 11i	17ft 10i	21ft 5in	27ft 6in	35ft 6in	40ft 5in	50ft 6in	75ft 2in	100ft 3i	150ft 2in

SUPER 35mm for 1.85:1 RELEASE

SUBJECT HEIGHT / CAMERA DISTANCE

	LENS FOCAL LENGTH (mm)										
	10	14.5	17.5	21	27	35	40	50	75	100	150
	LENS ANGLE (° from front entrance pupil)										
SUBJECT	66	48.2	40.7	34.3	27	21	18.4	14.8	9.9	7.4	5
HEIGHT	DISTANCE FROM FOCAL PLANE TO SUBJECT										
1ft				2ft 1in	2ft 7in	3ft 2in	3ft 6in	4ft 5in	6ft 0in	7ft 11in	11ft 9in
2ft	2ft 0in	2ft 8in	3ft 1in	3ft 8in	4ft 8in	5ft 10in	6ft 7in	8ft 3in	11ft 9in	15ft 8in	23ft 4in
3ft	2ft 10in	3ft 9in	4ft 5in	5ft 3in	6ft 9in	8ft 7in	9ft 8in	12ft 1in	17ft 7in	23ft 4in	34ft 10in
4ft	3ft 7in	4ft 10in	5ft 9in	6ft 11in	8ft 10in	11ft 3in	12ft 9in	15ft 11i	23ft 4in	31ft 1in	46ft 5in
5ft	4ft 4in	6ft 0in	7ft 1in	8ft 6in	10ft 11in	13ft 11in	15ft 10i	19ft 9in	29ft 1in	38ft 9in	58ft 0in
6ft	5ft 1in	7ft 1in	8ft 5in	10ft 2in	13ft 0in	16ft 8in	18ft 11i	23ft 8in	34ft 11i	46ft 6in	69ft 6in
7ft	5ft 11in	8ft 3in	9ft 10in	11ft 9in	15ft 1in	19ft 4in	22ft 0in	27ft 6in	40ft 8in	54ft 2in	81ft 1in
8ft	6ft 8in	9ft 4in	11ft 2in	13ft 4in	17ft 2in	22ft 1in	25ft 1in	31ft 4in	46ft 5in	61ft 10i	92ft 8in
10ft	8ft 2in	11ft 7in	13ft 10i	16ft 7in	21ft 3in	27ft 5in	31ft 3in	39ft 1in	58ft 0in	77ft 3in	115ft 9in

SUPER 35mm for 70mm RELEASE

SUBJECT HEIGHT / CAMERA DISTANCE

	LENS FOCAL LENGTH (mm)										
	10	14.5	17.5	21	27	35	40	50	75	100	150
	LENS ANGLE (° from front entrance pupil)										
SUBJECT	66	48.2	40.7	34.3	27	21	18.4	14.8	9.9	7.4	5
HEIGHT	DISTANCE FROM FOCAL PLANE TO SUBJECT										
1ft				2ft 4in	3ft 0in	3ft 8in	4ft 1in	5ft 1in	7ft 1in	9ft 5in	13ft 11in
2ft	2ft 4in	3ft 1in	3ft 7in	4ft 3in	5ft 5in	6ft 11in	7ft 9in	9ft 8in	13ft 11i	18ft 7in	27ft 8in
3ft	3ft 3in	4ft 5in	5ft 2in	6ft 2in	7ft 11in	10ft 1in	11ft 5in	14ft 3in	20ft 10i	27ft 9in	41ft 5in
4ft	4ft 2in	5ft 9in	6ft 9in	8ft 1in	10ft 5in	13ft 4in	15ft 1in	18ft 10i	27ft 8in	36ft 10i	55ft 2in
5ft	5ft 1in	7ft 0in	8ft 5in	10ft 1in	12ft 10in	16ft 6in	18ft 9in	23ft 5in	34ft 7in	46ft 0in	68ft 11in
6ft	6ft 0in	8ft 4in	10ft 0in	11ft 12i	15ft 4in	19ft 8in	22ft 5in	28ft 0in	41ft 5in	55ft 2in	82ft 7in
7ft	6ft 11in	9ft 8in	11ft 7in	13ft 11i	17ft 10in	22ft 11in	26ft 1in	32ft 7in	48ft 3in	64ft 4in	96ft 4in
8ft	7ft 10in	11ft 0in	13ft 2in	15ft 10i	20ft 3in	26ft 1in	29ft 9in	37ft 2in	55ft 2in	73ft 6in	110ft 1in
10ft	9ft 8in	13ft 8in	16ft 5in	19ft 8in	25ft 3in	32ft 6in	37ft 1in	46ft 4in	68ft 11i	91ft 10i	137ft 7in

Subject Size/Camera Distance Tables — TV & Anamorphic

35mm - TV TRANSMITTED AREA
SUBJECT WIDTH / CAMERA DISTANCE

	LENS FOCAL LENGTH (mm)										
	10	14.5	17.5	21	27	35	40	50	75	100	150
	HORIZONTAL LENS ANGLE (°from front entrance pupil)										
SUBJECT	90.3	69.5	59.8	51.2	40.9	32.1	28.2	22.8	15.3	11.5	7.7
WIDTH	DISTANCE FROM FOCAL PLANE TO SUBJECT										
1ft						2ft 3in	2ft 5in	3ft 0in	3ft 11in	5ft 3in	7ft 8in
2ft		1ft 10in	2ft 1in	2ft 6in	3ft 2in	3ft 11in	4ft 5in	5ft 6in	7ft 8in	10ft 2in	15ft 1in
3ft		2ft 7in	3ft 0in	3ft 7in	4ft 6in	5ft 8in	6ft 5in	8ft 0in	11ft 5in	15ft 2in	22ft 7in
4ft	2ft 6in	3ft 3in	3ft 10in	4ft 7in	5ft 10in	7ft 5in	8ft 5in	10ft 6in	15ft 1in	20ft 1in	30ft 0in
5ft	3ft 0in	4ft 0in	4ft 9in	5ft 8in	7ft 2in	9ft 2in	10ft 5in	12ft 11i	18ft 10i	25ft 1in	37ft 6in
6ft	3ft 6in	4ft 9in	5ft 7in	6ft 8in	8ft 6in	10ft 11in	12ft 5in	15ft 5in	22ft 7in	30ft 1in	44ft 11in
7ft	4ft 0in	5ft 5in	6ft 5in	7ft 9in	9ft 11in	12ft 8in	14ft 4in	17ft 11i	26ft 4in	35ft 0in	52ft 5in
8ft	4ft 6in	6ft 2in	7ft 4in	8ft 9in	11ft 3in	14ft 5in	16ft 4in	20ft 5in	30ft 0in	40ft 0in	59ft 10in
10ft	5ft 6in	7ft 7in	9ft 1in	10ft 10i	13ft 11in	17ft 10in	20ft 4in	25ft 5in	37ft 6in	49ft 11i	74ft 9in
12ft	6ft 6in	9ft 1in	10ft 10i	12ft 11i	16ft 7in	21ft 4in	24ft 4in	30ft 4in	44ft 11i	59ft 11i	89ft 8in
15ft	7ft 11in	11ft 3in	13ft 5in	16ft 1in	20ft 7in	26ft 7in	30ft 3in	37ft 10i	56ft 1in	74ft 9in	112ft 0in
20ft	10ft 5in	14ft 10i	17ft 9in	21ft 4in	27ft 4in	35ft 3in	40ft 2in	50ft 3in	74ft 9in	99ft 8in	149ft 4in
30ft	15ft 5in	22ft 0in	26ft 5in	31ft 9in	40ft 9in	52ft 8in	60ft 1in	75ft 1in	112ft 0i	149ft 4i	223ft 10i
60ft	30ft 4in	43ft 8in	52ft 7in	63ft 1in	81ft 0in	104ft 10i	119ft 9i	149ft 8i	23ft 10i	298ft 5i	447ft 6in

35mm - TV TRANSMITTED AREA
SUBJECT HEIGHT / CAMERA DISTANCE

	LENS FOCAL LENGTH (mm)										
	10	14.5	17.5	21	27	35	40	50	75	100	150
	LENS ANGLE (°from front entrance pupil)										
SUBJECT	74.1	55	46.6	39.5	31.2	24.3	21.4	17.2	11.5	8.6	5.8
HEIGHT	DISTANCE FROM FOCAL PLANE TO SUBJECT										
1ft					2ft 3in	2ft 10in	3ft 1in	3ft 10in	5ft 2in	6ft 10in	10ft 2in
2ft		2ft 4in	2ft 8in	3ft 3in	4ft 1in	5ft 1in	5ft 9in	7ft 2in	10ft 2in	13ft 6in	20ft 1in
3ft	2ft 6in	3ft 3in	3ft 10in	4ft 7in	5ft 10in	7ft 5in	8ft 5in	10ft 6in	15ft 1in	20ft 1in	30ft 0in
4ft	3ft 2in	4ft 3in	5ft 0in	6ft 0in	7ft 8in	9ft 9in	11ft 1in	13ft 9in	20ft 1in	26ft 9in	40ft 0in
5ft	3ft 10in	5ft 2in	6ft 2in	7ft 5in	9ft 5in	12ft 1in	13ft 8in	17ft 1in	25ft 1in	33ft 4in	49ft 11in
6ft	4ft 6in	6ft 2in	7ft 4in	8ft 9in	11ft 3in	14ft 5in	16ft 4in	20ft 5in	30ft 0in	40ft 0in	59ft 10in
7ft	5ft 2in	7ft 2in	8ft 6in	10ft 2in	13ft 0in	16ft 9in	19ft 0in	23ft 9in	35ft 0in	46ft 8in	69ft 9in
8ft	5ft 10in	8ft 1in	9ft 8in	11ft 7in	14ft 10in	19ft 0in	21ft 8in	27ft 0in	40ft 0in	53ft 3in	79ft 9in
10ft	7ft 1in	10ft 0in	12ft 0in	14ft 4in	18ft 5in	23ft 8in	26ft 11i	33ft 8in	49ft 11i	66ft 6in	99ft 7in

35mm ANAMORPHIC

SUBJECT WIDTH / CAMERA DISTANCE

SUBJECT WIDTH	LENS FOCAL LENGTH (mm)				
	35	40	50	75	100
	HORIZONTAL LENS ANGLE (°)				
	67.6	59.6	48	32.4	24.4
	DISTANCE				
1ft					
2ft				3ft 6in	4ft 8in
3ft			3ft 6in	5ft 3in	7ft 1in
4ft		3ft 9in	4ft 8in	7ft 1in	9ft 5in
5ft	4ft 1in	4ft 8in	5ft 10in	8ft 10in	11ft 9in
6ft	4ft 11in	5ft 8in	7ft 1in	10ft 7in	14ft 1in
7ft	5ft 9in	6ft 7in	8ft 3in	12ft 4in	16ft 5in
8ft	6ft 7in	7ft 6in	9ft 5in	14ft 1in	18ft 9in
10ft	8ft 3in	9ft 5in	11ft 9in	17ft 7in	23ft 6in
12ft	9ft 10in	11ft 3in	14ft 1in	21ft 2in	28ft 2in
15ft	12ft 4in	14ft 1in	17ft 7in	26ft 5in	35ft 3in
20ft	16ft 5in	18ft 9in	23ft 6in	35ft 3in	47ft 0in
30ft	24ft 8in	28ft 2in	35ft 3in	52ft 10i	70ft 5in
60ft	49ft 4in	56ft 4in	70ft 5in	105ft 8i	140ft 11in

35mm ANAMORPHIC

SUBJECT HEIGHT / CAMERA DISTANCE

SUBJECT HEIGHT	LENS FOCAL LENGTH (mm)				
	35	40	50	75	100
	VERTICAL LENS ANGLE (°)				
	28.5	25.1	20.2	13.5	10.2
	DISTANCE				
1ft				4ft 3in	5ft 7in
2ft	3ft 11in	4ft 6in	5ft 7in	8ft 5in	11ft 3in
3ft	5ft 11in	6ft 9in	8ft 5in	12ft 8in	16ft 10in
4ft	7ft 10in	9ft 0in	11ft 3in	16ft 10i	22ft 6in
5ft	9ft 10in	11ft 3in	14ft 1in	21ft 1in	28ft 1in
6ft	11ft 10i	13ft 6in	16ft 10i	25ft 4in	33ft 9in
7ft	13ft 9in	15ft 9in	19ft 8in	29ft 6in	39ft 4in
8ft	15ft 9in	18ft 0in	22ft 6in	33ft 9in	45ft 0in
10ft	19ft 8in	22ft 6in	28ft 1in	42ft 2in	56ft 3in

Camera Distance/Subject Size Tables — Academy, 1.66:1 & 1.85:1

The following tables may be used as a set-up guide to determine how wide or high the picture area will be when the camera is set up from a known distance from the focal plane.

35mm ACADEMY, 1.66:1 and 1.85:1
CAMERA DISTANCE / SCENE WIDTH

	LENS FOCAL LENGTH (mm)										
	10	14.5	17.5	21	27	35	40	50	75	100	150
	HORIZONTAL LENS ANGLE (° from front entrance pupil)										
FOCUS	92.7	71.7	61.8	53	42.4	33.3	29.4	23.7	15.9	12	8
DISTANCE	SCENE WIDTH										
2ft 0in	3ft 2in	2ft 4in	2ft 0in	1ft 7in	1ft 2in	0ft 11in	0ft 10in	0ft 7in	0ft 6in		
2ft 6in	4ft 2in	3ft 0in	2ft 7in	2ft 1in	1ft 7in	1ft 3in	1ft 1in	0ft 10in	0ft 8in		
3ft 0in	5ft 3in	3ft 9in	3ft 2in	2ft 7in	1ft 11in	1ft 6in	1ft 4in	1ft 0in	0ft 9in	0ft 7in	
4ft 0in	7ft 4in	5ft 2in	4ft 4in	3ft 7in	2ft 9in	2ft 1in	1ft 10in	1ft 5in	1ft 1in	0ft 9in	
5ft 0in	9ft 5in	6ft 8in	5ft 7in	4ft 7in	3ft 6in	2ft 9in	2ft 5in	1ft 11in	1ft 4in	1ft 0in	
6ft 0in	11ft 6in	8ft 1in	6ft 9in	5ft 7in	4ft 3in	3ft 4in	2ft 11in	2ft 4in	1ft 7in	1ft 2in	0ft 10in
7ft 0in	13ft 8in	9ft 6in	7ft 11in	6ft 7in	5ft 1in	3ft 11in	3ft 5in	2ft 9in	1ft 11in	1ft 5in	0ft 11in
8ft 0in	15ft 9in	11ft 0in	9ft 2in	7ft 7in	5ft 10in	4ft 6in	3ft 11in	3ft 2in	2ft 2in	1ft 8in	1ft 1in
9ft 0in	17ft 10in	12ft 5in	10ft 4in	8ft 7in	6ft 7in	5ft 1in	4ft 6in	3ft 7in	2ft 5in	1ft 10in	1ft 3in
10ft 0in	19ft 11in	13ft 11in	11ft 6in	9ft 7in	7ft 5in	5ft 8in	5ft 0in	4ft 0in	2ft 9in	2ft 1in	1ft 4in
12ft 0in	24ft 1in	16ft 9in	13ft 11in	11ft 7in	8ft 11in	6ft 11in	6ft 1in	4ft 10in	3ft 4in	2ft 6in	1ft 8in
15ft 0in	30ft 5in	21ft 1in	17ft 6in	14ft 7in	11ft 3in	8ft 8in	7ft 7in	6ft 1in	4ft 2in	3ft 1in	2ft 1in
20ft 0in	40ft 11in	28ft 4in	23ft 6in	19ft 6in	15ft 2in	11ft 8in	10ft 3in	8ft 2in	5ft 6in	4ft 2in	2ft 9in
30ft 0in	61ft 10in	42ft 9in	35ft 6in	29ft 6in	22ft 11in	17ft 8in	15ft 6in	12ft 4in	8ft 4in	6ft 3in	4ft 2in
60ft 0in	124ft 9in	86ft 2in	71ft 5in	59ft 6in	46ft 2in	35ft 8in	31ft 2in	24ft 11in	16ft 9in	12ft 6in	8ft 4in

35mm ACADEMY
CAMERA DISTANCE / SCENE HEIGHT

FOCUS DISTANCE	LENS FOCAL LENGTH (mm)										
	10	14.5	17.5	21	27	35	40	50	75	100	150
	VERTICAL LENS ANGLE (° from front entrance pupil)										
	74.8	55.6	47.2	40	31.6	24.6	21.6	17.4	11.6	8.7	5.8
	SCENE HEIGHT										
2ft 0in	2ft 4in	1ft 8in	1ft 5in	1ft 2in	0ft 10in	0ft 8in	0ft 7in	0ft 5in	0ft 4in		
2ft 6in	3ft 1in	2ft 1in	1ft 10in	1ft 6in	1ft 2in	0ft 11in	0ft 9in	0ft 7in	0ft 6in		
3ft 0in	3ft 10in	2ft 9in	2ft 4in	1ft 10in	1ft 5in	1ft 1in	1ft 0in	0ft 9in	0ft 7in	0ft 5in	
4ft 0in	5ft 4in	3ft 10in	3ft 2in	2ft 7in	2ft 0in	1ft 6in	1ft 4in	1ft 1in	0ft 9in	0ft 7in	
5ft 0in	6ft 11in	4ft 10in	4ft 1in	3ft 4in	2ft 7in	2ft 0in	1ft 9in	1ft 4in	1ft 0in	0ft 9in	
6ft 0in	8ft 5in	5ft 11in	4ft 11in	4ft 1in	3ft 1in	2ft 5in	2ft 1in	1ft 8in	1ft 2in	0ft 11in	0ft 7in
7ft in	9ft 11in	7ft 0in	5ft 10in	4ft 9in	3ft 8in	2ft 10in	2ft 6in	2ft 0in	1ft 5in	1ft 0in	0ft 8in
8ft 0in	11ft 6in	8ft 0in	6ft 8in	5ft 6in	4ft 3in	3ft 3in	2ft 11in	2ft 3in	1ft 7in	1ft 2in	0ft 10in
9ft 0in	13ft 0in	9ft 1in	7ft 7in	6ft 3in	4ft 10in	3ft 9in	3ft 3in	2ft 7in	1ft 10in	1ft 4in	0ft 11in
10ft 0in	14ft 6in	10ft 1in	8ft 5in	7ft 0in	5ft 5in	4ft 2in	3ft 8in	2ft 11in	2ft 0in	1ft 6in	1ft 0in

35mm 1.66:1
CAMERA DISTANCE / SCENE HEIGHT

FOCUS DISTANCE	LENS FOCAL LENGTH (mm)										
	10	14.5	17.5	21	27	35	40	50	75	100	150
	VERTICAL LENS ANGLE (° from front entrance pupil)										
	64.5	47	39.7	33.4	26.3	20.4	17.9	14.4	9.6	7.2	4.8
	SCENE HEIGHT										
2ft 0in	1ft 11in	1ft 5in	1ft 2in	0ft 11in	0ft 8in	0ft 7in	0ft 6in	0ft 4in	0ft 4in		
2ft 6in	2ft 6in	1ft 10in	1ft 6in	1ft 3in	0ft 11in	0ft 9in	0ft 8in	0ft 6in	0ft 5in		
3ft 0in	3ft 2in	2ft 3in	1ft 11in	1ft 7in	1ft 2in	0ft 11in	0ft 10in	0ft 7in	0ft 6in	0ft 4in	
4ft 0in	4ft 5in	3ft 2in	2ft 7in	2ft 2in	1ft 8in	1ft 3in	1ft 1in	0ft 11in	0ft 8in	0ft 6in	
5ft 0in	5ft 8in	4ft 0in	3ft 4in	2ft 9in	2ft 1in	1ft 8in	1ft 5in	1ft 2in	0ft 10in	0ft 7in	
6ft 0in	6ft 11in	4ft 10in	4ft 1in	3ft 4in	2ft 7in	2ft 0in	1ft 9in	1ft 5in	1ft 0in	0ft 9in	0ft 6in
7ft in	8ft 3in	5ft 9in	4ft 9in	3ft 11in	3ft 1in	2ft 4in	2ft 1in	1ft 8in	1ft 2in	1ft 0in	0ft 7in
8ft 0in	9ft 6in	6ft 7in	5ft 6in	4ft 7in	3ft 6in	2ft 9in	2ft 5in	1ft 11in	1ft 4in	1ft 0in	0ft 8in
9ft 0in	10ft 9in	7ft 6in	6ft 3in	5ft 2in	4ft 0in	3ft 1in	2ft 8in	2ft 2in	1ft 6in	1ft 1in	0ft 9in
10ft 0in	12ft 0in	8ft 4in	6ft 11in	5ft 9in	4ft 5in	3ft 5in	3ft 0in	2ft 5in	1ft 8in	1ft 3in	0ft 10in

35mm 1.85:1
CAMERA DISTANCE / SCENE HEIGHT

FOCUS DISTANCE	LENS FOCAL LENGTH (mm)										
	10	14.5	17.5	21	27	35	40	50	75	100	150
	VERTICAL LENS ANGLE (° from front entrance pupil)										
	59.1	42.7	35.9	30.2	23.7	18.4	16.1	12.9	8.6	6.5	4.3
	SCENE HEIGHT										
2ft 0in	1ft in	1ft 3in	1ft 1in	0ft 10in	0ft 8in	0ft 6in	0ft 5in	0ft 4in	0ft 3in		
2ft 6in	2ft 3in	1ft 8in	1ft 5in	1ft 1in	0ft 10in	0ft 8in	0ft 7in	0ft 5in	0ft 4in		
3ft 0in	2ft 10in	2ft 0in	1ft 8in	1ft 5in	1ft 1in	0ft 10in	0ft 9in	0ft 7in	0ft 6in	0ft 4in	
4ft 0in	4ft 0in	2ft 10in	2ft 4in	1ft 11in	1ft 6in	1ft 2in	1ft 0in	0ft 9in	0ft 7in	0ft 5in	
5ft 0in	5ft 1in	3ft 7in	3ft 0in	2ft 6in	1ft 11in	1ft 6in	1ft 3in	1ft 0in	0ft 9in	0ft 6in	
6ft 0in	6ft 3in	4ft 5in	3ft 8in	3ft 0in	2ft 4in	1ft 9in	1ft 7in	1ft 3in	0ft 11in	0ft 8in	0ft 5in
7ft in	7ft 4in	5ft 2in	4ft 4in	3ft 7in	2ft 9in	2ft 1in	1ft 10in	1ft 6in	1ft 0in	0ft 9in	0ft 6in
8ft 0in	8ft 6in	5ft 11in	4ft 11in	4ft 1in	3ft 2in	2ft 5in	2ft 2in	1ft 8in	1ft 2in	0ft 11in	0ft 7in
9ft 0in	9ft 8in	6ft 9in	5ft 7in	4ft 8in	3ft 7in	2ft 9in	2ft 5in	1ft 11in	1ft 4in	1ft 0in	0ft 8in
10ft 0in	10ft 9in	7ft 6in	6ft 3in	5ft 2in	4ft 0in	3ft 1in	2ft 8in	2ft 2in	1ft 6in	1ft 1in	0ft 9in

Camera Distance/Subject Size Tables — Super 35

SUPER 35 - SCENE WIDTH for ALL FORMATS
CAMERA DISTANCE / SCENE WIDTH

	LENS FOCAL LENGTH (mm)										
	10	14.5	17.5	21	27	35	40	50	75	100	150
	LENS ANGLE (° from front entrance pupil)										
FOCUS	100.4	79.2	68.9	59.5	47.9	37.8	33.4	27	18.2	13.7	9.1
DISTANCE	SCENE WIDTH										
2ft 0in	3ft 7in	2ft 8in	2ft 3in	1ft 10in	1ft 4in	1ft 1in	0ft 11in	0ft 9in	0ft 7in		
2ft 6in	4ft 10in	3ft 6in	2ft 11in	2ft 4in	1ft 9in	1ft 5in	1ft 3in	0ft 11in	0ft 9in		
3ft 0in	6ft 0in	4ft 4in	3ft 7in	2ft 11in	2ft 3in	1ft 9in	1ft 6in	1ft 2in	0ft 11in	0ft 8in	
4ft 0in	8ft 5in	5ft 11in	5ft 0in	4ft 1in	3ft 1in	2ft 5in	2ft 2in	1ft 8in	1ft 3in	0ft 11in	
5ft 0in	10ft 10in	7ft 7in	6ft 4in	5ft 3in	4ft 0in	3ft 1in	2ft 9in	2ft 2in	1ft 6in	1ft 2in	
6ft 0in	13ft 3in	9ft 3in	7ft 9in	6ft 4in	4ft 11in	3ft 9in	3ft 4in	2ft 8in	1ft 10in	1ft 5in	0ft 11in
7ft 0in	15ft 7in	10ft 11in	9ft 1in	7ft 6in	5ft 9in	4ft 6in	3ft 11in	3ft 1in	2ft 2in	1ft 7in	1ft 1in
8ft 0in	18ft 0in	12ft 7in	10ft 6in	8ft 8in	6ft 8in	5ft 2in	4ft 6in	3ft 7in	2ft 6in	1ft 10in	1ft 3in
9ft 0in	20ft 5in	14ft 3in	11ft 10in	9ft 10in	7ft 7in	5ft 10in	5ft 2in	4ft 1in	2ft 10in	2ft 1in	1ft 5in
10ft 0in	22ft 10in	15ft 11in	13ft 3in	10ft 11in	8ft 5in	6ft 6in	5ft 9in	4ft 7in	3ft 2in	2ft 4in	1ft 7in
12ft 0in	27ft 7in	19ft 2in	15ft 11in	13ft 3in	10ft 3in	7ft 11in	6ft 11in	5ft 6in	3ft 9in	2ft 10in	1ft 11in
15ft 0in	34ft 10in	24ft 2in	20ft 1in	16ft 8in	12ft 11in	10ft 0in	8ft 9in	6ft 11in	4ft 9in	3ft 7in	2ft 4in
20ft 0in	46ft 10in	32ft 5in	26ft 11in	22ft 4in	17ft 4in	13ft 5in	11ft 9in	9ft 4in	6ft 4in	4ft 9in	3ft 2in
30ft 0in	70ft 10in	49ft 0in	40ft 8in	33ft 10in	26ft 3in	20ft 3in	17ft 9in	14ft 2in	9ft 6in	7ft 2in	4ft 9in
60ft 0in	42ft 10i	98ft 8in	81ft 9in	68ft 1in	52ft 11in	40ft 10in	35ft 9in	28ft 7in	19ft 2in	14ft 4in	9ft 7in

SUPER 35 for ANAMORPHIC RELEASE
CAMERA DISTANCE / SCENE HEIGHT

FOCUS DISTANCE	LENS FOCAL LENGTH (mm)										
	10	14.5	17.5	21	27	35	40	50	75	100	150
	LENS ANGLE (° from front entrance pupil)										
	53.1	38.1	31.9	26.8	21	16.3	14.3	11.4	7.6	5.7	3.8
	SCENE HEIGHT										
2ft 0in	1ft 6in	1ft 1in	0ft 11in	0ft 9in	0ft 7in	0ft 5in	0ft 5in	0ft 4in	0ft 3in		
2ft 6in	2ft 0in	1ft 5in	1ft 3in	1ft 0in	0ft 9in	0ft 7in	0ft 6in	0ft 5in	0ft 4in		
3ft 0in	2ft 6in	1ft 10in	1ft 6in	1ft 3in	0ft 11in	0ft 9in	0ft 8in	0ft 6in	0ft 4in	0ft 3in	
4ft 0in	3ft 6in	2ft 6in	2ft 1in	1ft 8in	1ft 4in	1ft 0in	0ft 11in	0ft 8in	0ft 6in	0ft 5in	
5ft 0in	4ft 6in	3ft 2in	2ft 8in	2ft 2in	1ft 8in	1ft 4in	1ft 2in	0ft 11in	0ft 8in	0ft 6in	
6ft 0in	5ft 6in	3ft 10in	3ft 3in	2ft 8in	2ft 0in	1ft 7in	1ft 5in	1ft 1in	0ft 9in	0ft 7in	0ft 5in
7ft in	6ft 6in	4ft 7in	3ft 9in	3ft 2in	2ft 5in	1ft 10in	1ft 8in	1ft 4in	0ft 11in	0ft 8in	0ft 5in
8ft 0in	7ft 6in	5ft 3in	4ft 4in	3ft 7in	2ft 9in	2ft 2in	1ft 11in	1ft 6in	1ft 0in	0ft 9in	0ft 6in
9ft 0in	8ft 6in	5ft 11in	4ft 11in	4ft 1in	3ft 2in	2ft 5in	2ft 2in	1ft 8in	1ft 2in	0ft 11in	0ft 7in
10ft 0in	9ft 6in	6ft 7in	5ft 6in	4ft 7in	3ft 6in	2ft 9in	2ft 5in	1ft 11in	1ft 4in	1ft 0in	0ft 8in

SUPER 35 FOR 1.85:1 RELEASE
CAMERA DISTANCE / SCENE HEIGHT

FOCUS DISTANCE	LENS FOCAL LENGTH (mm)										
	10	14.5	17.5	21	27	35	40	50	75	100	150
	LENS ANGLE (° from front entrance pupil)										
	64.5	47	39.7	33.4	26.3	20.4	17.9	14.4	9.6	7.2	4.8
	SCENE HEIGHT										
2ft 0in	1ft 11in	1ft 5in	1ft 3in	1ft 0in	0ft 9in	0ft 7in	0ft 6in	0ft 5in	0ft 4in		
2ft 6in	2ft 7in	1ft 11in	1ft 7in	1ft 3in	1ft 0in	0ft 9in	0ft 8in	0ft 6in	0ft 5in		
3ft 0in	3ft 3in	2ft 4in	1ft 11in	1ft 7in	1ft 2in	0ft 11in	0ft 10in	0ft 8in	0ft 6in	0ft 4in	
4ft 0in	4ft 7in	3ft 3in	2ft 8in	2ft 2in	1ft 8in	1ft 4in	1ft 2in	0ft 11in	0ft 8in	0ft 6in	
5ft 0in	5ft 10in	4ft 1in	3ft 5in	2ft 10in	2ft 2in	1ft 8in	1ft 6in	1ft 2in	0ft 10in	0ft 7in	
6ft 0in	7ft 2in	5ft 0in	4ft 2in	3ft 5in	2ft 8in	2ft 1in	1ft 10in	1ft 5in	1ft 0in	0ft 9in	0ft 6in
7ft 0in	8ft 5in	5ft 11in	4ft 11in	4ft 1in	3ft 2in	2ft 5in	2ft 2in	1ft 8in	1ft 2in	0ft 11in	0ft 7in
8ft 0in	9ft 9in	6ft 10in	5ft 8in	4ft 8in	3ft 7in	2ft 9in	2ft 5in	1ft 11in	1ft 4in	1ft 0in	0ft 8in
9ft 0in	11ft 0in	7ft 8in	6ft 5in	5ft 4in	4ft 1in	3ft 2in	2ft 9in	2ft 2in	1ft 6in	1ft 2in	0ft 9in
10ft 0in	12ft 4in	8ft 7in	7ft 2in	5ft 11in	4ft 7in	3ft 6in	3ft 1in	2ft 6in	1ft 8in	1ft 3in	0ft 10in

35mm for 70mm RELEASE
CAMERA DISTANCE / SCENE HEIGHT

FOCUS DISTANCE	LENS FOCAL LENGTH (mm)										
	10	14.5	17.5	21	27	35	40	50	75	100	150
	LENS ANGLE (° from front entrance pupil)										
	57.3	41.3	34.7	29.1	22.9	17.7	15.5	12.5	8.3	6.3	4.2
	DISTANCE FROM FOCAL PLANE TO SUBJECT										
2ft 0in	1ft 8in	1ft 2in	1ft 0in	0ft 10in	0ft 7in	0ft 6in	0ft 5in	0ft 4in	0ft 3in		
2ft 6in	2ft 2in	1ft 7in	1ft 4in	1ft 1in	0ft 10in	0ft 8in	0ft 7in	0ft 5in	0ft 4in		
3ft 0in	2ft 9in	1ft 11in	1ft 8in	1ft 4in	1ft 0in	0ft 9in	0ft 8in	0ft 6in	0ft 5in	0ft 4in	
4ft 0in	3ft 10in	2ft 9in	2ft 3in	1ft 10in	1ft 5in	1ft 1in	0ft 12in	0ft 9in	0ft 7in	0ft 5in	
5ft 0in	4ft 11in	3ft 6in	2ft 11in	2ft 5in	1ft 10in	1ft 5in	1ft 3in	0ft 12in	0ft 8in	0ft 6in	
6ft 0in	6ft 0in	4ft 3in	3ft 6in	2ft 11in	2ft 3in	1ft 9in	1ft 6in	1ft 2in	0ft 10in	0ft 8in	0ft 5in
7ft in	7ft 1in	5ft 0in	4ft 2in	3ft 5in	2ft 8in	2ft 0in	1ft 9in	1ft 5in	0ft 12in	0ft 9in	0ft 6in
8ft 0in	8ft 2in	5ft 9in	4ft 9in	4ft 0in	3ft 0in	2ft 4in	2ft 1in	1ft 8in	1ft 2in	0ft 10in	0ft 7in
9ft 0in	9ft 3in	6ft 6in	5ft 5in	4ft 5in	3ft 5in	2ft 8in	2ft 4in	1ft 10in	1ft 3in	1ft 0in	0ft 8in
10ft 0in	10ft 5in	7ft 3in	6ft 0in	4ft 12in	3ft 10in	2ft 12in	2ft 7in	2ft 1in	1ft 5in	1ft 1in	0ft 9in

Camera Distance/Subject Size Tables — TV & Anamorphic

35mm - TV TRANSMITTED AREA
CAMERA DISTANCE / SCENE WIDTH

	LENS FOCAL LENGTH (mm)										
	10	14.5	17.5	21	27	35	40	50	75	100	150
	HORIZONTAL LENS ANGLE (°from front entrance pupil)										
FOCUS	90.3	69.5	59.8	51.2	40.9	32.1	28.2	22.8	15.3	11.5	7.7
DISTANCE	SCENE WIDTH										
2ft 0in	3ft 0in	2ft 3in	1ft 11in	1ft 6in	1ft 2in	0ft 11in	0ft 9in	0ft 7in	0ft 6in		
2ft 6in	4ft 0in	2ft 11in	2ft 5in	1ft 12in	1ft 6in	1ft 2in	1ft 0in	0ft 10in	0ft 7in		
3ft 0in	5ft 0in	3ft 7in	3ft 0in	2ft 6in	1ft 10in	1ft 5in	1ft 3in	1ft 0in	0ft 9in	0ft 7in	
4ft 0in	7ft 1in	5ft 0in	4ft 2in	3ft 5in	2ft 7in	2ft 0in	1ft 9in	1ft 5in	1ft 0in	0ft 9in	
5ft 0in	9ft 1in	6ft 5in	5ft 4in	4ft 5in	3ft 4in	2ft 7in	2ft 3in	1ft 10in	1ft 3in	0ft 11in	
6ft 0in	11ft 1in	7ft 9in	6ft 6in	5ft 4in	4ft 1in	3ft 2in	2ft 10in	2ft 2in	1ft 7in	1ft 2in	0ft 9in
7ft 0in	13ft 1in	9ft 2in	7ft 8in	6ft 4in	4ft 10in	3ft 9in	3ft 4in	2ft 7in	1ft 10in	1ft 4in	0ft 11in
8ft 0in	15ft 1in	10ft 7in	8ft 9in	7ft 3in	5ft 7in	4ft 4in	3ft 10in	3ft 0in	2ft 1in	1ft 7in	1ft 1in
9ft 0in	17ft 1in	11ft 11in	9ft 11in	8ft 3in	6ft 4in	4ft 11in	4ft 4in	3ft 5in	2ft 4in	1ft 9in	1ft 2in
10ft 0in	19ft 1in	13ft 4in	11ft 1in	9ft 2in	7ft 1in	5ft 6in	4ft 10in	3ft 10in	2ft 8in	1ft 12in	1ft 4in
12ft 0in	23ft 2in	16ft 1in	13ft 5in	11ft 1in	8ft 7in	6ft 8in	5ft 10in	4ft 7in	3ft 2in	2ft 4in	1ft 7in
15ft 0in	29ft 2in	20ft 3in	16ft 10in	14ft 0in	10ft 10in	8ft 4in	7ft 4in	5ft 10in	4ft 0in	3ft 0in	2ft 0in
20ft 0in	39ft 3in	27ft 2in	22ft 7in	18ft 9in	14ft 6in	11ft 3in	9ft 10in	7ft 10in	5ft 4in	4ft 0in	2ft 8in
30ft 0in	59ft 4in	41ft 1in	34ft 1in	28ft 4in	22ft 0in	17ft 0in	14ft 10in	11ft 10in	8ft 0in	6ft 0in	4ft 0in
60ft 0in	119ft 9in	82ft 8in	68ft 7in	57ft 1in	44ft 4in	34ft 3in	29ft 11in	23ft 11in	16ft 0in	12ft 0in	8ft 0in

35mm - TV TRANSMITTED AREA
CAMERA DISTANCE / SCENE HEIGHT

	LENS FOCAL LENGTH (mm)										
	10	14.5	17.5	21	27	35	40	50	75	100	150
	LENS ANGLE (°from front entrance pupil)										
FOCUS	74.1	55	46.6	39.5	31.2	24.3	21.4	17.2	11.5	8.6	5.8
DISTANCE	SCENE HEIGHT										
2ft 0in	2ft 3in	1ft 8in	1ft 5in	1ft 2in	0ft 10in	0ft 8in	0ft 7in	0ft 5in	0ft 4in		
2ft 6in	3ft 0in	2ft 2in	1ft 10in	1ft 6in	1ft 1in	0ft 10in	0ft 9in	0ft 7in	0ft 6in		
3ft 0in	3ft 9in	2ft 8in	2ft 3in	1ft 10in	1ft 5in	1ft 1in	1ft 0in	0ft 9in	0ft 7in	0ft 5in	
4ft 0in	5ft 3in	3ft 9in	3ft 2in	2ft 7in	2ft 0in	1ft 6in	1ft 4in	1ft 1in	0ft 9in	0ft 7in	
5ft 0in	6ft 10in	4ft 9in	4ft 0in	3ft 3in	2ft 6in	1ft 11in	1ft 9in	1ft 4in	1ft 0in	0ft 9in	
6ft 0in	8ft 4in	5ft 10in	4ft 10in	4ft 0in	3ft 1in	2ft 5in	2ft 1in	1ft 8in	1ft 2in	0ft 10in	0ft 7in
7ft in	9ft 10in	6ft 10in	5ft 9in	4ft 9in	3ft 8in	2ft 10in	2ft 6in	1ft 11in	1ft 4in	1ft 0in	0ft 8in
8ft 0in	11ft 4in	7ft 11in	6ft 7in	5ft 5in	4ft 2in	3ft 3in	2ft 10in	2ft 3in	1ft 7in	1ft 2in	0ft 9in
9ft 0in	12ft 10in	8ft 11in	7ft 5in	6ft 2in	4ft 9in	3ft 8in	3ft 3in	2ft 7in	1ft 9in	1ft 4in	0ft 11in
10ft 0in	14ft 4in	10ft 0in	8ft 4in	6ft 11in	5ft 4in	4ft 1in	3ft 7in	2ft 10in	2ft 0in	1ft 6in	1ft 1in

35mm ANAMORPHIC
CAMERA DISTANCE / SCENE WIDTH

FOCUS DISTANCE	LENS FOCAL LENGTH (mm)				
	35	40	50	75	100
	HORIZONTAL LENS ANGLE				
	(° from front entrance pupil)				
	67.6	59.6	48	32.4	24.4
	SCENE WIDTH				
	(from entrance pupil to subject)				
3ft 6in				1ft 5in	1ft 1in
3ft 6in	4ft 3in	3ft 9in	3ft 0in	2ft 0in	1ft 6in
4ft 0in	4ft 10in	4ft 3in	3ft 5in	2ft 3in	1ft 8in
5ft 0in	6ft 1in	5ft 4in	4ft 3in	2ft 10in	2ft 2in
6ft 0in	7ft 4in	6ft 5in	5ft 1in	3ft 5in	2ft 7in
7ft 0in	8ft 6in	7ft 5in	6ft 0in	4ft 0in	3ft 0in
8ft 0in	9ft 9in	8ft 6in	6ft 10in	4ft 7in	3ft 5in
9ft 0in	10ft 11in	9ft 7in	7ft 8in	5ft 1in	3ft 10in
10ft 0in	12ft 2in	10ft 8in	8ft 6in	5ft 8in	4ft 3in
12ft 0in	14ft 7in	12ft 9in	10ft 3in	6ft 10in	5ft 1in
15ft 0in	18ft 3in	16ft 0in	12ft 9in	8ft 6in	6ft 5in
20ft 0in	24ft 4in	21ft 3in	17ft 0in	11ft 4in	8ft 6in
30ft 0in	36ft 6in	31ft 11in	25ft 7in	17ft 0in	12ft 9in
60ft 0in	73ft 0in	63ft 10in	51ft 1in	34ft 1in	25ft 7in

35mm ANAMORPHIC
CAMERA DISTANCE / SCENE HEIGHT

FOCUS DISTANCE	LENS FOCAL LENGTH (mm)				
	35	40	50	75	100
	VERTICAL LENS ANGLE				
	(° from front entrance pupil)				
	28.5	25.1	20.2	13.5	10.2
	SCENE HEIGHT				
	(from entrance pupil to subject)				
2ft 6in				0ft 7in	0ft 5in
3ft 6in	1ft 9in	1ft 7in	1ft 3in	0ft 10in	0ft 7in
4ft 0in	2ft 0in	1ft 9in	1ft 5in	0ft 11in	0ft 9in
5ft 0in	2ft 6in	2ft 3in	1ft 9in	1ft 2in	0ft 11in
6ft 0in	3ft 1in	2ft 8in	2ft 2in	1ft 5in	1ft 1in
7ft in	3ft 7in	3ft 1in	2ft 6in	1ft 8in	1ft 3in
8ft 0in	4ft 1in	3ft 7in	2ft 10in	1ft 11in	1ft 5in
9ft 0in	4ft 7in	4ft 0in	3ft 2in	2ft 2in	1ft 7in
10ft 0in	5ft 1in	4ft 5in	3ft 7in	2ft 4in	1ft 9in

Depth of Field Tables

The following tables may equally be considered to be "Focus Split" or even "Circle of Confusion Tables." Depending upon which way they are used they may be used to determine:

• Depth of Field. (Given the focus distance together with the lens focal length, the acceptable c of c and the lens aperture, *determine the Near and Far Distances in acceptable focus.)*

• Focus Split. (Given the near and far distances, the lens focal length, the acceptable c of c and the lens aperture, *determine the Focus Distance to hold that Focus Split.)*

• Minimum Aperture. (Given the near and far distances, the lens focal length, the acceptable c of c and the lens aperture, *determine the minimum aperture required to hold that focus split.)*

• Maximum Focal Length. (Given the near and far distances, the acceptable c of c and the lens aperture, *determine the longest focal length with which it is possible to hold that split.)*

• Acceptable Circle of Confusion. (Given an acceptable degree of 'out-of-focusness' of a known near and far distance, and the lens focal length and aperture, *determine with what minimum c of c it is possible to hold that focus split in acceptable focus.)*

Choice of Circle of Confusion

The c of c used in practical cinematography is as much a measure of acceptable 'out-of-focusness' as it is of 'what-you-can-get-away-with.'

With older type lenses and/or with diffusion filters, fog filters, star filters and nets in front of the lens, and/or with smoke all over the set, etc., everything is unsharp and it is possible to get away with a c of c of 1/500", or even larger. With average lenses, 1/1000" is a reasonable starting point but with PANAVISION PRIMO lenses, be they prime or zoom, with no diffusion of any kind, contrasty lighting and wanting a maximum hard look then 1/2000", or even smaller, is what is needed.

There is only one sure way to tell what is the correct c of c to work to and that is to know what you did and what you expected on a previous test or take and then to look at properly projected dailies to make a subjective judgement to apply to future set-ups.

Using these tables

To use the following tables it is recommended that the user first determine the largest c of c that is safe to use (top left of the table), then move along the line to the aperture to be used, then down the column to select the closest near and far distances to what is required and from there move to the left to note the Focus Distance. It will still be necessary to make a mental adjustment according to how close to reality the selected near and far distances are.

Note: The following tables are computer generated. They take into consideraton Entrance Pupil positions and the fact that we measure focus distances from the film plane. They should, however, only be taken as a guide and a basis for photographic tests.

Depth of Field — Prime lenses

10 mm   PANAVISION PRIMO-L PRIME

Entrance pupil rearwards from front vertex = 49 mm   Lens length, vertex to focal plane = 200 mm

Circle of Confusion	Aperture										
1/500in					2	2.8	4	5.6	8	11	16
1/710in				2	2.8	4	5.6	8	11	16	22
1/1000in			2	2.8	4	5.6	8	11	16	22	
1/1420in		2	2.8	4	5.6	8	11	16	22		
1/2000in	2	2.8	4	5.6	8	11	16	22			

Focus Distance — Extreme distances in acceptable focus

Focus Distance											
2' 0" Near	1'10.2"	1'9.5"	1'8.6"	1'7.6"	1'6.3"	1'5.0"	1'3.4"	1'2"	1'0"	0'11"	0'9.8"
Far	2'2.3"	2'3.4"	2'5.3"	2'8.5"	3'3"	4'7"	17'6"	INF	INF	INF	INF
2' 6" Near	2'2.8"	2'1.8"	2'0.4"	1'10.8"	1'8.9"	1'6.9"	1'4"	1'2"	1'0"	0'11"	0'10.0"
Far	2'10.3"	3'0.5"	3'4"	4'0"	5'7"	14'3"	INF	INF	INF	INF	INF
3' 0" Near	2'7.2"	2'5.6"	2'3.7"	2'1.5"	1'11.0"	1'8"	1'5"	1'3"	1'1"	0'11"	0'10.2"
Far	3'7.1"	3'11"	4'6"	5'10"	11'2"	INF	INF	INF	INF	INF	0'0.1"
3' 6" Near	2'11.3"	2'9.2"	2'6.6"	2'3.9"	2'0.7"	1'9"	1'6"	1'4"	1'1"	0'11"	0'10.3"
Far	4'4"	4'11"	6'0"	8'11"	38'2"	INF	INF	INF	INF	INF	0'0.3"
4' 0" Near	3'3.1"	3'0.5"	2'9.3"	2'5.9"	2'2"	1'10"	1'7"	1'4"	1'1"	1'0"	0'10.3"
Far	5'3"	6'1"	8'0"	14'8"	INF	INF	INF	INF	INF	INF	0'0.4"
4' 6" Near	3'6.7"	3'3.5"	2'11.7"	2'7.8"	2'3"	1'11"	1'7"	1'4"	1'2"	1'0"	0'10.4"
Far	6'3"	7'6"	10'10"	29'3"	INF	INF	INF	INF	INF	INF	0'0.5"
5' 0" Near	3'10.1"	3'6.4"	3'1.9"	2'9.4"	2'4"	2'0"	1'8"	1'5"	1'2"	1'0"	0'10.4"
Far	7'4"	9'2"	15'1"	>100'	INF	INF	INF	INF	INF	INF	0'0.6"
6' 0" Near	4'4.3"	3'11.4"	3'5.7"	3'0"	2'6"	2'1"	1'9"	1'5"	1'2"	1'0"	0'10.5"
Far	10'0"	14'0"	36'6"	INF	INF	INF	INF	INF	INF	INF	0'0.7"
7' 0" Near	4'9.9"	4'3.8"	3'8"	3'2"	2'7"	2'2"	1'9"	1'5"	1'2"	1'0"	0'10.5"
Far	13'6"	22'3"	INF	INF	INF	INF	INF	INF	INF	INF	0'0.7"
8' 0" Near	5'3.0"	4'7.7"	3'11"	3'4"	2'9"	2'3"	1'9"	1'6"	1'2"	1'0"	0'10.6"
Far	18'3"	39'11"	INF	INF	INF	INF	INF	INF	INF	INF	0'0.8"
10' Near	5'11.7"	5'2"	4'4"	3'7"	2'10"	2'4"	1'10"	1'6"	1'2"	1'0"	0'10.6"
Far	36'1"	INF	INF	INF	INF	INF	INF	INF	INF	INF	0'0.9"
12' Near	6'7.1"	5'7"	4'7"	3'9"	3'0"	2'5"	1'11"	1'6"	1'3"	1'0"	0'10.6"
Far	>100'	INF	INF	INF	INF	INF	INF	INF	INF	INF	0'0.9"
15' Near	7'4"	6'1"	4'11"	4'0"	3'1"	2'5"	1'11"	1'7"	1'3"	1'0"	0'10.7"
Far	INF	INF	INF	INF	INF	INF	INF	INF	INF	INF	0'0.9"
20' Near	8'3"	6'9"	5'4"	4'2"	3'3"	2'6"	1'11"	1'7"	1'3"	1'0"	0'10.7"
Far	INF	INF	INF	INF	INF	INF	INF	INF	INF	INF	0'1.0"
30' Near	9'5"	7'6"	5'9"	4'5"	3'4"	2'7"	2'0"	1'7"	1'3"	1'0"	0'10.7"
Far	INF	INF	INF	INF	INF	INF	INF	INF	INF	INF	0'1.0"
60' Near	11'1"	8'5"	6'3"	4'9"	3'6"	2'8"	2'0"	1'7"	1'3"	1'0"	0'10.8"
Far	INF	INF	INF	INF	INF	INF	INF	INF	INF	INF	INF
Hyperfocal distance	13'5"	9'3"	6'5"	4'7"	3'3"	2'4"	1'7"	1'2"	0'10"	0'7"	0'5"

Depth of Field — Prime lenses

14.5 mm   PANAVISION PRIMO-L PRIME

Entrance pupil rearwards from front vertex = 41 mm   Lens length, vertex to focal plane = 164 mm

Circle of Confusion	Aperture										
1/500in					2	2.8	4	5.6	8	11	16
1/710in				2	2.8	4	5.6	8	11	16	22
1/1000in			2	2.8	4	5.6	8	11	16	22	
1/1420in		2	2.8	4	5.6	8	11	16	22		
1/2000in	2	2.8	4	5.6	8	11	16	22			

Focus Distance		Extreme distances in acceptable focus										
2' 0"	Near	1' 11.0"	1' 10.6"	1' 10.0"	1' 9.4"	1' 8.4"	1' 7.4"	1' 6.0"	1' 4.6"	1' 2.9"	1' 1"	0' 11"
	Far	2' 1.2"	2' 1.7"	2' 2.5"	2' 3.6"	2' 5.7"	2' 9.0"	3' 4"	4' 8"	18' 7"	INF	INF
2' 6"	Near	2' 4.2"	2' 3.6"	2' 2.7"	2' 1.6"	2' 0.2"	1' 10.5"	1' 8.5"	1' 6.6"	1' 4"	1' 2"	1' 0"
	Far	2' 8.1"	2' 9.0"	2' 10.5"	3' 0.7"	3' 4"	4' 0"	5' 8"	12' 8"	INF	INF	INF
3' 0"	Near	2' 9.3"	2' 8.4"	2' 7.1"	2' 5.5"	2' 3.5"	2' 1.3"	1' 10.6"	1' 8"	1' 5"	1' 3"	1' 0"
	Far	3' 3.2"	3' 4.7"	3' 7.2"	3' 11"	4' 6"	5' 10"	10' 9"	INF	INF	INF	INF
3' 6"	Near	3' 2.2"	3' 1.0"	2' 11.2"	2' 9.1"	2' 6.5"	2' 3.7"	2' 0.4"	1' 9"	1' 6"	1' 3"	1' 0"
	Far	3' 10.7"	4' 0.9"	4' 4"	4' 11"	6' 0"	8' 8"	30' 9"	INF	INF	INF	INF
4' 0"	Near	3' 7.0"	3' 5.3"	3' 3.1"	3' 0.4"	2' 9.2"	2' 5.8"	2' 1"	1' 10"	1' 6"	1' 4"	1' 1"
	Far	4' 6.5"	4' 9"	5' 3"	6' 0"	7' 11"	13' 9"	INF	INF	INF	INF	INF
4' 6"	Near	3' 11.6"	3' 9.5"	3' 6.7"	3' 3.5"	2' 11.6"	2' 7.6"	2' 3"	1' 11"	1' 7"	1' 4"	1' 1"
	Far	5' 2.6"	5' 7"	6' 2"	7' 5"	10' 6"	25' 2"	INF	INF	INF	INF	INF
5' 0"	Near	4' 4.1"	4' 1.5"	3' 10.2"	3' 6.4"	3' 1.9"	2' 9.3"	2' 4"	2' 0"	1' 7"	1' 4"	1' 1"
	Far	5' 11.1"	6' 4"	7' 3"	9' 0"	14' 4"	74'	INF	INF	INF	INF	INF
6' 0"	Near	5' 0.6"	4' 9.1"	4' 4.5"	3' 11.6"	3' 5.8"	3' 0"	2' 6"	2' 1"	1' 8"	1' 5"	1' 1"
	Far	7' 5"	8' 2"	9' 10"	13' 5"	31' 0"	INF	INF	INF	INF	INF	INF
7' 0"	Near	5' 8.6"	5' 4.0"	4' 10.2"	4' 4.1"	3' 9.1"	3' 2"	2' 7"	2' 2"	1' 9"	1' 5"	1' 1"
	Far	9' 1"	10' 4"	13' 1"	20' 8"	>100'	INF	INF	INF	INF	INF	INF
8' 0"	Near	6' 4.2"	5' 10.5"	5' 3.4"	4' 8.1"	4' 0"	3' 4"	2' 9"	2' 3"	1' 9"	1' 5"	1' 2"
	Far	10' 11"	12' 10"	17' 6"	34' 8"	INF	INF	INF	INF	INF	INF	INF
10'	Near	7' 6.0"	6' 10.0"	6' 0.5"	5' 2.9"	4' 4"	3' 7"	2' 11"	2' 4"	1' 10"	1' 6"	1' 2"
	Far	15' 2"	19' 3"	32' 8"	>100'	INF	INF	INF	INF	INF	INF	INF
12'	Near	8' 6.5"	7' 8.1"	6' 8.0"	5' 8"	4' 8"	3' 10"	3' 0"	2' 5"	1' 10"	1' 6"	1' 2"
	Far	20' 7"	29' 0"	77'	INF	INF	INF	INF	INF	INF	INF	INF
15'	Near	9' 10.9"	8' 8.9"	7' 5"	6' 2"	5' 0"	4' 0"	3' 2"	2' 6"	1' 11"	1' 6"	1' 2"
	Far	31' 10"	58'	INF	INF	INF	INF	INF	INF	INF	INF	INF
20'	Near	11' 9"	10' 2"	8' 5"	6' 10"	5' 5"	4' 3"	3' 3"	2' 7"	1' 11"	1' 6"	1' 2"
	Far	70'	INF	INF	INF	INF	INF	INF	INF	INF	INF	INF
30'	Near	14' 6"	12' 1"	9' 8"	7' 8"	5' 11"	4' 6"	3' 5"	2' 8"	2' 0"	1' 7"	1' 2"
	Far	INF	INF	INF	INF	INF	INF	INF	INF	INF	INF	INF
60'	Near	19' 0"	15' 0"	11' 5"	8' 9"	6' 6"	4' 10"	3' 7"	2' 9"	2' 0"	1' 7"	1' 2"
	Far	INF	INF	INF	INF	INF	INF	INF	INF	INF	INF	INF
Hyperfocal distance		27' 6"	19' 5"	13' 7"	9' 9"	6' 10"	4' 10"	3' 5"	2' 6"	1' 8"	1' 3"	0' 10"

Depth of Field — Prime lenses

17.5 mm — PANAVISION PRIMO-L PRIME

Entrance pupil rearwards from front vertex = 40 mm
Lens length, vertex to focal plane = 151 mm

Circle of Confusion				Aperture						
1/500in				2	2.8	4	5.6	8	11	16
1/710in			2	2.8	4	5.6	8	11	16	22
1/1000in		2	2.8	4	5.6	8	11	16	22	
1/1420in	2	2.8	4	5.6	8	11	16	22		
1/2000in	2	2.8	4	5.6	8	11	16	22			

Focus Distance — Extreme distances in acceptable focus

Focus Distance											
2' 0" Near	1'11.2"	1'11.0"	1'10.5"	1'10.0"	1'9.3"	1'8.4"	1'7.3"	1'6.0"	1'4.4"	1'2.8"	1'1"
2' 0" Far	2'0.8"	2'1.2"	2'1.7"	2'2.5"	2'3.7"	2'5.6"	2'9.2"	3'3"	4'10"	13'9"	INF
2' 6" Near	2'4.7"	2'4.2"	2'3.6"	2'2.7"	2'1.5"	2'0.2"	1'10.4"	1'8.6"	1'6.3"	1'4"	1'1"
2' 6" Far	2'7.4"	2'8.0"	2'9.0"	2'10.4"	3'0.8"	3'4"	4'0"	5'5"	13'9"	INF	INF
3' 0" Near	2'10.1"	2'9.4"	2'8.4"	2'7.1"	2'5.5"	2'3.5"	2'1.2"	1'10.8"	1'7"	1'5"	1'2"
3' 0" Far	3'2.2"	3'3.2"	3'4.7"	3'7.1"	3'11"	4'6"	5'10"	9'8"	INF	INF	INF
3' 6" Near	3'3.3"	3'2.3"	3'0.9"	2'11.3"	2'9.1"	2'6.6"	2'3.6"	2'0.6"	1'9"	1'6"	1'3"
3' 6" Far	3'9.2"	3'10.6"	4'0.9"	4'4"	4'11"	5'11"	8'8"	22'1"	INF	INF	INF
4' 0" Near	3'8.4"	3'7.1"	3'5.3"	3'3.2"	3'0.4"	2'9.3"	2'5.7"	2'2.2"	1'10"	1'7"	1'3"
4' 0" Far	4'4.3"	4'6.3"	4'9"	5'2"	6'0"	7'8"	13'6"	>100'	INF	INF	INF
4' 6" Near	4'1.4"	3'11.7"	3'9.5"	3'6.9"	3'3.5"	2'11.8"	2'7.6"	2'3"	1'11"	1'7"	1'3"
4' 6" Far	4'11.7"	5'2.4"	5'6"	6'2"	7'4"	10'1"	23'11"	INF	INF	INF	INF
5' 0" Near	4'6.2"	4'4.2"	4'1.5"	3'10.4"	3'6.4"	3'2.1"	2'9.3"	2'4"	1'11"	1'8"	1'4"
5' 0" Far	5'7.3"	5'10.8"	6'4"	7'2"	9'0"	13'6"	62'	INF	INF	INF	INF
6' 0" Near	5'3.6"	5'0.8"	4'9.1"	4'4.9"	3'11.6"	3'6.2"	3'0"	2'6"	2'1"	1'8"	1'4"
6' 0" Far	6'11.1"	7'4"	8'2"	9'8"	13'3"	27'2"	INF	INF	INF	INF	INF
7' 0" Near	6'0.6"	5'9.0"	5'4.1"	4'10.7"	4'4.2"	3'9.6"	3'2"	2'8"	2'2"	1'9"	1'5"
7' 0" Far	8'3"	9'0"	10'3"	12'9"	20'2"	96'	INF	INF	INF	INF	INF
8' 0" Near	6'9.3"	6'4.6"	5'10.6"	5'4.0"	4'8.2"	4'0"	3'4"	2'9"	2'2"	1'9"	1'5"
8' 0" Far	9'9"	10'9"	12'8"	16'10"	33'0"	INF	INF	INF	INF	INF	INF
10' Near	8'1.5"	7'6.7"	6'10.3"	6'1.3"	5'3.1"	4'5"	3'7"	2'11"	2'4"	1'10"	1'5"
10' Far	13'0"	14'11"	19'0"	30'3"	>100'	INF	INF	INF	INF	INF	INF
12' Near	9'4.4"	8'7.4"	7'8.4"	6'9.1"	5'8"	4'9"	3'10"	3'1"	2'4"	1'11"	1'5"
12' Far	16'9"	20'0"	28'5"	64'	INF	INF	INF	INF	INF	INF	INF
15' Near	11'0"	10'0"	8'9.5"	7'6"	6'3"	5'1"	4'0"	3'3"	2'5"	1'11"	1'6"
15' Far	23'6"	30'7"	56'	INF	INF	INF	INF	INF	INF	INF	INF
20' Near	13'6"	11'11"	10'2"	8'7"	6'11"	5'6"	4'3"	3'4"	2'6"	2'0"	1'6"
20' Far	39'2"	64'	>100'	INF	INF	INF	INF	INF	INF	INF	INF
30' Near	17'3"	14'10"	12'2"	9'11"	7'9"	6'0"	4'7"	3'6"	2'7"	2'0"	1'6"
30' Far	>100'	INF	INF	INF	INF	INF	INF	INF	INF	INF	INF
60' Near	24'1"	19'6"	15'2"	11'9"	8'10"	6'8"	4'11"	3'9"	2'8"	2'1"	1'6"
60' Far	INF	INF	INF	INF	INF	INF	INF	INF	INF	INF	INF

Hyperfocal distance

39'11"	28'3"	19'10"	14'2"	9'11"	7'1"	5'0"	3'7"	2'6"	1'10"	1'3"

Depth of Field — Prime lenses

21 mm — PANAVISION PRIMO-L PRIME

Entrance pupil rearwards from front vertex = 48 mm Lens length, vertex to focal plane = 178 mm

Circle of Confusion / Aperture	C1	C2	C3	C4	C5	C6	C7	C8	C9	C10	C11
1/500in					2	2.8	4	5.6	8	11	16
1/710in				2	2.8	4	5.6	8	11	16	22
1/1000in			2	2.8	4	5.6	8	11	16	22	
1/1420in		2	2.8	4	5.6	8	11	16	22		
1/2000in	2	2.8	4	5.6	8	11	16	22			

Focus Distance — Extreme distances in acceptable focus

Focus Distance		C1	C2	C3	C4	C5	C6	C7	C8	C9	C10	C11
2' 0"	Near	1'11.5"	1'11.3"	1'11.1"	1'10.7"	1'10.2"	1'9.6"	1'8.7"	1'7.7"	1'6.4"	1'5.1"	1'3.4"
	Far	2'0.5"	2'0.7"	2'1.1"	2'1.5"	2'2.2"	2'3.3"	2'5.1"	2'7.7"	3'1"	4'2"	10'7"
2' 6"	Near	2'5.2"	2'4.8"	2'4.4"	2'3.8"	2'2.9"	2'1.9"	2'0.5"	1'11.1"	1'9.0"	1'7.1"	1'4"
	Far	2'6.9"	2'7.3"	2'7.9"	2'8.7"	2'10.1"	3'0.1"	3'3.7"	3'9"	5'2"	9'7"	INF
3' 0"	Near	2'10.7"	2'10.2"	2'9.5"	2'8.6"	2'7.4"	2'5.9"	2'4.0"	2'1.9"	1'11.2"	1'8.8"	1'5"
	Far	3'1.4"	3'2.0"	3'3.0"	3'4.3"	3'6.6"	3'10"	4'4"	5'4"	9'1"	79'	INF
3' 6"	Near	3'4.2"	3'3.5"	3'2.5"	3'1.3"	2'11.6"	2'9.6"	2'7.1"	2'4.5"	2'1.1"	1'10"	1'6"
	Far	3'8.1"	3'8.9"	3'10.3"	4'0.4"	4'3"	4'9"	5'8"	7'9"	20'1"	INF	INF
4' 0"	Near	3'9.5"	3'8.6"	3'7.3"	3'5.7"	3'3.5"	3'1.0"	2'9.9"	2'6.7"	2'2.7"	1'11"	1'7"
	Far	4'2.8"	4'4.0"	4'6.0"	4'8.9"	5'2"	5'10"	7'5"	11'5"	>100'	INF	INF
4' 6"	Near	4'2.8"	4'1.6"	4'0.0"	3'10.0"	3'7.3"	3'4.2"	3'0.4"	2'8.7"	2'4"	2'0"	1'8"
	Far	4'9.7"	4'11.3"	5'2.0"	5'6"	6'1"	7'1"	9'8"	18'4"	INF	INF	INF
5' 0"	Near	4'8.0"	4'6.5"	4'4.5"	4'2.1"	3'10.8"	3'7.2"	3'2.7"	2'10.5"	2'5"	2'1"	1'8"
	Far	5'4.7"	5'6.8"	5'10.3"	6'3"	7'1"	8'7"	12'10"	35'6"	INF	INF	INF
6' 0"	Near	5'6.1"	5'4.0"	5'1.2"	4'9.8"	4'5.4"	4'0.5"	3'6.8"	3'1"	2'7"	2'2"	1'9"
	Far	6'7.2"	6'10.5"	7'4"	8'0"	9'6"	12'6"	24'11"	INF	INF	INF	INF
7' 0"	Near	6'3.9"	6'1.1"	5'9.3"	5'4.9"	4'11.3"	4'5.2"	3'10.3"	3'4"	2'9"	2'3"	1'10"
	Far	7'10.2"	8'3"	8'11"	10'1"	12'6"	18'7"	76'	INF	INF	INF	INF
8' 0"	Near	7'1.4"	6'9.8"	6'5.0"	5'11.5"	5'4.6"	4'9.4"	4'1"	3'6"	2'10"	2'4"	1'10"
	Far	9'1.8"	9'8"	10'8"	12'5"	16'5"	29'3"	INF	INF	INF	INF	INF
10'	Near	8'7.6"	8'2.2"	7'7.3"	6'11.4"	6'2.0"	5'4.5"	4'6"	3'9"	3'0"	2'5"	1'11"
	Far	11'11"	12'11"	14'9"	18'4"	29'2"	>100'	INF	INF	INF	INF	INF
12'	Near	10'0"	9'5.4"	8'8.0"	7'9.8"	6'9.9"	5'10"	4'10"	4'0"	3'1"	2'6"	1'11"
	Far	14'11"	16'6"	19'10"	27'0"	60'	INF	INF	INF	INF	INF	INF
15'	Near	12'0"	11'2"	10'1"	8'11.2"	7'7"	6'5"	5'2"	4'3"	3'3"	2'7"	2'0"
	Far	19'11"	23'0"	30'1"	51'	INF	INF	INF	INF	INF	INF	INF
20'	Near	15'0"	13'7"	12'0"	10'5"	8'8"	7'1"	5'7"	4'6"	3'5"	2'8"	2'0"
	Far	30'2"	38'0"	62'	>100'	INF	INF	INF	INF	INF	INF	INF
30'	Near	19'10"	17'6"	14'11"	12'6"	10'0"	8'0"	6'2"	4'10"	3'7"	2'9"	2'1"
	Far	61'	>100'	INF	INF	INF	INF	INF	INF	INF	INF	INF
60'	Near	29'6"	24'7"	19'8"	15'7"	11'11"	9'1"	6'9"	5'2"	3'9"	2'10"	2'1"
	Far	INF	INF	INF	INF	INF	INF	INF	INF	INF	INF	INF
Hyperfocal distance		57'	40'9"	28'6"	20'5"	14'3"	10'2"	7'2"	5'3"	3'7"	2'7"	1'10"

Depth of Field — Prime lenses

27 mm   PANAVISION PRIMO-L PRIME

Entrance pupil rearwards from front vertex = 55 mm   Lens length, vertex to focal plane = 203 mm

Circle of Confusion				Aperture						
1/500in					2	2.8	4	5.6	8	11	16
1/710in				2	2.8	4	5.6	8	11	16	22
1/1000in			2	2.8	4	5.6	8	11	16	22	
1/1420in		2	2.8	4	5.6	8	11	16	22		
1/2000in	2	2.8	4	5.6	8	11	16	22			

Focus Distance		Extreme distances in acceptable focus									
2' 0"	Near	1' 11.7"	1' 11.6"	1' 11.5"	1' 11.3"	1' 11.0"	1' 10.6"	1' 10.0"	1' 9.4"	1' 8.5"	1' 7.5"	1' 6.1"
	Far	2' 0.3"	2' 0.4"	2' 0.6"	2' 0.8"	2' 1.2"	2' 1.7"	2' 2.5"	2' 3.6"	2' 5.8"	2' 9.1"	3' 5"
2' 6"	Near	2' 5.5"	2' 5.3"	2' 5.1"	2' 4.7"	2' 4.2"	2' 3.5"	2' 2.6"	2' 1.6"	2' 0.0"	1' 10.5"	1' 8.4"
	Far	2' 6.5"	2' 6.7"	2' 7.0"	2' 7.5"	2' 8.2"	2' 9.1"	2' 10.7"	3' 1.0"	3' 5"	4' 1"	6' 3"
3' 0"	Near	2' 11.2"	2' 10.9"	2' 10.5"	2' 10.0"	2' 9.2"	2' 8.2"	2' 6.8"	2' 5.3"	2' 3.2"	2' 1.1"	1' 10.4"
	Far	3' 0.8"	3' 1.1"	3' 1.6"	3' 2.3"	3' 3.5"	3' 5.1"	3' 7.8"	3' 11"	4' 9"	6' 3"	14' 9"
3' 6"	Near	3' 4.9"	3' 4.5"	3' 3.9"	3' 3.1"	3' 2.0"	3' 0.6"	2' 10.8"	2' 8.8"	2' 6.0"	2' 3.3"	2' 0.0"
	Far	3' 7.2"	3' 7.6"	3' 8.4"	3' 9.4"	3' 11.1"	4' 1.6"	4' 6"	5' 0"	6' 5"	10' 0"	>100'
4' 0"	Near	3' 10.5"	3' 10.0"	3' 9.1"	3' 8.1"	3' 6.6"	3' 4.9"	3' 2.5"	2' 11.9"	2' 8.5"	2' 5.3"	2' 1"
	Far	4' 1.6"	4' 2.3"	4' 3.3"	4' 4.8"	4' 7.2"	4' 10"	5' 5"	6' 4"	8' 10"	18' 1"	INF
4' 6"	Near	4' 4.1"	4' 3.3"	4' 2.3"	4' 1.0"	3' 11.1"	3' 8.9"	3' 6.0"	3' 2.9"	2' 10.7"	2' 7.0"	2' 2"
	Far	4' 8.1"	4' 9.0"	4' 10.4"	5' 0.4"	5' 3"	5' 8"	6' 6"	7' 10"	12' 6"	48' 11"	INF
5' 0"	Near	4' 9.6"	4' 8.7"	4' 7.3"	4' 5.7"	4' 3.4"	4' 0.7"	3' 9.2"	3' 5.5"	3' 0.7"	2' 8"	2' 3"
	Far	5' 2.7"	5' 3.8"	5' 5.6"	5' 8.2"	6' 0"	6' 7"	7' 8"	9' 10"	18' 8"	INF	INF
6' 0"	Near	5' 8.4"	5' 7.1"	5' 5.2"	5' 2.8"	4' 11.6"	4' 7.9"	4' 3.1"	3' 10.3"	3' 4.3"	2' 11"	2' 5"
	Far	6' 4.0"	6' 5.8"	6' 8.6"	7' 0"	7' 7"	8' 7"	10' 8"	15' 6"	71'	INF	INF
7' 0"	Near	6' 7.0"	6' 5.2"	6' 2.6"	5' 11.5"	5' 7.2"	5' 2.4"	4' 8.4"	4' 2.5"	3' 7"	3' 1"	2' 6"
	Far	7' 5.7"	7' 8.3"	8' 0"	8' 6"	9' 5"	11' 0"	14' 10"	26' 7"	INF	INF	INF
8' 0"	Near	7' 5.4"	7' 3.0"	6' 11.7"	6' 7.7"	6' 2.4"	5' 8.4"	5' 1.1"	4' 6.1"	3' 9"	3' 2"	2' 7"
	Far	8' 7.7"	8' 11.2"	9' 4.9"	10' 1"	11' 5"	13' 11"	20' 10"	57'	INF	INF	INF
10'	Near	9' 1.6"	8' 10.0"	8' 5.0"	7' 11.0"	7' 3.4"	6' 7.0"	5' 9.2"	5' 0"	4' 1"	3' 5"	2' 9"
	Far	11' 0"	11' 6"	12' 4"	13' 8"	16' 4"	22' 1"	48' 3"	INF	INF	INF	INF
12'	Near	10' 9"	10' 3"	9' 9.0"	9' 1.0"	8' 2.8"	7' 4.1"	6' 3.9"	5' 5"	4' 4"	3' 7"	2' 10"
	Far	13' 7"	14' 4"	15' 8"	17' 11"	22' 10"	36' 5"	>100'	INF	INF	INF	INF
15'	Near	13' 0"	12' 5"	11' 7"	10' 7"	9' 5.8"	8' 3.6"	7' 0"	5' 10"	4' 8"	3' 9"	2' 11"
	Far	17' 7"	18' 11"	21' 4"	25' 10"	37' 11"	>100'	INF	INF	INF	INF	INF
20'	Near	16' 8"	15' 7"	14' 3"	12' 10"	11' 2"	9' 6"	7' 10"	6' 5"	5' 0"	4' 0"	3' 0"
	Far	25' 0"	27' 11"	33' 8"	46' 8"	>100'	INF	INF	INF	INF	INF	INF
30'	Near	22' 11"	21' 0"	18' 7"	16' 2"	13' 7"	11' 2"	8' 11"	7' 1"	5' 4"	4' 2"	3' 2"
	Far	43' 5"	52'	79'	>100'	INF	INF	INF	INF	INF	INF	INF
60'	Near	36' 11"	32' 1"	26' 9"	21' 11"	17' 4"	13' 7"	10' 3"	7' 11"	5' 10"	4' 5"	3' 3"
	Far	>100'	>100'	INF	INF	INF	INF	INF	INF	INF	INF	INF
Hyperfocal distance		94'	67'	47' 2"	33' 8"	23' 7"	16' 10"	11' 10"	8' 7"	5' 11"	4' 4"	3' 0"

255

Depth of Field — Prime lenses

35 mm PANAVISION PRIMO-L PRIME

Entrance pupil rearwards from front vertex = 48 mm Lens length, vertex to focal plane = 193 mm

Circle of Confusion						Aperture					
1/500in					2	2.8	4	5.6	8	11	16
1/710in				2	2.8	4	5.6	8	11	16	22
1/1000in			2	2.8	4	5.6	8	11	16	22	
1/1420in		2	2.8	4	5.6	8	11	16	22		
1/2000in	2	2.8	4	5.6	8	11	16	22			
Focus Distance					Extreme distances in acceptable focus						
2' 0" Near	1' 11.8"	1' 11.8"	1' 11.7"	1' 11.6"	1' 11.4"	1' 11.1"	1' 10.8"	1' 10.4"	1' 9.7"	1' 9.0"	1' 7.9"
Far	2' 0.2"	2' 0.2"	2' 0.3"	2' 0.5"	2' 0.7"	2' 1.0"	2' 1.4"	2' 2.0"	2' 3.0"	2' 4.5"	2' 7.3"
2' 6" Near	2' 5.7"	2' 5.6"	2' 5.4"	2' 5.2"	2' 4.9"	2' 4.5"	2' 3.9"	2' 3.2"	2' 2.1"	2' 0.9"	1' 11.2"
Far	2' 6.3"	2' 6.4"	2' 6.6"	2' 6.8"	2' 7.2"	2' 7.8"	2' 8.6"	2' 9.7"	2' 11.8"	3' 2.8"	3' 9"
3' 0" Near	2' 11.5"	2' 11.4"	2' 11.1"	2' 10.8"	2' 10.3"	2' 9.6"	2' 8.7"	2' 7.7"	2' 6.1"	2' 4.4"	2' 2.1"
Far	3' 0.5"	3' 0.7"	3' 1.0"	3' 1.3"	3' 2.0"	3' 2.8"	3' 4.2"	3' 6.1"	3' 9"	4' 3"	5' 4"
3' 6" Near	3' 5.3"	3' 5.1"	3' 4.7"	3' 4.2"	3' 3.5"	3' 2.6"	3' 1.3"	2' 11.9"	2' 9.8"	2' 7.5"	2' 4.6"
Far	3' 6.7"	3' 7.0"	3' 7.4"	3' 8.0"	3' 8.9"	3' 10.2"	4' 0.3"	4' 3.2"	4' 9"	5' 6"	7' 9"
4' 0" Near	3' 11.1"	3' 10.8"	3' 10.3"	3' 9.6"	3' 8.6"	3' 7.4"	3' 5.8"	3' 3.9"	3' 1.2"	2' 10.4"	2' 6.7"
Far	4' 0.9"	4' 1.3"	4' 1.9"	4' 2.7"	4' 4.0"	4' 5.8"	4' 8.8"	5' 1"	5' 10"	7' 2"	11' 9"
4' 6" Near	4' 4.8"	4' 4.4"	4' 3.7"	4' 2.9"	4' 1.7"	4' 0.1"	3' 10.0"	3' 7.7"	3' 4.3"	3' 1.0"	2' 8.7"
Far	4' 7.2"	4' 7.7"	4' 8.5"	4' 9.6"	4' 11.3"	5' 1.8"	5' 5"	6' 0"	7' 1"	9' 3"	19' 8"
5' 0" Near	4' 10.5"	4' 10.0"	4' 9.1"	4' 8.1"	4' 6.6"	4' 4.7"	4' 2.1"	3' 11.3"	3' 7.3"	3' 3.4"	2' 10.4"
Far	5' 1.6"	5' 2.2"	5' 3.2"	5' 4.6"	5' 6.8"	5' 10.0"	6' 3"	7' 0"	8' 7"	12' 2"	42' 3"
6' 0" Near	5' 9.8"	5' 9.0"	5' 7.8"	5' 6.2"	5' 4.0"	5' 1.3"	4' 9.8"	4' 5.9"	4' 0.6"	3' 7.5"	3' 1"
Far	6' 2.3"	6' 3.3"	6' 4.9"	6' 7.0"	6' 10.5"	7' 3"	8' 1"	9' 4"	12' 8"	22' 9"	INF
7' 0" Near	6' 9.0"	6' 7.8"	6' 6.1"	6' 4.0"	6' 1.1"	5' 9.5"	5' 4.8"	4' 11.9"	4' 5.2"	3' 11.1"	3' 3"
Far	7' 3.3"	7' 4.7"	7' 6.9"	7' 10.0"	8' 3"	8' 11"	10' 1"	12' 2"	19' 0"	60'	INF
8' 0" Near	7' 8.0"	7' 6.4"	7' 4.3"	7' 1.5"	6' 9.8"	6' 5.2"	5' 11.4"	5' 5.3"	4' 9.3"	4' 2"	3' 5"
Far	8' 4.4"	8' 6.3"	8' 9.3"	9' 1.6"	9' 8"	10' 8"	12' 6"	15' 11"	30' 5"	INF	INF
10' Near	9' 5.6"	9' 3.2"	8' 11.9"	8' 7.7"	8' 2.0"	7' 7.4"	6' 11.2"	6' 2.8"	5' 4.3"	4' 7"	3' 9"
Far	10' 7"	10' 10"	11' 3"	11' 10"	12' 11"	14' 9"	18' 7"	28' 0"	>100'	INF	INF
12' Near	11' 2"	10' 11"	10' 6"	10' 0"	9' 5.0"	8' 8.2"	7' 9.4"	6' 10.8"	5' 9"	4' 11"	3' 11"
Far	12' 10"	13' 3"	13' 11"	14' 11"	16' 8"	19' 9"	27' 8"	56'	INF	INF	INF
15' Near	13' 9"	13' 4"	12' 9"	12' 0"	11' 1"	10' 1"	8' 10.5"	7' 8"	6' 4"	5' 3"	4' 2"
Far	16' 5"	17' 1"	18' 2"	19' 11"	23' 3"	30' 1"	53'	INF	INF	INF	INF
20' Near	17' 10"	17' 1"	16' 1"	15' 0"	13' 6"	12' 0"	10' 4"	8' 9"	7' 0"	5' 9"	4' 5"
Far	22' 8"	24' 0"	26' 4"	30' 2"	38' 9"	62'	>100'	INF	INF	INF	INF
30' Near	25' 4"	23' 10"	22' 0"	19' 10"	17' 4"	14' 11"	12' 4"	10' 2"	7' 10"	6' 3"	4' 8"
Far	36' 8"	40' 4"	47' 5"	62'	>100'	INF	INF	INF	INF	INF	INF
60' Near	43' 9"	39' 5"	34' 5"	29' 5"	24' 3"	19' 7"	15' 4"	12' 0"	8' 11"	6' 10"	5' 0"
Far	95'	>100'	>100'	INF	INF	INF	INF	INF	INF	INF	INF
Hyperfocal distance	158'	113'	79'	56'	39' 8"	28' 4"	19' 10"	14' 6"	10' 0"	7' 3"	5' 0"

Depth of Field — Prime lenses

40 mm PANAVISION PRIMO-L PRIME

Entrance pupil rearwards from front vertex = 55 mm Lens length, vertex to focal plane = 191 mm

Circle of Confusion		Aperture										
1/500in						2	2.8	4	5.6	8	11	16
1/710in					2	2.8	4	5.6	8	11	16	22
1/1000in				2	2.8	4	5.6	8	11	16	22	
1/1420in			2	2.8	4	5.6	8	11	16	22		
1/2000in		2	2.8	4	5.6	8	11	16	22			
Focus Distance		**Extreme distances in acceptable focus**										
2' 0"	Near	1' 11.9"	1' 11.8"	1' 11.7"	1' 11.6"	1' 11.5"	1' 11.3"	1' 11.0"	1' 10.7"	1' 10.2"	1' 9.5"	1' 8.6"
	Far	2' 0.1"	2' 0.2"	2' 0.3"	2' 0.4"	2' 0.5"	2' 0.7"	2' 1.1"	2' 1.5"	2' 2.3"	2' 3.3"	2' 5.3"
2' 6"	Near	2' 5.8"	2' 5.7"	2' 5.5"	2' 5.4"	2' 5.1"	2' 4.8"	2' 4.3"	2' 3.7"	2' 2.8"	2' 1.8"	2' 0.3"
	Far	2' 6.2"	2' 6.3"	2' 6.5"	2' 6.7"	2' 7.0"	2' 7.4"	2' 8.0"	2' 8.8"	2' 10.3"	3' 0.3"	3' 4"
3' 0"	Near	2' 11.6"	2' 11.5"	2' 11.3"	2' 11.0"	2' 10.6"	2' 10.1"	2' 9.4"	2' 8.5"	2' 7.2"	2' 5.7"	2' 3.6"
	Far	3' 0.4"	3' 0.5"	3' 0.7"	3' 1.0"	3' 1.5"	3' 2.2"	3' 3.2"	3' 4.5"	3' 7.1"	3' 10"	4' 6"
3' 6"	Near	3' 5.5"	3' 5.3"	3' 5.0"	3' 4.6"	3' 4.0"	3' 3.3"	3' 2.3"	3' 1.1"	2' 11.2"	2' 9.3"	2' 6.6"
	Far	3' 6.5"	3' 6.7"	3' 7.1"	3' 7.5"	3' 8.2"	3' 9.2"	3' 10.7"	4' 0.8"	4' 4"	4' 10"	6' 0"
4' 0"	Near	3' 11.3"	3' 11.0"	3' 10.6"	3' 10.1"	3' 9.4"	3' 8.4"	3' 7.0"	3' 5.4"	3' 3.1"	3' 0.6"	2' 9.2"
	Far	4' 0.7"	4' 1.0"	4' 1.5"	4' 2.1"	4' 3.0"	4' 4.4"	4' 6.5"	4' 9.5"	5' 3"	6' 0"	8' 0"
4' 6"	Near	4' 5.1"	4' 4.7"	4' 4.2"	4' 3.5"	4' 2.6"	4' 1.3"	3' 11.6"	3' 9.6"	3' 6.7"	3' 3.7"	2' 11.6"
	Far	4' 6.9"	4' 7.3"	4' 7.9"	4' 8.7"	4' 10.0"	4' 11.8"	5' 2.7"	5' 6"	6' 3"	7' 4"	10' 9"
5' 0"	Near	4' 10.9"	4' 10.4"	4' 9.8"	4' 8.9"	4' 7.7"	4' 6.2"	4' 4.0"	4' 1.6"	3' 10.1"	3' 6.5"	3' 1.8"
	Far	5' 1.2"	5' 1.7"	5' 2.4"	5' 3.5"	5' 5.1"	5' 7.4"	5' 11.3"	6' 4"	7' 4"	9' 0"	14' 10"
6' 0"	Near	5' 10.3"	5' 9.6"	5' 8.7"	5' 7.4"	5' 5.7"	5' 3.5"	5' 0.4"	4' 9.1"	4' 4.3"	3' 11.6"	3' 5.6"
	Far	6' 1.8"	6' 2.5"	6' 3.7"	6' 5.3"	6' 7.8"	6' 11.5"	7' 5"	8' 3"	10' 0"	13' 7"	35' 0"
7' 0"	Near	6' 9.6"	6' 8.7"	6' 7.4"	6' 5.7"	6' 3.3"	6' 0.3"	5' 8.3"	5' 4.0"	4' 9.9"	4' 4.1"	3' 8.8"
	Far	7' 2.5"	7' 3.6"	7' 5.2"	7' 7.5"	7' 11.2"	8' 4"	9' 2"	10' 4"	13' 5"	21' 2"	>100'
8' 0"	Near	7' 8.9"	7' 7.7"	7' 5.9"	7' 3.7"	7' 0.6"	6' 8.8"	6' 3.8"	5' 10.3"	5' 2.9"	4' 8.0"	3' 11"
	Far	8' 3.4"	8' 4.8"	8' 7.0"	8' 10.1"	9' 3.2"	9' 10"	11' 0"	12' 11"	18' 2"	36' 5"	INF
10'	Near	9' 7.0"	9' 5.1"	9' 2.4"	8' 11.0"	8' 6.3"	8' 0.7"	7' 5.4"	6' 9.7"	5' 11.6"	5' 2"	4' 4"
	Far	10' 5"	10' 7"	10' 11"	11' 4"	12' 1"	13' 3"	15' 5"	19' 7"	35' 9"	INF	INF
12'	Near	11' 4"	11' 2"	10' 10"	10' 5"	9' 10.9"	9' 3.2"	8' 5.5"	7' 7.6"	6' 6.9"	5' 7"	4' 7"
	Far	12' 8"	12' 11"	13' 5"	14' 1"	15' 3"	17' 2"	21' 1"	29' 11"	>100'	INF	INF
15'	Near	14' 0"	13' 8"	13' 2"	12' 7"	11' 9"	10' 10"	9' 9.4"	8' 8.2"	7' 3"	6' 2"	4' 11"
	Far	16' 1"	16' 6"	17' 4"	18' 6"	20' 7"	24' 4"	33' 4"	63'	INF	INF	INF
20'	Near	18' 3"	17' 8"	16' 10"	15' 11"	14' 7"	13' 3"	11' 7"	10' 0"	8' 3"	6' 9"	5' 3"
	Far	22' 0"	22' 11"	24' 6"	26' 11"	31' 9"	41' 8"	79'	INF	INF	INF	INF
30'	Near	26' 3"	25' 1"	23' 5"	21' 6"	19' 3"	16' 10"	14' 3"	11' 11"	9' 5"	7' 7"	5' 9"
	Far	34' 10"	37' 4"	41' 9"	49' 7"	69'	>100'	INF	INF	INF	INF	INF
60'	Near	46' 8"	42' 10"	38' 3"	33' 5"	28' 1"	23' 3"	18' 5"	14' 9"	11' 1"	8' 6"	6' 3"
	Far	84'	>100'	>100'	>100'	INF	INF	INF	INF	INF	INF	INF
Hyperfocal distance		207'	147'	103'	73'	51'	37' 0"	25' 11"	18' 11"	13' 0"	9' 6"	6' 7"

Depth of Field — Prime lenses

50 mm   PANAVISION PRIMO-L PRIME

Entrance pupil rearwards from front vertex = 51 mm   Lens length, vertex to focal plane = 115 mm

Circle of Confusion						Aperture					
1/500in					2	2.8	4	5.6	8	11	16
1/710in				2	2.8	4	5.6	8	11	16	22
1/1000in			2	2.8	4	5.6	8	11	16		
1/1420in		2	2.8	4	5.6	8	11	16	22		
1/2000in	2	2.8	4	5.6	8	11	16	22			

Focus Distance — Extreme distances in acceptable focus

Focus Distance												
2' 0"	Near	1' 11.9"	1' 11.8"	1' 11.8"	1' 11.7"	1' 11.6"	1' 11.4"	1' 11.2"	1' 10.9"	1' 10.4"	1' 9.9"	1' 9.0"
	Far	2' 0.1"	2' 0.2"	2' 0.2"	2' 0.3"	2' 0.4"	2' 0.6"	2' 0.9"	2' 1.3"	2' 1.9"	2' 2.7"	2' 4.1"
2' 6"	Near	2' 5.8"	2' 5.7"	2' 5.6"	2' 5.5"	2' 5.3"	2' 5.0"	2' 4.6"	2' 4.1"	2' 3.4"	2' 2.5"	2' 1.2"
	Far	2' 6.2"	2' 6.3"	2' 6.4"	2' 6.5"	2' 6.7"	2' 7.1"	2' 7.5"	2' 8.1"	2' 9.2"	2' 10.7"	3' 1.3"
3' 0"	Near	2' 11.7"	2' 11.6"	2' 11.5"	2' 11.3"	2' 10.9"	2' 10.5"	2' 10.0"	2' 9.3"	2' 8.1"	2' 6.9"	2' 5.1"
	Far	3' 0.3"	3' 0.4"	3' 0.6"	3' 0.8"	3' 1.1"	3' 1.6"	3' 2.3"	3' 3.3"	3' 5.0"	3' 7.3"	3' 11"
3' 6"	Near	3' 5.6"	3' 5.5"	3' 5.3"	3' 5.0"	3' 4.5"	3' 4.0"	3' 3.2"	3' 2.2"	3' 0.7"	2' 11.1"	2' 8.7"
	Far	3' 6.4"	3' 6.5"	3' 6.8"	3' 7.1"	3' 7.6"	3' 8.3"	3' 9.3"	3' 10.7"	4' 1.2"	4' 4"	4' 11"
4' 0"	Near	3' 11.5"	3' 11.3"	3' 11.0"	3' 10.6"	3' 10.0"	3' 9.3"	3' 8.3"	3' 7.0"	3' 5.1"	3' 3.0"	3' 0.0"
	Far	4' 0.5"	4' 0.7"	4' 1.0"	4' 1.5"	4' 2.1"	4' 3.1"	4' 4.5"	4' 6.4"	4' 10"	5' 2"	6' 1"
4' 6"	Near	4' 5.4"	4' 5.1"	4' 4.7"	4' 4.2"	4' 3.5"	4' 2.6"	4' 1.2"	3' 11.7"	3' 9.3"	3' 6.7"	3' 3.1"
	Far	4' 6.7"	4' 6.9"	4' 7.4"	4' 7.9"	4' 8.8"	4' 10.0"	4' 11.9"	5' 2.4"	5' 7"	6' 2"	7' 5"
5' 0"	Near	4' 11.2"	4' 10.9"	4' 10.4"	4' 9.8"	4' 8.9"	4' 7.7"	4' 6.1"	4' 4.2"	4' 1.3"	3' 10.2"	3' 5.9"
	Far	5' 0.8"	5' 1.2"	5' 1.7"	5' 2.4"	5' 3.5"	5' 5.0"	5' 7.4"	5' 10.8"	6' 5"	7' 2"	9' 0"
6' 0"	Near	5' 10.8"	5' 10.3"	5' 9.7"	5' 8.8"	5' 7.5"	5' 5.8"	5' 3.5"	5' 0.8"	4' 8.9"	4' 4.7"	3' 11.1"
	Far	6' 1.2"	6' 1.7"	6' 2.5"	6' 3.6"	6' 5.2"	6' 7.5"	6' 11.3"	7' 4"	8' 2"	9' 7"	13' 3"
7' 0"	Near	6' 10.4"	6' 9.7"	6' 8.8"	6' 7.6"	6' 5.8"	6' 3.6"	6' 0.5"	5' 9.0"	5' 3.9"	4' 10.7"	4' 3.7"
	Far	7' 1.7"	7' 2.4"	7' 3.5"	7' 5.0"	7' 7.3"	7' 10.6"	8' 4"	8' 11"	10' 3"	12' 7"	19' 11"
8' 0"	Near	7' 9.8"	7' 9.0"	7' 7.8"	7' 6.2"	7' 3.9"	7' 1.1"	6' 9.1"	6' 4.7"	5' 10.4"	5' 4.0"	4' 7.8"
	Far	8' 2.3"	8' 3.2"	8' 4.6"	8' 6.6"	8' 9.8"	9' 2.2"	9' 9"	10' 8"	12' 8"	16' 5"	32' 1"
10'	Near	9' 8.6"	9' 7.3"	9' 5.4"	9' 2.9"	8' 11.5"	8' 7.2"	8' 1.4"	7' 7.0"	6' 10.1"	6' 1.5"	5' 2.6"
	Far	10' 3"	10' 5"	10' 7"	10' 10"	11' 3"	11' 11"	13' 0"	14' 9"	18' 11"	28' 7"	>100'
12'	Near	11' 7"	11' 5"	11' 2"	10' 11"	10' 6"	10' 0"	9' 4.4"	8' 7.9"	7' 8.3"	6' 9.5"	5' 8"
	Far	12' 5"	12' 7"	12' 11"	13' 3"	13' 11"	14' 11"	16' 9"	19' 8"	28' 0"	56'	INF
15'	Near	14' 4"	14' 1"	13' 9"	13' 4"	12' 8"	12' 0"	11' 0"	10' 1"	8' 9.4"	7' 7.4"	6' 3"
	Far	15' 8"	16' 0"	16' 5"	17' 1"	18' 3"	20' 0"	23' 4"	29' 8"	53'	>100'	INF
20'	Near	18' 10"	18' 5"	17' 10"	17' 1"	16' 1"	14' 11"	13' 6"	12' 0"	10' 2"	8' 8"	6' 11"
	Far	21' 3"	21' 10"	22' 8"	24' 0"	26' 4"	30' 2"	38' 8"	59'	>100'	INF	INF
30'	Near	27' 6"	26' 7"	25' 4"	23' 10"	22' 0"	19' 10"	17' 4"	15' 0"	12' 3"	10' 1"	7' 9"
	Far	33' 0"	34' 4"	36' 8"	40' 3"	47' 3"	61'	>100'	INF	INF	INF	INF
60'	Near	50'	47' 8"	43' 10"	39' 7"	34' 7"	29' 7"	24' 4"	19' 11"	15' 4"	12' 0"	8' 10"
	Far	73'	80'	95'	>100'	>100'	INF	INF	INF	INF	INF	INF

Hyperfocal distance

322'	230'	161'	115'	80'	57'	40' 6"	29' 6"	20' 4"	14' 10"	10' 3"	

Depth of Field — Prime lenses

75 mm — PANAVISION PRIMO-L PRIME

Entrance pupil rearwards from front vertex = 51 mm   Lens length, vertex to focal plane = 115 mm

Circle of Confusion	Aperture										
1/500in					2	2.8	4	5.6	8	11	16
1/710in				2	2.8	4	5.6	8	11	16	22
1/1000in			2	2.8	4	5.6	8	11	16	22	
1/1420in		2	2.8	4	5.6	8	11	16	22		
1/2000in	2	2.8	4	5.6	8	11	16	22			

Focus Distance		Extreme distances in acceptable focus										
2' 0"	Near	2' 0.0"	1' 11.9"	1' 11.9"	1' 11.9"	1' 11.8"	1' 11.7"	1' 11.6"	1' 11.5"	1' 11.3"	1' 11.0"	1' 10.6"
	Far	2' 0.0"	2' 0.1"	2' 0.1"	2' 0.1"	2' 0.2"	2' 0.3"	2' 0.4"	2' 0.5"	2' 0.8"	2' 1.1"	2' 1.6"
2' 6"	Near	2' 5.9"	2' 5.9"	2' 5.8"	2' 5.8"	2' 5.7"	2' 5.6"	2' 5.4"	2' 5.2"	2' 4.8"	2' 4.4"	2' 3.7"
	Far	2' 6.1"	2' 6.1"	2' 6.2"	2' 6.2"	2' 6.3"	2' 6.4"	2' 6.6"	2' 6.9"	2' 7.3"	2' 7.8"	2' 8.7"
3' 0"	Near	2' 11.9"	2' 11.8"	2' 11.8"	2' 11.7"	2' 11.5"	2' 11.4"	2' 11.1"	2' 10.8"	2' 10.2"	2' 9.6"	2' 8.6"
	Far	3' 0.1"	3' 0.2"	3' 0.2"	3' 0.3"	3' 0.5"	3' 0.7"	3' 1.0"	3' 1.3"	3' 2.0"	3' 2.8"	3' 4.2"
3' 6"	Near	3' 5.8"	3' 5.8"	3' 5.7"	3' 5.5"	3' 5.3"	3' 5.1"	3' 4.7"	3' 4.3"	3' 3.5"	3' 2.7"	3' 1.3"
	Far	3' 6.2"	3' 6.2"	3' 6.3"	3' 6.5"	3' 6.7"	3' 6.9"	3' 7.4"	3' 7.9"	3' 8.8"	3' 10.0"	4' 0.1"
4' 0"	Near	3' 11.8"	3' 11.7"	3' 11.6"	3' 11.4"	3' 11.1"	3' 10.8"	3' 10.3"	3' 9.7"	3' 8.7"	3' 7.6"	3' 5.9"
	Far	4' 0.2"	4' 0.3"	4' 0.4"	4' 0.6"	4' 0.9"	4' 1.3"	4' 1.8"	4' 2.6"	4' 3.8"	4' 5.5"	4' 8.4"
4' 6"	Near	4' 5.7"	4' 5.6"	4' 5.4"	4' 5.2"	4' 4.9"	4' 4.4"	4' 3.8"	4' 3.0"	4' 1.8"	4' 0.4"	3' 10.2"
	Far	4' 6.3"	4' 6.4"	4' 6.6"	4' 6.8"	4' 7.2"	4' 7.7"	4' 8.4"	4' 9.4"	4' 11.0"	5' 1.2"	5' 5"
5' 0"	Near	4' 11.6"	4' 11.5"	4' 11.3"	4' 11.0"	4' 10.6"	4' 10.1"	4' 9.3"	4' 8.3"	4' 6.8"	4' 5.0"	4' 2.4"
	Far	5' 0.4"	5' 0.5"	5' 0.7"	5' 1.0"	5' 1.5"	5' 2.1"	5' 3.0"	5' 4.2"	5' 6.4"	5' 9.2"	6' 2"
6' 0"	Near	5' 11.5"	5' 11.3"	5' 11.0"	5' 10.5"	5' 9.9"	5' 9.2"	5' 8.0"	5' 6.6"	5' 4.4"	5' 2.0"	4' 10.4"
	Far	6' 0.5"	6' 0.8"	6' 1.1"	6' 1.5"	6' 2.2"	6' 3.1"	6' 4.5"	6' 6.4"	6' 9.7"	7' 2"	7' 10"
7' 0"	Near	6' 11.3"	6' 11.0"	6' 10.6"	6' 10.0"	6' 9.2"	6' 8.1"	6' 6.5"	6' 4.7"	6' 1.7"	5' 10.5"	5' 5.8"
	Far	7' 0.7"	7' 1.0"	7' 1.5"	7' 2.1"	7' 3.0"	7' 4.3"	7' 6.3"	7' 9.0"	8' 1"	8' 8"	9' 9"
8' 0"	Near	7' 11.0"	7' 10.7"	7' 10.1"	7' 9.4"	7' 8.3"	7' 6.9"	7' 4.8"	7' 2.4"	6' 10.7"	6' 6.6"	6' 0.7"
	Far	8' 1.0"	8' 1.4"	8' 2.0"	8' 2.8"	8' 4.1"	8' 5.8"	8' 8.5"	9' 0.1"	9' 6"	10' 3"	11' 10"
10'	Near	9' 10.5"	9' 9.9"	9' 9.0"	9' 7.8"	9' 6.1"	9' 4.0"	9' 0.8"	8' 9.2"	8' 3.6"	7' 9.7"	7' 1.2"
	Far	10' 1"	10' 2"	10' 3"	10' 4"	10' 6"	10' 9"	11' 1"	11' 7"	12' 7"	13' 11"	17' 1"
12'	Near	11' 9"	11' 8"	11' 7"	11' 6"	11' 3"	11' 0"	10' 8"	10' 3"	9' 7.3"	8' 11.4"	8' 0.3"
	Far	12' 2"	12' 3"	12' 4"	12' 6"	12' 9"	13' 1"	13' 8"	14' 6"	16' 0"	18' 4"	24' 2"
15'	Near	14' 8"	14' 7"	14' 5"	14' 2"	13' 10"	13' 6"	12' 11"	12' 4"	11' 4"	10' 5"	9' 2.7"
	Far	15' 3"	15' 5"	15' 7"	15' 10"	16' 3"	16' 10"	17' 9"	19' 2"	21' 11"	26' 7"	41' 4"
20'	Near	19' 5"	19' 3"	18' 11"	18' 7"	18' 0"	17' 4"	16' 5"	15' 5"	14' 0"	12' 7"	10' 10"
	Far	20' 6"	20' 9"	21' 1"	21' 7"	22' 4"	23' 6"	25' 5"	28' 3"	34' 11"	48' 8"	>100'
30'	Near	28' 10"	28' 4"	27' 9"	26' 11"	25' 10"	24' 5"	22' 8"	20' 9"	18' 3"	15' 11"	13' 1"
	Far	31' 3"	31' 9"	32' 7"	33' 9"	35' 9"	38' 9"	44' 4"	54'	85'	>100'	INF
60'	Near	55'	53'	51'	48' 10"	45' 2"	41' 2"	36' 3"	31' 7"	26' 0"	21' 6"	16' 8"
	Far	65'	67'	71'	77'	89'	>100'	>100'	>100'	INF	INF	INF

Hyperfocal distance										
726'	519'	363'	259'	181'	129'	91'	66'	45' 7"	33' 3"	22' 11"

Depth of Field — Prime lenses

100 mm · PANAVISION PRIMO-L PRIME

Entrance pupil rearwards from front vertex = 72 mm Lens length, vertex to focal plane = 145 mm

Circle of Confusion						Aperture					
1/500in						2	2.8	4	5.6	8	11	16
1/710in					2	2.8	4	5.6	8	11	16	22
1/1000in				2	2.8	4	5.6	8	11	16	22	
1/1420in		2	2.8	4	5.6	8	11	16	22			
1/2000in	2	2.8	4	5.6	8	11	16	22				

Focus Distance		Extreme distances in acceptable focus										
3' 0"	Near	2' 0.0"	2' 0.0"	2' 0.0"	1' 11.9"	1' 11.9"	1' 11.9"	1' 11.8"	1' 11.7"	1' 11.6"	1' 11.5"	1' 11.3"
	Far	2' 0.0"	2' 0.0"	2' 0.0"	2' 0.1"	2' 0.1"	2' 0.1"	2' 0.2"	2' 0.3"	2' 0.4"	2' 0.5"	2' 0.8"
3' 6"	Near	2' 6.0"	2' 5.9"	2' 5.9"	2' 5.9"	2' 5.8"	2' 5.8"	2' 5.7"	2' 5.6"	2' 5.4"	2' 5.1"	2' 4.8"
	Far	2' 6.0"	2' 6.1"	2' 6.1"	2' 6.1"	2' 6.2"	2' 6.2"	2' 6.3"	2' 6.5"	2' 6.7"	2' 6.9"	2' 7.4"
4' 0"	Near	2' 11.9"	2' 11.9"	2' 11.9"	2' 11.8"	2' 11.8"	2' 11.7"	2' 11.5"	2' 11.3"	2' 11.0"	2' 10.7"	2' 10.1"
	Far	3' 0.1"	3' 0.1"	3' 0.1"	3' 0.2"	3' 0.3"	3' 0.4"	3' 0.5"	3' 0.7"	3' 1.0"	3' 1.4"	3' 2.1"
4' 6"	Near	3' 5.9"	3' 5.9"	3' 5.8"	3' 5.8"	3' 5.6"	3' 5.5"	3' 5.3"	3' 5.0"	3' 4.6"	3' 4.1"	3' 3.4"
	Far	3' 6.1"	3' 6.1"	3' 6.2"	3' 6.3"	3' 6.4"	3' 6.5"	3' 6.7"	3' 7.0"	3' 7.5"	3' 8.1"	3' 9.1"
5' 0"	Near	3' 11.9"	3' 11.8"	3' 11.8"	3' 11.7"	3' 11.5"	3' 11.3"	3' 11.1"	3' 10.7"	3' 10.2"	3' 9.5"	3' 8.5"
	Far	4' 0.1"	4' 0.2"	4' 0.2"	4' 0.3"	4' 0.5"	4' 0.7"	4' 1.0"	4' 1.4"	4' 2.0"	4' 2.8"	4' 4.2"
6' 0"	Near	4' 5.8"	4' 5.8"	4' 5.7"	4' 5.6"	4' 5.4"	4' 5.1"	4' 4.8"	4' 4.3"	4' 3.6"	4' 2.8"	4' 1.5"
	Far	4' 6.2"	4' 6.2"	4' 6.3"	4' 6.4"	4' 6.6"	4' 6.9"	4' 7.3"	4' 7.8"	4' 8.6"	4' 9.7"	4' 11.5"
7' 0"	Near	4' 11.8"	4' 11.7"	4' 11.6"	4' 11.5"	4' 11.2"	4' 10.9"	4' 10.5"	4' 9.9"	4' 9.0"	4' 8.0"	4' 6.3"
	Far	5' 0.2"	5' 0.3"	5' 0.4"	5' 0.6"	5' 0.8"	5' 1.1"	5' 1.6"	5' 2.2"	5' 3.3"	5' 4.7"	5' 7.0"
8' 0"	Near	5' 11.7"	5' 11.6"	5' 11.4"	5' 11.2"	5' 10.9"	5' 10.4"	5' 9.7"	5' 8.9"	5' 7.6"	5' 6.1"	5' 3.8"
	Far	6' 0.3"	6' 0.4"	6' 0.6"	6' 0.8"	6' 1.2"	6' 1.7"	6' 2.4"	6' 3.4"	6' 5.0"	6' 7.0"	6' 10.7"
10'	Near	6' 11.6"	6' 11.4"	6' 11.2"	6' 10.9"	6' 10.4"	6' 9.8"	6' 8.9"	6' 7.8"	6' 6.0"	6' 4.0"	6' 0.8"
	Far	7' 0.4"	7' 0.6"	7' 0.8"	7' 1.1"	7' 1.6"	7' 2.3"	7' 3.4"	7' 4.7"	7' 7.0"	7' 10.0"	8' 3"
12'	Near	7' 11.5"	7' 11.3"	7' 10.9"	7' 10.5"	7' 9.9"	7' 9.1"	7' 7.9"	7' 6.5"	7' 4.1"	7' 1.5"	6' 9.5"
	Far	8' 0.5"	8' 0.8"	8' 1.1"	8' 1.5"	8' 2.2"	8' 3.1"	8' 4.5"	8' 6.3"	8' 9.4"	9' 1.5"	9' 9"
15'	Near	9' 11.2"	9' 10.8"	9' 10.3"	9' 9.7"	9' 8.7"	9' 7.4"	9' 5.5"	9' 3.3"	8' 11.7"	8' 7.8"	8' 1.8"
	Far	10' 0"	10' 1"	10' 1"	10' 2"	10' 3"	10' 5"	10' 7"	10' 10"	11' 3"	11' 10"	12' 11"
20'	Near	11' 10"	11' 10"	11' 9"	11' 8"	11' 7"	11' 5"	11' 2"	10' 11"	10' 6"	10' 1"	9' 4.9"
	Far	12' 1"	12' 1"	12' 2"	12' 3"	12' 5"	12' 7"	12' 10"	13' 3"	13' 11"	14' 10"	16' 7"
25'	Near	14' 10"	14' 9"	14' 8"	14' 6"	14' 4"	14' 1"	13' 9"	13' 4"	12' 9"	12' 1"	11' 1"
	Far	15' 2"	15' 2"	15' 4"	15' 5"	15' 8"	15' 11"	16' 5"	17' 0"	18' 2"	19' 9"	23' 2"
30'	Near	19' 8"	19' 7"	19' 5"	19' 2"	18' 10"	18' 5"	17' 10"	17' 2"	16' 2"	15' 1"	13' 6"
	Far	20' 3"	20' 5"	20' 7"	20' 10"	21' 3"	21' 9"	22' 8"	23' 11"	26' 3"	29' 9"	38' 4"
40'	Near	29' 4"	29' 1"	28' 8"	28' 2"	27' 6"	26' 7"	25' 4"	24' 0"	22' 0"	20' 0"	17' 5"
	Far	30' 8"	30' 11"	31' 5"	32' 0"	32' 11"	34' 4"	36' 7"	39' 11"	47' 0"	59'	>100'
60'	Near	57'	56'	54'	53'	50'	47' 9"	43' 11"	39' 11"	34' 7"	29' 11"	24' 4"
	Far	62'	64'	66'	68'	73'	80'	94'	>100'	>100'	INF	INF

Hyperfocal distance											
1292'	922'	646'	461'	323'	230'	161'	117'	81'	59'	40' 8"

150 mm

PANAVISION PRIMO-L PRIME

Entrance pupil rearwards from front vertex = 133 mm

Lens length, vertex to focal plane = 195 mm

Circle of Confusion	Aperture										
1/500in					2	2.8	4	5.6	8	11	16
1/710in				2	2.8	4	5.6	8	11	16	22
1/1000in			2	2.8	4	5.6	8	11	16	22	
1/1420in		2	2.8	4	5.6	8	11	16	22		
1/2000in	2	2.8	4	5.6	8	11	16	22			

Focus Distance		Extreme distances in acceptable focus										
5' 6"	Near	2' 0.0"	2' 0.0"	2' 0.0"	2' 0.0"	2' 0.0"	1' 11.9"	1' 11.9"	1' 11.9"	1' 11.8"	1' 11.8"	1' 11.7"
	Far	2' 0.0"	2' 0.0"	2' 0.0"	2' 0.0"	2' 0.0"	2' 0.1"	2' 0.1"	2' 0.1"	2' 0.2"	2' 0.2"	2' 0.3"
6' 0"	Near	2' 6.0"	2' 6.0"	2' 6.0"	2' 6.0"	2' 5.9"	2' 5.9"	2' 5.9"	2' 5.8"	2' 5.7"	2' 5.6"	2' 5.5"
	Far	2' 6.0"	2' 6.0"	2' 6.0"	2' 6.0"	2' 6.1"	2' 6.1"	2' 6.1"	2' 6.2"	2' 6.3"	2' 6.4"	2' 6.6"
6' 6"	Near	3' 0.0"	3' 0.0"	2' 11.9"	2' 11.9"	2' 11.9"	2' 11.9"	2' 11.8"	2' 11.7"	2' 11.6"	2' 11.4"	2' 11.2"
	Far	3' 0.0"	3' 0.0"	3' 0.1"	3' 0.1"	3' 0.1"	3' 0.1"	3' 0.2"	3' 0.3"	3' 0.4"	3' 0.6"	3' 0.9"
7' 0"	Near	3' 6.0"	3' 5.9"	3' 5.9"	3' 5.9"	3' 5.8"	3' 5.8"	3' 5.7"	3' 5.6"	3' 5.4"	3' 5.2"	3' 4.8"
	Far	3' 6.0"	3' 6.1"	3' 6.1"	3' 6.1"	3' 6.2"	3' 6.2"	3' 6.3"	3' 6.4"	3' 6.6"	3' 6.9"	3' 7.3"
7' 6"	Near	3' 11.9"	3' 11.9"	3' 11.9"	3' 11.9"	3' 11.8"	3' 11.7"	3' 11.6"	3' 11.4"	3' 11.2"	3' 10.9"	3' 10.4"
	Far	4' 0.1"	4' 0.1"	4' 0.1"	4' 0.1"	4' 0.2"	4' 0.3"	4' 0.4"	4' 0.6"	4' 0.8"	4' 1.2"	4' 1.7"
8' 0"	Near	4' 5.9"	4' 5.9"	4' 5.9"	4' 5.8"	4' 5.7"	4' 5.6"	4' 5.5"	4' 5.3"	4' 4.9"	4' 4.6"	4' 3.9"
	Far	4' 6.1"	4' 6.1"	4' 6.1"	4' 6.2"	4' 6.3"	4' 6.4"	4' 6.5"	4' 6.8"	4' 7.1"	4' 7.5"	4' 8.3"
9' 0"	Near	4' 11.9"	4' 11.9"	4' 11.8"	4' 11.8"	4' 11.7"	4' 11.5"	4' 11.3"	4' 11.1"	4' 10.7"	4' 10.2"	4' 9.4"
	Far	5' 0.1"	5' 0.1"	5' 0.2"	5' 0.2"	5' 0.3"	5' 0.5"	5' 0.7"	5' 1.0"	5' 1.4"	5' 1.9"	5' 2.9"
10'	Near	5' 11.9"	5' 11.8"	5' 11.7"	5' 11.6"	5' 11.5"	5' 11.3"	5' 11.0"	5' 10.6"	5' 10.0"	5' 9.3"	5' 8.2"
	Far	6' 0.1"	6' 0.2"	6' 0.3"	6' 0.4"	6' 0.5"	6' 0.7"	6' 1.0"	6' 1.4"	6' 2.1"	6' 2.9"	6' 4.3"
12'	Near	6' 11.8"	6' 11.8"	6' 11.6"	6' 11.5"	6' 11.3"	6' 11.0"	6' 10.6"	6' 10.1"	6' 9.3"	6' 8.3"	6' 6.7"
	Far	7' 0.2"	7' 0.2"	7' 0.4"	7' 0.5"	7' 0.7"	7' 1.0"	7' 1.4"	7' 2.0"	7' 2.9"	7' 4.1"	7' 6.1"
14'	Near	7' 11.8"	7' 11.7"	7' 11.5"	7' 11.3"	7' 11.1"	7' 10.7"	7' 10.2"	7' 9.5"	7' 8.4"	7' 7.1"	7' 5.0"
	Far	8' 0.2"	8' 0.3"	8' 0.5"	8' 0.7"	8' 1.0"	8' 1.3"	8' 1.9"	8' 2.7"	8' 3.9"	8' 5.5"	8' 8.2"
17'	Near	9' 11.6"	9' 11.5"	9' 11.3"	9' 11.0"	9' 10.5"	9' 9.9"	9' 9.1"	9' 8.0"	9' 6.3"	9' 4.3"	9' 1.1"
	Far	10' 0"	10' 0"	10' 0"	10' 1"	10' 1"	10' 2"	10' 3"	10' 4"	10' 6"	10' 8"	11' 1"
20'	Near	11' 11"	11' 11"	11' 10"	11' 10"	11' 9"	11' 9"	11' 7"	11' 6"	11' 3"	11' 0"	10' 8"
	Far	12' 0"	12' 0"	12' 1"	12' 1"	12' 2"	12' 3"	12' 4"	12' 6"	12' 9"	13' 1"	13' 8"
25'	Near	14' 11"	14' 10"	14' 10"	14' 9"	14' 8"	14' 7"	14' 5"	14' 2"	13' 11"	13' 6"	12' 11"
	Far	15' 0"	15' 1"	15' 1"	15' 2"	15' 3"	15' 5"	15' 7"	15' 10"	16' 3"	16' 9"	17' 9"
30'	Near	19' 10"	19' 9"	19' 8"	19' 7"	19' 5"	19' 3"	19' 0"	18' 7"	18' 1"	17' 5"	16' 6"
	Far	20' 1"	20' 2"	20' 3"	20' 4"	20' 6"	20' 9"	21' 1"	21' 6"	22' 4"	23' 4"	25' 4"
40'	Near	29' 8"	29' 7"	29' 4"	29' 2"	28' 10"	28' 4"	27' 9"	27' 0"	25' 10"	24' 7"	22' 8"
	Far	30' 3"	30' 5"	30' 7"	30' 10"	31' 3"	31' 9"	32' 7"	33' 8"	35' 8"	38' 5"	44' 2"
60'	Near	58'	58'	57'	56'	55'	53'	51'	49' 0"	45' 3"	41' 5"	36' 4"
	Far	61'	61'	62'	63'	65'	67'	71'	77'	88'	>100'	>100'

Hyperfocal distance

2906'	2076'	1453'	1038'	727'	519'	363'	264'	182'	132'	91'

Depth of Field — 17.5 - 75mm Zoom

17.5 mm   PANAVISION PRIMO 17.5 - 75mm ZOOM

Entrance pupil rearwards from front ve 62 mm   Lens length, vertex to focal plane = 352 mm

Circle of Confusion										
					Aperture					
1/500in					2.8	4	5.6	8	11	16
1/710in				2.8	4	5.6	8	11	16	22
1/1000in			2.8	4	5.6	8	11	16	22	
1/1420in		2.8	4	5.6	8	11	16	22		
1/2000in	2.8	4	5.6	8	11	16	22			
Focus Distance										
2' 6" Near	2' 5.1"	2' 4.7"	2' 4.2"	2' 3.6"	2' 2.8"	2' 1.7"	2' 0.6"	1' 11.0"	1' 9.6"	1' 7"
2' 6" Far	2' 7.0"	2' 7.5"	2' 8.2"	2' 9.3"	2' 11.0"	3' 2.0"	3' 7"	4' 10"	10' 0"	INF
2' 9" Near	2' 7.7"	2' 7.3"	2' 6.6"	2' 5.8"	2' 4.7"	2' 3.4"	2' 2.0"	2' 0.1"	1' 10.4"	1' 8"
2' 9" Far	2' 10.4"	2' 11.1"	3' 0.0"	3' 1.6"	3' 4.1"	3' 8"	4' 5"	7' 0"	57'	INF
3' 0" Near	2' 10.4"	2' 9.8"	2' 9.0"	2' 7.9"	2' 6.6"	2' 4.9"	2' 3.2"	2' 1.0"	1' 11"	1' 8"
3' 0" Far	3' 1.9"	3' 2.8"	3' 4.0"	3' 6.2"	3' 9.6"	4' 4"	5' 6"	11' 5"	INF	INF
3' 6" Near	3' 3.5"	3' 2.6"	3' 1.4"	2' 11.8"	2' 10.0"	2' 7.8"	2' 5.5"	2' 2"	2' 0"	1' 9"
3' 6" Far	3' 9.0"	3' 10.4"	4' 0.5"	4' 4"	4' 10"	6' 1"	9' 2"	INF	INF	INF
4' 0" Near	3' 8.5"	3' 7.2"	3' 5.6"	3' 3.5"	3' 1.1"	2' 10.2"	2' 7.4"	2' 4"	2' 1"	1' 10"
4' 0" Far	4' 4.3"	4' 6.5"	4' 9"	5' 3"	6' 2"	8' 8"	19' 0"	INF	INF	INF
4' 6" Near	4' 1.3"	3' 11.6"	3' 9.6"	3' 6.9"	3' 3.9"	3' 0.4"	2' 9.0"	2' 5"	2' 1"	1' 10"
4' 6" Far	5' 0.0"	5' 3.1"	5' 8"	6' 5"	7' 11"	13' 0"	>100'	INF	INF	INF
5' 0" Near	4' 6.0"	4' 3.8"	4' 1.3"	3' 10.0"	3' 6.5"	3' 2.3"	2' 10"	2' 6"	2' 2"	1' 10"
5' 0" Far	5' 8.0"	6' 0"	6' 7"	7' 8"	10' 3"	21' 11"	INF	INF	INF	INF
6' 0" Near	5' 2.9"	4' 11.8"	4' 8.2"	4' 3.7"	3' 10.9"	3' 5"	3' 0"	2' 7"	2' 3"	1' 11"
6' 0" Far	7' 1"	7' 8"	8' 9"	11' 1"	18' 1"	INF	INF	INF	INF	INF
7' 0" Near	5' 11.3"	5' 7.1"	5' 2.4"	4' 8.6"	4' 2.7"	3' 8"	3' 2"	2' 8"	2' 4"	1' 11"
7' 0" Far	8' 7"	9' 7"	11' 5"	16' 3"	40' 9"	INF	INF	INF	INF	INF
8' 0" Near	6' 7.2"	6' 1.9"	5' 8.0"	5' 1.0"	4' 5.9"	3' 10"	3' 4"	2' 9"	2' 4"	2' 0"
8' 0" Far	10' 3"	11' 10"	14' 10"	25' 0"	>100'	INF	INF	INF	INF	INF
10' Near	7' 9.8"	7' 2.1"	6' 5.8"	5' 8.3"	4' 11"	4' 1"	3' 6"	2' 10"	2' 5"	2' 0"
10' Far	14' 2"	17' 6"	25' 10"	>100'	INF	INF	INF	INF	INF	INF
12' Near	8' 10.9"	8' 0.6"	7' 2.0"	6' 2"	5' 3"	4' 4"	3' 8"	2' 11"	2' 6"	2' 0"
12' Far	19' 0"	25' 9"	50'	INF	INF	INF	INF	INF	INF	INF
15' Near	10' 4"	9' 2.2"	8' 0.1"	6' 9"	5' 8"	4' 7"	3' 9"	3' 0"	2' 6"	2' 1"
15' Far	28' 9"	48' 11"	>100'	INF	INF	INF	INF	INF	INF	INF
20' Near	12' 4"	10' 8"	9' 0"	7' 5"	6' 1"	4' 10"	3' 11"	3' 1"	2' 7"	2' 1"
20' Far	59'	>100'	INF	INF	INF	INF	INF	INF	INF	INF
30' Near	15' 3"	12' 8"	10' 5"	8' 4"	6' 7"	5' 2"	4' 1"	3' 2"	2' 7"	2' 1"
30' Far	INF	INF	INF	INF	INF	INF	INF	INF	INF	INF
60' Near	20' 0"	15' 9"	12' 4"	9' 5"	7' 3"	5' 6"	4' 4"	3' 3"	2' 8"	2' 2"
60' Far	INF	INF	INF	INF	INF	INF	INF	INF	INF	INF
	28' 3"	19' 10"	14' 2"	9' 11"	7' 1"	5' 0"	3' 7"	2' 6"	1' 10"	1' 3"

Depth of Field — 17.5 - 75mm Zoom

26 mm PANAVISION PRIMO 17.5 - 75mm ZOOM

Entrance pupil rearwards from front ve 74 mm   Lens length, vertex to focal plane = 352 mm

Circle of Confusion	Aperture									
1/500in					2.8	4	5.6	8	11	16
1/710in				2.8	4	5.6	8	11	16	22
1/1000in			2.8	4	5.6	8	11	16	22	
1/1420in		2.8	4	5.6	8	11	16	22		
1/2000in	2.8	4	5.6	8	11	16	22			
Focus Distance										
2' 6" Near	2' 5.6"	2' 5.4"	2' 5.1"	2' 4.8"	2' 4.3"	2' 3.7"	2' 3.0"	2' 1.9"	2' 0.8"	1' 11.2"
2' 6" Far	2' 6.5"	2' 6.7"	2' 7.0"	2' 7.4"	2' 8.0"	2' 9.0"	2' 10.4"	3' 1.2"	3' 5"	4' 5"
2' 9" Near	2' 8.4"	2' 8.1"	2' 7.8"	2' 7.4"	2' 6.8"	2' 5.9"	2' 5.0"	2' 3.6"	2' 2.2"	2' 0.4"
2' 9" Far	2' 9.6"	2' 9.9"	2' 10.3"	2' 10.9"	2' 11.8"	3' 1.2"	3' 3.2"	3' 7"	4' 2"	6' 0"
3' 0" Near	2' 11.2"	2' 10.9"	2' 10.5"	2' 9.9"	2' 9.1"	2' 8.1"	2' 7.0"	2' 5.3"	2' 3.6"	2' 1.4"
3' 0" Far	3' 0.8"	3' 1.2"	3' 1.7"	3' 2.5"	3' 3.7"	3' 5.6"	3' 8.5"	4' 2"	5' 1"	8' 9"
3' 6" Near	3' 4.8"	3' 4.3"	3' 3.7"	3' 2.8"	3' 1.7"	3' 0.2"	2' 10.6"	2' 8.2"	2' 6.0"	2' 3.1"
3' 6" Far	3' 7.3"	3' 7.9"	3' 8.7"	3' 10.0"	3' 11.9"	4' 3.2"	4' 8"	5' 8"	7' 11"	32' 1"
4' 0" Near	3' 10.3"	3' 9.6"	3' 8.7"	3' 7.5"	3' 6.0"	3' 4.0"	3' 1.8"	2' 10.8"	2' 8.0"	2' 4"
4' 0" Far	4' 1.9"	4' 2.7"	4' 3.9"	4' 5.9"	4' 8.8"	5' 2"	5' 10"	7' 9"	13' 7"	INF
4' 6" Near	4' 3.7"	4' 2.8"	4' 1.7"	4' 0.0"	3' 10.1"	3' 7.5"	3' 4.8"	3' 1.2"	2' 9.8"	2' 5"
4' 6" Far	4' 8.6"	4' 9.8"	4' 11.4"	5' 2.2"	5' 6"	6' 2"	7' 4"	10' 11"	31' 5"	INF
5' 0" Near	4' 9.0"	4' 7.9"	4' 6.4"	4' 4.4"	4' 2.0"	3' 10.8"	3' 7.6"	3' 3.2"	2' 11"	2' 6"
5' 0" Far	5' 3.4"	5' 5.0"	5' 7.2"	5' 11.0"	6' 4"	7' 4"	9' 1"	16' 3"	INF	INF
6' 0" Near	5' 7.5"	5' 5.7"	5' 3.6"	5' 0.6"	4' 9.2"	4' 4.8"	4' 0.4"	3' 6.8"	3' 2"	2' 8"
6' 0" Far	6' 5.3"	6' 7.9"	6' 11.7"	7' 6"	8' 4"	10' 3"	14' 8"	61'	INF	INF
7' 0" Near	6' 5.6"	6' 3.2"	6' 0.2"	5' 8.2"	5' 3.7"	4' 10.1"	4' 4.5"	3' 9"	3' 4"	2' 9"
7' 0" Far	7' 7.8"	7' 11.6"	8' 5"	9' 3"	10' 9"	14' 5"	25' 10"	INF	INF	INF
8' 0" Near	7' 3.4"	7' 0.2"	6' 8.4"	6' 3.3"	5' 9.6"	5' 2.8"	4' 8.1"	4' 0"	3' 5"	2' 10"
8' 0" Far	8' 10.8"	9' 4.2"	10' 0"	11' 4"	13' 9"	20' 8"	61'	INF	INF	INF
10' Near	8' 10.2"	8' 5.4"	7' 11.6"	7' 4.2"	6' 8.1"	5' 10.7"	5' 2"	4' 4"	3' 8"	3' 0"
10' Far	11' 6"	12' 4"	13' 8"	16' 4"	22' 5"	52'	INF	INF	INF	INF
12' Near	10' 4"	9' 2"	9' 1.3"	8' 3.4"	7' 5.0"	6' 5"	5' 6"	4' 7"	3' 10"	3' 1"
12' Far	14' 4"	15' 8"	18' 0"	23' 3"	38' 7"	INF	INF	INF	INF	INF
15' Near	12' 5"	11' 6"	10' 7"	9' 5.9"	8' 4.0"	7' 1"	6' 0"	4' 10"	4' 0"	3' 2"
15' Far	19' 0"	21' 7"	26' 5"	40' 2"	>100'	INF	INF	INF	INF	INF
20' Near	15' 6"	14' 2"	12' 9"	11' 1"	9' 6"	7' 10"	6' 6"	5' 2"	4' 2"	3' 3"
20' Far	28' 4"	34' 8"	49' 9"	>100'	INF	INF	INF	INF	INF	INF
30' Near	20' 9"	18' 4"	15' 11"	13' 4"	11' 1"	8' 10"	7' 2"	5' 6"	4' 5"	3' 5"
30' Far	55'	87'	>100'	INF	INF	INF	INF	INF	INF	INF
60 Near	31' 3"	26' 0"	21' 4"	16' 10"	13' 3"	10' 1"	7' 11"	5' 11"	4' 7"	3' 6"
60 Far	>100'	INF	INF	INF	INF	INF	INF	INF	INF	INF

| | 62' | 43' 8" | 31' 3" | 21' 11" | 15' 8" | 11' 0" | 8' 0" | 5' 6" | 4' 0" | 2' 9" |

Depth of Field — 17.5 - 75mm Zoom

34 mm — PANAVISION PRIMO 17.5 - 75mm ZOOM

Entrance pupil rearwards from front vertex = 84 mm   Lens length, vertex to focal plane = 352 mm

Circle of Confusion	Aperture									
1/500in					2.8	4	5.6	8	11	16
1/710in				2.8	4	5.6	8	11	16	22
1/1000in			2.8	4	5.6	8	11	16	22	
1/1420in		2.8	4	5.6	8	11	16	22		
1/2000in	2.8	4	5.6	8	11	16	22			
Focus Distance										
2' 6" Near	2' 5.7"	2' 5.6"	2' 5.5"	2' 5.2"	2' 5.0"	2' 4.5"	2' 4.1"	2' 3.3"	2' 2.5"	2' 1.2"
2' 6" Far	2' 6.3"	2' 6.4"	2' 6.6"	2' 6.8"	2' 7.2"	2' 7.7"	2' 8.4"	2' 9.8"	2' 11.6"	3' 3"
2' 9" Near	2' 8.6"	2' 8.5"	2' 8.3"	2' 8.0"	2' 7.6"	2' 7.1"	2' 6.4"	2' 5.4"	2' 4.4"	2' 2.9"
2' 9" Far	2' 9.4"	2' 9.5"	2' 9.8"	2' 10.1"	2' 10.6"	2' 11.3"	3' 0.3"	3' 2.2"	3' 4.9"	3' 10"
3' 0" Near	2' 11.5"	2' 11.3"	2' 11.1"	2' 10.7"	2' 10.2"	2' 9.5"	2' 8.7"	2' 7.5"	2' 6.2"	2' 4.3"
3' 0" Far	3' 0.5"	3' 0.7"	3' 1.0"	3' 1.4"	3' 2.1"	3' 3.1"	3' 4.4"	3' 7.0"	3' 10"	4' 7"
3' 6" Near	3' 5.3"	3' 5.0"	3' 4.6"	3' 4.0"	3' 3.3"	3' 2.3"	3' 1.1"	2' 11.3"	2' 9.5"	2' 7.0"
3' 6" Far	3' 6.8"	3' 7.1"	3' 7.6"	3' 8.3"	3' 9.3"	3' 10.9"	4' 1.1"	4' 5"	5' 0"	6' 6"
4' 0" Near	3' 11.0"	3' 10.5"	3' 10.0"	3' 9.2"	3' 8.2"	3' 6.8"	3' 5.2"	3' 2.9"	3' 0.5"	2' 9.3"
4' 0" Far	4' 1.1"	4' 1.6"	4' 2.2"	4' 3.3"	4' 4.8"	4' 7.2"	4' 10"	5' 5"	6' 5"	9' 8"
4' 6" Near	4' 4.6"	4' 4.0"	4' 3.3"	4' 2.3"	4' 0.9"	3' 11.1"	3' 9.1"	3' 6.1"	3' 3.2"	2' 11.4"
4' 6" Far	4' 7.5"	4' 8.1"	4' 9.1"	4' 10.5"	5' 0.6"	5' 4"	5' 9"	6' 8"	8' 4"	15' 5"
5' 0" Near	4' 10.2"	4' 9.5"	4' 8.5"	4' 7.2"	4' 5.5"	4' 3.3"	4' 0.7"	3' 9.1"	3' 5.6"	3' 1.1"
5' 0" Far	5' 1.9"	5' 2.8"	5' 4.0"	5' 5.9"	5' 8.8"	6' 1"	6' 8"	8' 1"	10' 11"	30' 1"
6' 0" Near	5' 9.2"	5' 8.1"	5' 6.7"	5' 4.7"	5' 2.3"	4' 11.0"	4' 7.4"	4' 2.5"	3' 9.9"	3' 4"
6' 0" Far	6' 3.0"	6' 4.4"	6' 6.4"	6' 9.5"	7' 2"	7' 10"	8' 11"	11' 11"	20' 5"	INF
7' 0" Near	6' 8.1"	6' 6.5"	6' 4.6"	6' 1.8"	5' 10.5"	5' 6.1"	5' 1.5"	4' 7.2"	4' 1.5"	3' 6"
7' 0" Far	7' 4.4"	7' 6.4"	7' 9.3"	8' 2"	8' 9"	9' 10"	11' 10"	18' 0"	54'	INF
8' 0" Near	7' 6.7"	7' 4.7"	7' 2.1"	6' 10.5"	6' 6.2"	6' 0.7"	5' 6.9"	4' 11.3"	4' 4"	3' 8"
8' 0" Far	8' 6.0"	8' 8.9"	9' 0.9"	9' 7"	10' 6"	12' 3"	15' 7"	29' 5"	INF	INF
10' Near	9' 3.5"	9' 0.2"	8' 8.2"	8' 2.7"	7' 8.4"	7' 0.4"	6' 4.3"	5' 6.2"	4' 9"	3' 11"
10' Far	10' 10"	11' 3"	11' 10"	12' 10"	14' 7"	18' 6"	28' 0"	>100'	INF	INF
12' Near	10' 11"	10' 6"	10' 1"	9' 5.6"	8' 9.0"	7' 10.5"	7' 0.2"	5' 11"	5' 1"	4' 2"
12' Far	13' 3"	13' 11"	14' 10"	16' 7"	19' 9"	27' 11"	59'	INF	INF	INF
15' Near	13' 4"	12' 9"	12' 0"	11' 1"	10' 1"	8' 11.3"	7' 9"	6' 6"	5' 5"	4' 4"
15' Far	17' 1"	18' 3"	20' 0"	23' 5"	30' 7"	57'	INF	INF	INF	INF
20' Near	17' 1"	16' 1"	14' 11"	13' 6"	12' 0"	10' 4"	8' 10"	7' 2"	5' 10"	4' 7"
20' Far	24' 1"	26' 6"	30' 7"	39' 10"	67'	INF	INF	INF	INF	INF
30' Near	23' 9"	21' 10"	19' 8"	17' 3"	14' 9"	12' 3"	10' 1"	7' 11"	6' 4"	4' 11"
30' Far	40' 10"	48' 6"	64'	>100'	INF	INF	INF	INF	INF	INF
60' Near	38' 11"	33' 10"	28' 11"	23' 9"	19' 3"	15' 1"	11' 11"	8' 11"	6' 11"	5' 2"
60' Far	>100'	>100'	INF	INF	INF	INF	INF	INF	INF	INF
	106'	74'	53'	37' 5"	26' 9"	18' 9"	13' 8"	9' 5"	6' 10"	4' 9"

Depth of Field — 17.5 - 75mm Zoom

44 mm PANAVISION PRIMO 17.5 - 75mm ZOOM

Entrance pupil rearwards from front vertex = 93 mm   Lens length, vertex to focal plane = 352 mm

Circle of Confusion	Aperture									
1/500in					2.8	4	5.6	8	11	16
1/710in				2.8	4	5.6	8	11	16	22
1/1000in			2.8	4	5.6	8	11	16	22	
1/1420in		2.8	4	5.6	8	11	16	22		
1/2000in	2.8	4	5.6	8	11	16	22			

Focus Distance											
2' 6"	Near	2' 5.8"	2' 5.8"	2' 5.7"	2' 5.5"	2' 5.4"	2' 5.1"	2' 4.8"	2' 4.3"	2' 3.7"	2' 2.8"
	Far	2' 6.2"	2' 6.2"	2' 6.3"	2' 6.5"	2' 6.7"	2' 7.0"	2' 7.4"	2' 8.1"	2' 9.0"	2' 10.7"
2' 9"	Near	2' 8.8"	2' 8.7"	2' 8.6"	2' 8.4"	2' 8.1"	2' 7.8"	2' 7.4"	2' 6.7"	2' 5.9"	2' 4.8"
	Far	2' 9.2"	2' 9.3"	2' 9.5"	2' 9.7"	2' 9.9"	2' 10.4"	2' 10.9"	2' 11.9"	3' 1.2"	3' 3.6"
3' 0"	Near	2' 11.7"	2' 11.6"	2' 11.4"	2' 11.2"	2' 10.9"	2' 10.4"	2' 9.9"	2' 9.1"	2' 8.1"	2' 6.7"
	Far	3' 0.3"	3' 0.4"	3' 0.6"	3' 0.9"	3' 1.2"	3' 1.8"	3' 2.5"	3' 3.8"	3' 5.5"	3' 8.9"
3' 6"	Near	3' 5.6"	3' 5.4"	3' 5.1"	3' 4.8"	3' 4.3"	3' 3.6"	3' 2.8"	3' 1.6"	3' 0.3"	2' 10.3"
	Far	3' 6.5"	3' 6.7"	3' 6.9"	3' 7.3"	3' 7.9"	3' 8.8"	3' 9.9"	4' 0.1"	4' 3.0"	4' 9"
4' 0"	Near	3' 11.4"	3' 11.1"	3' 10.8"	3' 10.3"	3' 9.6"	3' 8.7"	3' 7.6"	3' 5.9"	3' 4.1"	3' 1.5"
	Far	4' 0.6"	4' 0.9"	4' 1.3"	4' 1.9"	4' 2.7"	4' 4.0"	4' 5.8"	4' 9.0"	5' 1"	5' 11"
4' 6"	Near	4' 5.2"	4' 4.8"	4' 4.3"	4' 3.7"	4' 2.8"	4' 1.6"	4' 0.1"	3' 10.0"	3' 7.7"	3' 4.4"
	Far	4' 6.9"	4' 7.3"	4' 7.8"	4' 8.6"	4' 9.7"	4' 11.5"	5' 2.0"	5' 6"	6' 1"	7' 5"
5' 0"	Near	4' 10.9"	4' 10.5"	4' 9.9"	4' 9.0"	4' 7.9"	4' 6.3"	4' 4.5"	4' 1.8"	3' 11.0"	3' 7.1"
	Far	5' 1.1"	5' 1.6"	5' 2.3"	5' 3.4"	5' 4.9"	5' 7.3"	5' 10.7"	6' 5"	7' 3"	9' 4"
6' 0"	Near	5' 10.3"	5' 9.6"	5' 8.7"	5' 7.4"	5' 5.8"	5' 3.5"	5' 0.8"	4' 9.0"	4' 5.1"	3' 11.9"
	Far	6' 1.8"	6' 2.6"	6' 3.7"	6' 5.4"	6' 7.8"	6' 11.8"	7' 5"	8' 5"	10' 0"	15' 2"
7' 0"	Near	6' 9.6"	6' 8.6"	6' 7.3"	6' 5.5"	6' 3.3"	6' 0.1"	5' 8.6"	5' 3.5"	4' 10.5"	4' 3.9"
	Far	7' 2.6"	7' 3.7"	7' 5.3"	7' 7.8"	7' 11.5"	8' 5"	9' 2"	10' 10"	13' 10"	27' 5"
8' 0"	Near	7' 8.8"	7' 7.4"	7' 5.8"	7' 3.4"	7' 0.4"	6' 8.3"	6' 3.8"	5' 9.4"	5' 3.3"	4' 7.4"
	Far	8' 3.5"	8' 5.1"	8' 7.3"	8' 10.8"	9' 4.0"	10' 0"	11' 2"	13' 9"	19' 5"	69'
10'	Near	9' 6.7"	9' 4.6"	9' 1.9"	8' 10.2"	8' 5.6"	7' 11.4"	7' 4.8"	6' 7.9"	5' 11.5"	5' 1"
	Far	10' 5"	10' 8"	11' 0"	11' 6"	12' 3"	13' 8"	16' 0"	22' 5"	44' 10"	INF
12'	Near	11' 4"	11' 1"	10' 9"	10' 4"	9' 9.5"	9' 1.2"	8' 4.4"	7' 4.7"	6' 6.2"	5' 5"
	Far	12' 8"	13' 0"	13' 6"	14' 4"	15' 7"	18' 0"	22' 5"	38' 6"	>100'	INF
15'	Near	13' 11"	13' 6"	13' 1"	12' 4"	11' 7"	10' 7"	9' 7.3"	8' 3.7"	7' 2"	5' 11"
	Far	16' 2"	16' 9"	17' 7"	19' 1"	21' 5"	26' 5"	37' 8"	>100'	INF	INF
20'	Near	18' 1"	17' 5"	16' 7"	15' 6"	14' 3"	12' 9"	11' 3"	9' 5"	8' 0"	6' 5"
	Far	22' 3"	23' 5"	25' 2"	28' 4"	34' 2"	49' 8"	>100'	INF	INF	INF
30'	Near	25' 11"	24' 6"	22' 10"	20' 9"	18' 6"	15' 11"	13' 7"	11' 0"	9' 0"	7' 0"
	Far	35' 7"	38' 9"	44' 0"	55'	84'	>100'	INF	INF	INF	INF
60'	Near	45' 3"	41' 0"	36' 5"	31' 3"	26' 4"	21' 4"	17' 3"	13' 2"	10' 4"	7' 9"
	Far	89'	>100'	>100'	>100'	INF	INF	INF	INF	INF	INF
		178'	125'	89'	62'	44' 9"	31' 4"	22' 10"	15' 9"	11' 6"	7' 11"

Depth of Field — 17.5 - 75mm Zoom

52 mm PANAVISION PRIMO 17.5 - 75mm ZOOM

Entrance pupil rearwards from front vertex = 99 mm   Lens length, vertex to focal plane = 352 mm

Circle of Confusion		Aperture									
1/500in						2.8	4	5.6	8	11	16
1/710in					2.8	4	5.6	8	11	16	22
1/1000in				2.8	4	5.6	8	11	16	22	
1/1420in			2.8	4	5.6	8	11	16	22		
1/2000in		2.8	4	5.6	8	11	16	22			

Focus Distance											
2' 6"	Near	2'5.9"	2'5.8"	2'5.8"	2'5.7"	2'5.5"	2'5.3"	2'5.1"	2'4.7"	2'4.3"	2'3.6"
	Far	2'6.1"	2'6.2"	2'6.2"	2'6.4"	2'6.5"	2'6.7"	2'7.0"	2'7.5"	2'8.1"	2'9.2"
2' 9"	Near	2'8.8"	2'8.8"	2'8.7"	2'8.5"	2'8.4"	2'8.1"	2'7.8"	2'7.3"	2'6.7"	2'5.8"
	Far	2'9.2"	2'9.2"	2'9.3"	2'9.5"	2'9.7"	2'10.0"	2'10.3"	2'11.0"	2'11.9"	3'1.4"
3' 0"	Near	2'11.8"	2'11.7"	2'11.6"	2'11.4"	2'11.2"	2'10.9"	2'10.5"	2'9.8"	2'9.1"	2'8.0"
	Far	3'0.2"	3'0.3"	3'0.4"	3'0.6"	3'0.9"	3'1.2"	3'1.7"	3'2.6"	3'3.8"	3'5.8"
3' 6"	Near	3'5.7"	3'5.5"	3'5.4"	3'5.1"	3'4.8"	3'4.3"	3'3.7"	3'2.7"	3'1.6"	3'0.0"
	Far	3'6.3"	3'6.5"	3'6.7"	3'6.9"	3'7.3"	3'7.9"	3'8.7"	3'10.1"	4'0.0"	4'3.5"
4' 0"	Near	3'11.5"	3'11.4"	3'11.1"	3'10.7"	3'10.3"	3'9.6"	3'8.7"	3'7.4"	3'6.0"	3'3.8"
	Far	4'0.5"	4'0.7"	4'0.9"	4'1.4"	4'1.9"	4'2.8"	4'4.0"	4'6.1"	4'8.9"	5'2"
4' 6"	Near	4'5.4"	4'5.1"	4'4.8"	4'4.3"	4'3.7"	4'2.7"	4'1.6"	3'11.9"	3'10.0"	3'7.3"
	Far	4'6.6"	4'6.9"	4'7.3"	4'7.8"	4'8.6"	4'9.8"	4'11.5"	5'2.4"	5'6"	6'2"
5' 0"	Near	4'11.2"	4'10.9"	4'10.4"	4'9.8"	4'9.0"	4'7.8"	4'6.4"	4'4.3"	4'1.9"	3'10.6"
	Far	5'0.8"	5'1.2"	5'1.7"	5'2.4"	5'3.4"	5'5.0"	5'7.2"	5'11.2"	6'4"	7'4"
6' 0"	Near	5'10.8"	5'10.3"	5'9.6"	5'8.6"	5'7.4"	5'5.6"	5'3.6"	5'0.4"	4'9.1"	4'4.5"
	Far	6'1.3"	6'1.8"	6'2.6"	6'3.8"	6'5.4"	6'8.0"	6'11.6"	7'6"	8'4"	10'4"
7' 0"	Near	6'10.3"	6'9.5"	6'8.6"	6'7.2"	6'5.5"	6'3.1"	6'0.2"	5'8.0"	5'3.7"	4'9.7"
	Far	7'1.8"	7'2.6"	7'3.7"	7'5.5"	7'7.9"	7'11.8"	8'5"	9'4"	10'9"	14'6"
8' 0"	Near	7'9.7"	7'8.7"	7'7.4"	7'5.6"	7'3.3"	7'0.1"	6'8.5"	6'3.1"	5'9.7"	5'2.4"
	Far	8'2.5"	8'3.6"	8'5.1"	8'7.5"	8'10.9"	9'4.4"	10'0"	11'4"	13'7"	20'9"
10'	Near	9'8.2"	9'6.6"	9'4.6"	9'1.7"	8'10.1"	8'5.2"	7'11.7"	7'3.9"	6'8.2"	5'10.3"
	Far	10'4"	10'6"	10'8"	11'0"	11'6"	12'4"	13'7"	16'5"	22'0"	53'
12'	Near	11'6"	11'4"	11'1"	10'9"	10'3"	9'9.0"	9'1.5"	8'3.1"	7'5.1"	6'4"
	Far	12'6"	12'9"	13'1"	13'7"	14'4"	15'9"	17'11"	23'4"	37'2"	INF
15'	Near	14'3"	13'11"	13'6"	13'0"	12'4"	11'6"	10'8"	9'5.6"	8'4.3"	7'0"
	Far	15'10"	16'2"	16'9"	17'8"	19'1"	21'8"	26'2"	40'4"	>100'	INF
20'	Near	18'7"	18'1"	17'5"	16'6"	15'6"	14'2"	12'9"	11'1"	9'6"	7'9"
	Far	21'7"	22'4"	23'5"	25'4"	28'4"	34'9"	48'6"	>100'	INF	INF
30'	Near	26'11"	25'10"	24'6"	22'8"	20'8"	18'4"	16'0"	13'4"	11'1"	8'9"
	Far	33'10"	35'9"	38'10"	44'6"	55'	87'	>100'	INF	INF	INF
60'	Near	48'8"	45'0"	41'0"	36'1"	31'2"	25'11"	21'6"	16'9"	13'4"	10'0"
	Far	78'	90'	>100'	>100'	>100'	INF	INF	INF	INF	INF
		249'	174'	124'	87'	62'	43'9"	31'11"	22'0"	16'0"	11'1"

Depth of Field — 17.5 - 75mm Zoom

75 mm PANAVISION PRIMO 17.5 - 75mm ZOOM

Entrance pupil rearwards from front vertex = 112 mm Lens length, vertex to focal plane = 352 mm

Circle of Confusion	Aperture									
1/500in					2.8	4	5.6	8	11	16
1/710in				2.8	4	5.6	8	11	16	22
1/1000in			2.8	4	5.6	8	11	16	22	
1/1420in		2.8	4	5.6	8	11	16	22		
1/2000in	2.8	4	5.6	8	11	16	22			
Focus Distance										
2' 6" Near	2' 5.9"	2' 5.9"	2' 5.9"	2' 5.8"	2' 5.8"	2' 5.7"	2' 5.6"	2' 5.4"	2' 5.1"	2' 4.8"
Far	2' 6.1"	2' 6.1"	2' 6.1"	2' 6.2"	2' 6.2"	2' 6.3"	2' 6.5"	2' 6.7"	2' 7.0"	2' 7.4"
2' 9" Near	2' 8.9"	2' 8.9"	2' 8.8"	2' 8.8"	2' 8.7"	2' 8.6"	2' 8.4"	2' 8.1"	2' 7.8"	2' 7.3"
Far	2' 9.1"	2' 9.1"	2' 9.2"	2' 9.2"	2' 9.3"	2' 9.5"	2' 9.6"	2' 9.9"	2' 10.3"	2' 10.9"
3' 0" Near	2' 11.9"	2' 11.9"	2' 11.8"	2' 11.7"	2' 11.6"	2' 11.4"	2' 11.2"	2' 10.9"	2' 10.5"	2' 9.9"
Far	3' 0.1"	3' 0.1"	3' 0.2"	3' 0.3"	3' 0.4"	3' 0.6"	3' 0.8"	3' 1.2"	3' 1.7"	3' 2.5"
3' 6" Near	3' 5.8"	3' 5.8"	3' 5.7"	3' 5.6"	3' 5.4"	3' 5.1"	3' 4.8"	3' 4.3"	3' 3.7"	3' 2.8"
Far	3' 6.2"	3' 6.2"	3' 6.3"	3' 6.4"	3' 6.6"	3' 6.9"	3' 7.3"	3' 7.9"	3' 8.6"	3' 10.0"
4' 0" Near	3' 11.8"	3' 11.7"	3' 11.6"	3' 11.4"	3' 11.1"	3' 10.8"	3' 10.3"	3' 9.6"	3' 8.8"	3' 7.5"
Far	4' 0.2"	4' 0.3"	4' 0.4"	4' 0.6"	4' 0.9"	4' 1.3"	4' 1.8"	4' 2.7"	4' 3.8"	4' 5.8"
4' 6" Near	4' 5.7"	4' 5.6"	4' 5.4"	4' 5.2"	4' 4.8"	4' 4.4"	4' 3.8"	4' 2.8"	4' 1.8"	4' 0.1"
Far	4' 6.3"	4' 6.4"	4' 6.6"	4' 6.9"	4' 7.2"	4' 7.8"	4' 8.5"	4' 9.7"	4' 11.2"	5' 2.0"
5' 0" Near	4' 11.6"	4' 11.5"	4' 11.2"	4' 10.9"	4' 10.5"	4' 9.9"	4' 9.1"	4' 7.9"	4' 6.6"	4' 4.5"
Far	5' 0.4"	5' 0.6"	5' 0.8"	5' 1.1"	5' 1.6"	5' 2.3"	5' 3.2"	5' 4.8"	5' 6.9"	5' 10.7"
6' 0" Near	5' 11.4"	5' 11.2"	5' 10.8"	5' 10.3"	5' 9.7"	5' 8.8"	5' 7.6"	5' 5.8"	5' 3.8"	5' 0.8"
Far	6' 0.6"	6' 0.9"	6' 1.2"	6' 1.8"	6' 2.5"	6' 3.6"	6' 5.1"	6' 7.7"	6' 11.1"	7' 5"
7' 0" Near	6' 11.2"	6' 10.8"	6' 10.3"	6' 9.6"	6' 8.7"	6' 7.4"	6' 5.8"	6' 3.3"	6' 0.6"	5' 8.5"
Far	7' 0.9"	7' 1.2"	7' 1.8"	7' 2.5"	7' 3.6"	7' 5.2"	7' 7.4"	7' 11.3"	8' 4"	9' 2"
8' 0" Near	7' 10.9"	7' 10.4"	7' 9.7"	7' 8.8"	7' 7.6"	7' 5.8"	7' 3.7"	7' 0.5"	6' 8.9"	6' 3.7"
Far	8' 1.2"	8' 1.7"	8' 2.4"	8' 3.5"	8' 4.9"	8' 7.2"	8' 10.2"	9' 3.7"	9' 11"	11' 2"
10' Near	9' 10.1"	9' 9.3"	9' 8.3"	9' 6.8"	9' 4.9"	9' 2.1"	8' 10.8"	8' 5.8"	8' 0.4"	7' 4.7"
Far	10' 1"	10' 2"	10' 4"	10' 5"	10' 8"	11' 0"	11' 5"	12' 3"	13' 5"	16' 0"
12' Near	11' 9"	11' 8"	11' 6"	11' 4"	11' 1"	10' 9"	10' 4"	9' 9.8"	9' 2.5"	8' 4.2"
Far	12' 2"	12' 4"	12' 5"	12' 8"	13' 0"	13' 6"	14' 2"	15' 6"	17' 6"	22' 5"
15' Near	14' 7"	14' 5"	14' 3"	13' 11"	13' 7"	13' 1"	12' 6"	11' 7"	10' 9"	9' 7.0"
Far	15' 4"	15' 6"	15' 9"	16' 2"	16' 8"	17' 7"	18' 9"	21' 3"	25' 5"	37' 8"
20' Near	19' 3"	19' 0"	18' 8"	18' 2"	17' 6"	16' 8"	15' 8"	14' 4"	12' 11"	11' 3"
Far	20' 8"	21' 0"	21' 6"	22' 2"	23' 3"	25' 0"	27' 8"	33' 9"	45' 11"	>100'
30' Near	28' 5"	27' 10"	27' 0"	25' 11"	24' 8"	22' 11"	21' 1"	18' 7"	16' 4"	13' 7"
Far	31' 8"	32' 6"	33' 8"	35' 6"	38' 4"	43' 8"	52'	81'	>100'	INF
60' Near	53'	51'	49' 0"	45' 5"	41' 6"	36' 8"	32' 0"	26' 6"	22' 0"	17' 3"
Far	67'	71'	77'	88'	>100'	>100'	>100'	INF	INF	INF
	519'	363'	259'	181'	129'	91'	66'	45' 7"	33' 3"	22' 11"

267

Depth of Field — 11:1 Zoom

24 mm PANAVISION PRIMO 11:1, 24-275mm, ZOOM

Entrance pupil rearwards from front vertex = 113 mm   Lens length, vertex to focal plane = 418 mm

Circle of Confusion	Aperture									
1/500in					2.8	4	5.6	8	11	16
1/710in				2.8	4	5.6	8	11	16	22
1/1000in			2.8	4	5.6	8	11	16	22	
1/1420in		2.8	4	5.6	8	11	16	22		
1/2000in	2.8	4	5.6	8	11	16	22			
Focus Distance										
4' 0" Near	3' 10.1"	3' 9.4"	3' 8.4"	3' 7.1"	3' 5.5"	3' 3.4"	3' 1.1"	2' 10.1"	2' 7.3"	2' 4"
Far	4' 2.1"	4' 3.1"	4' 4.4"	4' 6.7"	4' 10"	5' 4"	6' 3"	9' 0"	22' 11"	INF
4' 6" Near	4' 3.5"	4' 2.5"	4' 1.2"	3' 11.5"	3' 9.4"	3' 6.7"	3' 3.9"	3' 0.2"	2' 8"	2' 5"
Far	4' 8.9"	4' 10.3"	5' 0.2"	5' 3.5"	5' 8"	6' 6"	8' 1"	14' 2"	INF	INF
5' 0" Near	4' 8.7"	4' 7.4"	4' 5.8"	4' 3.6"	4' 1.1"	3' 9.8"	3' 6.4"	3' 2.0"	2' 10"	2' 5"
Far	5' 3.8"	5' 5.7"	5' 8.3"	6' 0"	6' 8"	7' 11"	10' 6"	26' 6"	INF	INF
6' 0" Near	5' 6.9"	5' 5.0"	5' 2.6"	4' 11.4"	4' 7.8"	4' 3.2"	3' 10.7"	3' 5"	3' 0"	2' 7"
Far	6' 6.1"	6' 9.1"	7' 1"	7' 9"	8' 11"	11' 7"	19' 4"	INF	INF	INF
7' 0" Near	6' 4.8"	6' 2.1"	5' 10.9"	5' 6.6"	5' 1.8"	4' 8.0"	4' 2.4"	3' 7"	3' 2"	2' 8"
Far	7' 9.0"	8' 1"	8' 8"	9' 9"	11' 9"	17' 6"	49' 1"	INF	INF	INF
8' 0" Near	7' 2.3"	6' 10.8"	6' 6.6"	6' 1.2"	5' 7.2"	5' 0.2"	4' 5"	3' 9"	3' 3"	2' 9"
Far	9' 0.6"	9' 7"	10' 5"	12' 1"	15' 7"	28' 4"	INF	INF	INF	INF
10' Near	8' 8.5"	8' 3.1"	7' 8.9"	7' 1.0"	6' 4.6"	5' 7.1"	4' 10"	4' 1"	3' 5"	2' 10"
Far	11' 9"	12' 10"	14' 6"	18' 3"	28' 4"	>200'	INF	INF	INF	INF
12' Near	10' 1"	9' 6.0"	8' 9.6"	7' 11.2"	7' 0.5"	6' 0"	5' 2"	4' 3"	3' 7"	2' 11"
Far	14' 10"	16' 6"	19' 8"	27' 7"	62' 9"	INF	INF	INF	INF	INF
14' Near	11' 5"	10' 7"	9' 9.0"	8' 8.1"	7' 7.1"	6' 5"	5' 5"	4' 5"	3' 8"	2' 11"
Far	18' 2"	20' 11"	26' 3"	43' 6"	>200'	INF	INF	INF	INF	INF
17' Near	13' 3"	12' 2"	11' 0"	9' 7.5"	8' 3"	6' 10"	5' 9"	4' 7"	3' 9"	3' 0"
Far	23' 10"	28' 11"	40' 11"	>100'	INF	INF	INF	INF	INF	INF
20' Near	15' 0"	13' 7"	12' 1"	10' 5"	8' 10"	7' 3"	6' 0"	4' 9"	3' 10"	3' 1"
Far	30' 6"	39' 8"	66' 11"	INF	INF	INF	INF	INF	INF	INF
25' Near	17' 6"	15' 7"	13' 7"	11' 6"	9' 6"	7' 8"	6' 3"	4' 10"	3' 11"	3' 1"
Far	44' 7"	68' 2"	>200'	INF	INF	INF	INF	INF	INF	INF
30' Near	19' 9"	17' 3"	14' 10"	12' 4"	10' 1"	8' 0"	6' 6"	5' 0"	4' 0"	3' 1"
Far	64' 7"	131'	INF	INF	INF	INF	INF	INF	INF	INF
40' Near	23' 6"	20' 0"	16' 9"	13' 7"	10' 11"	8' 6"	6' 9"	5' 2"	4' 1"	3' 2"
Far	146'	INF	INF	INF	INF	INF	INF	INF	INF	INF
60' Near	28' 11"	23' 10"	19' 4"	15' 1"	11' 10"	9' 0"	7' 0"	5' 3"	4' 2"	3' 2"
Far	INF	INF	INF	INF	INF	INF	INF	INF	INF	INF
120' Near	37' 9"	29' 4"	22' 8"	17' 1"	12' 11"	9' 7"	7' 4"	5' 5"	4' 3"	3' 3"
Far	INF	INF	INF	INF	INF	INF	INF	INF	INF	INF
	53'	37' 3"	26' 7"	18' 8"	13' 4"	9' 4"	6' 10"	4' 8"	3' 5"	2' 4"

Depth of Field — 11:1 Zoom

50 mm — PANAVISION PRIMO 11:1, 24-275mm, ZOOM

Entrance pupil rearwards from front vertex = 182 mm   Lens length, vertex to focal plane = 418 mm

Aperture (Circle of Confusion staircase)

Circle of Confusion										
Aperture					2.8	4	5.6	8	11	16
1/500in					2.8	4	5.6	8	11	16
1/710in				2.8	4	5.6	8	11	16	22
1/1000in			2.8	4	5.6	8	11	16	22	
1/1420in		2.8	4	5.6	8	11	16	22		
1/2000in	2.8	4	5.6	8	11	16	22			

Focus Distance (Near / Far)

Focus Distance	N/F										
4' 0"	Near	3' 11.5"	3' 11.3"	3' 11.0"	3' 10.6"	3' 10.0"	3' 9.3"	3' 8.3"	3' 6.9"	3' 5.3"	3' 3.0"
	Far	4' 0.5"	4' 0.7"	4' 1.1"	4' 1.5"	4' 2.2"	4' 3.2"	4' 4.5"	4' 6.9"	4' 10"	5' 4"
4' 6"	Near	4' 5.3"	4' 5.0"	4' 4.7"	4' 4.1"	4' 3.4"	4' 2.4"	4' 1.2"	3' 11.3"	3' 9.3"	3' 6.3"
	Far	4' 6.7"	4' 7.0"	4' 7.4"	4' 8.1"	4' 8.9"	4' 10.3"	5' 0.2"	5' 3"	5' 8"	6' 6"
5' 0"	Near	4' 11.1"	4' 10.8"	4' 10.3"	4' 9.6"	4' 8.7"	4' 7.4"	4' 5.8"	4' 3.5"	4' 1.0"	3' 9.4"
	Far	5' 0.9"	5' 1.3"	5' 1.9"	5' 2.7"	5' 3.8"	5' 5.7"	5' 8.1"	6' 0"	6' 7"	7' 10"
6' 0"	Near	5' 10.7"	5' 10.1"	5' 9.4"	5' 8.3"	5' 6.9"	5' 5.0"	5' 2.8"	4' 11.4"	4' 7.9"	4' 3.1"
	Far	6' 1.4"	6' 2.0"	6' 2.9"	6' 4.2"	6' 6.0"	6' 9.0"	7' 1"	7' 9"	8' 9"	11' 3"
7' 0"	Near	6' 10.1"	6' 9.3"	6' 8.3"	6' 6.8"	6' 4.9"	6' 2.2"	5' 11.2"	5' 6.7"	5' 2.2"	4' 8.0"
	Far	7' 2.0"	7' 2.9"	7' 4.1"	7' 6.1"	7' 8.8"	8' 1"	8' 7"	9' 8"	11' 4"	16' 4"
8' 0"	Near	7' 9.4"	7' 8.4"	7' 7.0"	7' 5.0"	7' 2.5"	6' 11.1"	6' 7.2"	6' 1.5"	5' 7.8"	5' 0.3"
	Far	8' 2.7"	8' 4.0"	8' 5.7"	8' 8.3"	9' 0.1"	9' 6"	10' 3"	11' 10"	14' 8"	24' 10"
10'	Near	9' 7.8"	9' 6.1"	9' 3.9"	9' 0.8"	8' 9.0"	8' 3.7"	7' 9.9"	7' 1.7"	6' 5.7"	5' 7.6"
	Far	10' 4"	10' 6"	10' 9"	11' 2"	11' 8"	12' 8"	14' 1"	17' 6"	24' 10"	91' 2"
12'	Near	11' 5"	11' 3"	11' 0"	10' 7"	10' 2"	9' 7.0"	8' 11.1"	8' 0.3"	7' 2.1"	6' 1"
	Far	12' 6"	12' 9"	13' 2"	13' 9"	14' 8"	16' 2"	18' 9"	25' 7"	46' 4"	INF
14'	Near	13' 3"	13' 0"	12' 7"	12' 1"	11' 6"	10' 9"	9' 11.1"	8' 9.6"	7' 9.3"	6' 6"
	Far	14' 9"	15' 2"	15' 8"	16' 6"	17' 10"	20' 3"	24' 7"	38' 3"	120'	INF
17'	Near	15' 11"	15' 6"	15' 0"	14' 3"	13' 5"	12' 4"	11' 3"	9' 9.7"	8' 6"	7' 0"
	Far	18' 2"	18' 9"	19' 7"	21' 0"	23' 3"	27' 8"	36' 7"	80'	INF	INF
20'	Near	18' 6"	17' 11"	17' 3"	16' 3"	15' 2"	13' 10"	12' 5"	10' 7"	9' 1"	7' 5"
	Far	21' 8"	22' 6"	23' 9"	25' 11"	29' 5"	37' 2"	55' 7"	>200'	INF	INF
25'	Near	22' 8"	21' 10"	20' 9"	19' 5"	17' 10"	15' 11"	14' 1"	11' 9"	9' 11"	7' 11"
	Far	27' 9"	29' 2"	31' 4"	35' 3"	42' 4"	60' 9"	135'	INF	INF	INF
30'	Near	26' 8"	25' 6"	24' 1"	22' 3"	20' 2"	17' 9"	15' 5"	12' 9"	10' 7"	8' 3"
	Far	34' 2"	36' 5"	39' 10"	46' 5"	59' 8"	105'	>200'	INF	INF	INF
40'	Near	34' 3"	32' 4"	30' 0"	27' 2"	24' 1"	20' 8"	17' 7"	14' 1"	11' 5"	8' 9"
	Far	48' 0"	52' 6"	60' 1"	76' 9"	122'	>200'	INF	INF	INF	INF
60'	Near	47' 11"	44' 1"	39' 11"	34' 11"	30' 0"	24' 9"	20' 5"	15' 10"	12' 6"	9' 5"
	Far	80'	94'	>100'	>100'	INF	INF	INF	INF	INF	INF
120'	Near	79' 4"	69' 4"	59' 5"	48' 11"	39' 8"	30' 11"	24' 4"	18' 0"	13' 10"	10' 1"
	Far	>200'	>200'	INF	INF	INF	INF	INF	INF	INF	INF
Hyperfocal		230'	161'	115'	80'	57'	40' 6"	29' 6"	20' 4"	14' 10"	10' 3"

Depth of Field — 11:1 Zoom

100 mm   PANAVISION PRIMO 11:1, 24-275mm, ZOOM

Entrance pupil rearwards from front vertex = 313 mm   Lens length, vertex to focal plane = 418 mm

Circle of Confusion	Aperture									
1/500in					2.8	4	5.6	8	11	16
1/710in				2.8	4	5.6	8	11	16	22
1/1000in			2.8	4	5.6	8	11	16	22	
1/1420in		2.8	4	5.6	8	11	16	22		
1/2000in	2.8	4	5.6	8	11	16	22			
Focus Distance										
4' 0" Near	3' 11.8"	3' 11.8"	3' 11.7"	3' 11.6"	3' 11.4"	3' 11.1"	3' 10.8"	3' 10.3"	3' 9.6"	3' 8.7"
Far	4' 0.2"	4' 0.2"	4' 0.3"	4' 0.5"	4' 0.6"	4' 0.9"	4' 1.3"	4' 1.9"	4' 2.6"	4' 3.9"
4' 6" Near	4' 5.8"	4' 5.7"	4' 5.6"	4' 5.4"	4' 5.2"	4' 4.8"	4' 4.4"	4' 3.7"	4' 2.9"	4' 1.7"
Far	4' 6.2"	4' 6.3"	4' 6.4"	4' 6.6"	4' 6.8"	4' 7.2"	4' 7.7"	4' 8.5"	4' 9.5"	4' 11.2"
5' 0" Near	4' 11.7"	4' 11.6"	4' 11.5"	4' 11.3"	4' 11.0"	4' 10.5"	4' 10.0"	4' 9.2"	4' 8.2"	4' 6.6"
Far	5' 0.3"	5' 0.4"	5' 0.5"	5' 0.8"	5' 1.1"	5' 1.5"	5' 2.1"	5' 3.2"	5' 4.4"	5' 6.7"
6' 0" Near	5' 11.6"	5' 11.4"	5' 11.2"	5' 10.9"	5' 10.5"	5' 9.8"	5' 9.1"	5' 7.8"	5' 6.4"	5' 4.1"
Far	6' 0.4"	6' 0.6"	6' 0.8"	6' 1.1"	6' 1.6"	6' 2.3"	6' 3.2"	6' 4.8"	6' 6.8"	6' 10.3"
7' 0" Near	6' 11.5"	6' 11.2"	6' 10.9"	6' 10.5"	6' 9.9"	6' 9.0"	6' 7.9"	6' 6.2"	6' 4.2"	6' 1.2"
Far	7' 0.6"	7' 0.8"	7' 1.1"	7' 1.6"	7' 2.3"	7' 3.3"	7' 4.5"	7' 6.8"	7' 9.6"	8' 2"
8' 0" Near	7' 11.3"	7' 11.0"	7' 10.6"	7' 10.0"	7' 9.2"	7' 8.0"	7' 6.6"	7' 4.4"	7' 1.8"	6' 9.9"
Far	8' 0.7"	8' 1.1"	8' 1.5"	8' 2.1"	8' 3.0"	8' 4.4"	8' 6.1"	8' 9.2"	9' 1.1"	9' 8"
10' Near	9' 10.8"	9' 10.4"	9' 9.7"	9' 8.7"	9' 7.5"	9' 5.7"	9' 3.5"	9' 0.0"	8' 8.1"	8' 2.3"
Far	10' 1"	10' 1"	10' 2"	10' 3"	10' 4"	10' 7"	10' 10"	11' 3"	11' 9"	12' 10"
12' Near	11' 10"	11' 9"	11' 8"	11' 7"	11' 5"	11' 2"	10' 11"	10' 6"	10' 1"	9' 5.4"
Far	12' 1"	12' 2"	12' 3"	12' 5"	12' 7"	12' 10"	13' 2"	13' 10"	14' 9"	16' 6"
14' Near	13' 9"	13' 8"	13' 7"	13' 5"	13' 3"	12' 11"	12' 7"	12' 0"	11' 5"	10' 7"
Far	14' 2"	14' 3"	14' 4"	14' 7"	14' 10"	15' 2"	15' 9"	16' 8"	18' 0"	20' 8"
17' Near	16' 8"	16' 7"	16' 5"	16' 2"	15' 10"	15' 5"	14' 11"	14' 2"	13' 4"	12' 2"
Far	17' 3"	17' 5"	17' 7"	17' 10"	18' 3"	18' 10"	19' 8"	21' 2"	23' 5"	28' 3"
20' Near	19' 7"	19' 5"	19' 2"	18' 10"	18' 5"	17' 10"	17' 2"	16' 2"	15' 1"	13' 7"
Far	20' 5"	20' 7"	20' 10"	21' 3"	21' 9"	22' 8"	23' 10"	26' 2"	29' 7"	38' 0"
25' Near	24' 4"	24' 1"	23' 9"	23' 3"	22' 7"	21' 9"	20' 9"	19' 3"	17' 9"	15' 8"
Far	25' 8"	25' 11"	26' 4"	27' 0"	27' 10"	29' 4"	31' 5"	35' 7"	42' 5"	62' 4"
30' Near	29' 1"	28' 8"	28' 2"	27' 6"	26' 7"	25' 5"	24' 0"	22' 1"	20' 1"	17' 6"
Far	30' 11"	31' 4"	32' 0"	32' 11"	34' 3"	36' 7"	39' 10"	46' 11"	59' 7"	108'
40' Near	38' 4"	37' 8"	36' 10"	35' 8"	34' 2"	32' 2"	30' 0"	27' 0"	24' 1"	20' 5"
Far	41' 9"	42' 6"	43' 8"	45' 6"	48' 1"	52' 9"	59' 11"	77' 8"	120'	>200'
60' Near	56'	54'	53'	50'	47' 9"	43' 11"	39' 11"	34' 8"	30' 0"	24' 6"
Far	64'	66'	68'	73'	80'	94'	>100'	>100'	INF	INF
120' Near	106'	101'	95' 4"	87' 8"	79' 2"	69' 1"	59' 8"	48' 7"	39' 9"	30' 7"
Far	137'	147'	161'	190'	>200'	>200'	INF	INF	INF	INF
	922'	646'	461'	323'	230'	161'	117'	81'	59'	40' 8"

Depth of Field — 11:1 Zoom

150 mm   PANAVISION PRIMO 11:1, 24-275mm, ZOOM

Entrance pupil rearwards from front vertex =   555 mm   Lens length, vertex to focal plane =   418 mm

Circle of Confusion	Aperture									
1/500in					2.8	4	5.6	8	11	16
1/710in				2.8	4	5.6	8	11	16	22
1/1000in			2.8	4	5.6	8	11	16	22	
1/1420in		2.8	4	5.6	8	11	16	22		
1/2000in	2.8	4	5.6	8	11	16	22			

Focus Distance										
4' 0" Near	3' 11.9"	3' 11.9"	3' 11.8"	3' 11.7"	3' 11.6"	3' 11.4"	3' 11.2"	3' 10.9"	3' 10.4"	3' 9.8"
Far	4' 0.1"	4' 0.1"	4' 0.2"	4' 0.3"	4' 0.4"	4' 0.6"	4' 0.8"	4' 1.2"	4' 1.6"	4' 2.4"
4' 6" Near	4' 5.9"	4' 5.8"	4' 5.7"	4' 5.6"	4' 5.5"	4' 5.3"	4' 5.0"	4' 4.6"	4' 4.1"	4' 3.2"
Far	4' 6.1"	4' 6.2"	4' 6.3"	4' 6.4"	4' 6.5"	4' 6.7"	4' 7.0"	4' 7.5"	4' 8.1"	4' 9.1"
5' 0" Near	4' 11.8"	4' 11.8"	4' 11.7"	4' 11.6"	4' 11.4"	4' 11.1"	4' 10.8"	4' 10.3"	4' 9.6"	4' 8.6"
Far	5' 0.2"	5' 0.2"	5' 0.3"	5' 0.4"	5' 0.6"	5' 0.9"	5' 1.3"	5' 1.8"	5' 2.5"	5' 3.8"
6' 0" Near	5' 11.8"	5' 11.7"	5' 11.6"	5' 11.4"	5' 11.1"	5' 10.8"	5' 10.3"	5' 9.5"	5' 8.7"	5' 7.2"
Far	6' 0.2"	6' 0.3"	6' 0.4"	6' 0.6"	6' 0.9"	6' 1.3"	6' 1.8"	6' 2.6"	6' 3.7"	6' 5.4"
7' 0" Near	6' 11.7"	6' 11.6"	6' 11.4"	6' 11.2"	6' 10.8"	6' 10.3"	6' 9.7"	6' 8.7"	6' 7.5"	6' 5.6"
Far	7' 0.3"	7' 0.4"	7' 0.6"	7' 0.9"	7' 1.2"	7' 1.7"	7' 2.4"	7' 3.6"	7' 5.0"	7' 7.4"
8' 0" Near	7' 11.6"	7' 11.4"	7' 11.2"	7' 10.9"	7' 10.5"	7' 9.8"	7' 9.0"	7' 7.7"	7' 6.2"	7' 3.8"
Far	8' 0.4"	8' 0.6"	8' 0.8"	8' 1.1"	8' 1.6"	8' 2.3"	8' 3.1"	8' 4.6"	8' 6.5"	8' 9.7"
10' Near	9' 11.4"	9' 11.1"	9' 10.8"	9' 10.3"	9' 9.6"	9' 8.7"	9' 7.4"	9' 5.5"	9' 3.2"	8' 11.6"
Far	10' 0"	10' 0"	10' 1"	10' 1"	10' 2"	10' 3"	10' 4"	10' 7"	10' 10"	11' 3"
12' Near	11' 11"	11' 10"	11' 10"	11' 9"	11' 8"	11' 7"	11' 5"	11' 2"	10' 11"	10' 6"
Far	12' 0"	12' 1"	12' 1"	12' 2"	12' 3"	12' 5"	12' 7"	12' 10"	13' 2"	13' 10"
14' Near	13' 10"	13' 10"	13' 9"	13' 8"	13' 7"	13' 5"	13' 3"	12' 11"	12' 7"	12' 0"
Far	14' 1"	14' 1"	14' 2"	14' 3"	14' 4"	14' 6"	14' 9"	15' 2"	15' 8"	16' 7"
17' Near	16' 10"	16' 9"	16' 8"	16' 7"	16' 5"	16' 2"	15' 11"	15' 6"	15' 0"	14' 3"
Far	17' 1"	17' 2"	17' 3"	17' 5"	17' 7"	17' 10"	18' 2"	18' 9"	19' 6"	21' 0"
20' Near	19' 9"	19' 8"	19' 7"	19' 5"	19' 2"	18' 11"	18' 6"	17' 11"	17' 3"	16' 3"
Far	20' 2"	20' 3"	20' 4"	20' 6"	20' 9"	21' 2"	21' 8"	22' 6"	23' 7"	25' 9"
25' Near	24' 8"	24' 6"	24' 4"	24' 1"	23' 10"	23' 4"	22' 9"	21' 11"	20' 11"	19' 6"
Far	25' 3"	25' 5"	25' 7"	25' 10"	26' 3"	26' 10"	27' 7"	29' 0"	30' 11"	34' 7"
30' Near	29' 6"	29' 4"	29' 1"	28' 9"	28' 4"	27' 8"	26' 10"	25' 8"	24' 4"	22' 5"
Far	30' 5"	30' 7"	30' 10"	31' 3"	31' 10"	32' 8"	33' 10"	36' 0"	38' 11"	44' 11"
40' Near	39' 2"	38' 11"	38' 6"	37' 10"	37' 1"	35' 11"	34' 8"	32' 8"	30' 7"	27' 7"
Far	40' 9"	41' 1"	41' 7"	42' 4"	43' 4"	45' 0"	47' 2"	51' 4"	57' 6"	71' 9"
60' Near	58'	57'	56'	55'	53'	51'	48' 9"	45' 0"	41' 1"	35' 11"
Far	61'	62'	63'	65'	67'	71'	77'	89'	>100'	>100'
120' Near	113'	110'	107'	102'	97' 4"	90' 1"	82' 4"	72' 1"	62' 8"	51' 5"
Far	127'	130'	135'	143'	156'	179'	>200'	>200'	>200'	INF

	2076'	1453'	1038'	727'	519'	363'	264'	182'	132'	91'

Depth of Field — 11:1 Zoom

275 mm PANAVISION PRIMO 11:1, 24-275mm, ZOOM

Entrance pupil rearwards from front vertex = 682 mm   Lens length, vertex to focal plane = 418 mm

Circle of Confusion				Aperture						
1/500in					2.8	4	5.6	8	11	16
1/710in				2.8	4	5.6	8	11	16	22
1/1000in			2.8	4	5.6	8	11	16	22	
1/1420in		2.8	4	5.6	8	11	16	22		
1/2000in	2.8	4	5.6	8	11	16	22			
Focus Distance										
4' 0" Near	4' 0.0"	4' 0.0"	3' 11.9"	3' 11.9"	3' 11.9"	3' 11.8"	3' 11.7"	3' 11.6"	3' 11.5"	3' 11.3"
Far	4' 0.0"	4' 0.0"	4' 0.1"	4' 0.1"	4' 0.1"	4' 0.2"	4' 0.3"	4' 0.4"	4' 0.5"	4' 0.8"
4' 6" Near	4' 6.0"	4' 5.9"	4' 5.9"	4' 5.9"	4' 5.8"	4' 5.8"	4' 5.7"	4' 5.5"	4' 5.4"	4' 5.1"
Far	4' 6.0"	4' 6.1"	4' 6.1"	4' 6.1"	4' 6.2"	4' 6.2"	4' 6.3"	4' 6.5"	4' 6.7"	4' 7.0"
5' 0" Near	4' 11.9"	4' 11.9"	4' 11.9"	4' 11.9"	4' 11.8"	4' 11.7"	4' 11.6"	4' 11.4"	4' 11.2"	4' 10.9"
Far	5' 0.1"	5' 0.1"	5' 0.1"	5' 0.1"	5' 0.2"	5' 0.3"	5' 0.4"	5' 0.6"	5' 0.8"	5' 1.2"
6' 0" Near	5' 11.9"	5' 11.9"	5' 11.9"	5' 11.8"	5' 11.7"	5' 11.6"	5' 11.5"	5' 11.2"	5' 10.9"	5' 10.4"
Far	6' 0.1"	6' 0.1"	6' 0.1"	6' 0.2"	6' 0.3"	6' 0.4"	6' 0.6"	6' 0.8"	6' 1.1"	6' 1.6"
7' 0" Near	6' 11.9"	6' 11.9"	6' 11.8"	6' 11.7"	6' 11.6"	6' 11.5"	6' 11.3"	6' 10.9"	6' 10.5"	6' 9.9"
Far	7' 0.1"	7' 0.1"	7' 0.2"	7' 0.3"	7' 0.4"	7' 0.5"	7' 0.7"	7' 1.1"	7' 1.5"	7' 2.2"
8' 0" Near	7' 11.9"	7' 11.8"	7' 11.8"	7' 11.7"	7' 11.5"	7' 11.3"	7' 11.1"	7' 10.6"	7' 10.1"	7' 9.3"
Far	8' 0.1"	8' 0.2"	8' 0.2"	8' 0.3"	8' 0.5"	8' 0.7"	8' 1.0"	8' 1.4"	8' 1.9"	8' 2.9"
10' Near	9' 11.8"	9' 11.7"	9' 11.6"	9' 11.5"	9' 11.3"	9' 10.9"	9' 10.6"	9' 9.9"	9' 9.1"	9' 7.9"
Far	10' 0"	10' 0"	10' 0"	10' 0"	10' 0"	10' 1"	10' 1"	10' 2"	10' 3"	10' 4"
12' Near	11' 11"	11' 11"	11' 11"	11' 11"	11' 10"	11' 10"	11' 9"	11' 9"	11' 7"	11' 6"
Far	12' 0"	12' 0"	12' 0"	12' 0"	12' 1"	12' 1"	12' 2"	12' 3"	12' 4"	12' 6"
14' Near	13' 11"	13' 11"	13' 11"	13' 11"	13' 10"	13' 10"	13' 9"	13' 8"	13' 6"	13' 4"
Far	14' 0"	14' 0"	14' 0"	14' 1"	14' 1"	14' 2"	14' 2"	14' 4"	14' 5"	14' 8"
17' Near	16' 11"	16' 11"	16' 11"	16' 10"	16' 9"	16' 9"	16' 8"	16' 6"	16' 4"	16' 0"
Far	17' 0"	17' 0"	17' 1"	17' 1"	17' 2"	17' 3"	17' 4"	17' 6"	17' 8"	18' 0"
20' Near	19' 11"	19' 11"	19' 10"	19' 10"	19' 9"	19' 8"	19' 6"	19' 4"	19' 1"	18' 8"
Far	20' 0"	20' 1"	20' 1"	20' 2"	20' 2"	20' 4"	20' 5"	20' 8"	20' 11"	21' 5"
25' Near	24' 10"	24' 10"	24' 9"	24' 8"	24' 7"	24' 5"	24' 3"	23' 11"	23' 7"	23' 0"
Far	25' 1"	25' 1"	25' 2"	25' 3"	25' 4"	25' 6"	25' 9"	26' 1"	26' 6"	27' 3"
30' Near	29' 10"	29' 9"	29' 8"	29' 7"	29' 5"	29' 3"	28' 11"	28' 6"	28' 0"	27' 2"
Far	30' 1"	30' 2"	30' 3"	30' 4"	30' 6"	30' 9"	31' 0"	31' 7"	32' 2"	33' 4"
40' Near	39' 9"	39' 8"	39' 6"	39' 4"	39' 1"	38' 8"	38' 2"	37' 5"	36' 7"	35' 3"
Far	40' 2"	40' 4"	40' 5"	40' 8"	40' 11"	41' 4"	41' 11"	42' 10"	44' 0"	46' 1"
60' Near	59'	59'	58'	58'	57'	57'	56'	54'	52'	50'
Far	60'	60'	61'	61'	62'	63'	64'	66'	69'	74'
120' Near	117'	117'	115'	114'	112'	109'	105'	100'	94' 3"	85' 10"
Far	122'	123'	124'	126'	128'	133'	138'	149'	164'	198'
	6978'	4885'	3489'	2442'	1745'	1221'	888'	611'	444'	306'

Depth of Field — 3:1 Zoom

135 mm   PANAVISION PRIMO 3:1, 135-420mm, ZOOM

Entrance pupil rearwards from front vertex = 636 mm   Lens length, vertex to focal plane = 565 mm

Circle of Confusion	Aperture									
1/500in					2.8	4	5.6	8	11	16
1/710in				2.8	4	5.6	8	11	16	22
1/1000in			2.8	4	5.6	8	11	16	22	
1/1420in		2.8	4	5.6	8	11	16	22		
1/2000in	2.8	4	5.6	8	11	16	22			
Focus Distance										
8' 0" Near	7' 11.5"	7' 11.4"	7' 11.1"	7' 10.7"	7' 10.2"	7' 9.5"	7' 8.5"	7' 7.0"	7' 5.3"	7' 2.5"
Far	8' 0.5"	8' 0.7"	8' 0.9"	8' 1.3"	8' 1.9"	8' 2.7"	8' 3.7"	8' 5.5"	8' 7.8"	8' 11"
8' 6" Near	8' 5.5"	8' 5.3"	8' 5.0"	8' 4.5"	8' 4.0"	8' 3.1"	8' 2.1"	8' 0.4"	7' 10.5"	7' 7.4"
Far	8' 6.5"	8' 6.7"	8' 7.0"	8' 7.5"	8' 8.1"	8' 9.0"	8' 10.2"	9' 0.3"	9' 2.8"	9' 7"
9' 0" Near	8' 11.4"	8' 11.2"	8' 10.9"	8' 10.4"	8' 9.7"	8' 8.8"	8' 7.6"	8' 5.8"	8' 3.6"	8' 0.2"
Far	9' 0.6"	9' 0.8"	9' 1.2"	9' 1.7"	9' 2.4"	9' 3.4"	9' 4.7"	9' 7.0"	9' 9.9"	10' 3"
10' Near	9' 11.3"	9' 11.0"	9' 10.6"	9' 10.0"	9' 9.2"	9' 8.0"	9' 6.6"	9' 4.3"	9' 1.7"	8' 9.6"
Far	10' 0"	10' 1"	10' 1"	10' 2"	10' 2"	10' 4"	10' 5"	10' 8"	11' 0"	11' 6"
11' Near	10' 11"	10' 10"	10' 10"	10' 9"	10' 8"	10' 7"	10' 5"	10' 2"	9' 11.7"	9' 6.8"
Far	11' 0"	11' 1"	11' 1"	11' 2"	11' 3"	11' 5"	11' 7"	11' 10"	12' 3"	12' 11"
12' Near	11' 11"	11' 10"	11' 10"	11' 9"	11' 8"	11' 6"	11' 4"	11' 1"	10' 9"	10' 3"
Far	12' 1"	12' 1"	12' 2"	12' 3"	12' 4"	12' 6"	12' 8"	13' 0"	13' 6"	14' 4"
13' Near	12' 10"	12' 10"	12' 9"	12' 8"	12' 7"	12' 5"	12' 3"	11' 11"	11' 7"	11' 0"
Far	13' 1"	13' 1"	13' 2"	13' 3"	13' 5"	13' 7"	13' 10"	14' 3"	14' 9"	15' 9"
14' Near	13' 10"	13' 10"	13' 9"	13' 8"	13' 6"	13' 4"	13' 1"	12' 9"	12' 4"	11' 9"
Far	14' 1"	14' 2"	14' 2"	14' 4"	14' 5"	14' 8"	14' 11"	15' 5"	16' 1"	17' 3"
15' Near	14' 10"	14' 9"	14' 8"	14' 7"	14' 5"	14' 3"	14' 0"	13' 7"	13' 1"	12' 5"
Far	15' 1"	15' 2"	15' 3"	15' 4"	15' 6"	15' 9"	16' 1"	16' 8"	17' 5"	18' 10"
17' Near	16' 10"	16' 9"	16' 8"	16' 6"	16' 4"	16' 0"	15' 9"	15' 2"	14' 8"	13' 9"
Far	17' 2"	17' 3"	17' 4"	17' 6"	17' 8"	18' 0"	18' 5"	19' 2"	20' 2"	22' 1"
20' Near	19' 9"	19' 8"	19' 6"	19' 4"	19' 1"	18' 8"	18' 3"	17' 7"	16' 10"	15' 8"
Far	20' 2"	20' 4"	20' 5"	20' 8"	21' 0"	21' 5"	22' 0"	23' 1"	24' 7"	27' 5"
25' Near	24' 7"	24' 5"	24' 3"	23' 11"	23' 7"	23' 0"	22' 4"	21' 4"	20' 3"	18' 7"
Far	25' 4"	25' 6"	25' 9"	26' 1"	26' 7"	27' 3"	28' 3"	30' 1"	32' 7"	37' 9"
30' Near	29' 5"	29' 3"	28' 11"	28' 6"	28' 0"	27' 2"	26' 3"	24' 10"	23' 5"	21' 3"
Far	30' 6"	30' 9"	31' 1"	31' 7"	32' 3"	33' 4"	34' 10"	37' 8"	41' 8"	50' 6"
40' Near	39' 0"	38' 8"	38' 2"	37' 5"	36' 6"	35' 2"	33' 8"	31' 5"	29' 1"	25' 10"
Far	40' 11"	41' 4"	42' 0"	42' 11"	44' 2"	46' 3"	49' 2"	54' 11"	63' 9"	87' 4"
60' Near	57'	57'	56'	54'	52'	49' 9"	46' 10"	42' 7"	38' 4"	32' 11"
Far	62'	63'	64'	66'	69'	75'	83'	>100'	>100'	>100'
120' Near	112'	108'	105'	99' 8"	93' 4"	85' 2"	76' 10"	66' 0"	56' 5"	45' 6"
Far	129'	133'	139'	150'	167'	>200'	>200'	>200'	INF	INF
	1681'	1177'	841'	588'	420'	294'	214'	147'	107'	74'

Depth of Field — 3:1 Zoom

200 mm   PANAVISION PRIMO 3:1, 135-420mm, ZOOM

Entrance pupil rearwards from front vertex = 817 mm   Lens length, vertex to focal plane = 565 mm

Circle of Confusion	Aperture									
1/500in					2.8	4	5.6	8	11	16
1/710in				2.8	4	5.6	8	11	16	22
1/1000in			2.8	4	5.6	8	11	16	22	
1/1420in		2.8	4	5.6	8	11	16	22		
1/2000in	2.8	4	5.6	8	11	16	22			

Focus Distance											
8' 0" Near	7' 11.8"	7' 11.7"	7' 11.5"	7' 11.3"	7' 11.1"	7' 10.7"	7' 10.2"	7' 9.4"	7' 8.4"	7' 6.9"
Far	8' 0.2"	8' 0.3"	8' 0.5"	8' 0.7"	8' 0.9"	8' 1.4"	8' 1.9"	8' 2.7"	8' 3.8"	8' 5.6"
8' 6" Near	8' 5.7"	8' 5.6"	8' 5.5"	8' 5.3"	8' 5.0"	8' 4.5"	8' 4.0"	8' 3.1"	8' 2.0"	8' 0.3"
Far	8' 6.3"	8' 6.4"	8' 6.5"	8' 6.8"	8' 7.1"	8' 7.5"	8' 8.1"	8' 9.1"	8' 10.3"	9' 0.4"
9' 0" Near	8' 11.7"	8' 11.6"	8' 11.4"	8' 11.2"	8' 10.8"	8' 10.3"	8' 9.7"	8' 8.7"	8' 7.6"	8' 5.7"
Far	9' 0.3"	9' 0.4"	9' 0.6"	9' 0.8"	9' 1.2"	9' 1.7"	9' 2.3"	9' 3.4"	9' 4.8"	9' 7.1"
10' Near	9' 11.6"	9' 11.5"	9' 11.3"	9' 11.0"	9' 10.6"	9' 10.0"	9' 9.2"	9' 8.0"	9' 6.6"	9' 4.3"
Far	10' 0"	10' 0"	10' 0"	10' 1"	10' 1"	10' 2"	10' 2"	10' 4"	10' 5"	10' 8"
11' Near	10' 11"	10' 11"	10' 11"	10' 10"	10' 10"	10' 9"	10' 8"	10' 7"	10' 5"	10' 2"
Far	11' 0"	11' 0"	11' 0"	11' 1"	11' 1"	11' 2"	11' 3"	11' 5"	11' 7"	11' 10"
12' Near	11' 11"	11' 11"	11' 11"	11' 10"	11' 10"	11' 9"	11' 8"	11' 6"	11' 4"	11' 1"
Far	12' 0"	12' 0"	12' 1"	12' 1"	12' 2"	12' 3"	12' 4"	12' 6"	12' 8"	13' 0"
13' Near	12' 11"	12' 11"	12' 10"	12' 10"	12' 9"	12' 8"	12' 7"	12' 5"	12' 3"	11' 11"
Far	13' 0"	13' 0"	13' 1"	13' 1"	13' 2"	13' 3"	13' 4"	13' 7"	13' 9"	14' 2"
14' Near	13' 11"	13' 11"	13' 10"	13' 10"	13' 9"	13' 8"	13' 6"	13' 4"	13' 1"	12' 9"
Far	14' 0"	14' 1"	14' 1"	14' 2"	14' 2"	14' 4"	14' 5"	14' 8"	14' 11"	15' 5"
15' Near	14' 11"	14' 10"	14' 10"	14' 9"	14' 8"	14' 7"	14' 6"	14' 3"	14' 0"	13' 7"
Far	15' 0"	15' 1"	15' 1"	15' 2"	15' 3"	15' 4"	15' 6"	15' 9"	16' 1"	16' 7"
17' Near	16' 11"	16' 10"	16' 10"	16' 9"	16' 8"	16' 6"	16' 4"	16' 1"	15' 9"	15' 3"
Far	17' 1"	17' 1"	17' 2"	17' 2"	17' 4"	17' 5"	17' 8"	18' 0"	18' 4"	19' 1"
20' Near	19' 10"	19' 10"	19' 9"	19' 8"	19' 6"	19' 4"	19' 1"	18' 9"	18' 4"	17' 8"
Far	20' 1"	20' 2"	20' 2"	20' 4"	20' 5"	20' 8"	20' 11"	21' 4"	21' 11"	22' 11"
25' Near	24' 9"	24' 9"	24' 7"	24' 6"	24' 3"	24' 0"	23' 8"	23' 1"	22' 6"	21' 6"
Far	25' 2"	25' 3"	25' 4"	25' 6"	25' 8"	26' 0"	26' 5"	27' 2"	28' 1"	29' 9"
30' Near	29' 9"	29' 7"	29' 6"	29' 3"	29' 0"	28' 7"	28' 1"	27' 4"	26' 5"	25' 1"
Far	30' 3"	30' 4"	30' 6"	30' 8"	31' 0"	31' 6"	32' 1"	33' 2"	34' 6"	37' 1"
40' Near	39' 6"	39' 4"	39' 1"	38' 9"	38' 3"	37' 7"	36' 9"	35' 5"	34' 0"	31' 10"
Far	40' 5"	40' 7"	40' 10"	41' 3"	41' 10"	42' 8"	43' 9"	45' 9"	48' 5"	53' 6"
60' Near	59'	58'	58'	57'	56'	54'	53'	50'	47' 7"	43' 5"
Far	61'	61'	62'	62'	64'	66'	68'	73'	80'	96'
120' Near	116'	114'	112'	109'	106'	101'	95' 4"	87' 2"	79' 1"	68' 5"
Far	124'	125'	128'	132'	138'	147'	161'	191'	>200'	>200'
	3691'	2583'	1845'	1292'	923'	646'	470'	323'	235'	162'

Depth of Field — 3:1 Zoom

270 mm PANAVISION PRIMO 3:1, 135-420mm, ZOOM

Entrance pupil rearwards from front vertex = 975 mm   Lens length, vertex to focal plane = 565 mm

Circle of Confusion	Aperture									
1/500in					2.8	4	5.6	8	11	16
1/710in				2.8	4	5.6	8	11	16	22
1/1000in			2.8	4	5.6	8	11	16	22	
1/1420in		2.8	4	5.6	8	11	16	22		
1/2000in	2.8	4	5.6	8	11	16	22			

Focus Distance										
8' 0" Near	7' 11.9"	7' 11.8"	7' 11.7"	7' 11.6"	7' 11.4"	7' 11.2"	7' 10.9"	7' 10.4"	7' 9.8"	7' 8.9"
Far	8' 0.1"	8' 0.2"	8' 0.3"	8' 0.4"	8' 0.6"	8' 0.8"	8' 1.1"	8' 1.6"	8' 2.3"	8' 3.3"
8' 6" Near	8' 5.8"	8' 5.8"	8' 5.7"	8' 5.6"	8' 5.4"	8' 5.1"	8' 4.8"	8' 4.2"	8' 3.6"	8' 2.5"
Far	8' 6.2"	8' 6.2"	8' 6.3"	8' 6.5"	8' 6.6"	8' 6.9"	8' 7.2"	8' 7.8"	8' 8.5"	8' 9.7"
9' 0" Near	8' 11.8"	8' 11.8"	8' 11.7"	8' 11.5"	8' 11.3"	8' 11.0"	8' 10.6"	8' 10.0"	8' 9.3"	8' 8.1"
Far	9' 0.2"	9' 0.2"	9' 0.4"	9' 0.5"	9' 0.7"	9' 1.0"	9' 1.4"	9' 2.0"	9' 2.8"	9' 4.1"
10' Near	9' 11.8"	9' 11.7"	9' 11.6"	9' 11.4"	9' 11.2"	9' 10.8"	9' 10.4"	9' 9.6"	9' 8.8"	9' 7.3"
Far	10' 0"	10' 0"	10' 0"	10' 0"	10' 0"	10' 1"	10' 1"	10' 2"	10' 3"	10' 5"
11' Near	10' 11"	10' 11"	10' 11"	10' 11"	10' 11"	10' 10"	10' 10"	10' 9"	10' 8"	10' 6"
Far	11' 0"	11' 0"	11' 0"	11' 0"	11' 1"	11' 1"	11' 2"	11' 2"	11' 4"	11' 6"
12' Near	11' 11"	11' 11"	11' 11"	11' 11"	11' 10"	11' 10"	11' 9"	11' 8"	11' 7"	11' 5"
Far	12' 0"	12' 0"	12' 0"	12' 0"	12' 1"	12' 1"	12' 2"	12' 3"	12' 4"	12' 7"
13' Near	12' 11"	12' 11"	12' 11"	12' 11"	12' 10"	12' 10"	12' 9"	12' 8"	12' 6"	12' 4"
Far	13' 0"	13' 0"	13' 0"	13' 1"	13' 1"	13' 2"	13' 2"	13' 4"	13' 5"	13' 8"
14' Near	13' 11"	13' 11"	13' 11"	13' 10"	13' 10"	13' 9"	13' 8"	13' 7"	13' 6"	13' 3"
Far	14' 0"	14' 0"	14' 0"	14' 1"	14' 1"	14' 2"	14' 3"	14' 4"	14' 6"	14' 9"
15' Near	14' 11"	14' 11"	14' 11"	14' 10"	14' 10"	14' 9"	14' 8"	14' 7"	14' 5"	14' 2"
Far	15' 0"	15' 0"	15' 0"	15' 1"	15' 1"	15' 2"	15' 3"	15' 5"	15' 7"	15' 10"
17' Near	16' 11"	16' 11"	16' 10"	16' 10"	16' 9"	16' 8"	16' 7"	16' 5"	16' 3"	15' 11"
Far	17' 0"	17' 0"	17' 1"	17' 1"	17' 2"	17' 3"	17' 4"	17' 6"	17' 9"	18' 1"
20' Near	19' 11"	19' 10"	19' 10"	19' 9"	19' 8"	19' 7"	19' 6"	19' 3"	19' 0"	18' 7"
Far	20' 0"	20' 1"	20' 1"	20' 2"	20' 3"	20' 4"	20' 6"	20' 9"	21' 0"	21' 7"
25' Near	24' 10"	24' 10"	24' 9"	24' 8"	24' 7"	24' 5"	24' 2"	23' 10"	23' 6"	22' 10"
Far	25' 1"	25' 1"	25' 2"	25' 3"	25' 4"	25' 7"	25' 9"	26' 2"	26' 8"	27' 5"
30' Near	29' 10"	29' 9"	29' 8"	29' 7"	29' 5"	29' 2"	28' 11"	28' 5"	27' 11"	27' 0"
Far	30' 1"	30' 2"	30' 3"	30' 4"	30' 6"	30' 10"	31' 1"	31' 8"	32' 4"	33' 7"
40' Near	39' 9"	39' 7"	39' 6"	39' 3"	39' 0"	38' 7"	38' 1"	37' 4"	36' 5"	35' 0"
Far	40' 3"	40' 4"	40' 6"	40' 8"	41' 0"	41' 5"	42' 0"	43' 0"	44' 3"	46' 7"
60' Near	59'	59'	58'	58'	57'	57'	55'	54'	52'	49' 6"
Far	60'	60'	61'	61'	62'	63'	64'	67'	70'	75'
120' Near	117'	116'	115'	114'	111'	108'	105'	99' 4"	93' 4"	84' 9"
Far	122'	123'	124'	126'	129'	133'	139'	151'	167'	>200'
	6726'	4709'	3363'	2354'	1682'	1177'	856'	589'	428'	295'

Depth of Field — 3:1 Zoom

420 mm — PANAVISION PRIMO 3:1, 135-420mm, ZOOM

Entrance pupil rearwards from front vertex = 1,198 mm   Lens length, vertex to focal plane = 565 mm

Circle of Confusion	Aperture									
1/500in					2.8	4	5.6	8	11	16
1/710in				2.8	4	5.6	8	11	16	22
1/1000in			2.8	4	5.6	8	11	16	22	
1/1420in		2.8	4	5.6	8	11	16	22		
1/2000in	2.8	4	5.6	8	11	16	22			

Focus Distance										
8' 0" Near	7' 11.9"	7' 11.9"	7' 11.9"	7' 11.8"	7' 11.7"	7' 11.6"	7' 11.5"	7' 11.3"	7' 11.0"	7' 10.5"
8' 0" Far	8' 0.1"	8' 0.1"	8' 0.1"	8' 0.2"	8' 0.3"	8' 0.4"	8' 0.5"	8' 0.7"	8' 1.0"	8' 1.5"
8' 6" Near	8' 5.9"	8' 5.9"	8' 5.9"	8' 5.8"	8' 5.7"	8' 5.6"	8' 5.4"	8' 5.2"	8' 4.9"	8' 4.4"
8' 6" Far	8' 6.1"	8' 6.1"	8' 6.1"	8' 6.2"	8' 6.3"	8' 6.4"	8' 6.6"	8' 6.8"	8' 7.1"	8' 7.7"
9' 0" Near	8' 11.9"	8' 11.9"	8' 11.8"	8' 11.8"	8' 11.7"	8' 11.5"	8' 11.4"	8' 11.1"	8' 10.8"	8' 10.2"
9' 0" Far	9' 0.1"	9' 0.1"	9' 0.2"	9' 0.2"	9' 0.3"	9' 0.5"	9' 0.6"	9' 0.9"	9' 1.3"	9' 1.8"
10' Near	9' 11.9"	9' 11.9"	9' 11.8"	9' 11.7"	9' 11.6"	9' 11.5"	9' 11.3"	9' 10.9"	9' 10.5"	9' 9.9"
10' Far	10' 0"	10' 0"	10' 0"	10' 0"	10' 0"	10' 0"	10' 0"	10' 1"	10' 1"	10' 2"
11' Near	10' 11"	10' 11"	10' 11"	10' 11"	10' 11"	10' 11"	10' 11"	10' 10"	10' 10"	10' 9"
11' Far	11' 0"	11' 0"	11' 0"	11' 0"	11' 0"	11' 0"	11' 0"	11' 1"	11' 1"	11' 2"
12' Near	11' 11"	11' 11"	11' 11"	11' 11"	11' 11"	11' 11"	11' 11"	11' 10"	11' 10"	11' 9"
12' Far	12' 0"	12' 0"	12' 0"	12' 0"	12' 0"	12' 0"	12' 1"	12' 1"	12' 2"	12' 3"
13' Near	12' 11"	12' 11"	12' 11"	12' 11"	12' 11"	12' 11"	12' 10"	12' 10"	12' 9"	12' 8"
13' Far	13' 0"	13' 0"	13' 0"	13' 0"	13' 0"	13' 0"	13' 1"	13' 1"	13' 2"	13' 3"
14' Near	13' 11"	13' 11"	13' 11"	13' 11"	13' 11"	13' 11"	13' 10"	13' 10"	13' 9"	13' 8"
14' Far	14' 0"	14' 0"	14' 0"	14' 0"	14' 0"	14' 1"	14' 1"	14' 2"	14' 2"	14' 4"
15' Near	14' 11"	14' 11"	14' 11"	14' 11"	14' 11"	14' 10"	14' 10"	14' 9"	14' 8"	14' 7"
15' Far	15' 0"	15' 0"	15' 0"	15' 0"	15' 0"	15' 1"	15' 1"	15' 2"	15' 3"	15' 4"
17' Near	16' 11"	16' 11"	16' 11"	16' 11"	16' 11"	16' 10"	16' 10"	16' 9"	16' 8"	16' 6"
17' Far	17' 0"	17' 0"	17' 0"	17' 0"	17' 1"	17' 1"	17' 2"	17' 2"	17' 4"	17' 5"
20' Near	19' 11"	19' 11"	19' 11"	19' 11"	19' 10"	19' 10"	19' 9"	19' 8"	19' 6"	19' 4"
20' Far	20' 0"	20' 0"	20' 0"	20' 1"	20' 1"	20' 1"	20' 2"	20' 3"	20' 5"	20' 7"
25' Near	24' 11"	24' 11"	24' 11"	24' 10"	24' 10"	24' 9"	24' 8"	24' 6"	24' 4"	24' 0"
25' Far	25' 0"	25' 0"	25' 1"	25' 1"	25' 2"	25' 3"	25' 4"	25' 6"	25' 8"	26' 0"
30' Near	29' 11"	29' 11"	29' 10"	29' 9"	29' 9"	29' 7"	29' 6"	29' 3"	29' 0"	28' 8"
30' Far	30' 0"	30' 1"	30' 1"	30' 2"	30' 2"	30' 4"	30' 5"	30' 8"	30' 11"	31' 5"
40' Near	39' 10"	39' 10"	39' 9"	39' 8"	39' 7"	39' 4"	39' 2"	38' 10"	38' 4"	37' 8"
40' Far	40' 1"	40' 1"	40' 2"	40' 3"	40' 5"	40' 7"	40' 10"	41' 2"	41' 8"	42' 6"
60' Near	59'	59'	59'	59'	59'	58'	58'	57'	56'	55'
60' Far	60'	60'	60'	60'	60'	61'	61'	62'	63'	65'
120' Near	119'	118'	118'	117'	116'	115'	113'	110'	107'	102'
120' Far	120'	121'	121'	122'	123'	125'	127'	131'	136'	144'
	16276'	11393'	8138'	5697'	4070'	2849'	2072'	1425'	1037'	713'

The
Sound Recordists'
PANAFLEX

Creating the Quietest Possible Recording Conditions

From the Sound Recordist's point of view, the most important aspect of the choice of camera for a particular production is 'how much noise is the principal camera going to make when shooting close in to the leading artist who is speaking in whispers in absolutely quiet surroundings?'

With a PANAFLEX camera the chances are that the noisiest thing around will be the Nagra recorder.

Vast amounts of time, money, energy and ingenuity have been expended by PANAVISION to develop and refine the quiet running aspect of the PANAFLEX range of cameras in order that the maximum percentage of original sound is usable and does not have to be looped because there is unacceptable camera noise in the background.

This has been done without compromise to the weight and the size of the camera, the way the lenses are mounted, the steadiness of the image or the size of the registration pins and the usability of the camera in general.

The PLATINUM PANAFLEX, in particular, requires no extra blimping for even the closest microphone positioning.

Just as the quietness of the camera has been achieved by a scientific approach and a team effort at the factory, so the maintenance of that state of quietness requires good servicing, a knowledgeable use of the equipment in the field and the cooperation of all the crew.

Measuring camera noise

All cameras make a noise, especially with film running through them in the intermittent manner that film runs through a camera, and this is measured over a wide range of frequencies.

PANAVISION measures the noise level of its cameras with a full roll of film running through the camera, with the microphone placed 3' (0.914m) from the film plane, with the magazine in the top position so that it is not hidden from the microphone, with any lens on and in an exceptionally quiet sound-proof chamber.

This test is significantly more exacting than making measurements with the microphone 1 meter (3' 3.37") away and using only a short focal length lens.

PANAVISION also make polar graphs of the camera noise so they can check the amount of noise emerging from the camera in all directions (because the microphone is rarely placed directly in front of the lens) and measure the spectrum of camera noise, from which they can determine the amount of noise being generated by every individual moving component within the camera.

278

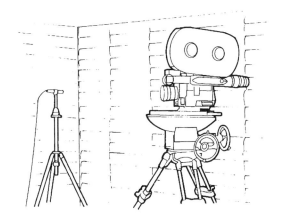

1

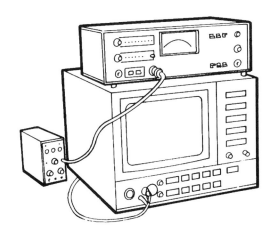

2

1. PANAFLEX camera in noise test room, 2. Noise data recording instrument.

Camera Noise Control

If a camera becomes noisier than it should be, then there are a number of possible causes that can be checked immediately, viz.:

Is the filter door closed?
Is the film running over the sprocket teeth correctly?
Are both loops as large as possible?
Has the pitch control been set for optimum quietness?
Is the de-anamorphoser lever set properly?
Are the aperture plate locking levers touching the camera door?
Is anything creating a mechanical link between the mechanism plate and the camera body?
Are all the internal circuit boards secure?
Is the motor touching the motor cover?
Does the movement require lubricating?

If none of the above is the answer to the problem then the camera should be returned to PANAVISION, or its representative, for attention.

Minimizing camera noise

Although the noise generated by PANAFLEX cameras is reasonably even all around there is a slight advantage to be gained by positioning the microphone forward of the film plane (rather than behind the camera) and at '10 o'clock' or '5 o'clock' relative to, and looking at, the front of the camera.

Most of what little noise comes from PANAFLEX cameras is confined to a few very narrow frequency bands. Much can be done, particularly at the dubbing stage, to minimize any recorded camera noise by putting in notch filters at 24 Hz and 12 KHz and their harmonics.

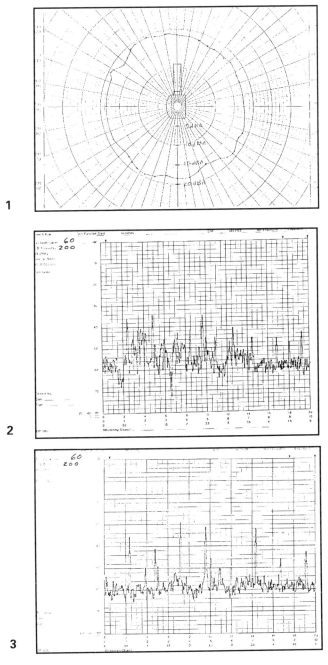

1. Polar camera noise graph showing noise level three feet forward from the film plane, 2. Noise spectrum graph of a PLATINUM PANAFLEX, 3. Noise spectrum graph of a GII PANAFLEX.

The
Production Managers'
PANAFLEX

Ordering PANAVISION Equipment

To the Production Manager falls the task of ordering the Camera and associated equipment, and of making sure that what is needed is where it has to be, when it has to be. Equally he or she must make sure that whatever is no longer needed is returned as soon as possible, so that money is not spent renting equipment unnecessarily.

To make the operation run as efficiently as possible PANAVISION, and its Representatives worldwide, have specially trained client liaison personnel who are never more than a telephone call, or a fax, or a telex away. Equally, all of PANAVISION's equipment is only a truck or an aircraft journey away.

At the start of a production it is always advantageous to try to have a personal meeting with the person who is going to look after your project, so that when you make telephone calls later on you both know who you are talking to.

Whenever practical PANAVISION's client contact person will appreciate being invited to visit the set or the location to meet and to talk to the people who are actually using the equipment. It not only helps to make the current production run more smoothly but also affords an opportunity to hear comments and suggestions which can be incorporated into PANAVISION's product range in the future.

Ordering over the telephone

When you place an order over the telephone PANAVISION's client contact person will write it down on a special form he or she has for the purpose. It is not necessary but it does make life easier, and there is less likely to be an error, if you state your requirements in the same order as is printed on the form. To this end PANAVISION will always supply you with copies of their order form so that everyone is using the same document.

Rep.:_____ Order#: _____ Production I.D.#: _____

Producer:_____ Ordered By: _____Date: _____ Time: _____

Picture:_____Telephone:_____

Prep: _____Ship _____Start _____Ret._____

Shipping Instructions		P.O. _____D.P. _____
		WILL COMP. P.M. _____
		REVISIONS A.C. _____
	P/U Time	1 2 3 4

G.G. FORMAT		GG-X	MONITOR 3 4 8 9	FTZC#
		HCM10 M5 M2	PRS	PMSC#
		PM10 REV	RSB(TACHO)	SRM
PFX-P	SCCD/PCV	M10	PCLAHP HHPCH	SSCB2#
PFX-GII	SCCD/PCV	M5	FSE	PL 650 1000
PFX-G	SCCD/PCV	M2	PLL	PL2#
PFX-X	CCD-X	M20	MFFGB MFF2SK	PT2
PSTR-P	SCCD/PCV	STM10 REV	EPI-P	PSC2#
PSTR	SCCD/PCV	STM5	FFD	PFL#
PFXLW-II		M5-PG	TSCU	PNPS/FVSC#
PFX-	W/CONVR KIT	SCM3# SCJB/SCVM	ARF	TLS
PFX-XPG		PGA/PGV/SCGS	MBP	PVE
RFTC		SCNB(8)/SCNBC(2)	ECMB	PWP (L) (S)
SPSR	PSR	MIT10	MBS/MBSA6.6X3	CHB
PSRCCD		M-PS	FA	CSDF# HHSD#
MKIIT		NS/HS/FRIES	MBM 4X5 6X6	WB#
PAIII		AM1000	AIIIAEV	IP/IP2/IP3#
PAII		AM400 REV HH	AUSS	HV/MIIV/HV2/-V#
CE BASE		AM200 HH	AWP	1.4 XE 2XE
CCD-J	CCD-JC		NI	RDM# CPP#
				ZC SZC
SL10	FILT/HLDR	SL35 T1.9 CF#	SL150 T1.9	LWZ#
SL14.5 T1.9#	CF#	SL40 T1.9	SLZ3 T2.8#	Z5S T3.1
SL17.5 T1.9	CF#	SL50 T1.9	SLZ T2.3#	Z6 S T3
SL21 T1.9	CF#	SL75 T1.9	SLZ11 T2.8#	Z10S T4
SL27 T1.9	CF#	SL100 T.19	VFL4X T6.3#	ZC10 T3.8
USZ14 T1.9	SZ T1.9	SS14 T1.9	SM50-MF T1.4	PH PH-S
USZ24 T1.3	SZ T1.9	SS17 T1.9	SM100-MF T2#	PHDTP
USZ29 T1.3	SZ T1.9	SS20 T1.9	SM200-MF T4#	OH100/OHU#
USZ35 T1.4	SZ T1.9	SS24 T1.3		SH/SHS80/SH80#
USZ50 T1.4	SZ T1.9	SS29 T1.3	SR24-SF T3.5#	C40H/C40DH#
USZ85 T1.4	SZ T1.9	US35 T1.3	SR45-SF T2.8#	WSH# WSRAM
USZ100 T2#	SZ T2	SS40 T1.3		RHF7#
USZ135 T2#	SZ T2	US50 T1.0	SP9.8 T2.8 (ARRI)	BAZ
USZ180 T2.8	SZ T2	SS75 T1.6	SPN8 T2.8#	PTATE#
		SS100 T1.6		PUB
SPN200 T2#		SS125 T1.6#	MS40 T2.8#	PCM/PCOB (L/XL)
SPN300 T2#		SS150 T1.5	MC60 T2.8	PRK PTLT
SPC200 T2#		SS200 T2	MS90 T2.8#	PUAB PAB
SPC300 T2.8#		SS300 T2.8	MC100 T2.8#	
SPC400 T2.8#		SP400 T4	SM90-MF T2#	PTP-S RST
SPC600 T4.5#		SP500 T4		PTP-B RST-B
SPC800 T5.6			VCLS#	MHH (H) (L)
			ST24	RBS
			ST35	
85 N3,6,9		4 X 5/6 X 6/138/4.5	ST50	24LA12
OPTICAL FLAT		4 X 5/6 X 6/138/4.5	ST80	24GC17A/U
PROMIST 1/8-5BLK/WHT		4 X 5/6 X 6/138/4.5	ST180	24LA10
CON.UL,L,S 1/8 - 5		4 X 5/6 X 6/138/4.5		B4C
SOFT F/X 1/2 - 5		4 X 5/6 X 6/138/4.5	FLS#	3GGC17
ND .30 .60 .90		4 X 5/6 X 6/138/4.5		CHRG (24) (36)
DIOPTERS FL, SP		138/4.5		SCNB(8) SCNBC(2)
POLA WARM		138/4.5		PINKED OUT BY:

1. PANAVISION Camera Equipment Dept.'s Order Form

Shipping Equipment Overseas

Whenever equipment is sent overseas, shipping lists, detailing the equipment's description, serial number, country of origin, size, weight and value, etc., must be prepared in advance for the benefit of all the Customs Officers and Shipping Agents who are likely to be encountered along the way. The permutations of what items go together on any particular job are so vast that it is impossible to have shipping lists printed in advance but every detail is listed on PANAVISION's mainframe computer so that any shipping list is only a keyboard away.

For equipment being exported temporarily to many countries the most convenient method of coping with the problems of Import/Export is to use an International Carnet de Passage, a sort of 'Passport for Camera Equipment.' PANAVISION is able to supply your Shipping Agent with all the necessary information to apply for such documentation.

Goods shipped to European EEC countries from elsewhere in the world require only customs clearance at their first point of entry and at their last point of exit. There are no customs requirements for goods shipped within the EEC.

It is vitally important to get the Carnet document stamped and signed when leaving a country to obtain proof of export (other than within the EEC going to another EEC country) or else the full amount of customs duty will be payable later.

Carnet countries

The following countries accept the International Carnet de Passage:

Algeria	Hungary	Portugal*
Australia	Iceland	Romania
Austria*	Ireland, Republic of*	Senegal
Belgium*	Israel	Singapore
Bulgaria	Italy*	Slovak Republic
Canada	Ivory Coast	Slovenia
Cyprus	Japan	South Africa
Czech Republic	Luxembourg*	South Korea
Denmark*	Malaysia	Spain*
Finland*	Malta	Sweden*
France*	Mauritius	Switzerland
Germany*	Netherlands*	Turkey
Gibraltar	New Zealand	United Kingdom*
Greece*	Norway	United States of America
Hong Kong	Poland	

* EEC countries

286

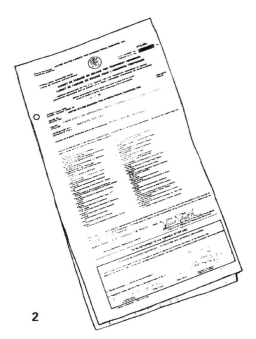

1. Portion of a PANAVISION shipping list, 2. Cover of an International Carnet de Passage.

Camera Equipment Reminder List

As an aide memoire to ordering PANAVISION CAMERA EQUIPMENT the following is a general listing of the principal items of equipment that are available from PANAVISION Inc. in Los Angeles:

Cameras:

35mm CAMERAS
PLATINUM PANAFLEX
GII GOLDEN PANAFLEX
GOLDEN PANAFLEX
PANAFLEX-X
LIGHTWEIGHT PANAFLEX for Steadicam system
PLATINUM PANASTAR
PANASTAR
SUPER PSR-200
PSR-200
PAN-ARRI III with PANAVISION lens mount

PAN ARRI IIC with PANAVISION hardfront
LOW PROFILE PAN-ARRI CAMERA
PAN-MITCHELL Mk.II with PANAVISION hardfront

65mm CAMERAS
PANAVISION 65mm cameras for principal photography, for backgraound plates and for special effects.

16mm CAMERAS:
PANAVISION 16

PANAFLEX camera accessories:

AATONCODE TIME CODE SYSTEM
AUTOMOBILE BASE
BALANCE PLATE
BARNIES, rain and dust covers
- lens heater type, long and short
- lens weather protectors, long and short
- magazine covers, 250, 500 and 1000 ft.
- magazine heater, 250, 500 and 1000 ft.
- weather proof camera covers
BATTERIES:
- additional 24v Nicad type
- 24v belt type
- 24v solid Lead Acid type, complete with chargers
- 36v
BATTERY CHARGERS
BATTERY ELIMINATOR
CAMERA REMOTE CONTROL UNIT
CHANGING BAG
CINEMATOGRAPHERS' COMPUTER PROGRAM
DIOPTERS, Full or split
- sliding type
DIRECTORS' VIEWFINDERS:
- adjustable type
- PANAFINDER type
- Mitchell type
ELECTRONIC ACCESSORIES:
- field to frame synchronizer

- flash synchronizer
- line to film (50/60 Hz) synchronizer
- projector to camera synchronizer
- precision speed control (4-34 fps)
- remote on-off switch.
- remote speed control
- Stop Motion Package (PANASTAR only)
- time lapse (¼ sec. - 10 min. per frame)
- video to camera synchronizer
EXTENSION VIEWFINDER:
- intermediate length
EYEPIECE POUCH
FILTERS:
- various types and sizes
- Net frames - Optical flats
- Sliding diffusers
- Special holders for wide angle lenses
FOLLOW FOCUS CONTROL:
- modular type
- regular type
- super type
- extension cable for above
GELATIN FILTER PUNCH
GROUND GLASS:
- additional PANAGLOW type
- matte cutter
HAND GRIPS and HANDLES:

288

- adjustable, left hand
- adjustable, right hand
- "T" type handle
- Auxiliary carrying handle to use with PANACLEAR
HEADS:
- PANAHEAD
- Super PANAHEAD
- PANABALL leveler
- Worrall head spacer
- O'Connor 200 - O'Connor 100
- O'Connor 50
- O'Connor slide
- O'Connor Ball Leveller
- Ronford 15/S
- Sachtler 7+7
- Sachtler 25
- Eyepiece leveler for use with fluid heads
LENS ACCESSORIES:
- Bellows lens attachment, shift type
- Bellows lens attachment
- Distortion attachment
- Dyna Lens anti-vibration attachment
- Electronic zoom controller (additional)
- Focus control, Type FF
- Focus control high speed
- Flange focal depth gage set
- Inclining Prism
- Matte Box lens hood front flap
- Range extender, 1.5x focal length
- Primo 1.4x
- 2x
- 2x for Canon lenses
- Revolving mesmerizer lens
- Rifle sight attachment
- Split diopter system
- Zoom control battery complement
- Zoom lens control, foot pedal type
LOUMA CAMERA CRANE SYSTEM
MAGAZINES:
- 250, 500 AND 1000'
- 1000' reversible (for PLATINUM PANAFLEX only)
- 1000' high speed (for PANASTAR only)
- 1000' high speed reversible (for PANASTAR only)
MATTE BOXES:
- standard 5.650 x 4" type
- wide angle 5.650 x 4" type
- hand held type
- clamp-on type
- tiltable type
- 4 x 4" type (for PANAFLEX 16)
- 6.6 x 6.6", 2 x grad type
- 6.6 x 6.6", 3 x grad type
- 6.6 x 6.6", Modular type
- Tilting filter module
- Dual motorized sliding grads module
- Double rotating filter module, additional
- Single rotating filter module, additional
- 6.6 x 8" tiltable type
- Super sunshade extension
- Sunshade extension

PANAFADE in-shot exposure control system
PANAFLASHER in-camera negative flashing device
PANAGLIDE floating camera system
- PANAFLEX type
- Pan-Arri type
PANALENS LIGHT
PANALITE camera mounted controllable Obie light
PANALUX nightvision viewfinder
PANAROCK near ground level pan and tilt device
PANATAPE electronic tape measure
PANATATE nodal turn-over mount
PANATILT/BALANCE PLATE
PROJECTOR LENSES, 35mm spherical
- 35mm Anamorphic attachment
- 70mm
RAIN and SPRAY DEFLECTORS:
- Compact type
REMOTE APERTURE CONTROL
REMOTE FOCUS AND APERTURE CONTROL UNIT
REMOTE SHUTTER LOCK CABLE
REMOTE SYNC CONTROL CABLE
RISER PLATE, 45° type
SLATE (CLAP BOARD):
- many types and sizes
SLIDING BASE PLATE
SUPER 35 modification
"T" STOP CONTROLS:
- for 5:1 & 10:1 zoom lenses
THREE PERF MOVEMENT
TILT PLATE, geared type
TRIPODS, PANAPOD
- Standard
- Baby
- Hi-hat
- Spreader
UNDERWATER HOUSINGS
- Pan-Arri type
- Anamorphic type
VIDEO ASSIST CAMERAS:
- CCD FLICKER-FREE PANAVID
- PANAVID
- as above, with control unit (GII & X cameras only)
- CEI type (Pan-Arri III only)
VIDEO ASSIST SYSTEMS - recorders
- monitors
- enhancer
- frame line generator
WATER BOX
WEATHER PROOF COVER
WEDGE PLATE

SPHERICAL LENS REMINDER LIST

The decision to go Anamorphic or Spherical is one that the Producer will undoubtedly make, the choice of individual lenses is one that the Director and the Director of Photography will want to have a major say in but, no doubt, in the end it will be the Production Manager who will sign the order.

PANAVISION spherical (non-anamorphic) lenses:

PANAVISION PRIMO LENSES

Focal Length	Aperture	Min. Focus Distance
10mm	T1.9	2'
14.5mm	T1.9	2'
17.5mm	T1.9	2'
21mm	T1.9	2'
27mm	T1.9	2'
35mm	T1.9	2'
40mm	T1.9	2'
50mm	T1.9	2'
75mm	T1.9	2'
100mm[1]	T1.9	2'
150mm[1]	T1.9	5'

PANAVISION PRIMO ZOOM LENSES

Focus Range	Aperture	Min Focus Distance
17.5 - 75mm[1]	T2.3	2' 6"
24 - 275mm[1]	T2.8	4'
135 - 400mm[1]	T2.8	8' 6"

PRIMO MATCHED LIGHTWEIGHT ZOOM LENS

Focus Range	Aperture	Min Focus Distance
27 - 68mm	T2.8	3'

PRIMO CLOSE FOCUS LENSES

Focal Length	Aperture	Min. Focus Distance
14.5mm	T1.9	8"
17.5mm	T1.9	7.5"
21mm	T1.9	9.5"
27mm	T1.9	9.5
35mm	T1.9	11"

PRIMO MATCHED MACRO LENSES

Focal Length	Aperture	Min. focus Distance	Magnification
50mm	T1.4	9"	1:2
90mm[1]	T2	14.75"	1:0.7
100mm[1]	T2	1' 6"	1:2.5
200mm[1]	T4	2' 4"	1:2

PRIMO MATCHED SLANT FOCUS LENSES

Focal Length	Aperture	Min. focus Distance	Lens Type
24mm[1]	T3.5	1'	Close focus

45mm[1]	T2.8	1' 4"	Close focus
90mm[1]	T2.8	1' 6"	Close focus

[1]Particularly suitable for use with a PANAVISION PRIMO 1.4x Range Extender

PANAVISION Mk II ULTRA SPEED LENSES

Focal Length	Aperture	Min Focus Distance
14mm	T1.9	2'
17mm	T1.9	2'
20mm	T1.9	2' 6"
24mm	T1.2	2'
29mm	T1.2	2' 3"
35mm	T1.3	2'
40mm	T1.3	2'
50mm	T1.0	2'
75mm	T1.6	2'
100mm	T1.6	4'
125mm	T1.6	3' 6"
150mm	T1.5	5'

Mk II SUPER SPEED LENSES

Focal length	Aperture	Min. focus distance
24mm	T2.0	2'
28mm	T2.0	2'
35mm	T1.6	2'
50mm	T1.4	2'6"
55mm	T1.1	2'6"

PANAVISION NORMAL SPEED LENSES

Focal length	Aperture	Min. focus distance
8mm[1]	T2.8	1'
9.8mm[2]	T2.8	2'
16mm	T2.8	1' 9"
20mm	T3	2' 6"
20mm	T4	2' 3"
24mm	T2.8	2' 3"
28mm	T2.8	2'
32mm	T2.8	2'
35mm	T2	2'
40mm	T2	2'
50mm	T2	2' 6"
75mm	T2	2' 9"
100mm	T2.4	3' 6"
150mm	T2.8	5'

[2]Nikkor Fisheye, [3]For Pan-Arri only

ULTRA SPEED Mk II "Z" SERIES LENSES

Focal Length	Aperture	Min. Focus Distance
14˙mm	T1.9	2'
17mm[4]	T1.9	2'
20mm[4]	T1.9	2' 6"
24mm[5]	T1.3	2'
29mm[5]	T1.3	2'
35mm[5]	T1.4	2'
50mm[5]	T1.4	2'
85mm[5]	T1.4	2'
100mm	T2	3'
135mm	T2.8	5'
180mm	T2.8	5'

SUPER SPEED Mk II "Z" SERIES LENSES

Focal Length	Aperture	Min.Focus Distance
14mm	T1.9	2'
17mm[4]	T1.9	2'
20mm[4]	T1.9	2' 6"
24mm[5]	T1.9	2'
29mm[5]	T1.9	2'
35mm[5]	T1.9	2'
50mm[5]	T1.9	2'
85mm[5]	T1.9	2'
100mm	T2	3'
135mm	T2.8	5'
180mm	T2.8	5'

CANON BNC MOUNTED LENSES

Focal Length	Aperture	Min. Focus Distance	Lens Type
14mm	T2.8	1' 6"	
15mm	T2.8	0' 7"	Fisheye
18mm[5]	T1.5	1'	
24mm[5]	T1.5	1'	
35mm[5]	T1.3	2'	
50mm[5]	T1.3	2'	
85mm[5]	T1.4	3'	
135mm	T2	4' 6"	
200mm	T2.8	5'	

PANAVISION PRIMO 1.4x range extender

[4] Non-Zeiss glass but color & MTF matched to complement Z series
[5] Available as a set of five lenses only.

Suitable only for cameras with a BNC lens mount.

TELEPHOTO LENSES

Focal Length	Aperture	Min. Focus Distance	Lens Type
200mm	T2	6'	Ultra Speed
300mm	T2.8	15'	Ultra Speed
300mm	T2.8	10'	Canon
300mm	T2	13'	Nikkor
400mm	T2.8	15'	Canon
400mm	T4	15'	
500mm	T4	23'	
600mm	T4.5	27'	Canon
800mm	T5	45'	Canon
1000mm	T6	22'	
1000mm	T9	22'	
150-600mm	T6	10'	Canon Varifocal

CLOSE FOCUS & MACRO LENSES

Focal Length	Aperture	Min. focus Distance	Magnification Factor
17mm	T1.9	10"	
20mm	T4	8"	
24mm	T2.8	8"	
28mm	T2.8	8"	
35mm	T2	8"	
40mm	T2.8		1:2
60mm	T2.8		1:2
90mm	T2.8		1:2
100mm	T2.8		1:2

SLANT FOCUS LENSES

Focal Length	Aperture	Min. focus Distance	Lens Type
24mm[5]	T1.4	1'	Close focus
45mm[3]	T2.8	1' 4"	Close focus
90mm[5]	T2.8	1' 6"	Close focus

SPECIAL PURPOSE LENSES

PANAVISION/FRAZIER lens system
Innovision Lens system
View camera lens system

35mm ZOOM LENSES

Focal Range	Aperture	Zoom Ratio	Optical Details	Min. Focus Distance
17.5 - 75mm	T2.5	4.3;1	PANAVISION PRIMO	3'
20 - 60mm	T3	3:1	Cooke/PANAVISION	2'3"
20 - 100mm	T3.1	5:1	Cooke/PANAVISION	2'6"
20 - 120mm	T3	6:1	Angenieux/PANAVISION	3'6"
20 - 125mm	T1.9	6.25:1	PANAVISION ULTRA-ZOOM	4'
24 - 275mm[1]	T2.8	11:1	PANAVISION PRIMO	4'
35 - 140mm	T4.5	4:1		4'
25 - 250mm	T4	10:1	Cooke/PANAVISION SUPER ZOOM	5'6"
25 - 250mm	T4	10:1	Angenieux/PANAVISION	5'6"
25 - 250mm	T4	10:1	Helicopter mount type	5'6"
23 - 460mm	T10	20:1		5'6"
27 - 68mm	T2.8	2.5:11	Lightweight type	3'
35 - 140mm	T4.5	4:1	Angenieux/PANAVISION	4'
135 - 420mm[1]	T4	3:1	PANAVISION PRIMO	8'6"
150 - 600mm	T6.3	4:1	Canon/PANAVISION	10'

ANAMORPHIC LENS REMINDER LIST

As with spherical lenses, PANAVISION has the widest possible range of anamorphic lenses to choose from.

PANAVISION anamorphic lenses

PANAVISION PRIMO ANAMORPHIC LENSES

Focal Length	Aperture	Min. Focus Distance
35mm	T2	3' 6"
40mm	T2	3' 6"
50mm	T2	3' 6"
75mm	T2	5' 6"
100mm[1]	T2	3' 6"

PANAVISION PRIMO ANAMORPHIC ZOOM LENSES

Focal Range	Aperture	Zoom Ratio	Min. Focus Distance
48 - 550mm	T4.5	11:1	4' 1"
270 - 840mm	T4.5	3:1	8' 7"

"E" SERIES COLOR MATCHED AUTO PANATAR LENSES

Focal Length	Aperture	Min. Focus Distance
28mm	T2.3	5'
35mm	T2	5'
40mm	T2	5'
50mm	T2	5'
75mm	T2	5'
85mm	T2	5'
100mm	T2.3	5'
180mm[1]	T2.8	4' 6"

[1]Particularly suitable for use with a PANAVISION PRIMO 1.4x Range Extender

"C" SERIES LENSES

Focal Length	Aperture	Min. Focus Distance
30mm	T3	4'
35mm	T2.3	2' 9"
40mm	T2.8	2' 6"
50mm	T2.3	2' 6"
75mm	T2.5	4' 6"
100mm	T2.8	4' 6"
150mm	T3.5	5'
180mm[1]	T2.8	4' 6"

SUPER SPEED LENSES

Focal Length	Aperture	Min. Focus Distance
24mm	T1.6	6'
35mm	T1.4	4' 6"
50mm	T1.1	4'
50mm	T1.4	4'
55mm	T1.4	4'
75mm	T1.8	4' 6"
100mm	T1.8	4' 6" - 5''

TELEPHOTO LENSES

Focal Length		Aperture	Min. Focus Distance
360mm		T4	5' 6"
400mm	Nikon	T3.5	9'
400mm	Canon	T3	8'
600mm	Nikon	T4	13'
600mm	Canon	T4.5	27'
800mm	Canon	T5.6	15'
1000mm		T5.6	22'
1200mm	Canon	T6	27'
2000mm		T9	30'

ANAMORPHIC ZOOM LENSES

Focal Range	Aperture	Zoom Ratio	Optical Details	Min. Focus Distance
40 - 200mm	T4.5	5:1	Cooke/PANAVISION Super Panazoom	2' 6"
48 - 550mm	T4.5	11:1	PANAVISION Anamorphic PRIMO zoom	4' 1"
50 - 500mm	T5.6	10;1	Cooke/PANAVISION Super Panazoom	5' 6"
50 - 500mm	T5.6	10:1	Angenieux/PANAVISION Anamorphic zoom	5' 6"
270 - 840mm	T4.5	3:1	PANAVISION Anamorphic PRIMO zoom	8' 7"

SPECIAL PURPOSE ANAMORPHIC LENSES

Focal Length	Aperture	Macro Ratio	Optical Details	Min. Focus Distance
90mm	T4.3		Anamorphic Slant Focus with Close Focus	1' 5"
25mm	T2.5		Wide Angle Distoortion lens	5'
55mm	T2.5		Close Focus	10"
100mm	T2.8		Insert or Process lens	4' 6"
150mm	T3.2	1:1.5	Macro Panatar	1' 5"
200mm	T3.2	1:2	Macro Panatar	1' 6"
250mm	T3..2	1:2	Macro Panatar	2' 5"

PANAVISION REPRESENTATIVES

Wherever in the world a film has to be made be sure there is a PANAVISION representative nearby to supply you with all your camera equipment needs.

Because the local PANAVISION representative is usually the major equipment supplier in his local area it follows that they can also supply you with lighting and many other of the myriad of technical items you will need to make your production go smoothly.

In the phone and fax numbers listed below the International Dialing Code is preceded by "+". When dialing locally it may sometimes be necessary to precede the number with "0."

PANAVISION corporate headquarters:

PANAVISION INTERNATIONAL L.P.
6219 DE SOTO AVE
WOODLAND HILLS
LOS ANGELES, CA 91367
Phone: +1 818 316 1000
Fax: +1 818 316 1111

PANAVISION subsidiaries, U.S.A.:

PANAVISION, FLORIDA
2000 UNIVERSAL STUDIOS PLAZA STE. 900
ORLANDO, FL 32819-7606
Phone: +1 407-363-0990
Fax: +1 407-363-0180

PANAVISION, HOLLYWOOD
6779 HAWTHORN
HOLLYWOOD, CA 90028
Phone: +1 213-464-3800
Fax: +1 213-467-0522

PANAVISION, NEW YORK
540 W. 36th STREET
NEW YORK, NY 10018
Phone: +1 212-594-8700
Fax: +1 212-564-4918

PANAVISION, NORTH CAROLINA
1223 N. 23rd STREET
WILMINGTON, NC 28405
Phone: +1 910-343-8796
Fax: +1 910-343-8275

PANAVISION representatives, U.S.A.:

ATLANTA, GEORGIA
VICTOR DUNCAN INC. - ATLANTA
3752 DEKALB TECHNOLOGY
PARKWAY
ATLANTA, GA 30340-3603
Phone: +1 404-457-4550
Fax: +1 404-457-4758

CHICAGO, ILLINOIS
VICTOR DUNCAN INC.- CHICAGO
3650 W. BRADLEY PLACE, Unit A
CHICAGO, IL 60618
Phone: +1 312-267-1500
Fax: +1 312-267-9026

DALLAS, TEXAS
VICTOR DUNCAN INC.- DALLAS
6305 N. O'CONNOR, Suite 100
IRVING, TX 75039-3510
Phone: +1 214-869-0200
Fax: +1 214-556-1862

DETROIT, MICHIGAN
VICTOR DUNCAN INC.- DETROIT
23801 INDUSTRIAL PARK DRIVE, Suite 100
FARMINGTON HILLS, MI 48024-1132
Phone: +1 810-471-1600
Fax: +1 810-471-1940

MIAMI, FLORIDA
PRO GEAR INC.
15101 N.E. 21st AVENUE
NORTH MIAMI BEACH, FL 33162
Phone: +1 305-956-9870
Fax: +1 305-956-9871

294

PANAVISION representatives, U.S.A.,
continued:

SAN FRANCISCO, CALIFORNIA
CINE RENT/STAGE A
155 FELL STREET
SAN FRANCISCO, CA 94102
Phone: +1 415-695-3100
Fax: +1 415-552-9474

PANAVISION subsidiaries worldwide:

CANADA:
PANAVISION CANADA - MONTREAL
5620 FERRIER STREET
MONTREAL, QUEBEC H4P 1M7
CANADA
Phone: +1 514-866-7262
Fax: +1 514-866-2297

PANAVISION CANADA - TORONTO
CINE SPACE, 629 EASTERN AVENUE
TORONTO, ONTARIO M4M 1E4
CANADA
Phone: +1 416-752-7670
Fax: +1 416-752-7599

PANAVISION CANADA - VANCOUVER
3999 E.2ND AVENUE
BURNABY, B.C. V5C 3W9
CANADA
Tel: +1 604-291-7262
Fax: +1 604-291-0422

IRELAND:
PANAVISION IRELAND Ltd.
MTM ARDMORE STUDIOS
BRAY, COUNTY WICKLOW
REPUBLIC OF IRELAND
Phone: +353 12-860-811
Fax: +353 12-863-425

U.K.:
PANAVISION U.K. - LONDON
WYCOMBE ROAD
WEMBLEY, MIDDLESEX
U.K.
Phone: +44 181-902-8835
Fax: +44 181-902-3273

PANAVISION U.K. - SHEPPERTON
SHEPPERTON STUDIOS
SHEPPERTON, MIDDX, TW17 0Q7.
U.K.
Phone: +44 1732-572-440
Fax: +44 1732-572-450

PANAVISION representatives
worldwide:

AUSTRALIA:
SAMUELSON FILM SERVICE - SYDNEY
1 MCLACHAN AVENUE
ARTARMON, N.S.W. 2064
AUSTRALIA
Phone: +61 2-436-1844
Fax: +61 2-438-2583

SAMUELSON FILM SERVICE - MELBOURNE
245-247 NORMANBY ROAD
SOUTH MELBOURNE, VICTORIA 3205
AUSTRALIA
Phone: +61 39-646-3044
Fax: +61 39-646-4636

CHINA:
BEIJING SALON FILMS Ltd.
19 BEI SAN HUAN WEST ROAD
BEIJING 100088
CHINA
Phone: +86 10-201-0134
Fax: +86 10-204-0977

SALON FILMS (SHANGHAI) Ltd.
RM. 103, SHANGHAI EVERGREEN
MANSION
68 LANE 569 XINHUA RA
SHANGHAI
CHINA
Phone: +86 21-280-8751
Fax: +86 21-280-8749

GD PEARL RIVER SALON FILMS & TV EQUIPMENT Co. Ltd.
352 XINKONG ROAD
CENTRAL, GUANGZHOU
CHINA
Phone:
Fax:

FRANCE:
SAMUELSON ALGA CINEMA S.A.
24-26 RUE JEAN MOULIN,
94300 VINCENNES, PARIS
FRANCE
Phone: +33 14 813 2550
Fax: +33 14 813 2551

HONG KONG:
SALON FILMS (H.K.) LTD.
6 DEVON ROAD
KOWLOON TONG
KOWLOON, HONG KONG
Phone: +852 2-338-6311
Fax: +852 2-338-2539

ITALY:
TRIO S.R.L.
VIA DELLE CAPANNELLE, 95
00178 ROMA
ITALY
Phone: +39 6-72-90-02-35
Fax: +39 6-72-90-02-42

JAPAN:
SANWA CINE EQUIPMENT RENTAL
Co. Ltd.
5-5 KOJIMACHI
CHIYODA-KU, TOKYO 102
JAPAN
Phone: +81 3-5210-3322
Fax: +81 3-5210-2270

SANWA CINE EQUIPMENT RENTAL
Co. Ltd.
3 - 1 TOYOSAKI 5 - HOME
KITA-KU, OSAKA 531
JAPAN
Phone: +81 6-375-3838
Fax: +81 6-375-3010

SANWA CINE EQUIPMENT RENTAL
Co. Ltd.
56-1 GOORI-CHO, NISHIKYOGOKU
UKYO-KU, KYOTO 615
JAPAN
Phone: +81 75-321-5200
Fax: +81 75-321-4133

MALAYSIA
SALON FILMS (M) SDN BHD:
2B JALAN GURNEY
54000, KUALA LUMPUR
MALAYSIA
Phone: +60 3-293-7482
Fax: +60 3-293-1728

MEXICO:
TRATA FILMS, S.A.
ATLETAS No. 2 COL. COUNTRY CLUB
DELEGACION COYOACAN
04420 MEXICO CITY D.F.
MEXICO
Phone: +52 525-549-3060
Fax: +52 525-689-5231

PHILIPPINES:
SALON FILMS (PHILIPPINES) LTD.
NATIVDAD 1 BUILDING
2308 PASONG TAMO EXT.
MAKITA, METRO MANILA
PHILLIPINES
Phone: +63 2-881-6 91
Fax: +63 2-889-237

SOUTH AFRICA:
LOGICAL DESIGNS (PTY) LTD.
P.O. BOX 2700, HALFWAY HOUSE
1685 S. TRANSVAAL
JOHANNESBURG, SOUTH AFRICA
Phone: +27 11-466-2380
Fax: +27 11-466-2387

SPAIN:
CAMARA RENT - MADRID
MAURICIO LEGENDRE, 36
MADRID-28046
SPAIN
Phone: +34 91-733-4131
Fax: +34 91-315-6036

CAMARA RENT - BARCELONA
CONCILIO DE TRENTE 242
BARCELONA-08020
SPAIN
Phone: +34 93-314-5000
Fax: +34 3-9313-9113

THAILAND:
SALON FILMS (THAILAND) LTD.
NO. 149/4 RAMA VI ROAD
PHAYATHAI
BANGKOK 10400
THAILAND
Phone: +66 2-278-3380
Fax: +66 2-278-4524

Index